MySQL/PHP Database Applications

Jay Greenspan and Brad Bulger

M&T Books

An imprint of IDG Books Worldwide, Inc.

Foster City, CA • Chicago, IL • Indianapolis, IN • New York, NY

MySQL/PHP Database Applications

Published by
M&T Books
An imprint of IDG Books Worldwide, Inc.
919 E. Hillsdale Blvd., Suite 400
Foster City, CA 94404
www.idgbooks.com (IDG Books Worldwide Web site)

ISBN: 0-7645-3537-4

Printed in the United States of America

10 9 8 7 6 5 4 3 2 1

1O/QZ/QR/QR/FC

Distributed in the United States by IDG Books Worldwide, Inc.

Distributed by CDG Books Canada Inc. for Canada; by Transworld Publishers Limited in the United Kingdom; by IDG Norge Books for Norway; by IDG Sweden Books for Sweden; by IDG Books Australia Publishing Corporation Pty. Ltd. for Australia and New Zealand; by TransQuest Publishers Pte Ltd. for Singapore, Malaysia, Thailand, Indonesia, and Hong Kong; by Gotop Information Inc. for Taiwan; by ICG Muse, Inc. for Japan; by Intersoft or South Africa; by Eyrolles for France; by International Thomson Publishing for Germany, Austria, and Switzerland; by Distribuidora Cuspide for Argentina; by LR International for Brazil; by Galileo Libros for Chile; by Ediciones ZETA S.C.R. Ltda. for Peru; by WS Computer Publishing Corporation, Inc., for the Philippines; by Contemporanea de Ediciones for Venezuela; by Express Computer Distributors for the Caribbean and West Indies; by Micronesia Media Distributor, Inc. for Micronesia; by Chips Computadoras S.A. de C.V. for Mexico; by Editorial Norma de Panama S.A. for Panama; by American Bookshops for Finland.

For general information on IDG Books Worldwide's books in the U.S., please call our Consumer Customer Service department at 800-762-2974. For reseller information, including discounts and premium sales, please call our Reseller Customer Service department at 800-434-3422.

For information on where to purchase IDG Books Worldwide's books outside the U.S., please contact our International Sales department at 317-572-3993 or fax 317-572-4002.

For consumer information on foreign language translations, please contact our Customer Service department at 800-434-3422, fax 317-572-4002, or e-mail rights@idgbooks.com.

For information on licensing foreign or domestic rights, please phone +1-650-653-7098.

For sales inquiries and special prices for bulk quantities, please contact our Order Services department at 800-434-3422 or write to the address above.

For information on using IDG Books Worldwide's books in the classroom or for ordering examination copies, please contact our Educational Sales department at 800-434-2086 or fax 317-572-4005.

For press review copies, author interviews, or other publicity information, please contact our Public Relations department at 650-653-7000 or fax 650-653-7500.

For authorization to photocopy items for corporate, personal, or educational use, please contact Copyright Clearance Center, 222 Rosewood Drive, Danvers, MA 01923, or fax 978-750-4470.

Library of Congress Cataloging-in-Publication Data
Greenspan, Jay, 1968-
    My SQL/PHP database applications / Jay Greenspan and Brad Bulger.
        p. cm.
    ISBN 0-7645-3537-4 (alk. paper)
    1. SQL (Computer program language) 2. PHP (Computer program language 3. Web databases.
I. Bulger, Brad, 1959- II. Title.
QA76.73.S67G73   2001
005.13'3--dc21   00-053995

is a registered trademark or trademark under exclusive license to IDG Books Worldwide, Inc. from International Data Group, Inc. in the United States and/or other countries.

is a trademark of IDG Books Worldwide, Inc.

ABOUT IDG BOOKS WORLDWIDE

Welcome to the world of IDG Books Worldwide.

IDG Books Worldwide, Inc., is a subsidiary of International Data Group, the world's largest publisher of computer-related information and the leading global provider of information services on information technology. IDG was founded more than 30 years ago by Patrick J. McGovern and now employs more than 9,000 people worldwide. IDG publishes more than 290 computer publications in over 75 countries. More than 90 million people read one or more IDG publications each month.

Launched in 1990, IDG Books Worldwide is today the #1 publisher of best-selling computer books in the United States. We are proud to have received eight awards from the Computer Press Association in recognition of editorial excellence and three from Computer Currents' First Annual Readers' Choice Awards. Our best-selling ...For Dummies® series has more than 50 million copies in print with translations in 31 languages. IDG Books Worldwide, through a joint venture with IDG's Hi-Tech Beijing, became the first U.S. publisher to publish a computer book in the People's Republic of China. In record time, IDG Books Worldwide has become the first choice for millions of readers around the world who want to learn how to better manage their businesses.

Our mission is simple: Every one of our books is designed to bring extra value and skill-building instructions to the reader. Our books are written by experts who understand and care about our readers. The knowledge base of our editorial staff comes from years of experience in publishing, education, and journalism — experience we use to produce books to carry us into the new millennium. In short, we care about books, so we attract the best people. We devote special attention to details such as audience, interior design, use of icons, and illustrations. And because we use an efficient process of authoring, editing, and desktop publishing our books electronically, we can spend more time ensuring superior content and less time on the technicalities of making books.

You can count on our commitment to deliver high-quality books at competitive prices on topics you want to read about. At IDG Books Worldwide, we continue in the IDG tradition of delivering quality for more than 30 years. You'll find no better book on a subject than one from IDG Books Worldwide.

John Kilcullen
Chairman and CEO
IDG Books Worldwide, Inc.

Eighth Annual
Computer Press
Awards ≥1992

Ninth Annual
Computer Press
Awards ≥1993

Tenth Annual
Computer Press
Awards ≥1994

Eleventh Annual
Computer Press
Awards ≥1995

IDG is the world's leading IT media, research and exposition company. Founded in 1964, IDG had 1997 revenues of $2.05 billion and has more than 9,000 employees worldwide. IDG offers the widest range of media options that reach IT buyers in 75 countries representing 95% of worldwide IT spending. IDG's diverse product and services portfolio spans six key areas including print publishing, online publishing, expositions and conferences, market research, education and training, and global marketing services. More than 90 million people read one or more of IDG's 290 magazines and newspapers, including IDG's leading global brands — Computerworld, PC World, Network World, Macworld and the Channel World family of publications. IDG Books Worldwide is one of the fastest-growing computer book publishers in the world, with more than 700 titles in 36 languages. The "...For Dummies®" series alone has more than 50 million copies in print. IDG offers online users the largest network of technology-specific Web sites around the world through IDG.net (http://www.idg.net), which comprises more than 225 targeted Web sites in 55 countries worldwide. International Data Corporation (IDC) is the world's largest provider of information technology data, analysis and consulting, with research centers in over 41 countries and more than 400 research analysts worldwide. IDG World Expo is a leading producer of more than 168 globally branded conferences and expositions in 35 countries including E3 (Electronic Entertainment Expo), Macworld Expo, ComNet, Windows World Expo, ICE (Internet Commerce Expo), Agenda, DEMO, and Spotlight. IDG's training subsidiary, ExecuTrain, is the world's largest computer training company, with more than 230 locations worldwide and 785 training courses. IDG Marketing Services helps industry-leading IT companies build international brand recognition by developing global integrated marketing programs via IDG's print, online and exposition products worldwide. Further information about the company can be found at www.idg.com.   1/26/00

Credits

ACQUISITIONS EDITOR
Debra Williams Cauley

PROJECT EDITOR
Neil Romanosky

TECHNICAL EDITORS
Richard Lynch
Michael Widenius

COPY EDITOR
S. B. Kleinman

PROJECT COORDINATORS
Louigene A. Santos
Danette Nurse

GRAPHICS AND PRODUCTION
SPECIALISTS
Robert Bilhmayer
Rolly Delrosario
Jude Levinson
Michael Lewis
Ramses Ramirez
Victor Pérez-Varela

QUALITY CONTROL TECHNICIAN
Dina F Quan

PERMISSIONS EDITOR
Laura Moss

MEDIA DEVELOPMENT SPECIALIST
Angela Denny

MEDIA DEVELOPMENT COORDINATOR
Marisa Pearman

BOOK DESIGNER
Jim Donohue

ILLUSTRATORS
Gabriele McCann
Ronald Terry

PROOFREADING AND INDEXING
York Production Services

COVER IMAGE
© Noma/Images.com

About the Authors

Jay Greenspan made his living as a technical consultant and editor before finding his way into Wired Digital's Webmonkey. There he learned everything he knows about Web technology and gained an appreciation for electronic music, the color orange, and a "cute top." He now makes his living as a writer and consultant. He will neither confirm nor deny the rumors that he once worked for a prime-time game show.

Brad Bulger can remember when computers were as big as refrigerators and old-timers would come into the machine room and call them "mini." He learned more than anyone really should about database systems by working for Relational Technology nee Ingres nee CA for many years. After an interregnum, he got a job with Wired. He would still like to know when the future is going to get here, but has a sneaking suspicion he already knows.

In memory of Dr. Jonathan B. Postel

Preface

Welcome. If you are thumbing through these pages, you're probably considering writing Web-based applications with PHP and MySQL. If you decide to go with these tools, you'll be in excellent company. Thousands of developers – from total newbies to programmers with years of experience – are turning to PHP and MySQL for their Web-based projects; and for good reason.

Both PHP and MySQL are easy to use, fast, free, and powerful. If you want to get a dynamic Web site up quickly, there are no better choices. The PHP scripting language was built for the Web. All the tasks common to Web development can be accomplished in PHP with an absolute minimum of effort. Similarly, MySQL excels at tasks common to dynamic Web sites. Whether you're creating a content-management system or an e-commerce application, MySQL is a great choice for your data storage.

Is This Book for You?

There are quite a few books that deal with PHP and a few that cover MySQL. We've read some of these and found a few to be quite helpful. If you're looking for a book that deals with gory details of either of these packages, you should probably look elsewhere.

The focus of this book is applications development. We are concerned with what it takes to get data-driven Web sites up and running in an organized and efficient way. The book does not go into arcane detail of every aspect of either of these tools. For example, in this book, you will not find a discussion of PHP's LDAP functions or MySQL's C application program interface (API). Instead, we will focus on the pieces of both packages that affect one another. We hope that by the time you're done with this book you'll know what it takes to get an application up and running using PHP and MySQL.

How This Book Is Organized

We have organized the book into four parts.

Part 1: Using MySQL

Before you code any PHP scripts, you will need to know how to design a database, create tables in your database, and get the information you want from the database. Part I of this book will show you about all you need to know to work with MySQL.

Part II: Using PHP

As an applications developer, the bulk of your time will be spent writing scripts that access the database and present HTML to a user's browser. Part II will start by showing you the basics of the PHP scripting language, covering how PHP works with variables, conditions, and control structures. Part II will also cover many of PHP's functions and discuss techniques for writing clean, manageable code.

Part III: Simple Applications

In this part, we present two of the seven applications in this book: a guestbook and a survey. Here you will see the lessons from Parts I and II put into practice as we build working applications.

Part IV: Not So Simple Applications

Here the applications will be more complex, as we present applications commonly used on the Web. You will see how you can design a content management system, a discussion board, a shopping cart, and other useful applications. Along the way, we will show some tips and techniques that should be helpful as you write your applications.

Part V: Appendixes

The appendixes cover several topics of interest to the MySQL/PHP developer. In the appendixes, you will find installation and configuration instructions, quick reference guides to PHP and MySQL functions, a regular expressions overview, and guides to MySQL administration. In addition, there are a few helpful resources, snippets of code, and instructions on using the CD-ROM.

Tell Us What You Think

Both the publisher and authors of this book hope you find it a valuable resource. Please feel free to register this book at the IDG Books Web site (http://www.idgbooks.com) and give us your feedback. Also check in at the site we've dedicated to this book, http://www.mysqlphpapps.com/, where you will be able to contact the authors and find updates to the applications created for this book.

Acknowledgments

This book would never have happened if not for the efforts of Debra Williams Cauley. I thank her for her patience and persistence. The efforts and talents of Neil Romanosky, S. B. Kleinman, and many others at IDG Books have made this book more lucid and attractive than we could have hoped. Richard Lynch's exacting eye and technical acumen kept our code clean, fast, and readable.

Any book on open-source software owes debt to those who have created these great tools. So I thank everyone involved with PHP and MySQL, from the core developers to those who contribute to the documentation. Special thanks to Michael (Monty) Widenius, MySQL's lead developer. He has not only created a terrific relational database, but has offered his advice and expertise to the authors of this book.

Contents at a Glance

Contents

Introduction

SOON WE WILL HEAD OFF on a fabulous journey, a journey on which we will explore the ins and outs of MySQL and PHP database applications in great detail. It's going to be a fun trip; we just know it.

OK, maybe we're being a bit optimistic. If you're anything like us, there will be points when this particular journey will be a lot more tedious than it is exciting. Let's face facts: application development isn't always the most exciting thing in the world. And as with any other venture that involves programming, there are sure to be some very frustrating times, whether because of a syntax error you can't find or a piece of code that won't do what you think it ought to do. But despite all that, here you are, and I think there is a very good reason for your being here.

Web applications are the present and the future. No matter your background, whether it be Visual Basic or COBOL, or maybe you know just some HTML and JavaScript, your résumé is only going to improve with some Web applications development experience. We don't think there's a better combination of tools to have under your belt than PHP and MySQL. The numbers bear us out. PHP and MySQL are becoming increasingly popular, and the demand for people who can use these tools will only increase.

But a bit later there will be more details on why you should use PHP and MySQL. Before we can get into the details of that, we want take a bit of time to go over the architecture of Web applications. Once we've done this, we will be able to explain in detail why PHP and MySQL should be the centerpieces of your application development environment. Once we've sold you on these tools, we'll present a very quick and grossly under-coded application. As you look over this application, you will see the basic syntax and principles behind PHP and MySQL.

 As we proceed with the book, we will assume that you have read and understand everything presented in this introduction.

Basic Architecture

At the most basic level, the Web works off of a client/server architecture. Simply stated, that means that both a central server and a client application are responsible for some amount of processing. This differs from a program such as Microsoft Word, which operates just fine without any help from a server. Those of you who used older VAX machines will remember the days of dumb terminals, which had no processing power whatsoever. Depending on where you work today, perhaps in a university or a bank, you may still use applications that are in no way dependent on the client. In other words, all the work is done on the central computer.

The client

The applications you can develop with MySQL and PHP make use of a single client: the Web browser. This is not the only possibility for Internet-based applications. For very sophisticated applications that require more client-side processing or that need to maintain state (we will talk about maintaining state later in the Introduction), a Java applet may be necessary. But unless you're coding something like a real-time chat program, client-side Java is completely unnecessary.

So the only client you should be concerned with is the Web browser. The applications will need to render in the browser. As you probably already know, the primary language of browsers is the hypertext markup language or HTML. HTML provides a set of tags that describe how a Web page should look. If you are new to the concept of HTML, get on the Web and read one of the many tutorials out there. It shouldn't take that much time to learn the basics.

Of course, most browsers will accept more than HTML. There are all kinds of plug-ins, including RealPlayer, Flash, and Shockwave. Most browsers also have some level of support for JavaScript, and some of the newer ones can work with XML. But, like most Web developers, we will be taking a lowest-common-denominator approach in this book. We're going to create applications that can be read in any browser. There will be no JavaScript, XML, or anything else that could prevent some users from rendering the pages we serve. HTML it is.

The server

Almost all of the work of Web applications takes place on the server. A specific application, called a Web server, will be responsible for communicating with the browser. A relational database server stores whatever information the application requires. Finally, you need a language to broker requests between the Web server and the database server; it will also be used to perform programmatic tasks on the information that comes to and from the Web server. Figure I-1 represents this system.

But of course none of this is possible without an operating system. The Web server, programming language, and database server you use must work well with your operating system.

OPERATING SYSTEM

There are many operating systems out there. Windows 98 and Macintosh OS are probably the most popular. But that's hardly the end of it. Circumstances may have forced you to work with some obscure OS for the past few years. You may even be under the impression that your OS is the best thing going. That's fine. But if you're planning on spending a lot of time on the Web and are planning on running applications, you're best off getting to know either Windows NT/2000 or Unix. These two account for well over 90 percent of all the Web servers on the Web. It is probably easier for you to learn a little NT/2000 or Unix than it is to convince everybody else that the AS/400 is the way to go.

Introduction   xxv

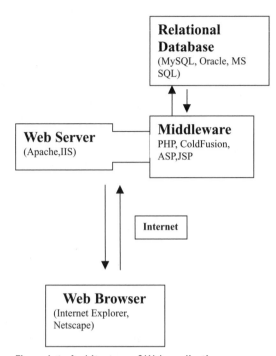

Figure I-1: Architecture of Web applications

Which should you use? Well, this is a complex question, and the answer for many will be based partially on religion. In case you're unaware of it, let's take a moment to talk about the broad topics in this religious war.

If you don't know what we are talking about, here are the basics. PHP and MySQL belong to a class of software known as *open source.* This means that the source code to the heart of their applications is available to anyone who wants to see it. They make use of an open-source development model, which allows anyone who is interested to participate in the development of the project. In the case of PHP, coders all over the world participate in the development of the language and see no immediate pay for their substantial work. Most of the people who participate are passionate about good software and code for the enjoyment of seeing people like you and me develop with their tools.

This method of development has been around for some time, but it has gained prominence as Linux has become increasingly popular. More often than not, open-source software is free. You can download the application, install it, and use it without getting permission from anyone or paying a dime to anyone.

Suffice it to say that Microsoft, Oracle, and other traditional software companies do not make use of this method of development.

If you are not an open-source zealot, there are excellent reasons to choose NT/2000. Usually, the thing that steers people towards NT/2000 is inertia. If you or your company has been developing with Microsoft products for years, it is probably going to be easier to stay within that environment. If you have a team of people who know Visual Basic, you are probably going to want to stick with NT/2000. Even if this is the case, there's nothing to prevent you from developing with PHP and MySQL. Both products run on Windows 95/98 and Windows NT/2000.

But in the real world, almost all PHP/MySQL applications are running off of some version of Unix, whether it be Linux, BSD, Irix, Solaris, HP-UX, or one of the other flavors. For that reason, the applications in this book will work with Unix. If you need to run these on Windows, minor alterations to the PHP scripts may be necessary. Most of the people who created PHP and MySQL are deeply involved with Unix, and most of their development is done on Unix machines, so it's not surprising that the software they have created works best on Linux, BSD, and other Unix boxes.

The major advantage of Unix is its inherent stability. Boxes loaded with Linux have been known to run months or years without crashing. Linux and BSD also have the advantage of being free and able to run on standard PC hardware. If you have any old 486, you can load it up with Linux, MySQL, PHP, and Apache and have yourself a well-outfitted Web server. You probably wouldn't want to put this on the Web, where a moderate amount of traffic might overwhelm it, but it will serve nicely as a development server, a place where you can test your applications.

WEB SERVER

The Web server has what seems to be a fairly straightforward job. It sits there, running on top of your operating system, listening for requests that somebody on the Web might make, responds to those requests, and serves out the appropriate Web pages. In reality, it is a bit more complicated than that, and because of the 24/7 nature of the Web, stability of the Web server is a major issue.

There are many Web servers out there, but two Web servers dominate the market. They are Apache and Microsoft's Internet Information Server (IIS).

INTERNET INFORMATION SERVER   IIS is deeply tied to the Windows environment and is a key component of Microsoft's Active Server Pages. If you've chosen to go the Microsoft way, you'll almost certainly end up using IIS.

There is a certain amount of integration between the programming language and Web server. At this point, PHP 4 integrates well with IIS. As of this writing, there is some concern about the stability of PHP/IIS under heavy load, but PHP is improving all the time, and by the time you read this there may no longer be a problem.

APACHE   The Apache Web server is the most popular Web server there is. It, like Linux, PHP, and MySQL, is an open-source project. Not surprisingly, Apache works best in Unix environments, but also runs just fine under Windows.

Apache makes use of third-party modules. Because it is open source, anyone with the skill can write code that extends the functionality of Apache. PHP will most often run as an Apache extension, known as an Apache module.

Apache is a great Web server. It is extremely quick and amazingly stable. The most frequently stated complaint about Apache is that, like many pieces of Unix software, there are limited graphical tools with which you can manipulate the application. You alter Apache by specifying options on the command line or by altering text files. When you come to Apache for the first time, all this can be a bit opaque.

Though Apache works best on Unix systems, there are also versions that run on Windows operating systems. Nobody, not even the Apache developers, recommends that Apache be run on a busy server under Windows. If you have decided to use the Windows platform for serving Web pages, you're better off using IIS.

But there are conditions under which you'll be glad Apache does run under Windows. You can run Apache, PHP, and MySQL on a Windows 98 machine and then transfer those applications to Linux with practically no changes to the scripts. This is the easiest way to go if you need to develop locally on Windows but to serve off a Unix/Apache server.

MIDDLEWARE

PHP belongs to a class of languages known as *middleware*. These languages work closely with the Web server to interpret the requests made from the World Wide Web, process these requests, interact with other programs on the server to fulfill the requests, and then indicate to the Web server exactly what to serve to the client's browser.

The middleware is where you'll be doing the vast majority of your work. With a little luck, you can have your Web server up and running without a whole lot of effort. And once it is up and running, you won't need to fool with it a whole lot.

But as you are developing your applications, you'll spend a lot of time writing code that makes your applications work. In addition to PHP, there are several languages that perform similar functions. Some of the more popular choices are ASP, Perl, and ColdFusion.

RELATIONAL DATABASES

Relational Database Management Systems (RDBMSs) provide a great way to store and access complex information. They have been around for quite a while. In fact, they predate the Web, Linux, and Windows NT, so it should be no surprise that there are many RDBMSs to choose from. All of the major databases make use of the Structured Query Language (SQL).

Some of the more popular commercial RDBMSs are Oracle, Sybase, Informix, Microsoft's SQL Server, and IBM's db2. In addition to MySQL, there are now two major open-source relational databases. Postgres has been the major alternative to MySQL in the open-source arena for some time. In August 1999, Borland released its Interbase product under an open-source license and allowed free download and use.

Why these Products?

Given the number of choices out there, you may be asking yourself why you should choose PHP and/or MySQL. We will answer this question in the following three sections.

Why PHP?

Programming languages are a lot like shoes. Some look good to some people yet look really ugly to others. To carry the analogy a little further, some shoes just fit well on some feet.

What we mean is this: when it comes to Web programming, all languages do pretty much the same thing: They all interact with relational databases; they all work with a filesystem; they all interact with a Web server. The question about which language is best is rarely a matter of a language's inability to perform certain actions. It's usually more a matter of how quickly you can do what you need to do with the least amount of pain.

IT'S FAST AND EASY

What about speed? There are really only three things that we know for sure when it comes to comparing speeds of Web programming languages. First, applications written in C will be the fastest. Second, programming in C is rather difficult and will take much longer than any of the other languages mentioned so far. Third, comparisons between languages are extremely difficult. From everything we know, we feel safe in saying the PHP is as fast as anything out there.

More often than not choosing a language comes back to the same issues involved in buying shoes. You'll want to go with what's most comfortable. If you're like us, you will find that PHP has managed the perfect mix of power, structure, and ease of use. Again, this is largely a matter of opinion, but we do believe the syntax of PHP is superior to that of ASP and JSP. And we believe it puts more power at your fingertips more quickly than ColdFusion and is not as difficult to learn as Perl.

In the end, we believe PHP offers the best opportunity to develop powerful Web applications quickly. That generalization made, we do believe there are other excellent reasons for choosing PHP.

IT'S CROSS-PLATFORM

In the rundown of Web architecture, we mentioned that PHP will run on Windows 2000/NT and Unix and with both IIS and Apache. But the cross-platform abilities of PHP go far beyond these platforms. If you happen to be using Netscape, Roxen, or just about anything else, it is likely PHP will work with it.

Yes, ASP can be run on Linux, and ColdFusion can work on Solaris and Linux, and JSP is adaptable across many platforms. At this point, PHP works as well on as wide a variety of systems as any other available product.

IT ACCESSES EVERYTHING

What do you need to access in the course of creating your Web applications? LDAP? IMAP mail server? Oracle? Informix? DB2? Or maybe you need an XML parser or WDDX functions.

Whatever you need to use, it is more than likely that PHP has a built-in set of functions that make getting whatever you need very easy. But what if it doesn't have something built in that you'd like? That brings us to our next point.

IT'S CONSTANTLY BEING IMPROVED

If you are new to open source development, you might be surprised by the high quality of the software. There are thousands of very technical, very talented programmers out there who love to spend their time creating great, and mostly free, software. In an active project such as PHP, there is a variety of developers looking to improve the product almost daily.

It is truly remarkable. If you happen to find a bug, you can submit a report to a mailing list that the core developers read. Depending on its severity, it is likely that the bug will be addressed within a couple of hours to a couple of days.

When PHP 4 was put together, it was done so in a modular fashion. This makes adding greater functionality reasonably easy. If there are sets of functions you'd like added to PHP, there's a good chance that someone will be able to do it with minimal effort.

YOUR PEERS WILL SUPPORT YOU

Most languages have active mailing lists and development sites. PHP is no exception. If you run into trouble – if there's a bug in your code you just can't figure out or you can't seem to fathom some function or another – someone among the hundreds subscribed to PHP mailing lists will be happy to check and fix your code.

The open-source nature of PHP creates a real feeling of community. When you get into trouble, your PHP-hacking brethren will feel your pain and ease it.

IT'S FREE

If you have a computer, Linux, Apache, and PHP are all completely free.

Why MySQL?

This one is perhaps a little tougher to answer. Although MySQL has much to recommend it, it also has a variety of competitors, many of whom may be better suited for a particular task.

In Part I of this book, MySQL is discussed in some detail. In these chapters, you'll see that we mention features available in other relational databases that MySQL does not support. (If you know your way around databases and are curious, these include stored procedures, triggers, referential integrity, and SQL unions and subqueries.) Given these limitations, there are definitely environments where MySQL would not be the best choice. If you are planning on starting, say, a bank (you know, a savings and loan), MySQL probably isn't for you.

But for the majority of people in the majority of applications, MySQL is a great choice. It is particularly well suited for Web applications.

IT'S COST-EFFECTIVE

Think you need an Oracle installation? Get ready to shell out somewhere between $30,000-$100,000 or more. There's no doubt that Oracle, Sybase, and Informix create terrific databases, but the cost involved will be prohibitive for many.

MySQL is free. You can install and use it and pay nothing in the process.

IT'S QUICK AND POWERFUL

MySQL may not have every bell and whistle available for a relational database, but for most users there is plenty. If you are serving out Web content or creating a moderately sized commerce site, MySQL has all the power you need.

For small-to-medium-sized databases, MySQL will be extremely fast. The developers of MySQL take great pride in the speed of their product. For applications like the ones presented in Parts III and IV of this book, it is unlikely you'll find a database that's any faster.

IT'S IMPROVING ALL THE TIME

MySQL is improving at a staggering rate. The developers release updates frequently and are adding impressive (and we do mean impressive) features all the time. Recently, MySQL added support for transactions; they are apparently at work now on stored procedures.

MySQL transaction support was added shortly before this writing. Therefore, applications in this book that might make use of transactions do not.

All in all, MySQL is an excellent product and getting better all the time.

Your First Application

Enough of the prelude. Let's get to writing an application so you can see how all of these parts come together in a real live application. By the time you have finished reading this intro, you should have a pretty good idea of how it all comes together.

Tool check

There are a few key elements you need to get going. We'll run through them here so you'll know what you need.

SOFTWARE

This is a Web-based application, so you're clearly going to need a Web server. You will probably be using Apache, whether you are using Windows or Unix. You will need to install Apache so that it can access the PHP language.

In addition, you will need to have MySQL installed. And PHP will have to be able to recognize MySQL. Apache, MySQL, and PHP are provided on the accompanying CD, and installation instructions are provided in Appendix B. You may want to install these packages before proceeding, or you could just read along to get an idea of what we're doing and install the packages later when you want to work with the more practical examples in this book.

TEXT EDITOR

As of this writing, there are no slick, integrated development environments (IDEs) for PHP. To code PHP and your Web pages, you will need a text editor. You could use Notepad or something similarly basic, but if you're starting without an allegiance to any particular editor, I suggest you get something with good syntax highlighting. On Windows, Allaire's Homesite (www.allaire.com) is a tool that works well with PHP, and we've heard excellent things about Editplus (www.editplus.com).

If you have been working on Unix for some time, it is likely that you already know and love some text editor or another, whether it be Emacs, vi , or Kedit. If not, any of these are fine, though the first two do take some getting used to. If you're woking on Unix, but don't have the patience to learn vi, try Pico. It's very easy to use.

TIP If you need a text editor under Unix but don't know your way around vi, try Pico. It's a very basic, easy-to-use text editor.

Application overview

We thought we would start this book with something really exotic, a Web application that's mind-blowingly original, something never before seen on the Web. After a great brainstorming session, when we contacted some of the brightest people on the Web, and geniuses in other creative fields, we found the perfect thing. We'd write an application that stores user information, a place where users can enter their names, e-mail addresses, URLs, and maybe even comments. After lengthy discussion, and deep prayer, we decided on a name for this application. It is now and forever to be known as a *guestbook*.

XREF The guestbook is a simplified example, something you would never want to run on a live Web server. We re-create this application in a more robust form in Chapter 8.

Create the database

Now that you know exactly what you need , the first step is to create a database that will store this information. To do this, you will use the language common to most every database server: the Structured Query Language (SQL). You will read a lot more about this later, so don't worry if you don't understand everything right away. Just read through the rest of the Introduction and then read Chapter 1.

Start up the MySQL command-line client. If you're working on Unix, typing **mysql** at the shell should do the trick (or you might have to go to the /mysql/bin directory). If you are on Windows, you will need to go to the DOS prompt, find the path to mysql.exe, and execute it. Then, at the prompt, create a new database. When you're done, you should have something that looks very much like this:

```
[jay@mybox jay]$ mysql
Welcome to the MySQL monitor.  Commands end with ; or \g.
Your MySQL connection id is 716 to server version: 3.22.27-log

Type 'help' for help.

mysql> create database guestbook;
Query OK, 1 row affected (0.00 sec)

mysql>
```

Now, within the database named guestbook, you will need a table that stores the user information. This table is also created in the MySQL monitor. The command to create the table isn't very complex. You basically need to let MySQL know what kind of information to expect, whether numbers or stings, and whether or not any of the information can be omitted (or NULL). The basic command is **create table**; it will look about like this when you make the table:

```
mysql> use guestbook
Database changed
mysql> create table guestbook
    -> (
    ->         name            varchar(40) null,
    ->         location        varchar(40) null,
    ->         email           varchar(40) null,
    ->         url             varchar(40) null,
    ->         comments        text null
    -> )
    -> ;
Query OK, 0 rows affected (0.00 sec)

mysql>
```

So now you have a database named guestbook and a table within the database named guestbook. Now it's time to write an application in PHP that will enable you to insert, edit, and view information kept in this guestbook.

Your PHP Script

Now's the time to move to the text editor. In the course of configuring your Web server, you will need to let it know which files should be handed off to PHP so the engine can interpret the page. Most often, these files will have a .php extension, though it is possible to have PHP interpret anything, including .html files. These scripts will live inside the folder designated to hold Web pages. For Apache, this will usually be /htdocs.

BASIC SYNTAX

One neat thing about PHP is that it lets you move between straight HTML and commands that are part of the PHP programming language. It works like this: The sections of your script between the opening tag <?php and a closing tag ?> will be interpreted by the PHP engine, and portions not within these tags will be treated as plain HTML. Check out the following PHP page.

```php
<?php
echo "Hi,";
?>
mom.
```

When run through the Web server, this would create a Web page that prints, simply, "Hi, mom." PHP's echo command manages the first part of the line. But, of course, PHP can do quite a bit more than that. Like any other programming language, it can work with variables and make decisions.

```php
<?php
echo "hi, mom. ";

$var = date("H");
if ($var <= 11)
{
    echo "good morning";
}
elseif ($var > 11 and $var < 18)
{
    echo "good afternoon";
}
else
{
    echo "good evening";
}
?>
```

In this page, after printing out the greeting, there is some real programming. I've used PHP's built-in date function to grab the hour of the day in 24-hour format. That value is immediately assigned to a variable named $var. Then a decision is made, and the appropriate text is printed, depending on the time of day. Notice the syntax here. Each PHP command ends with a semicolon. In the if statement, curly braces hold the commands to be executed depending on the condition. And the condition itself is held within parentheses.

The date() function and echo, which are used in the previous example, are just two of the hundreds of functions built into PHP, many of which you will learn to use in the course of this book. If you are going to access the database, you're going to need a few more.

CONNECTING TO THE DATABASE

While you're installing PHP, you should let it know that you plan on using MySQL with it. If you don't do this, what we will discuss now won't work. Even if PHP is aware that you're using MySQL, in your specific scripts you must identify the exact database you need access to. In this case, that will be the guestbook database you just created.

```
mysql_connect("localhost", "nobody","password") or
    die ("Could not connect to database");
mysql_select_db("guestbook") or
    die ("Could not select database");
```

The first line tells MySQL that the Web server (the entity running the script) is on the local machine, has a username of nobody, and has a password of password. Then, if the connection is successful, the specific database is selected with the mysql_select_db() command. With these lines safely tucked away in your scripts, you should be able to manipulate the database with your commands.

Because you're going to need these lines in every page in this application, it makes sense to save some typing and put them in a file of their own and include them in every page. If you've done any programming at all, you know that this involves dumping the entire contents of that file into the file being accessed. These lines will be kept in a file called dbconnect.php. At the top of every other file in this application will be the following line:

```
include('dbconnect.php');
```

INSERTING INFORMATION INTO THE DATABASE

Because you have yet to put any users in the database, we'll start by reviewing the script that will allow that. But first, we need to tell you a little bit more about PHP variables. A bit earlier, we showed that you can create variables within a PHP script, but as this is a client/server environment, you're going to need to get variable data from the client (the Web browser) to PHP. You'll usually do this with HTML forms.

There's a basic rundown of HTML forms in Appendix A. Check that if you need to. For now we will just point out that every form element has a name, and when a form is submitted the names of those form elements become available as variables in the PHP script the form was submitted to. With the following form, as soon as the form is submitted, the variables $surname and $submit will become available in the PHP script myscript.php. The value of $surname will be whatever the user enters into the text field. The value of $submit will be the text string "submit."

```
<form action="myscript.php">
    <input type="text" name="surnmae">
```

```
    <input type="submit" name="submit" value="submit">
</form>
```

Before we show the script itself, now is a good time to note that Web programming is slightly different from other types of programming in one important respect: It is stateless. To display a page, a Web server must first receive a request from a browser. The language they speak is called HTTP, the Hypertext Transfer Protocol. The request will include several things – the page the browser wishes to see, the form data, the type of browser being used, and the IP address the browser is using. Based on this information, the Web server will decide what to serve.

Once it has served this page, the server maintains no connection to the browser. It has absolutely no memory of what it served to whom. Each HTTP request is dealt with individually with no regard to what came before it. For this reason, in Web programming you need to come up with some way of maintaining state. That is, if you are progressing through an application, you will need some way of letting the server know what happened. Essentially, you will need ways of passing variables from page to page. This will come up in our applications. The applications will solve this problem in one of three ways: by passing hidden form elements, by using cookies, or by using sessions.

Now back to our script.

```
<form action="myscript.php">
    <input type="text" name="surnmae">
    <input type="submit" name="submit" value="submit">
</form>
```

You can decide what you will display on a page based on the variable information that comes from HTML forms. For instance, you could check if the preceding form had been submitted by checking if the variable name $submit had a value of "submit." This very technique will come into play when it comes to creating the page for inserting information into the database.

There is one page in our application, called sign.php, that has an HTML form. The action of the form in this page is create_entry.php. Here's the page in all its glory:

```
<h2>Sign my Guest Book!!!</h2>

<form method=post action="create_entry.php">

<b>Name:</b>
<input type=text size=40 name=name>
<br>
<b>Location:</b>
<input type=text size=40 name=location>
<br>
```

```
<b>Email:</b>
<input type=text size=40 name=email>
<br>
<b>Home Page URL:</b>
<input type=text size=40 name=url>
<br>
<b>Comments:</b>
<textarea name=comments cols=40 rows=4 wrap=virtual></textarea>
<br>

<input type=submit name=submit value="Sign!">
<input type=reset name=reset value="Start Over">

</form>
```

When the user fills out this form and submits it, the information will be sent to create_entry.php. The first thing to do on this page is to check that the form has been submitted. If it has, take the values entered into the form and use them to create a query that you will send to MySQL. Don't worry about the specifics of the query just yet. Just know that it will insert a row into the database table you created earlier.

```
<?php
include("dbconnect.php");

if ($submit == "Sign!")
{
    $query = "insert into guestbook
        (name,location,email,url,comments) values
        ('$name', '$location', '$email', '$url', '$comments')"
    ;
    mysql_query($query) or
            die (mysql_error());
?>
<h2>Thanks!!</h2>
<h2><a href="view.php">View My Guest Book!!!</a></h2>
<?php
}
else
{
    include("sign.php");
}
?>
```

If the form, which is in sign.php, hasn't been submitted, it is included and therefore will show the same form. You may notice that this page is submitted to itself.

The first time the create_entry.php page is called, the form in sign.php will be displayed. The next time, though, the data will be inserted into the database.

Figures I-2 and I-3 show the pages that this script will create.

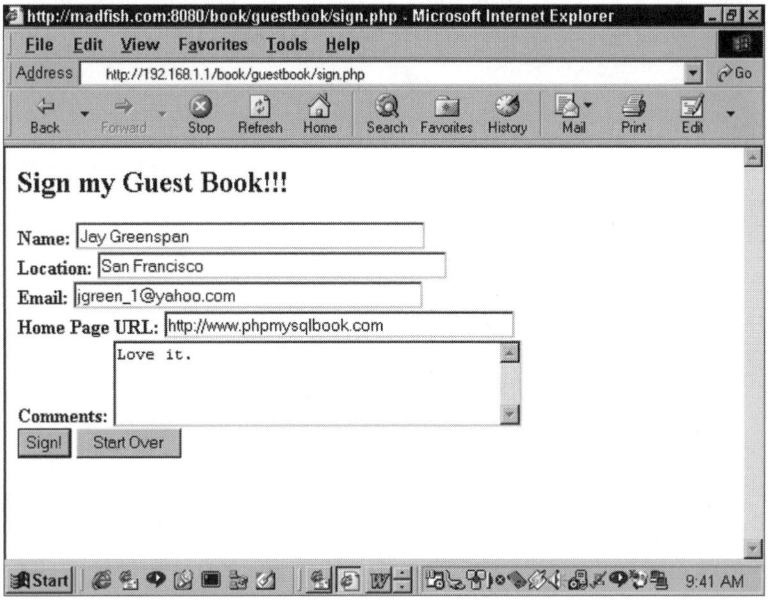

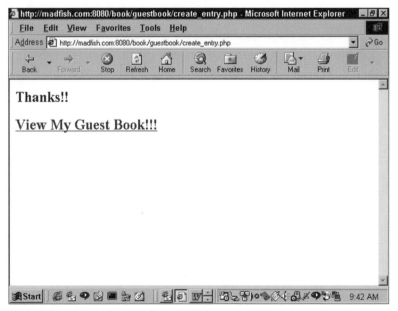

Figure I-2: create_entry.php the first time through

Figure I-3: create_entry.php after submission

VIEWING INFORMATION IN THE DATABASE

This shouldn't be too tough. You already know that the file will need to include dbconnect.php. Other than that, we've already mentioned that databases store information in tables. Each row of the table will contain information on a specific person who signed the guestbook, so to view all of the information, the page will need to retrieve and print out every row of data. Here's the script that will do it (you should notice that it's pretty sparse):

```php
<?php include("dbconnect.php"); ?>

<h2>View My Guest Book!!</h2>

<?php

$result = mysql_query("select * from guestbook") or
    die (mysql_error());
while ($row = mysql_fetch_array($result))
{
    echo "<b>Name:</b>";
 echo $row["name"];
 echo "<br>\n";
 echo "<b>Location:</b>";
 echo $row["location"];
 echo "<br>\n";
 echo "<b>Email:</b>";
 echo $row["email"];
 echo "<br>\n";
 echo "<b>URL:</b>";
 echo $row["url"];
 echo "<br>\n";
 echo "<b>Comments:</b>";
 echo $row["comments"];
 echo "<br>\n";
 echo "<br>\n";
 echo "<br>\n";
}
mysql_free_result($result);
?>

<h2><a href="sign.php">Sign My Guest Book!!</a></h2>
```

The query asks MySQL for every row in the database. Then the script enters a loop. Each row in the database is loaded into the variable $row, one row at a time. Rows will continue to be accessed until none is left. At that time, the script will drop out of the while loop.

As it works through the loop, each column in that row is displayed. For example

```
print $row["email"]
```

will print out the e-mail column for the row being accessed.

When run, this simple script will print out every row in the database. Figure I-4 shows what the page will look like.

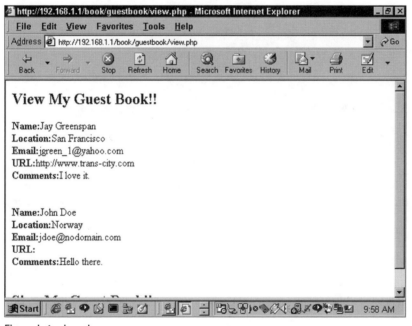

Figure I-4: view.php

And that about does it for our first application.

WHY YOU SHOULD NOT USE THIS APPLICATION

If you want to load this up on your own server to see if it works, fine; be our guest. But we wouldn't put it anywhere where the general public could get to it. No, if you were to do that there would be problems. For instance, you could end up with Figure I-5 on your view.php page. Not good at all!

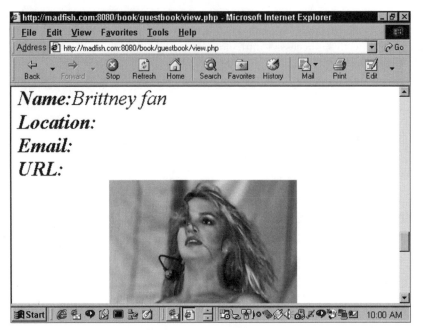

Figure I-5: Problematic guestbook entry

If you want a guestbook, you should use the super-hyper-coded application made exclusively for the readers of this book, which you will find in Chapter 8. We call this application Guestbook2k. But before we get there, it's time for some education.

Now get reading.

Part I

Working with MySQL

Chapter 1

Database Design with MySQL

IN THIS CHAPTER

- ◆ Identifying the problems that led to the creation of the relational database
- ◆ Learning the normalization process
- ◆ Taking a look at database features that MySQL does not currently support

THE BULK OF THIS CHAPTER is for those of you who have made it to the early 21st century without working with relational databases. If you're a seasoned database pro, having worked with Oracle, Sybase, or even something like Microsoft Access or Paradox, you may want to skip this little lesson on database theory. However, I do suggest that you look at the final section of this chapter, where I discuss some of MySQL's weirder points. MySQL's implementation of SQL is incomplete, so it may not support some of what you might be looking for.

Why Use a Relational Database?

If you're still here and are ready to read with rapt attention about database theory and the wonders of normalization, you probably don't know much about the history of the relational database. You may not even care. For that reason, I'll keep this very brief. Dr. E. F. Codd was a research scientist at IBM in the 1960s. A mathematician by training, he was unhappy with the available models of data storage. He found that all the available methods were prone to error and redundancy. He worked on these problems and then, in 1970, published a paper with the rousing title "A Relational Model of Data for Large Shared Databanks." In all honesty, nothing has been the same since.

A programmer named Larry Ellison read the paper and started work on software that could put Dr. Codd's theories into practice. If you've been a resident of this planet over the past 20 years, you may know that Ellison's product and company took the name Oracle and that he is now one of the richest men in the world. His earliest product was designed for huge mainframe systems. Responding to market demands over the years, Oracle, and many other companies that have sprung up since, have designed systems with a variety of features geared toward a variety of operating systems. Now, relational databases are so common that you can get one that runs on a Palm Pilot.

To understand why Dr. Codd's theories have revolutionized the data storage world, it's best to have an idea as to what the troubles are with other means of data storage. Take the example of a simple address book – nothing too complex, just something that stores names, addresses, phone numbers, e-mails, and the like. If there's no persistent, running program that we can put this information into, the file system of whatever OS is running becomes the natural choice for storage.

For a simple address book, a delimited text file can be created to store the information. If the first row serves as a header and commas are used as the delimiter, it might look something like this:

```
Name, Addr1, Addr2, City, State, Zip, Phone, E-mail
Jay Greenspan, 211 Some St, Apt 2, San Francisco, CA, 94107,
4155551212, jgreen_1@yahoo.com
Brad Bulger, 411 Some St, Apt 6, San Francisco, CA, 94109,
4155552222, bbulger@yahoo.com
John Doe, 444 Madison Ave, , New York, NY, 11234, 2125556666,
nobody@hotmail.com
```

This isn't much to look at, but it is at least machine-readable. Using whatever language you wish, you can write a script that opens this file and then parses the information. You will probably want it in some sort of two-dimensional or associative array so that you'll have some flexibility in addressing each portion of each line of this file. Any way you look at it, there's going to be a fair amount of code to write. If you want this information to be sortable and queryable by a variety of criteria, you're going to have to write scripts that will, for instance, sort the list alphabetically by name or find all people within a certain area code. What a pain.

You might face another major problem if your data needs to be used across a network by a variety of people. Presumably more than one person is going to need to write information to this file. What happens if two people try to make changes at once? For starters, it's quite possible that one person will overwrite another's changes. To prevent this from happening, the programmer has to specify file locking if the file is in use. While this might work, it's kind of a pain in the neck for the person who gets locked out. Obviously, the larger the system gets the more unmanageable this all becomes.

What you need is something more robust than the file system – a program or daemon that stays in memory seems to be a good choice. Further, you'll need a data storage system that reduces the amount of parsing and scripting that the programmer needs to be concerned with. No need for anything too arcane here. A plain, simple table like Table 1-1 should work just fine.

Now this is pretty convenient. It's easy to look at and, if there is a running program that accesses this table, it should be pretty quick. What else might this program do? First, it should be able to address one row at a time without affecting the others. That way, if two or more people want to insert information into this table, they won't be tripping over each other. It would be even spiffier if the program provided a simple and elegant way to extract information from a table such as this. There should be a quick way of finding all of the people from California that doesn't involve parsing and sorting the file. Furthermore, this wondrous program should be able to accept statements that describe what you want in a language very similar to English. That way you can just say: "Give me all rows where the contents of the State column equal 'CA'."

Yes, this would be great, but it isn't enough. There are still major problems that will need to be dealt with. These problems, which I'll discuss in the following pages, are the same ones that made Dr. Codd write his famous paper, and that made Larry Ellison a billionaire.

Blasted Anomalies

Dr. Codd's goal was to have a model of information that was dependable. All of the data-storage methods available to him had inherent problems. He referred to these problems as anomalies. There are three types of anomalies: Update, Delete, and Insert.

Update anomaly

Now that we can assume that a table structure can quickly and easily handle multiple requests, we need to see what happens when the information gets more complex. Adding some more information to the previous table introduces some serious problems (Table 1-2).

Table 1-2 is meant to store information for an entire office, not just a single person. Since this company deals with other large companies, there will be times when more than one contact will be at a single office location. For example, in Table 1-2, there are two contacts at 1121 43rd St. At first this may appear to be OK: we can still get at all the information available relatively easily. The problem comes when the BigCo Company decides to up and move to another address. In that case, we'd have to update the address for BigCo in two different rows. This may not sound like such an onerous task, but consider the trouble if this table has 3,000 rows instead of 3 – or 300,000 for that matter. Someone, or some program, has to make sure the data is changed in every appropriate place.

Another concern is the potential for error. It's very possible that one of these rows could be altered while the other one remained the same. Or, if changes are keyed in one row at a time, it's likely that somebody will introduce a typo. Then you're left wondering if the correct address is 1121 or 1211.

The better way to handle this data is to take the company name and address and put that information in its own table. The two resulting tables will resemble Table 1-3 and Table 1-4.

TABLE 1–1 SIMPLE TABLE FOR DATA STORAGE

name	addr1	addr2	city	state	zip	phone	e-mail
Jay Greenspan	211 Some St	Apt 2	San Francisco	CA	94107	4155551212	jgreen_1@yahoo.com
Brad Bulger	411 Some St	Apt 6	San Francisco	CA	94109	4155552222	bbulger@yahoo.com
John Doe	444 Madison Ave		New York	NY	11234	2125556666	nobody@hotmail.com

TABLE 1–2 PROBLEMATIC TABLE STORAGE

id	company_name	company_address	contact_name	contact_title	phone	email
1	BigCo Company	1121 43rd St	Jay Greenspan	Vice President	4155551212	jgreen_1@yahoo.com
2	BigCo Company	1121 43rd St	Brad Bulger	President	4155552222	bbulger@yahoo.com
3	LittleCo Company	4444 44th St	John Doe	Lackey	2125556666	nobody@hotmail.com

TABLE 1-3 COMPANIES

company_id	company_name	company_address
1	BigCo Company	1121 43rd St
2	LittleCo Company	4444 44th St

TABLE 1-4 CONTACTS

contact_id	company_id	contact_name	contact_title	phone	email
1	1	Jay Greenspan	Vice President	4155551212	jgreen_1@yahoo.com
2	1	Brad Bulger	President	4155552222	bbulger@yahoo.com
3	2	John Doe	Lackey	2125556666	nobody@hotmail.com

Now the information pertinent to BigCo Co. is in its own table, named Companies. If you look at the next table (Table 1-4), named Contacts, you'll see that we've inserted another column, called company_id. This column references the company_id column of the Company table. In Brad's row, we see that the company_id (the second column) equals 1. We can then go to the Companies table, look at the information for company_id 1 and see all the relevant address information. What's happened here is that we've created a relationship between these two tables — hence the name *relational database.*

We still have all the information we had in the previous setup, we've just segmented it. In this setup we can change the address for both Jay and Brad by altering only a single row. That's the kind of convenience we're after.

Perhaps this leaves you wondering how we get this information un-segmented. Relational databases give us the ability to merge, or join, tables. Consider the following statement, which is intended to give us all the available information for Brad: "Give me all the columns from the contacts table where contact_id is equal to 1, and while you're at it throw in all the columns from the Companies table where the company_id field equals the value shown in Brad's company_id column." In other words, in this statement, you are asking to join these two tables where the company_id fields are the same. The result of this request, or query, would look something like Table 1-5.

In the course of a couple of pages, you've learned how to solve a data-integrity problem by segmenting information and creating additional tables. But I have yet to give this problem a name. When I learned the vocabulary associated with relational databases from a very thick and expensive book, this sort of problem was called an *update anomaly.* There may or may not be people using this term in the real world; if there are, I haven't met them. However, I think this term is pretty apt. In the table presented earlier in this section, if we were to update one row in the table, other rows containing the same information would not be affected.

Delete anomaly

Now take a look at Table 1-6, focusing on row 3. Consider what happens if Mr. Doe is deleted from the database. This may seem like a simple change but suppose someone accessing the database wants a list of all the companies contacted over the previous year. In the current setup, when we remove row 3 we take out not only the information about John Doe, we remove information about the company as well. This problem is called a *deletion anomaly.*

If the company information is moved to its own table, as we saw in the previous section, this won't be a problem. We can remove Mr. Doe and then decide independently if we want to remove the company he's associated with.

TABLE 1-5 QUERY RESULTS

company_id	company_name	company_address	contact_id	Contact Name	Contact Title	Phone	E-mail
1	BigCo Company	1121 43rd St	2	Brad Bulger	President	4155552222	bbulger@yahoo.com

TABLE 1-6 TABLE WITH DELETION ANOMALY

company_id	company_name	company_address	contact_name	contact_title	phone	email
1	BigCo Company	1121 43rd St	Jay Greenspan	Vice President	4155551212	jgreen_1@yahoo.com
2	BigCo Company	1121 43rd St	Brad Bulger	President	4155552222	bbulger@yahoo.com
3	LittleCo Company	4444 44th St	John Doe	Lackey	2125556666	nobody@hotmail.com

Insert anomaly

Our final area of concern is problems that will be introduced during an insert. Looking again at the Table 1-6, we see that the purpose of this table is to store information on contacts, not companies. This becomes a drag if you want to add a company but not an individual. For the most part, you'll have to wait to have a specific contact to add to the data before you can add company information to the database. This is a ridiculous restriction.

Normalization

Now that we've shown you some of the problems you might encounter, you need to learn the ways to find and eliminate these anomalies. This process is known as normalization. Understanding normalization is vital to working with relational databases. But, to anyone who has database experience, normalization is not the be-all and end-all of data design. Experience and instinct also play a part in creating a good database. In the examples presented later in this book, the data will be normalized, for the most part — but there will also be occasions when an unnormalized structure is preferable.

One other quick caveat. The normalization process consists of several "normal forms." In this chapter we will cover 1st, 2nd, and 3rd normal forms. In addition to these, the normalization process can continue through four other normal forms. (For the curious, these are called Boyce-Codd normal form, 4th normal form, 5th normal form, and Domain/Key normal form). I know about these because I read about them in a book. In the real world, where real people actually develop database applications, these normal forms just don't get talked about. If you get your data into 3rd normal form that's about good enough. Yes, there is a possibility that anomalies will exist in 3rd normal form, but if you get this far you should be OK.

1st normal form

Getting data into 1st normal form is fairly easy. Data need to be in a table structure and meet the following criteria:

- Each column must contain an "atomic" value. That means that there will be only one value per cell. No arrays or any other manner of representing more than one value will exist in any cell.

- Each column must have a unique name.

- The table must have a set of values that uniquely identifies the row (This is known as the primary key of the table).

- No two rows can be identical.

- No repeating groups of data are allowed.

The final item here is the only one that may require some explanation. Take a look at Table 1-7:

TABLE 1-7 TABLE WITH REPEATING GROUPS OF DATA

company_id	company_ name	company_ address	contact_ name	contact_ title	phone	email
1	BigCo Company	1121 43rd St	Jay Greenspan	Vice President	4155551212	jgreen_1@yahoo.com
2	BigCo Company	1121 43rd St	Brad Bulger	President	4155552222	bbulger@yahoo.com
3	LittleCo Company	4444 44th St	John Doe	Lackey	2125556666	nobody@hotmail.com

As we've already seen, row 1 and row 2 contain two columns that contain identical information. This is a repeating group of data. Only when we remove these columns and place them in their own table will this data be first normal form. The separation of tables that we did in Tables 1-3 and 1-4 will move this data into 1st normal form.

Before we move on to chat about 2nd and 3rd normal form, you're going to need a couple of quick definitions. The first is *primary key*. The primary key is a column or set of columns by which each row can be uniquely identified. In the tables presented so far, I've included a column with sequential values, and as rows are added to these tables the database engine will automatically insert an integer one greater than the maximum value for the column. It's an easy way to make sure you have a unique field for every row. Every database in the world has some method of defining a column like this. In MySQL it's called an auto_increment field. Depending on your data, there are all kinds of values that will work for a primary key. Social Security numbers work great, as do e-mail addresses and URLs. The data just need to be unique. In some cases, two or more columns may comprise your primary key. For instance, continuing with our address book example, if contact information needs to be stored for a company with many locations, it will probably be best to store the switchboard number and mailing address information in a table that has the company_id and the company city as its primary key.

Next, we need to define the word *dependency,* which means pretty much what you think it means. A dependent column is one that is inexorably tied to the primary key. It can't exist in the table if the primary key is removed.

With that under our belts, we are ready to tackle 2nd normal form.

2nd normal form

This part of the process only comes into play when you end up with one of those multi-column primary keys that I just discussed. Assume that in the course of dividing up our address tables we end up with Table 1-8. Here, the company_name and comapany_location comprise the multi-column primary key.

TABLE 1-8 TABLE NOT IN 2ND NORMAL FROM

company_name	company_location	company_ceo	company_address
BigCo Company	San Francisco	Bill Hurt	1121 43rd St
LittleCo Company	LA	LittleCo Company	4444 44th st

You should be able to see pretty quickly that an insertion anomaly would work its way in here if we were to add another location for BigCo Co. We'd have the CEO name, Bill Hurt, repeated in an additional row, and that's no good.

We can get this table into 2nd normal form by removing rows that are only partially dependent on the primary key. Here, CEO is only dependent on the company_name column. It is not dependent on the company_location column. To get into 2nd normal form, we move rows that are only partially dependent on a multi-field primary key into their own table. 2nd normal form does not apply to tables that have a single-column primary key.

3rd normal form

Finishing up the normalization process, 3rd normal form is concerned with *transitive dependencies*. A transitive dependency is a situation where a column exists that is not directly reliant on the primary key. Instead, the field is reliant on some other field, which in turn is dependent on the primary key. A quick way to get into 3rd normal form is to look at the all fields in a table and ask if those fields describe the primary key. If not, you're not there.

If your address book needs to store more information on your contacts, you may find yourself with a table like this.

TABLE 1-9 TABLE NOT IN 3RD NORMAL FORM

contact_id	contact_ name	contact_ phone	assistant_ name	assistant_ phone
1	Bill Jones	4155555555	John Bills	2025554444
2	Carol Shaw	2015556666	Shawn Carlo	6505556666

You may think we're doing OK here. But look at the assistant_phone column and ask if that really describes the primary key (and the focus of this table), which is your contact. It's possible, even likely, that one assistant will serve many people, in which case it's possible that an assistant name and phone will end up listed in the table more than once. That would be a repeating group of data, which we already know we don't want.

Types of Relationships

Essentially, the deal with this book is that we're going to create a bunch of tables that don't have anomalies. We'll include columns that maintain relationships between these tables. There are three specific types of relationships that we'll encounter in database land.

One-to-many relationship

This is by far the most common type of relationship that occurs between tables. When one value in a column references several fields in another table, a one-to-many relationship is in effect (Figure 1-1).

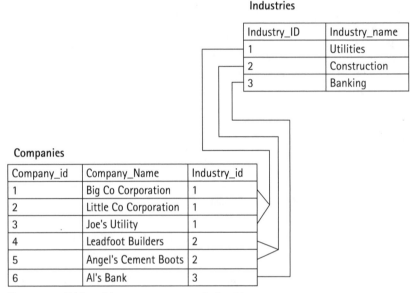

Figure 1-1: Tables with a one-to-many relationship

This is a classic one-to many relationship. Here, each company is associated with a certain industry. As you can see, one industry listed in the industry table can be associated with one or more rows in the company table. This in no way restricts what we can do with the companies. We are absolutely free to use this table as the basis for other one-to-many relationships. Figure 1-2 shows that the Companies table can be on the "one" side of a one-to-many relationship with a table that lists city locations for all the different companies.

One-to-one relationship

A one-to-one relationship is essentially a one-to-many relationship where only one row in a table is related to only one row in another table. During the normalization process, I mentioned a situation where one table holds information on corporate executives and another holds information on their assistants. This could very well be a one-to-one relationship if each executive has one assistant and each assistant works for only one executive. Figure 1-3 gives a visual representation

Industries

Industry_ID	Industry_name
1	Utilities
2	Construction
3	Banking

Companies

Company_id	Company_Name	Industry_id
1	Big Co Corporation	1
2	Little Co Corporation	1
3	Joe's Utility	1
4	Leadfoot Builders	2
5	Angel's Cement Boots	2
6	Al's Bank	3

Co_Location_id	Company_id	city
1	2	San Francisco
2	2	New York
3	2	Chicago
4	5	Dallas

Figure 1-2: Tables with two one-to-many relationships

Executives

ExecID	Exec_first_name	Exec_last_name
1	Jon	Dust
2	Melinda	Burns
3	Larry	Gains

Assistants

Asst_id	Exec_id	Asst_first_name	Asst_last_name
1	1	Walter	James
2	2	James	Walter
3	3	Nancy	Els

Figure 1-3: Tables with a one-to-one relationship

Many-to-many relationship

Many-to-many relationships work a bit differently from the other two. For instance, suppose that the company keeping the data has a variety of newsletters that it sends to its contacts, and it needs to add this information to the database. There's a weekly, a monthly, a bi-monthly, and an annual newsletter, and to keep from annoying clients, the newsletters must only be sent to those who request them.

To start, you could add a table that stores the newsletter types (Table 1-10)

TABLE 1-10 NEWSLETTERS TABLE

newsletter_id	newsletter_name
1	Weekly
2	Monthly
3	Bi-monthly
4	Annual

Table 1-10 can't be directly related to another table that stores contact information. The only way to make this work is to add a column that stores the newsletters that each contact receives. Right away, you should notice a problem with the Table 1-11.

TABLE 1-11 CONTACTS TABLE

contact_id	contact_first_name	contact_last_name	newsletters
1	Jon	Doe	1,3,4
2	Al	Banks	2,3,4

In this table the Newsletters column contains more than one value. The value looks a lot like an array. As mentioned earlier, this should never occur within your database — we want only atomic values in each column.

In situations like this you'll need to create another table. Figure 1-4 shows how the relationship between these values can be made to work.

Contact_id	Contact_first_name	Contact_last_name
1	Jon	Doe
2	Al	Banks

Newsletter_id	Newsletter_name
1	Weekly
2	Bi-Weekly
3	Annual
4	Semi-annual

Client_id	Newsletter_id
1	1
1	2
2	2
2	3
2	4

Figure 1-4: Tables with a many-to-many relationship

With this structure, any number of contacts can have any number of newsletters and any number of newsletters can be sent to any number of contacts.

Features MySQL Does Not Support

MySQL is a polarizing piece of software in the applications development community. It has aspects that many developers like: it's free, it doesn't take up a whole lot in the way of resources, it's very quick, and it's easy to learn compared to packages like Oracle and Sybase. However, MySQL achieves its speediness by doing without features common in other databases, and these shortcomings will keep many from adopting MySQL for their applications. But, for many, the lack of certain features shouldn't be much of a problem. Read and decide for yourself.

Referential integrity

Every example used in the previous pages made use of *foreign keys*. A foreign key is a column that references the primary key of another table in order to maintain a relationship. In Table 1-4, the Contacts table contains a company_id column, which references the primary key of the Companies table (Table 1-3). This column is a foreign key to the Companies table.

In Chapter 2 we demonstrate how to create tables in MySQL. It's easy enough to create tables with all the columns necessary for primary keys and foreign keys. However, in MySQL foreign keys do not have the significance they have in most database systems.

In packages like Oracle, Sybase, or PostGres, tables can be created that explicitly define foreign keys. For instance, using the tables 1-3 and 1-4 with Oracle, the database system could be made aware that the company_id column in the Contacts table had a relationship to the Companies table. This is potentially a very good thing. If the database system is aware of a relationship, it can check to make sure the value being inserted into the foreign key field exists in the referenced table. If it does not, the database system will reject the insert. This is known as referential integrity.

To achieve the same effect in MySQL, the application developer must add some extra steps before inserting or updating records. For example, to be ultra-safe, the programmer needs to go through the following steps in order to insert a row in the Contacts table (1-4):

1. Get all of the values for company_id in the Companies table.

2. Check to make sure the value for company_id you are going to insert into the Contacts table exists in the data you retrieved in step 1.

3. If it does, insert values.

The developers of MySQL argue that referential integrity is not necessary and that including it would slow down MySQL. Further, they argue that it is the responsibility of the application interacting with the database to ensure that the inserted data is correct. There is logic to this way of thinking. In Parts III and IV of this book we present several applications that all work just fine without enforcing referential integrity or the method of checking shown above. In general, in these applications, all the possible values are pulled from a database anyway and there's very little opportunity for errors to creep into the system.

For example, using PHP and HTML, the programmer might turn the Companies table into a drop-down box. That way the user can only choose a valid value.

Transactions

In relational databases, things change in groups. As shown in a variety of applications in this book, many changes require that rows be updated in several tables concurrently. In some cases, tables may be dropped as part of a series of statements that get the data where it needs to be. An e-commerce site may contain code like the following:

1. Insert customer into the Customers table.

2. Add invoice information into the Invoice table.

3. Remove a quantity of 1 of ordered item from the Items table.

By the time you read this book, there is a very good chance that MySQL will support transactions. The developers have been working with transaction-safe tables for some time. Check mysql.com to see if the current release can use transactions. We did not use transactions in any of the applications in this book.

When you're working with a series of steps like this, there is potential for serious problems. If the operating system crashes or power goes out between steps two and three, the database will contain bad data.

To prevent such a state, most sophisticated database systems make use of *transactions*. With transactions, the developer can identify a group of commands. If any one of these commands fails to go through, the whole group of commands is nixed and the database returns to the state it was in before the first command was attempted. This is known a COMMIT/ROLLBACK approach. Either all of the requests are committed to the database, or the database is rolled back to the state it was in prior to the transactions.

In Section 5.4.3 of the MySQL Reference Manual, there is a lengthy defense of MySQL's choice not to include transactions. It also includes techniques for achieving the same effect with logging and table locks. You can decide for yourself whether this argument makes sense. Many people feel that the lack of transactions makes MySQL a poor choice in certain environments. If you're the IT manager at a bank looking for a relational database management system (RDBMS), MySQL probably isn't the way to go.

Stored procedures

The big fancy database systems allow for procedural code (something very much like PHP or Perl) to be placed within the database. There are a couple of key advantages to using stored procedures. First, it can reduce that amount of code needed in middleware applications. If MySQL accepted stored procedures, a single PHP command can be sent to the database to query data, do some string manipulation, and then return a value ready to be displayed in your page.

The other major advantage comes from working in an environment where more than one front-end is accessing the same database. Consider a situation where there happens to be a front-end written for the Web and another in Visual C++ accessible on Windows machines. It would be a pain to write all the queries and transactions in two different places. You'd be much better off writing stored procedures and accessing those from your various applications.

 MySQL also does not support sub-selects. We will discuss how to work around this limitation in Chapter 3.

Summary

At this point you should have a pretty good idea of how relational databases work. The theory covered here is really important, as quality data design is one of the cornerstones of quality applications. If you fail in the normalization process, you could leave yourself with difficulties that will haunt you for months or years.

In the applications in Parts 3 and 4 of this book, you will see how we approached and normalized several sets of data.

Now that you know how tables in a relational database work, move on to Chapter 2, where you will see how to make these tables in MySQL.

Chapter 2

The Structured Query Language for Creating and Altering Tables

IN THIS CHAPTER

♦ Creating tables and databases in MySQL

♦ Choosing the proper column type and column attributes for tables

♦ Maintaining databases and tables

IN CHAPTER 1 YOU LEARNED that tables are the basis of all the good things that come from working with relational databases. There's a fair amount you can do with these tables, as you'll see throughout this book. So it should come as no surprise that the process of creating and maintaining the tables requires some knowledge. As Mom used to say, nothing good comes easy.

If you're coming to MySQL from Microsoft's SQL Server or a desktop package like Access, you may be used to creating tables with a slick WYSIWYG (what you see is what you get) interface. In fact, there is a package called phpMyadmin that will give you many of the niceties you're used to working with. We use this tool and love it. We'll discuss it in further detail at the end of this chapter. There's no doubt that working with a graphical interface can be a lot more pleasant than figuring out the syntax of a language – any language.

 In fact, there are many GUI tools you can use when working with MySQL. See http://www.mysql.com/downloads/contrib.html for a listing. The MySQL development team is working on an Access-like interface to MySQL. Check the mysql.com site for availability.

However, even if you plan on installing and using this tool, you should take some time to learn how to create and maintain tables using the Data Definition Language (DDL), which is part of SQL. Specifically, it will be a great help to you to know the `create` and `alter` commands. Before too long you will have to use these commands within your scripts. There also may be an occasion when you don't have access to the graphical interface, and you'll need this knowledge to fall back on.

Definitions

Before we get to creating tables and databases in MySQL, there are a couple of items you'll need to understand. The concepts I'm about to present are very important — make sure you understand how to deal with these before you move forward in your database design.

Null

One of the first decisions you will have to make for every column in your tables is whether or not you are going to allow null values. If you remember back to your ninth grade math, you may recall the null set, which is a grouping that contains nothing. In relational databases, null has the same meaning: a null field contains nothing.

Keep in mind that a null field is distinctly different from a text string with no characters (a zero-length string) or the numerical value of zero. The difference is that empty strings and zeros are values. In your programming you most likely have had an occasion where you have had to check whether a string contained any value, perhaps as part of an `if...` statement. In PHP, it would look like this:

```
$var //this is a variable used in the test
if ($var == "")
{
    echo "Var is an empty string";
} else {
    echo $var;
}
```

The same syntax would work for comparing zero against another value.

These sorts of comparisons will not work with null. Since null is the absence of value, any comparison with any value (including another null) is meaningless. In Chapter 3 you will see that null values require the application developer to be very careful when writing table joins. To give you a quick preview, consider what would happen if we wanted to join Table 2-1 and Table 2-2:

TIP

In your SQL select statements (covered in Chapter 3), there are a couple of ways you can check if a field contains a null value. First, you can use MySQL's `isnull()` function. For example to find rows in a table where the mid-dle_name column contains null values, you could run the following query:

select * from names where isnull(middle_name);

Or, to exclude null values in the query result:

```
select * from names where !isnull(middle_name);
```

The exclamation point means "not."

You can also use the `is null` and `is not null` statements. For example:

```
select * from users were addr2 is null;
select * from users where addr2 is not null;
```

TABLE 2-1 CONTACTS

first_name	last_name	spouse_id
Jay	Greenspan	1
Brad	Bulger	NULL

TABLE 2-2 SPOUSES

spouse_id	first_name	last_name
1	Melissa	Ramirez

If you wanted to find the authors of a great book on MySQL and PHP and their associated spouses, you would have to join these tables on the `spouse_id` field. (Don't worry if you don't understand the exact syntax, it will be covered in the next chapter.)

```
SELECT * FROM Contacts, Spouses
   WHERE Contacts.spouse_id = Spouses.spouse_id
```

This statement would work fine for Jay, but there's going to be a problem for Brad because he's not married and his `spouse_id` field is null. He will not show up in the result set even though the goal of the query is to get all the people in the contacts table and the associated spouses if they exist.

Again, this is just a preview, an example of why null is so important. In Chapter 3 you will see how the outer join solves problems like this.

Index

Arguably the single greatest advantage of a relational database is the speed with which it can query and sort tremendous amounts of information. To achieve these great speeds, MySQL and all other database servers make use of optimized data-storage mechanisms called indexes.

An index allows a database server to create a representation of a column that it can search with amazing speeds. Indexes are especially helpful in finding a single row or groups of rows from a large table. They can also speed up joins and aggregate functions, like `min()` and `max()`,which we'll cover in Chapter 3.

Given these advantages, why not just create an index for every column for every table? There are some very good reasons. First, indexes can actually slow some things down. It takes time for your database server to maintain indexes. You wouldn't want to create overhead for your server that is not going to be a benefit to you down the road. There are also occasions when the indexes themselves are slower. If you need to iterate through every row in a table, you're actually better off not using an index. Also, unnecessary indexes will use a lot of disk space.

A table's primary key is often the subject of searches (for obvious reasons). Thus, in a table definition, the column or columns that you declare as your primary key will automatically be indexed.

There will be more on creating indexes later in this chapter.

create database Statement

Before you can get to creating your tables, you'll need to create a database. This should take all of a second. The basic Create system is fairly simple and can be run from any interface that has access to MySQL.

The general syntax is:

```
create database database_name
```

In case you're wondering, after running this command MySQL creates a folder in which it stores all the files needed for your database. On my Linux machine, the database folders are stored in /var/lib/mysql/.

When naming databases, or for that matter columns or indexes, avoid using names that will cause confusion down the road. On operating systems where the file names are case sensitive, such as most Unix systems, database names will also be case sensitive. Come up with conventions that you plan on sticking to, such as using all lowercase names for tables and columns. Spaces are not allowed. Though MySQL can work around potentially bad choices, you should avoid using words that MySQL uses in the course of its business. For instance, naming a table "Select" is a really bad idea. In Chapter 7 of the MySQL reference manual, there is a list of over 150 reserved words. If you stay away from words used by SQL or MySQL functions you should be OK.

From the MySQL command line client, you can simply type in:

```
create database database_name;
```

 TIP The MySQL command-line client is in the /bin directory of your MySQL installation and has the file name mysql (on Unix) or mysql.exe on DOS/Windows.

From PHP, you can use either the `mysql_create_db ()` or the `mysql_query()` function. The following piece of code would create two databases. Keep in mind that you will need to be logged into MySQL as a user with the proper rights for the code to work.

```
$conn = mysql_connect("localhost","username", "password")
   or die ("Could not connect to localhost");


mysql_create_db("my_database") or
    die ("Could not create database");
$string = "create database my_other_db";
mysql_query($string) or
    die(mysql_error());
```

use database Statement

Before you can begin making tables in MySQL you must select a database that has been created. If you are accessing MySQL through the mysql command-line client, you will have to enter the statement:

```
use database_name
```

If you're accessing a database through PHP, use the `mysql_select_db()` function.

```
$conn = mysql_connect("localhost","username", "password")
  or die ("Could not connect to localhost");

mysql_select_db("test", $conn) or
    die ("Could not select database");
```

create table Statement

Once you have created and selected a database, you are ready to create a table. The basic Create Table system is fairly simple and takes this basic form.

```
create table table_name
(
    column_1 column_type column attributes,
    column_2 column_type column attributes,
    primary key (column_name),
    index index_name(column_name)
)
```

Column types, column attributes, and details on indexes are covered in the following sections. Before we get to those, there are two simple column attributes to discuss:

◆ null | not null

◆ default

The first gives you the opportunity to forbid or allow null values. If you don't specify "null" or "not null" it is assumed that null values are allowed. The second, if declared, sets a value if none is declared when you insert a row into the table.

Here's an example `create` statement where you can see these two attributes, and a few others, put to use. This one was lifted from Chapter 12 and changed slightly.

```
create table topics2 (
        topic_id        integer not null auto_increment,
        parent_id       integer default 0 not null,
        root_id         integer default 0,
        name            varchar(255),
        description     text null,
        create_dt       timestamp,
        modify_dt       timestamp,
```

```
        author              varchar(255) null,
        author_host         varchar(255) null,
primary key(topic_id),
index my_index(parent_id))
```

This statement creates a table named "topics" with nine columns and two indexes, one for the primary key and one for the parent_id column. In the above statement four column types are used: integer, varchar, text, and timestamp. These, and many other column types are discussed in further detail below. You should have a good understanding of all the column types available as well as ways to create indexes before you set out to create tables.

To create tables from the command line client, key in the entire command. From PHP, use the mysql_query() function.

```
$conn = mysql_connect("localhost","username", "password") or
    die ("Could not connect to localhost");

mysql_select_db("test", $conn) or
    die("could not select database");
$query = "create table my_table (
    col_1 int not null primary key,
    col_2 text
)";
mysql_query($query) or
    die(mysql_error());
```

Column Types

MySQL comes with a range of column types. Several are similar but have subtle yet important differences. Give this section a read and choose carefully when deciding on column types for your tables.

Text column types

MySQL has seven column types suitable for storing text strings:

- char
- varchar
- tinytext
- text

- ◆ mediumtext
- ◆ longtext
- ◆ enum

CHAR

Usage: `char(length)`

The char column type has a maximum length of 255 characters. This is a fixed-length type, meaning that when a value is inserted that has fewer characters than the maximum length of the column, the field will be right-padded with spaces. So if a column has been defined as char(10) and you want to store the value "happy", MySQL will actually store "happy" and then five spaces. The spaces are removed from the result when the value is retrieved from the table.

VARCHAR

Usage: `varchar(length)`

This is nearly identical to char and is used in many of the same places. It also has a maximum length of 255. The difference is that varchar is a variable-length column type. The values will not be padded with spaces. Instead MySQL will add one character to each varchar field, which stores the length of the field. MySQL removes spaces from the end of strings in varchar fields.

USING CHAR OR VARCHAR   For the most part there is little practical difference between char and varchar. Which one you decide to use will depend on which will require more space, the trailing spaces in a char column or the single character in varchar. If your field stores something like last names, you'll probably want to allow 25 characters, just to be safe. If you were to use the char column type and someone had the last name Smith, your column would contain 20 trailing spaces. There's no need for it; you're much better off using varchar and allowing MySQL to track the size of the column. However, when you want to store passwords of five to seven characters, it would be a waste to use varchar to track the size of the column. Every time a varchar field is updated, MySQL has to check the length of the field and change the character that stores the field length. You'd be better off using char(7).

If you define a column as varchar with a column length of less than four, MySQL will automatically change the column to the char type.

TINYTEXT
Usage: `tinytext`

This is first of the four binary (or blob) text character types. All of these types (tinytext, text, mediumtext, and largetext) are variable column types, similar to varchar. They differ only in the size of string they can contain. The tinytext type has a maximum length of 255, so in fact it serves the same purpose as varchar(255). An index can be created for an entire tinytext column

TEXT
Usage: `text`

The text type has a maximum length of 65,535 characters. Indexes can be created on the first 255 characters of a text column.

MEDIUMTEXT
Usage: `mediumtext`

The mediumtext type has a maximum length of 16,777,215 characters. Indexes can be created on the first 255 characters of a mediumtext column.

LONGTEXT
Usage: `longtext`

The longtext type has a maximum length of 4,294,967,295 characters. Indexes can be created on the first 255 characters of a longtext column. However, this column currently is not very useful, as MySQL allows string of only 16 million bytes.

ENUM
Usage: `enum ('value1', 'value2', 'value3' ...) [default 'value']`

With enum, you can limit the potential values of a column to those you specify. It allows for 65,535 values, though it's difficult to see a situation where you'd want to use this column with more than a few potential values. This type would be of use when, for example, you want to allow only values of "yes" or "no". The `create` statement that makes use of enum will look like this:

```
create table my_table (
   id int auto_increment primary key,
   answer enum ('yes', 'no') default 'no'
);
```

SET   Usage: `set ('value1', 'value2', 'value3' ...) [default 'value']`

This column type defines a superset of values. This allows for zero or more values from the list you specify to be included in a field.

You will not see this column type used in this book. We do not like to see multiple values in a single field as it violates very basic rules of database design. Re-read Chapter 1 if you don't know what this means.

Numeric column types

MySQL has seven column types suitable for storing numeric values. Note that the following are synonyms: int and integer; double, double precision, and real; and decimal and numeric.

- ◆ int/integer
- ◆ tinyint
- ◆ mediumint
- ◆ bigint
- ◆ float
- ◆ double/double precision/real
- ◆ decimal/numeric

For all numeric types the maximum display size is 255. For most numeric types you will have the option to *zerofill* a column – to left-pad it with zeros. For example, if you have an int column that has a display size of 10 and you insert a value of 25 into this column, MySQL will store and display 0000000025. The numeric column types may also be defined as signed or unsigned. Signed is the default definition.

INT/INTEGER
Usage: `int(display size) [unsigned] [zerofill]`
If you use the unsigned flag, this column type can store integers from 0 to 4,294,967,295. If signed, the range is from –2,147,483,648 to 2,147,483,647. Int will often be used with auto_increment to define the primary key of a table.

```
create table my_table (
    table_id int unsigned auto_increment primary key,
    next_column text
);
```

Note that I've used an unsigned column because an auto_increment column has no need for negative values.

TINYINT
Usage: `tinyint(display size) [unsigned] [zerofill]`
If unsigned, tinyint stores integers between 0 and 255. If signed, the range is from -128 to 127.

MEDIUMINT

Usage: `mediumint(display size) [unsigned] [zerofill]`

If unsigned, mediumint stores integers between -8,388,608 and 8,388,607. If signed, the range is from 0 to 1677215.

BIGINT

Usage: `bigint(display size) [unsigned] [zerofill]`

If unsigned, bigint stores integers between -9,223,372,036,854,775,808 to 9,223,372,036,854,775,807. If signed, the range is from 0 to 18,446,744,073,709, 551,615.

FLOAT

Usage: `FLOAT(precision) [zerofill]`

In this usage, float stores a floating-point number and cannot be unsigned. The precision attribute can be <=24 for a single-precision floating-point number and between 25 and 53 for a double-precision floating-point number. Starting in MySQL 3.23, this is a true floating-point value. In earlier MySQL versions, FLOAT(precision) always has two decimals.

Usage: `FLOAT[(M,D)] [ZEROFILL]`

This is a small (single-precision) floating-point number and cannot be unsigned. Allowable values are -3.402823466E+38 to -1.175494351E-38, zero, and 1.175494 351E-38 to 3.402823466E+38. M is the display width and D is the number of decimals. FLOAT without an argument or with an argument of <= 24 stands for a single-precision floating-point number.

DOUBLE/DOUBLE PRECISION/REAL

Usage: `DOUBLE[(M,D)] [zerofill]`

This is a double-precision floating-point number and cannot be unsigned. Allowable values are -1.7976931348623157E+308 to -2.2250738585072014E-308, zero, and 2.2250738585072014E-308 to 1.7976931348623157E+308. M is the display width and D is the number of decimals.

Usage: `DECIMAL[(M[,D])] [ZEROFILL]`

Numbers in a decimal column are stored as characters. Each number is stored as a string, with one character for each digit of the value. If D is 0, values will have no decimal point. The maximum range of DECIMAL values is the same as for DOUBLE, but the actual range for a given DECIMAL. If M is left out, it's set to 10.

Date and time types

MySQL has five column types suitable for storing dates and times.

- date
- datetime
- timestamp
- time
- year

MySQL date and time types are flexible, accepting either strings or numbers as part of insert statements. Additionally, MySQL is pretty good at interpreting dates that you give it. For instance, if we create this table:

```
create table date_test(
    id int unsigned auto_increment,
    the_date date
);
```

The following insert statements are all interpreted correctly by MySQL:

```
insert into date_test (a_date) values ('00-06-01');
insert into date_test (a_date) values ('2000-06-01');
insert into date_test (a_date) values ('20000601');
insert into test6 (a_date) values (000601);
```

 TIP MySQL prefers to receive dates as strings. So '000601' is a better choice than a similar integer. Using strings for date values may save you from encountering some errors down the road.

Extracting information from date and time columns can be a challenge. MySQL provides many functions that help manipulate these columns.

DATE
Usage: date
The date column type stores values in the format YYYY-MM-DD. It will allow values between 1000-01-01 and 9999-12-31.

DATETIME
Usage: datetime [null | not null] [default]
The datetime type stores values in the format: YYYY-MM-DD HH:MM:SS. It will allow values between 1000-01-01 00:00:00 and 9999-12-31 23:59:59.

TIMESTAMP
Usage: timestamp(size)
This is a handy column type that will automatically record the time of the most recent change to a row, whether it is an insert or an update. Size can be defined as any number between 2 and 14. Table 2-3 shows the values stored with each column size. The default value is 14.

TABLE 2-3 TIMESTAMP FORMATS

Size	Format
2	YY
4	YYMM
6	YYMMDD
8	YYYYMMDD
10	YYMMDDHHMM
12	YYMMDDHHMMSS
14	YYYYMMDDHHMMSS

TIME
Usage: `time`

Stores time in HH:MM:SS format and has a value range from –838:59:59 to 838:59:59. The reason for the large values is that the time column type can be used to store the result of mathematical equations involving times.

YEAR
Usage: `year[(2|4)]`

In these post-Y2K days it's hard to imagine that you'd want to store your years in two-digit format, but you can. In two-digit format, allowable dates are between 1970 and 2069. The digits 70-99 are prepended with 19 and 01–69 are prepended with 20.

Four-digit year format allows values from 1901 to 2155.

Creating Indexes

Starting in version 3.23.6 MySQL can create an index on any column. There can be a maximum of 16 columns for any table. The basic syntax is:

```
index index_name (indexed_column)
```

TIP Although the index name is optional, you should always name your indexes. It becomes very important should you want to delete or change your index using the SQL `alter` statement. If you don't specify a name, MySQL will base the index name on the first column in your index.

Another way to create an index is to declare a column as a primary key. Note that any auto_increment column must be indexed, and you'll probably want to declare it as your primary key. In the following table, the id_col column is indexed.

```
create table my_table (
    id_col int unsigned auto_increment primary key,
    another_col text
);
```

The primary key can also be declared like other indexes after the column definitions.

```
create table my_table (
    id_col int unsigned not null auto_increment,
    another_col text,
    primary key(id_col)
);
```

Indexes can span more than one row. If a query uses two rows in concert during a search, you could create an index that covers the two with this statement:

```
create table mytable(
    id_col int unsigned not null,
    another_col char(200) not null,
    index dual_col_index(id_col, another_col)
);
```

This index will be used for searches on id_col and another_col. These indexes work from left to right. So this index will be used for searches that are exclusively on id_col. However, it will not be used for searches on another_col.

Finally, you can create indexes on only part of a column. Starting in MySQL version 3.23 you can index tinytext, text, mediumtext, and longtext columns on the initial 255 characters. For char and varchar columns, you can create indexes for the initial portion of a column. Here the syntax is:

```
index index_name (column_name(column_length))
```

For example:

```
create table my_table(
    char_column char (255) not null,
    text_column text not null,
    index index_on_char (char_column(20)),
    index index_on_text (text_column(200))
);
```

An index can also assure that unique values exist in every row in a table by using the `unique` constraint.

```
create table my_table(
    char_column char (255) not null,
    text_column text not null,
    unique index index_on_char (char_column)
);
```

Table Types

MySQL offers three table types: ISAM, MyISAM, BDB, and Heap. ISAM is an older table type and is not recommended for new applications. The default table type is MyISAM. The syntax for declaring a table type is

```
create table table_name type=table_type(
    col_name column attribute
);
```

MyISAM tables are extremely fast and very stable. There's no need to declare another table type unless one of the other table type fits your specific needs.

Heaps are actually memory-resident hash tables. They are not stored in any physical location and therefore will disappear in the case of crash or power outage. But because of their nature, they are blazingly fast. You should only use these for temporary tables.

Starting in MySQL version 3.23.16, MySQL offers BDB tables. These tables are transaction safe and are integral to MySQL's efforts to include transactions. Check Section 8.4 of the MySQL reference manual to see the current state of BDB tables.

alter table Statement

If you're not happy with the form of your table, you can modify it with the `alter table` statement. Specifically, this statement allows you to rename tables, columns, and indexes; add or drop columns and indexes; and redefine the definitions of columns and indexes. This statement will always start with alter table table_name. The rest of the command will depend on the action needed as described below.

Changing a table name

The syntax for changing a table name is as follows:

```
alter table table_name rename new_table_name
```

 If you have MySQL version 3.23.27 or higher you can make use of the `rename` statement. The basic syntax is

```
rename table_name to new_table_name
```

Adding and dropping columns

When adding a column, you will need to include all the column definitions defined in the previous section. In addition, starting in version 3.22, MySQL allows you to specify where in the table the column will reside, although this specification is optional. The basic syntax is:

```
alter table table_name add column column_name column attributes
```

For example:

```
alter table my_table add column my_column text not null
```

To specify the location of the column, use `first` to specify your inserted column as the first column in the table or `after` to place the column following a column that already exists, as shown in the following examples.

```
alter table my_table add column my_next_col text not null first
alter table my_table add column my_next_col text not null after
my_other_column
```

To drop a column, you need only the following:

```
alter table table_name drop column column name
```

TIP When altering a table, try to get all of your changes into a single alter statement. It's better practice than, for example, deleting an index in one statement and creating a new one in another statement.

Adding and dropping indexes

You can add indexes using the `index`, `unique`, and `primary key` commands in the same way they are used in the `create` statement.

```
alter table my_table add index index_name (column_name1,
column_name2, ...)
alter table my_table add unique index_name(column_name)
alter table my_table add primary key(my_column)
```

Making your indexes go away is just as easy with the `drop` command.

```
alter table table_name drop index index_name
alter table_name test10 drop primary key
```

Changing column definitions

It is possible to change a column's name or attributes with either the `change` or `modify` commands. To change a column's name, you must also redefine the column's attributes. The following will work:

```
alter table table_name change original_column_name new_column_name
int not null
```

But this will not:

```
alter table table_name change my_col2 my_col3;
```

If you wish to change only the column's attributes, you can use the `change` command and make the new column name the same as the old column name. For instance, to change the column col_1 from a char(200) column to a varchar(200) column, you could use the following:

```
alter table table_name change col_1 col_1 varchar(200)
```

Starting in MySQL version 3.22.16, you could also use the `modify` command.

```
alter table table_name modify 1 col_1 varchar(200)
```

insert Statement

Now that you know all you need to know about creating and modifying tables, you're probably going to want to put some information into the table. You do this by using the `insert` statement.

The basic form of the SQL `insert` statement is:

```
insert into table_name (column_1, column2, column3,...) values
(value1, value2, value3 ...)
```

If a column in your table allows null values, you can leave it out of the `insert` statement.

Text strings must be surrounded by single quote marks ('). For example:

```
insert into table_name (text_col, int_col) values ('hello world', 1)
```

This can cause a problem because undoubtedly someone is going to want to insert a contraction into your database and that would confuse your database. Therefore you'll need a way of escaping the single quote character. In fact there are several characters that need to be escaped in order to be inserted into MySQL. If you want to insert any of the following characters into a text field they must be prepended with a backslash:

- ' (single quote)
- " (double quote)
- \ (backslash)
- % (percent sign)
- _ (underscore)

You can also escape single quotes by using two consecutive single quote marks (' ').

The following characters are identified in MySQL by their typical escape sequences:

- \n (newline)
- \t (tab)
- \r (carriage return)
- \b (back space)

It's worth noting here that, for the most part, you won't have to worry about escaping all of these characters while doing your PHP programming. As we'll see there are functions and settings built into PHP that handle this automatically. The `addslashes()` function and the magic quotes settings in the php.ini are particularly helpful.

update Statement

The SQL `update` statement is slightly different from the others we've seen so far, in that it makes use of a `where` clause. The general syntax is:

```
update table_name set col_1=value1, col_2=value_2 where col=value
```

Once again, if you're inserting a string, you'll need to surround it with single quotes and escape properly. Keep in mind that the `where` portion of the `update` statement can be about any comparison operator. Often it will be used to identify a single row by its primary key. In Table 2-4, id is the primary key.

TABLE 2-4 FOLKS TABLE

id	fname	lname	salary
1	Don	Ho	25,000
2	Don	Corleone	800,000
3	Don	Juan	32,000
4	Don	Johnson	44,500

This statement would affect only Don Corleone:

```
update folks set fname='Vito' where id=2
```

As you can see, it would be risky to run an `update` statement based on the fname column, as you could accidentally update every column in this table.

```
update folks set fname='Vito' where fname='don'
```

You could also use `update` to give your underpaid employees a raise:

```
update folks set salary=50000 where salary<50,000
```

drop table/drop database

If you wish to get rid of a table or an entire database, the drop command will do the trick. Keep in mind that if you drop a database you will lose all of the tables that exist within the database.

```
drop table table_name
drop database database_name
```

The drop table command can be from PHP through the mysql_query() function. If you wish to drop a database from PHP, you need to make use of the mysql_drop_db() function.

show tables

To get a list of the tables available in a database, use the show tables command. For this command to work, you must have already selected a database using the use database command.

Figure 2-1 shows the response to the show tables command from the MySQL command line client.

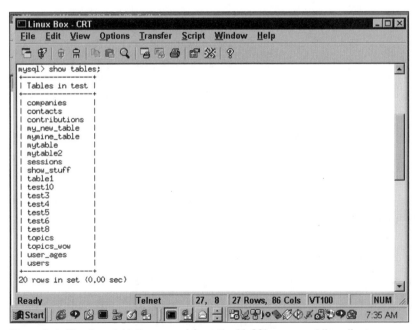

Figure 2-1: The show tables command from the MySQL command line client

From PHP, you can get a list of tables by using `mysql_list_tables()`.

```
<?
mysql_connect("localhost", "root", "");
$result = mysql_list_tables("test");

while($row = mysql_fetch_array($result))
{
    echo $row[0] . "<br>\n";
}
?>
```

NOTE You are better off not using mysql_list_tables(), as this function may not be available in the future. Running a show tables command through mysql_query() is a better choice.

show columns/show fields

These commands, which are synonymous, are very handy if you can't remember the column types and attributes you declared in your `create` statement. For example, let's say you created a table with the following command.

```
create table topics (
        topic_id        integer not null auto_increment primary key,
        parent_id       integer default 0 not null,
        root_id         integer default 0,
        name            varchar(255),
        description     text null,
        create_dt       timestamp,
        modify_dt       timestamp,
        author          varchar(255) null,
        author_host     varchar(255) null,
        index my_index(parent_id)
)
```

Figure 2-2 shows the results you would get after running `show fields` from topics from the MySQL command line client.

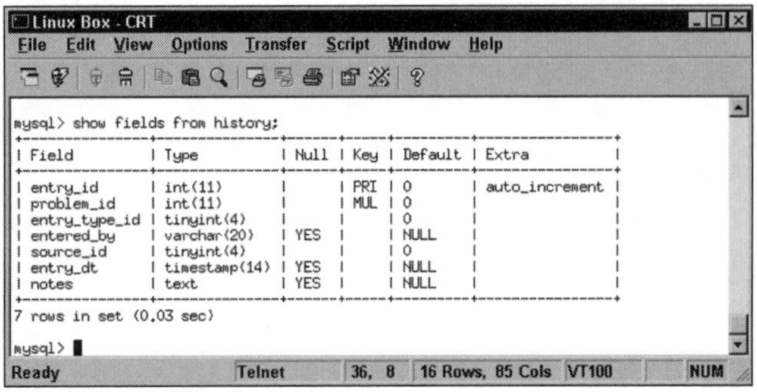

Figure 2-2: The show fields command from the MySQL command line client

You can get similar information through the PHP interface by using `mysql_field_name()`, `mysql_field_type()`, and `mysql_field_len()`. All of the syntax and functions in this code are covered in Part II of this book.

```
$db = mysql_connect("localhost","root", "")
  or die ("Could not connect to localhost");
mysql_select_db("test", $db)
  or die ("Could not find test");

$db_name ="topics";
$query = "select * from $db_name";
$result = mysql_query($query);
$num_fields = mysql_num_fields($result);

//create table header
echo "<table border = 1>";
echo "<tr>";
for ($i=0; $i<$num_fields; $i++)
{
    echo "<th>";
    echo mysql_field_name ($result, $i);
    echo "</th>";
}
echo "</tr>";
//end table header

//create table body

echo "<tr>";
for ($i=0; $i<$num_fields; $i++)
{
    echo "<td valign = top>";
```

```
    echo mysql_field_type ($result, $i) . "<br> \n";
    echo "(" . mysql_field_len ($result, $i) . ")<br> \n";
    echo mysql_field_flags ($result, $i) . "<br> \n";
    echo "</td>";
}
echo "</tr>";
//end table body

echo "</table>";
```

Using phpMyAdmin

If you are an old-time Unix guy or gal, you may be perfectly comfortable keying in all of your commands and sorting out the errors when you mistype something or screw up the syntax. But myself, I like the convenience of a graphical interface.

If you're like me, you will be thrilled to know that a couple of programmers have used PHP to create a great Web-based interface to MySQL. Best of all, they're giving their program away. All you need to do is cruise over to phpwizard.net and download the appropriate .tar, .gz, or .zip file. We would have included it on the CD, but you're really better off getting the most recent version off their site. It's constantly being improved.

This package will cover about all the MySQL administrative functions you'll come across. Figures 2-3 and 2-4 show a bit of what you can expect for phpMyAdmin.

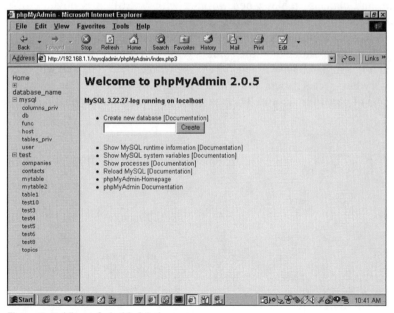

Figure 2-3: View of phpMyAdmin

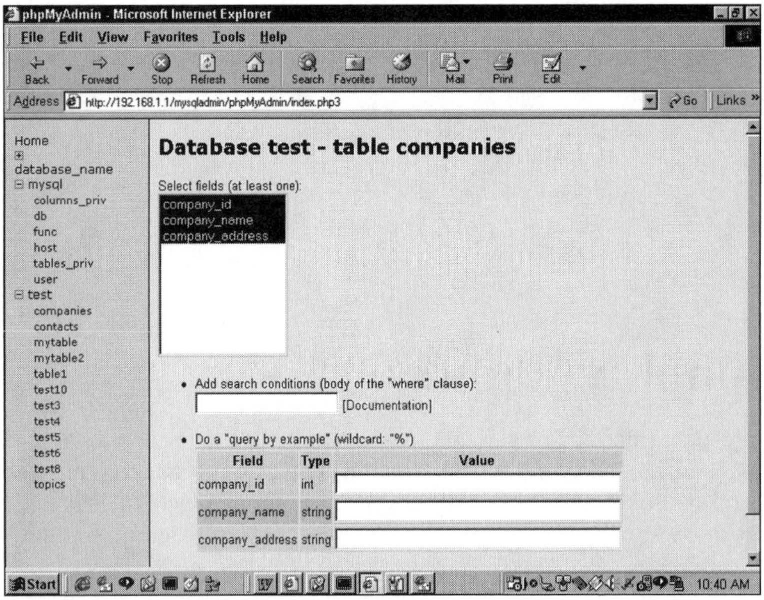

Figure 2-4: Another View of phpMyAdmin

Summary

This chapter discussed everything you need to know in order to create and maintain databases and database tables when working with MySQL. It is possible that you will never need to commit the details of the create statement to memory, as graphical tools like phpMyAdmin can help you create and alter tables.

Still, it is important to understand the column types and the purposes of indexes, as a quick and efficient database will always use the correct data type and will only include indexes when necessary. As you will see in Parts III and IV of this book, we take a good deal of care to make sure that we get the most out of our databases.

Chapter 3

Getting What You Want with select

THE select STATEMENT IS your key to getting exactly what you want from your database. It's amazingly agile, capable of getting about any set of data that you can imagine. Working with select can get a bit hairy when queries get extremely complex, but once you understand the basics, which are covered in this chapter, you should be able to get almost any group of data from your database.

There are very good books that spend a long time explaining the details of the select statement. If you find that this chapter doesn't cover something you need, we suggest you first turn to the MySQL manual, and then the MySQL mailing lists. In addition, *SQL For Dummies*, also published by IDG Books Worldwide, covers the ANSI standard in some pretty good detail.

Basic select

When it comes time to take the information from your database and lay it out on your Web pages, you'll need to limit the information returned from your tables and join tables together to get the proper information. So you'll start with your database, the superset of information, and return a smaller set. In the select statement you'll choose columns from one or more tables to assemble a result set. This result has columns and rows and thus can be effectively thought of as a table (or a two-dimensional array, if your mind works that way). This table doesn't actually exist in the database, but it helps to think about it this way.

The basic `select` statement requires you to indicate the table you are selecting from and the column names you require. If you wish to select all the columns from a given table, you can substitute an asterisk (*) for the field names.

```
select column_1, column_2, column_3 from table_name
```

or

```
select * from table_name
```

Keep in mind that with a `select` statement you are not actually altering the tables involved in the query. You are simply retrieving information. From PHP, you will send the query to MySQL from the `mysql_query()` function.

There are all sorts of ways you can choose to lay out the information, but at times you're going to want a simple HTML table with the column names put in a header row. The simple PHP code in Listing 3-1 will lay out any SQL query in an ultra-simple HTML table. It includes a simple form that will allow you to enter a query. If you don't understand this code just yet, don't worry about it; all the PHP functions will be covered in Chapter 6. Alter the `mysql_connect()` and `mysql_select_db()` functions if you wish to change the database used.

Listing 3-1: PHP script that converts an SQL query to an HTML table

```php
<?php

if(!isset($query) || empty($query))
   {$query = "select * from users";}
//stripslashes is necessary because the select statement is
//coming from a form. In most systems, the magic_quotes
//setting (see Appendix B) will prepend single quotes
//with backslashes, which could be problematic.
$query=stripslashes($query);

mysql_connect("username", "password", "")
   or die("Could not connect to database.");
mysql_select_db("test") or
   die("Cannot select database");
$result = mysql_query($query) or
   die( mysql_error() );

$number_cols = mysql_num_fields($result);

echo "<b>query: $query</b>";
//layout table header
echo "<table border = 1>\n";
echo "<tr align=center>\n";
```

```php
for ($i=0; $i<$number_cols; $i++)
{
    echo "<th>" . mysql_field_name($result, $i). "</th>\n";
}
echo "</tr>\n";//end table header

//layout table body
while ($row = mysql_fetch_row($result))
{
    echo "<tr align=left>\n";
    for ($i=0; $i<$number_cols; $i++)
    {
        echo "<td>";
        if (!isset($row[$i])) //test for null value
            {echo "NULL";}
        else
            {echo $row[$i];}
        echo "</td>\n";
    }
    echo "</tr>\n";
}

echo "</table>";

?>

<form action="<? echo $PHP_SELF?>" method="get">
  <input type="text" name="query" size="50"><br>
  <input type="submit">
</form>
```

For the remainder of this chapter you will see how to build on the complexity of the select statement. To see things in action, we created a table in MySQL against which we can run these queries. This is the create statement for a table named "users", which holds basic personal information:

```sql
CREATE TABLE users (
userid int(10) unsigned NOT NULL auto_increment,
fname varchar(25) NOT NULL,
lname varchar(25) NOT NULL,
addr varchar(255) NOT NULL,
addr2 varchar(255),
city varchar(40) NOT NULL,
state char(2) NOT NULL,
zip varchar(5) NOT NULL,
```

```
lastchanged timestamp(14),
PRIMARY KEY (userid)
);
```

To get things started, we loaded up the database with a few rows of information. When run through the PHP code above, the query `select * from users` will return the results shown in Figure 3-1.

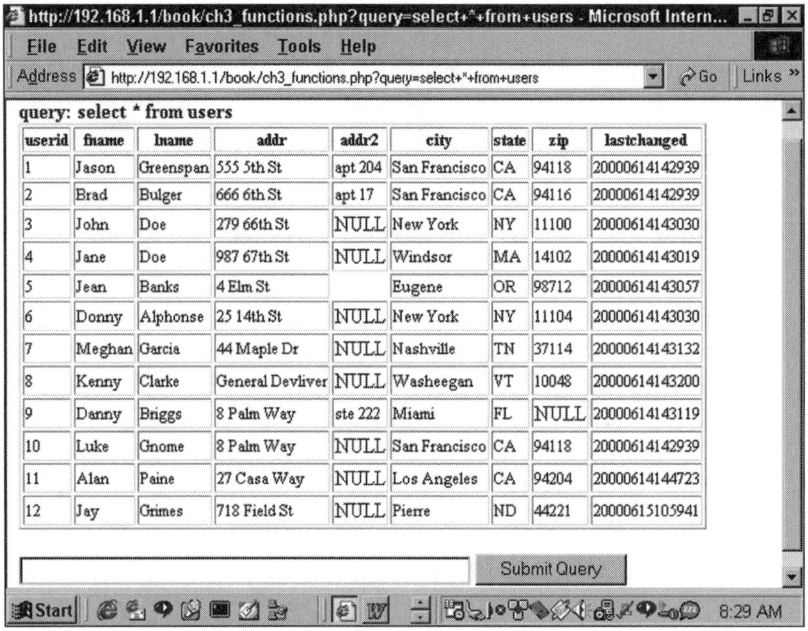

userid	fname	lname	addr	addr2	city	state	zip	lastchanged
1	Jason	Greenspan	555 5th St	apt 204	San Francisco	CA	94118	20000614142939
2	Brad	Bulger	666 6th St	apt 17	San Francisco	CA	94116	20000614142939
3	John	Doe	279 66th St	NULL	New York	NY	11100	20000614143030
4	Jane	Doe	987 67th St	NULL	Windsor	MA	14102	20000614143019
5	Jean	Banks	4 Elm St		Eugene	OR	98712	20000614143057
6	Donny	Alphonse	25 14th St	NULL	New York	NY	11104	20000614143030
7	Meghan	Garcia	44 Maple Dr	NULL	Nashville	TN	37114	20000614143132
8	Kenny	Clarke	General Devliver	NULL	Washeegan	VT	10048	20000614143200
9	Danny	Briggs	8 Palm Way	ste 222	Miami	FL	NULL	20000614143119
10	Luke	Gnome	8 Palm Way	NULL	San Francisco	CA	94118	20000614142939
11	Alan	Paine	27 Casa Way	NULL	Los Angeles	CA	94204	20000614144723
12	Jay	Grimes	718 Field St	NULL	Pierre	ND	44221	20000615105941

Figure 3-1: Results of query using select * from users

The where clause

The `where` clause limits the rows that are returned from your query. To get a single row from a table, you would a run the query against the primary key. For instance, to get all the information on Brad, you would use this query:

```
select * from users where userid = 2
```

Figure 3-2 shows the results of this query.

If you're doing a comparison to a column that stores a string (char, varchar, etc), you will need to surround the string used for comparison in the `where` clause by single quotes.

```
select * from users where city = 'San Francisco'
```

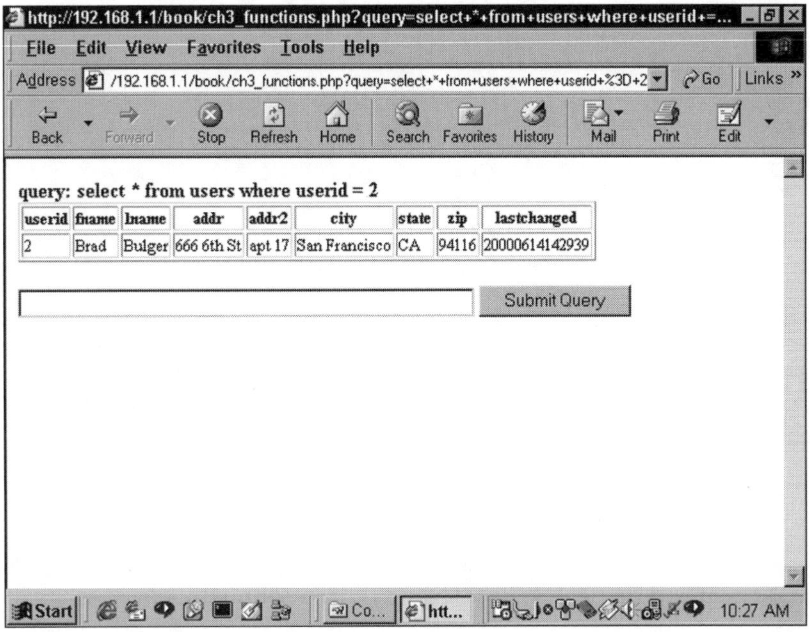

Figure 3-2: Results of query using select * from users where userid=2

MySQL has several comparison operators that can be used in the where clause. Table 3-1 lists these operators.

TABLE 3-1 MYSQL COMPARISON OPERATORS

Operator	Definition
=	equal to
<> or !=	not equal to
<	less than
<=	less than or equal to
>	greater than
>=	greater than or equal to
Like	Compares a string (discussed in detail later in this Chapter)

You can compare several operators at once by adding and or or to the where clause.

```
select * from users
where userid = 1 or
    .  city = 'San Francisco'

select * from users
where state = 'CA' and
      city = 'San Francisco'
```

It's important to note that fields with null values cannot be compared with any of the operators used in Table 3-1. For instance, in the table shown in Figure 3-1, you might think that the following statement would return every row in the table:

```
select * from users where zip <> '11111' or state = '11111'
```

But in fact, row 9 will not be returned by the query. Null values will test neither true nor false to any of these operators. Instead, to deal with null values, you will need to make use of the is null or is not null predicates.

To get the previous query to work as we had intended you'd need to augment your original query.

```
select * from users
where zip <> '11111' or
      zip = '11111' or
      zip is null
```

Or if you wanted to find all the rows where the zip contained any value (except null) you could use the following:

```
select * from table where zip is not null
```

USING DISTINCT

There will be times where your query will contain superfluous data. For instance, if your goal was to see all the cities in California, your first instinct might be to run a query like select city, state from users where state='CA'. But look at the result returned in Figure 3-3.

Notice that the first three rows are identical. This is no good, as there's no need for these extra rows. You can get by this by using select distinct. When you use distinct, the MySQL engine will remove rows with identical results. So here the better query is select distinct city, state from users where state='CA', which returns the data in Figure 3-4, which is exactly what you want.

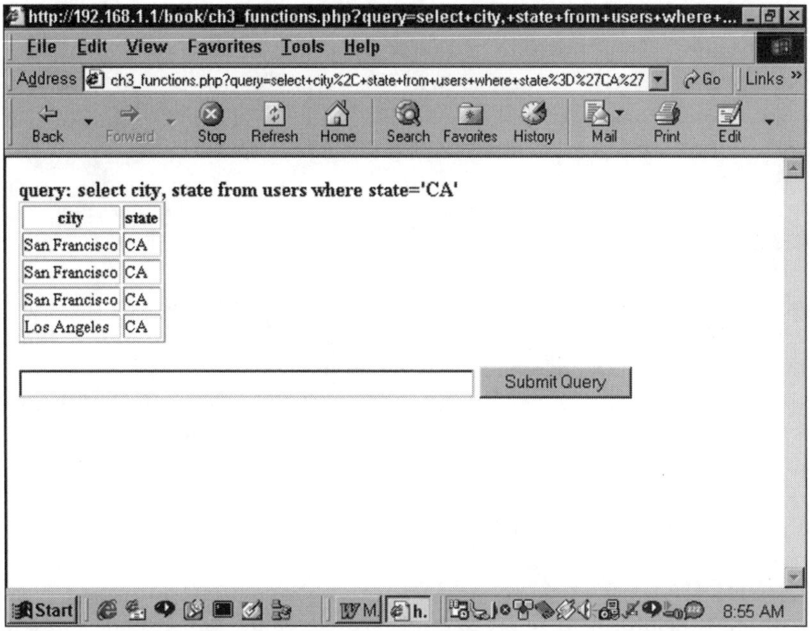

Figure 3-3: Results of query using select city, state from users where state='CA'

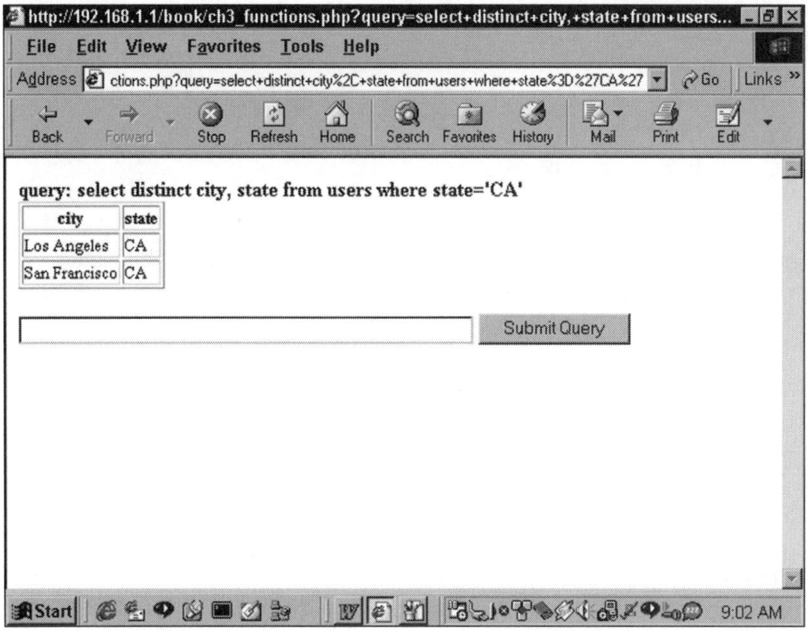

Figure 3-4: Results of query using select distinct city, state from users where state='CA'

USING BETWEEN

You can also choose values within a range by using the between predicate. between works for numeric values as well as dates. In the following query, lastchanged is a timestamp column. If you wanted to find the people who signed up on the day of June 14, 2000, you could use this query:

```
select * from users where lastchanged between 20000614000000 and
20000614235959
```

Remember that the default timestamp column type stores dates in the form YYYYMMDDHHMMSS, so to get all entries for a single day, you need to start your range at midnight (00:00:00) and end it at 11:59:59 pm (23:59:59).

You can also use between on text strings. If you wished to list all the last names in the first half of the alphabet, this query would work. Note that the following query will not include names that start with "m".

```
select * from users where lname between 'a' and 'm'
```

USING IN/NOT IN

The in predicate is helpful if there are several possible values for a single column that can be returned. If you queried the users table to get all the states in New England, you could write the query like this:

```
select * from users
 where state = 'RI' or
       state = 'NH' or
       state = 'VT' or
       state = 'MA' or
       state = 'ME'
```

Using in, you can specify a set of possible values and simplify this statement. The following query would achieve the same result.

```
select * from users
   where state in ('RI', 'NH', 'VT', 'MA', 'ME')
```

If you need to achieve the same effect but in reverse, you can use the not in predicate. To get a listing of all people in the table *not* living in New England, simple throw in the word 'not':

```
select * from user where
       state not in ('RI', 'NH', 'VT', 'MA', 'ME')
```

USING LIKE

Of course there will be occasions when you are searching for a string, but you're not exactly sure what the string looks like. In cases like these, you will need to use wildcard characters. In order to use wildcards, you need the like predicate.

There are two wildcard characters available, the underscore (_) and the percent sign (%). The underscore stands for a single character. The percent sign represents any number of characters, including none.

So, for example, if you were looking for someone with the first name of Daniel or Danny or Dan, you would use the percent sign.

```
select * from users where fname like 'Dan%'
```

Note that because the percent sign will match on zero characters, the preceding query would match the name "Dan".

However, if for some odd reason you needed to find all of the people in your database with four-letter first names beginning with the letter J, you'd construct your query like this: (Note that three underscores follow the letter J.)

```
select * from users where fname like 'J___'
```

The three underscores will match any characters and return names like Jean, John, and Jack. Jay and Johnny will not be returned.

 In MySQL the like comparison is not case sensitive. This is quite different from most implementations.

order by

There is one thing you should always keep in mind when working with relational databases: the storage of rows in any table is completely arbitrary. In general, you'll have no idea of the order in which your database has decided to put the rows you've inserted. When it matters, you can specify the order of rows returned in your query by tacking order by on the end of it.

This command can sort by any column type: alphabetical, chronological, or numeric. In addition, order by allows you to sort in either ascending or descending order by placing asc or desc after order by, respectively. If neither is included, asc is used by default.

To alphabetize the entries in the table, you would probably want to make sure that this list is sorted by both first name and last name:

```
select * from users order by lname, fname
```

You can sort by as many columns as you wish, and you can mix the `asc` and `desc` as you need. The following query isn't particularly useful, but it is possible:

```
select * from users order by lname asc, fname desc
```

limit

The `limit` predicate will restrict the number of rows returned from your query. It allows you to specify both the starting row and the number of rows you want returned. To get the first five rows from the table, run the following query:

```
select * from users limit 0,5
```

To find the first five rows alphabetically, you could use `limit` with `order by`:

```
select * from users order by lname, fname limit 0,5
```

You'll probably notice that the numbering is like arrays — the first row is row 0. To get the second five rows of the table, you'd run the following:

```
select * from users limit 5,5
```

`limit` is particularly useful in situations where you want to restrict the display on any one page. You'll see the use of `limit` throughout this book. Even Chapter 8, which is the first application in this book, uses `limit`.

group by and aggregate functions

Remember back to when we were talking about using `select` with `distinct` and how that removed rows we didn't need? That may have seemed pretty cool, but it's nothing compared to what you can get out of using `group by` and its associated aggregate functions.

Consider this task: you wish to know the number of entries from each state in our database (for example, six from California, seven from New York, two from Vermont). If you did a `select distinct state from users order by state`, you would get a listing of each state in the database, but there's no way to get the numbers. As MySQL goes through the table to process the query, it simply skips over rows that would return identical values.

However, with `group by`, MySQL creates a temporary table where it keeps all of the information on the rows and columns fitting your criteria. This allows the engine to perform some very key tasks on the temporary table. Probably the easiest way to show what `group by` can do is by showing one of the aggregate functions. We'll start with `count()`.

MySQL may not actually create a temporary table for each group by; however, the actual inner workings of a group by are pretty complex, and this is a good way to think about what MySQL is doing.

COUNT()

Once again, the goal of your query is to find out the number of people from each state that are in your users table. To do that you will use group by with count().

Remember that when the group by clause is used, you can imagine MySQL creating a temporary table where it assembles like rows. The count() function then (you guessed it) counts the number of rows in each of the groups. Check out the following query and the result returned in Figure 3-5.

```
select state, count(*) from users group by state
```

```
http://192.168.1.1/book/ch3_functions.php?query=select+state,+count(")+from+users+gro...

File   Edit   View   Favorites   Tools   Help

Address  ch3_functions.php?query=select+state%2C+count%28"%29+from+users+group+by+state+      Go    Links »

 Back    Forward    Stop   Refresh   Home     Search  Favorites  History    Mail    Print    Edit

query: select state, count(*) from users group by state

  state  count(*)
  CA     4
  FL     1
  MA     1
  ND     1
  NY     2
  OR     1
  TN     1
  VT     1

                                              Submit Query

 Start                                    h.  M              9:50 AM
```

Figure 3-5: Results of query using select state, count(*) from users group by state

Here the asterisk (*) indicates that all rows within the group should be counted. The count(*) function is also handy for getting the total number of rows in a table.

```
select count(*) from users
```

Within a group by, you can also indicate a specific field that is to be counted. count will look for the number of non-null values. Take, for example, the table in Figure 3-6.

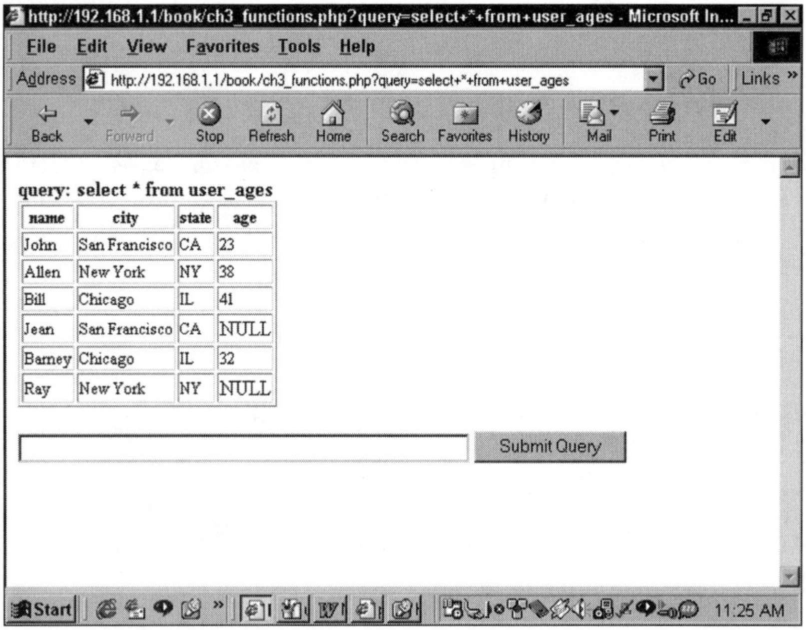

Figure 3-6: users_ages table

It may not seem that there's much use in counting non-null values from this table. However, if you're the type that's really into statistics, you could use this table to figure out what percentage from each city feels comfortable indicating its age. First you'd need a count of all the entries from each specific city and state; following that, you'd need a count of all the non-null values in the age field.

```
Select city, state, count(*), count(age) from user_ages
group by state, city
```

From the result in Figure 3-7, you can see that Chicagoans are far more forthcoming than those from the coasts.

This is as good a time as any to introduce aliases. There will be times, particularly when you're working with functions, when the column name returned by the query isn't what you'd like it to be. For example, in Figure 3-7 you may wish for a table header a bit more descriptive than count(*).

You can follow any function or column name with the word as and then specify a name you prefer. as simply designates an alias. If you need a column name that is more than one word, surround the text string with single quotes.

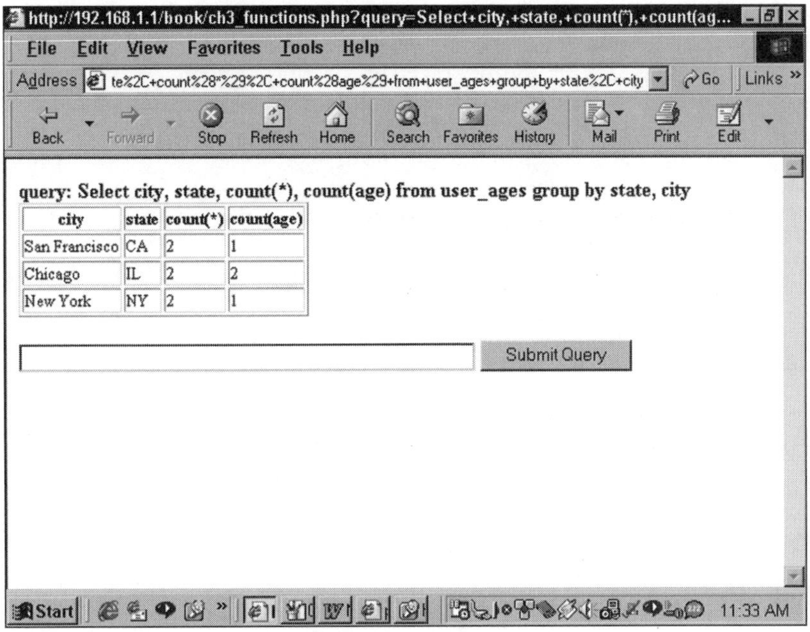

Figure 3-7: Results of query using count( ) function

While on the topic of aliases, I'll also mention that there are a variety of functions available in MySQL (see Appendix I). They range from simple math functions to more complex operations. Below I've thrown in some math to clarify the purpose of the query. Notice the use of the as clause and the way it affects the display of the query (shown in Figure 3-8).

```
Select city, state, count(*) as 'Total Rows',
       count(age) as 'The Willing',
       (count(age)/count(*)*100) as 'Percent Responding'
from user_ages
group by state, city
```

You can also use aliases on tables. This will be particularly helpful when dealing with multiple tables. I'll discuss this in further detail in the section "Multi-table join."

SUM( )

The sum( ) function returns the sum of a given column and is almost always used with a group by clause. For instance, if you are running an application for a non-profit, you might want to know the total contributions from each state. The table you're working with might look like the one in Figure 3-9.

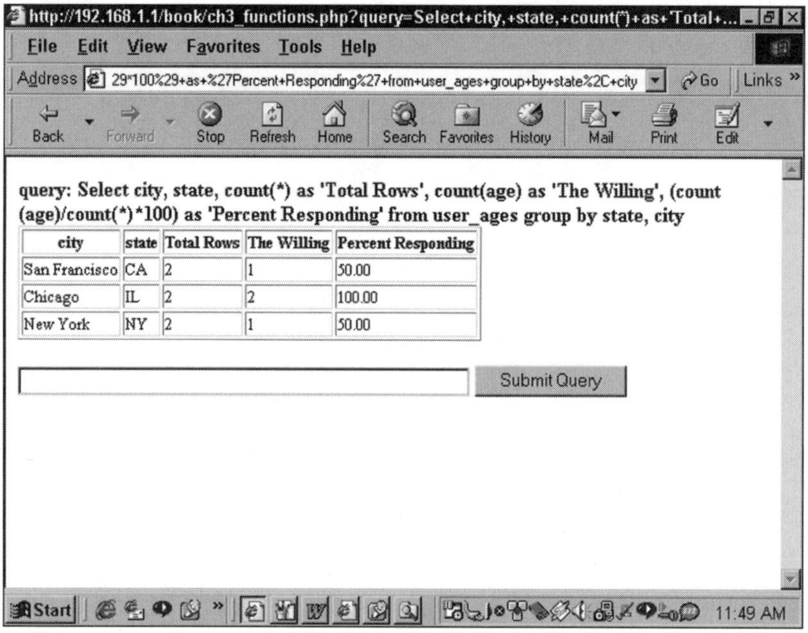

Figure 3-8: Results of query using functions and aliases

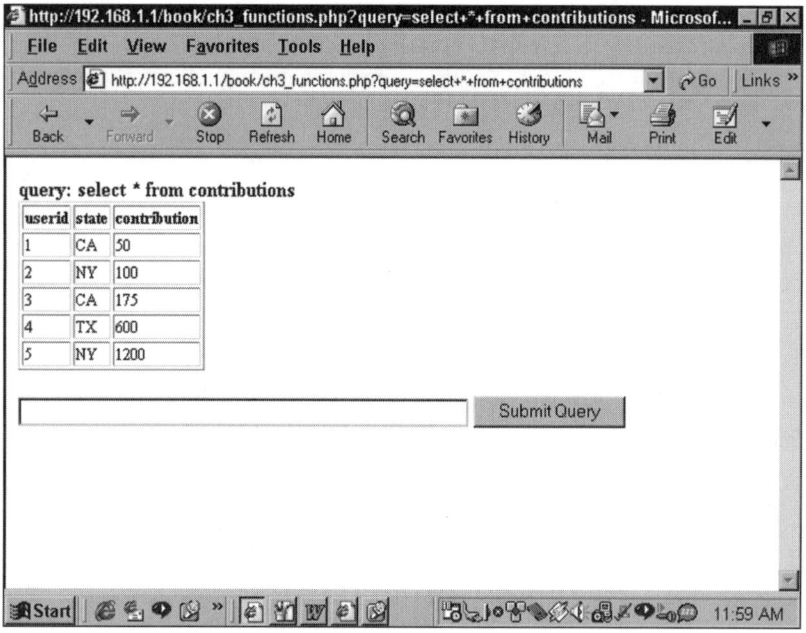

Figure 3-9: Table where using sum() would be helpful

To get the total from each state, you'd run the following query:

```
select state, sum(contribution) from contributions group by state
```

MIN()

The `min()` function pulls out the lowest value in each grouping. To find the lowest contribution from any state just make a small change to the previous query:

```
select state, min(contribution) from contributions group by state
```

MAX()

As you probably guessed, `max()` will return the highest value in a group:

```
select state, max(contribution) from contributions group by state
```

AVG()

`avg ()` returns the average of the group:

```
select state, sum(contribution) from contributions group by state
```

You could throw all these together to create a pretty useful query, as Figure 3-10 and the following query show.

```
select state, sum(contribution) as 'Total',
       avg(contribution) as 'Average',
       min(contribution) as 'Minimum',
       max(contribution) as 'Maximum'
from contributions
group by state
```

GROUP BY OPTIONS

Most relational databases require that fields listed in the `select` clause be used in the `group by` predicate. But MySQL gives you more options; you can group a subset of the columns listed. For instance, if you wanted to find out the number of people in one city and get a look at a sample Zip code from that city, you could run the following:

```
select city, zip, count(*) from users group by city
```

The query would return a listing of cities, the number of entries for each city, and one sample Zip code.

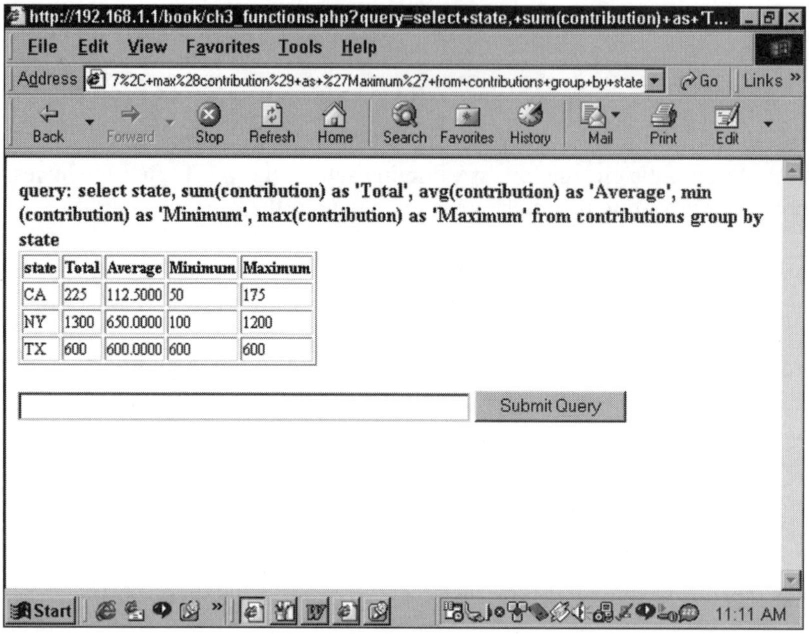

Figure 3-10: Using multiple aggregate functions together

This is quite different from the results from this query:

```
select city, zip, count(*) from users group by city, zip
```

This returns a separate row for each city/zip combination and provides a count for each unique combination.

having

The `having` predicate restricts the rows displayed by a `group by`. This is not the same as the `where` clause. The `where` clause actually restricts the rows that are used in the `group by`. The `having` clause only prevents their display.

If you needed to find the average amount of donations from each state for all those who contributed more than $100, you could run the following:

```
select avg(donations), state where donations> 100
```

However, if you wanted to display average contributions for all of the states where the average was over $100, you would have to use the `having` clause. Since the `having` clause does not restrict rows that go into the `group by`, the aggregate functions, in this case `avg()`, use all the rows in their calculations.

```
select avg(contribution) as avg_contrib, state
from contributions
group by state
having avg(contribution)>500
```

Joining Tables

If you read Chapter 1, you know that relational databases work so well because they segment information. Different tables hold information on different topics, and fields are inserted into the tables to maintain relationships. After you finish the normalization process, it's likely that none of your tables will be usable without the others. That is why you'll need to join tables in your SQL select statements.

Two-table join (the equi-join)

For the sake of continuity, we're going to reprise a couple of tables first seen in Chapter 1. Take a look at the familiar tables in Figure 3-11.

companies

company_id	company_name	address
1	Big Co Company	1121 43rd St
2	Little Co Company	4444 44th St

contracts

contract_id	company_id	Name	Title	Phone	Email
1	1	Jay Greenspan	Vice President	4155551212	1121 43rd St
2	1	Brad Bulber	President	4155552222	4444 44th St
3	2	John Doe	Lacky	2125556666	4444 44th St

Figure 3-11: Tables in need of a join

If you're looking to do a mailing to all of the people in the contacts table, you are going to need to join the contacts table to the companies table, because the street address is in the companies table (and it's exactly where it should be). The company_id column in the contacts table creates the relationship between these tables. And if you join these tables on occasions where the company_id field in the contacts table is equal to the company_id field in the contacts table, all of the information will be at your fingertips.

This is easy enough to accomplish in SQL. In the `from` portion of the `select` statement all of the tables to be joined must be listed. And in the `where` portion, the fields on which the join takes place must be shown:

```
select *
from companies, contacts
where companies.company_ID = contacts.company_ID
```

At times when a reference to a field name is ambiguous, you need to specify which table the column comes from the by using the syntax `table_name.column_name`. This is done in the `where` clause in Figure 3-12. If you fail to indicate the table from which you're pulling the company_id column in the SQL statements, MySQL will return an error.

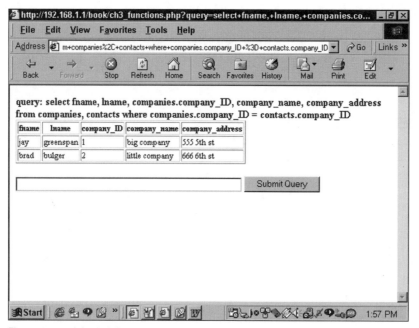

Figure 3-12: A basic join

This type of join, where tables are merged based on quality in a common field, is extremely common. It is known as an *equi-join*, or an *inner join*. The name "inner join" will make more sense once you learn about the *outer join* later in this chapter.

Once you begin performing joins, aliases become convenient. By specifying an alias in the `from` clause you could save yourself some typing. In the following code, `t1` is an alias for companies and `t2` is an alias for contacts.

```
select *
from companies t1, contacts t2
where t1.company_ID = t2.company_ID
```

Multi-table join

An equi-join can be applied to more than one table. Many of your SQL statements will join three, four, or more tables. All you'll need to do is add additional columns after select, additional tables in the from clause, and the additional join parameters in the where clause. Take a look at the tables that need multiple joins in Figure 3-13.

company_id	name
1	IBM
2	Xerox
3	Sun

expertise_id	area
1	Hardware
2	Software
3	Consulting

company_id	expertise_id
1	1
1	2
1	3
2	1
2	3
3	1
3	2

location_id	company_id	address	state
1	1	4 My Way, Durham	NC
2	2	44 Circle Dr, New York	NY
3	1	1 Front St, San Francisco	CA
4	2	Park Dr, Palo Alto	CA
5	2	48 Times Square, New York	NY
6	3	280 South, Sunnyvale	CA

Figure 3-13: Tables in need of multiple joins

If you wanted to find the addresses for all of the companies with offices in California who had expertise in consulting, you would have to join all four of these tables. The following query would get the job done. Here the where clause contains quite a few tests; the first two lines of the where clause limit the rows that will be returned to those companies that match our criteria. The remainder of the where clause takes care of the joins.

```
SQL-query:
Select *
from companies, locations, expertise, companies_expertise
where state = 'CA' and
    companies_expertise.expertise_ID = 3 and
    companies.company_ID = companies_expertise.company_ID and
    companies.company_ID = locations.company_ID and
    companies_expertise.expertise_ID = expertise.expertise_ID
```

outer join

The challenges presented by null values have shown themselves repeatedly in this book. In Chapter 2 we presented these two tables, seen in Figure 3-14.

first_name	last_name	spouse_id
Jay	Greenspan	1
Brad	Bulger	

spouse_id	spouse_first_name	spouse_last_name
1	Melissa	Ramirez

Figure 3-14: Tables in need of an outer join

Now imagine that you need to get a list of the authors of this book and their spouses, if they are married. The equi-join shown in the previous section will not work in this case. Take the following query:

```
select *
from contact, spouses
where contact.spouse_ID = spouses.spouse_ID
```

Only the first row of the contact table will be returned. The null value in the second row ensures that nothing can match the criteria in the where clause. In cases like this, where we need to preserve one table and join the second table when there are matching values, we will make use of the outer join (also known as the *left outer join*), which looks like this:

```
select *
from contact
left join spouses
on contact.spouse_ID = spouses.spouse_ID
```

This statement says, "I want to keep the entire contacts table, and tack on the spouses table when these two fields are equal." The word *left* in the term *left outer join* refers to the fact that when you visualize your database tables, you should visualize the first table, the one that appears in the `from` clause, on the right-most side, and the joined table on the left.

Depending on the database package you're using, the syntax of the outer join may vary. Some databases support left, right, and full (both left and right) outer joins. MySQL only has the left outer join, but in practice it's usually all you need. You can use the syntax seen in the previous query, or you can use `left outer join on`.

Outer joins will come up frequently out of necessity. Additionally, it is often good practice to use outer joins even when you feel an inner join will do the trick. It's just a matter of being safe. You'd rather not have important rows of data come up missing because you forgot to account for null values. Throughout the book, you will see occasions when we have used outer joins because we just wanted to be extra careful.

There may come times when you will need to do more than one outer join. Say, for instance (and for no particularly good reason), we wanted to store information regarding spouses' siblings. We'd add another table listing the siblings and a column to the spouses table, which maintained the relationship. So, if we were to design a query that maintained everyone in the contacts table, and maintained everyone returned from the spouses table, we'd have to throw in two outer joins:

```
select *
from contact
left join spouses on contact.spouse_ID = spouses.spouse_ID
left join on syblings spouses.sybling_ID = syblings.sybling_ID
```

self join

As bizarre as it may sound, the time will come when you'll need to join a table to a copy of itself. You'll usually run into the need for this when looking for duplicates in a table. If we had a sneaking suspicion that there was a bigamist in Table 3-2, how would we search out the two with the same spouse?

TABLE 3-2 CONTACTS

contact_id	first_name	last_name	spouse_id
1	jay	greenspan	1
2	brad	bulger	

Continued

TABLE 3-2 CONTACTS *(Continued)*

contact_id	first_name	last_name	spouse_id
3	john	james	2
4	elliot	simms	2

You would need to discover if the value in this spouse_id field was repeated (for instance, the number 2 appears more than once). You could do a `group by`, but then there would be no way of getting the names of the people involved. Using `group by` along with the `count()` function, you could find the occasions where one person appears more than once, but it would take a second query to find out who those people were. With a `self join`, you can do it all in one step. But it needs to be a carefully considered step.

You might think that the following query would do the trick. Notice that I again use an alias, so that we have two table names we can address.

```
select t1.first_name, t1.last_name, t2.first_name, t2.last_name
from contacts t1, contacts t2
where t1.spouse_id = t2.spouse_id
```

But this is going to return more rows than we need. Specifically, each name will match itself, providing duplicates of each returned entry. Given this query, when the row for Jay is compared to itself, it will test true and be returned in the result. You can eliminate redundancy here by ensuring that the contact_id field from the first table is not equal to the ID field in the second table.

```
select t1.first_name, t1.last_name
from contacts t1, contacts t2
where t1.spouse_id = t2.spouse_id
and t1.contact_id != t2.contact_id
```

This is good but not perfect. Take the example of Elliot and John. A row will be returned when the Elliot is in `t1` and John is in `t2`; another will be returned when John is in `t1` and Elliot is in `t2`. The easiest way to address that here is to make use of the numeric primary key. You know one ID will be greater than the other, and by using that information you can get rid of all duplicates.

```
select t1.first_name, t1.last_name
from contacts t1, contacts t2
where t1.spouse_id = t2.spouse_id
and t1.countact_id < t2.contact_id
```

Portions of SQL the SQL Standard that MySQL Doesn't Support

The MySQL developers are constantly working on improvements to the software. It is possible that within the next couple of years they will support most of the features you'd find in high-priced commercial software, like Oracle, Sybase, Informix, or Microsoft's SQL Server. But as of the writing of this book, there are a couple of portions of the select syntax that MySQL doesn't support.

Unions

Unions allow queries with the same number of columns to be returned in one result set. For instance, if you had two tables storing user names, you could have all of the names in one query returned with a statement like this:

```
select first_name, last_name
from table_1
union
select first_name, last_name
from table_2
```

Unions are convenient, but their absence in MySQL isn't that big of a deal. In the preceding example, you could easily run a second query.

Correlated subqueries

If you're coming from a background of using a package like Oracle, you may find the absence of correlated subqueries troubling. The good news is that subquery support is high on the developers' priority list. For those new to the concept, subqueries allow you to define an entire query in the where clause.

For example, using subqueries, if you had a table that stored students and their test scores, you could easily find all the students with better-than-average test scores:

```
select first_name, last_name, score
from test_scores
where score> (select avg(score) from test_scores)
```

You can achieve the same effect by running two queries. In all cases you can work around the absence of subqueries by running additional queries. You lose some elegance, but the effect is identical.

Make sure to check in at the mysql.com every now and then. Subqueries may be included in version 3.24. And by the time you're reading this, that version may be available.

In Chapter 10 there is more information on dealing with subqueries in MySQL.

Summary

You can get through the better part of your life without committing some portions of SQL to memory. If you are using graphical tools you may not need to learn the specifics of the `create` or `alter` command. The same cannot be said of the `select` statement.

Everything covered in this chapter is really important to your life as an applications developer. The `select` statement allows you efficiently retrieve and sort information from your databases, and if you understand the intricacies of the `select` statement, you'll be able to write applications more efficiently and elegantly.

Part II

Working with PHP

Chapter 4

Getting Started with PHP – Variables

IN THIS CHAPTER

♦ Assigning variables within PHP scripts

♦ Handling data passed from HTML forms

♦ Working with PHP's built-in variables, including Apache variables

♦ Testing for and assigning variable types

PHP MAKES WORKING WITH variables extremely easy. PHP is smart about understanding variable types and keeps the syntax to an absolute minimum. Those coming to PHP from a C, Java, or Perl background may find PHP easier to deal with, but the ease of syntax can present its own problems.

All variables in PHP start with a dollar sign ($). It doesn't matter what kind of variables they are, whether strings, integers, floating-point numbers, or even arrays. They all look identical in the code. The PHP engine keeps track of the type of information you are storing.

In general, variables will come from three places: they are either assigned within a script, passed from an HTML page (often from form input), or part of your PHP environment. We'll talk about each of these in the following sections. Note that variables can come from other places: URLs and sessions are also possible origins of variables.

Assigning Simple Variables Within a Script

PHP does not require explicit variable declaration. All you have to do is use a variable and it exists. And as we already mentioned, all variable types look identical. The following code shows how to assign variables of string, integer, and floating-point (double) types:

```
$a = "this is a string"; //this is a string
$b = 4; //this is an integer
```

71

```
$c = 4.837; //this is a floating-point number
$d = "2"; //this is another string
```

Notice that the = is the assignment operator. For comparison, you must use two consecutive equal signs (= =). For example, if($x==1).

Typing is flexible, and PHP is pretty smart about handling changes in types. For example, given the code you just saw, the following would evaluate as you'd probably hope:

```
$e = $b + $d;
echo $e;
```

PHP would recognize that you want to treat the string in $d as an integer. The variable $e will be an integer type and will equal 6. In fact, PHP will also evaluate the following as an integer:

```
$a = 2;
$b = "2 little piggies";
$c = $a + $b;
```

Here, $c will equal 4. If an integer or floating-point number is at the beginning of a string, PHP can evaluate it as such. Similarly, PHP will move smoothly among numeric types.

```
$f = 2; //$f is an integer
$g = 1.444; // $g is a double (floating-point) type
$f = $f + $g;   //$f is now a double type
```

This kind of flexibility is nice, but it can lead to some difficulty. There will be times when you're not sure what variable types you are working with. We'll show you how to deal with these circumstances in the section "Testing Variables."

Delimiting Strings

In the preceding code, all the strings were surrounded by double quotes. There are two other ways to delimt strings in PHP.

If you surround your strings with double quotes, variables within the string will be expanded. For instance,

```
$my_name = "Jay";
$phrase = "Hello, my name is, $my_name";
echo $phrase;
```

will print "Hello, my name is, Jay". But if you want to include any of the following characters within you string, they must be escaped with backslashes:

- " (double quotes)

- \ (backslash)

- $ (dollar sign)

For example, to print an opening form tag using double quotes you would have to do the following.

```
echo "<form action=\"mypage.php\" method=\"get\">";
```

You can also surround strings with single quotes. If a string is within single quotes, variables will not be expanded. So this code:

```
$my_name = "Jay";
echo 'Hello, my name is, $my_name';
```

will print "Hello, my name is, $my_name". The only characters that need to be escaped within single quotes are single quotes and backslashes.

Finally, starting in PHP 4, you can make use of Here documents. This is a hybrid of the single and double-quote style that can be convenient in many circumstances. Here docs are delimited at the start of the string with three less-than signs <<< and an identifier. In the book we use the identifier EOQ. The string is terminated with the same identifier followed by a semicolon. In the following, $my_string is a string properly delimited using Here doc syntax.

```
$my_string = <<<EOQ
My string is in here.
EOQ;
```

Using Here docs, variables will be expanded within string and double quotes do not need to be escaped. We make frequent use of Here docs when working with form elements.

```
$element = <<<EOQ
<textarea name="$name" cols="$cols" rows="$rows"
wrap="$wrap">$value</textarea>
EOQ;
```

In a case like this we don't need to litter the string with backslashes, and we still get the convenience of having variables expanded within the string.

Array elements accessed by associative keys cannot be expanded in Here docs. For example, the following will produce an error.

```
$array = array ("fname"=>"jay", "lname"=>"greenspan");
$str = <<<EOQ
print my string $array["fname"]
EOQ;
```

Assigning arrays within a script

Arrays are variables that contain multiple values. A simple array might store the months of the year. To assign this array, you could use the following:

```
$months = array("January", "February", "March", "May", "June",
"July", "August", "September", "October", "November", "December");
```

This array has 12 elements, and you can address them by their ordinal placement in the array, starting with 0. So the command echo $months[0] would print January and echo $months[11] would print December. To print out all of the values within an array, you could get the length of the array and then set up a loop.

```
for ($month_number=0; $i<count($months); $i++)
{
  echo $months[$month_number] . "<br>\n" ;
}
```

The for loop is explained in Chapter 5.

You can also assign values to arrays with a simple assignment operator. The following would work:

```
$dogs = array();
$dogs[0] = "shepherd";
$dogs[1] = "poodle";
```

If you don't specify the numeral, the value will be tacked on the end of the array. The following line would assign "retriever" to $dogs[2].

```
$dogs[] = "retriever";
```

There are a variety of functions that work with arrays (over 40 in PHP 4).
Many of these will be covered in Chapter 6.

Like many programming languages, PHP makes use of associative arrays. If you
are new to the concept, elements in associative arrays have "keys" that reference
individual elements. This is particularly important when you're dealing with databases. When you fetch rows from your database query you will usually refer to the
elements by their keys.

You can assign an associative array in this manner. Here, first_name,
last_name, and e-mail are the keys.

```
$person = array (
    "first_name" => "Jay",
    "last_name" => "Greenspan",
    "e-mail" => "jgreen_1@yahoo.com"
);
```

If you wanted to add to this array, you could assign another value. Notice that
the next line would add an integer into the array, so this array would contain four
values, three strings and one integer.

```
$person["age"] = 32;
```

Typically, if you want to access both the keys and the values in an associative
array, you would use list()=each(), as in the following code.

```
while (list($key, $value) = each($person))
{
    echo "<b>key :</b> $key, value = $value <br>\n";
}
```

Chapter 5 describes the list()=each() in more detail. Basically, each() pulls the
key and value of a single array element; list() takes those values and assigns
them to $key and $value, respectively. This process continues until each element in
the array has been accessed. If you want to go through the array a second time, you
will need to reset the array pointer with reset($person).

If you wanted to get only the value without the key, or if you were using a non-
associative array and wanted to use the list()=each() structure, you would have
to do this:

```
while (list( , $value) = each($person))
{
```

```
    echo "value = $value <br>\n";
}
```

Or, if you want to get at just the keys, you could do this.

```
while (list($key) = each($person))
{
    echo "key = $key <br>\n";
}
```

 Think about PHP arrays this way: all arrays are associative. A couple of pages back you saw you can assign a basic array without specifying associative keys. For example $myarray= array ("pug", "poodle").When this is done, PHP assigns $myarray consecutive numeric keys starting at zero. They behave just like associative keys. You step through them using list() =each(). They make use of the same array functions, many of which are explained in Chapter 6.

Assigning two-dimensional arrays in a script

PHP also supports multi-dimensional arrays. The most commonly used multi-dimensional array is the two-dimensional array. Two-dimensional arrays look a lot like tables. They store information that is based on two keys. For instance, if we wanted to store information on more than one person, a two-dimensional array would work well. We would assign an array named $people, and within $people there would be individual arrays addressing each person:

```
$people = array (
            "jay" => array (
                "last_name" => "greenspan",
                "age" => 32
            ),
            "john" => array (
                "last_name" => "doe",
                "age" => 52
            )
);
```

Here the $people array contains information on two people, Jay and John. To access information on any single value, you will need to use both keys. To print out John's last age, the following two commands would work:

```
echo $people["john"]["age"]; //prints 52
```

You could access all of the elements in a two-dimensional array by looping through both of the array's dimensions:

```
while(list($person, $person_array) = each($people))
{
    echo "<b>What I know about $person</b><br>\n";
    while(list($person_attribute, $value) = each($person_array))
    {
        echo "$person_attribute = $value<br>\n";
    }

}
```

Accessing Variables Passed from the Browser

The whole point of using PHP, or any other middleware package for that matter, is to deliver customized information based on user preferences and need. Often, the information will come via HTML forms. But information can come from other places, including HTML anchors, cookies, and sessions.

HTML forms variables

One of the most common ways in which variable information is delivered is through HTML forms.

 Appendix A presents detailed information on creating HTML forms. Refer to that appendix before you read this section if you are unfamiliar with this topic.

For each of your form elements you will have to assign a name and a value attribute. When the form is submitted, the name=value pairs are passed to PHP. They can be passed to PHP by either the GET or POST methods, depending on what you chose in your form action attribute.

Once a form is submitted, the form elements automatically become global variables in PHP. (Global variables and variable scope are discussed in Chapter 6). It is truly a no-muss, no-fuss way of doing business. Consider the following simple HTML form:

```
<form action=mypage.php action=post>
    <input type=text name=email>
```

```
<input type=text name=first_name>
<input type=submit name=submit value=add>
</form>
```

Once the user hits the submit button, variables named $email, $first_name, and $submit will be available in the called PHP page. You can then process these variables however you see fit. Note that in most of our applications we will be using the value of the submit button, to make sure the page understands what action the user has taken. The following is a brief example of how this will work. Assume the name of the page is mypage.php.

```
<?php
if (isset($submit) && $submit=="yes")
{
    echo "thank you for submitting your form."
} else {
?>
<form action=mypage.php action=post>
   <input type=text name=email>
   <input type=text name=first_name>
   <input type=submit name=submit value=yes>
</form>
<?php
}
?>
```

 In some browsers if there is only one submit button within a form, the user can hit the enter key and submit the form without the submit button information being sent.

On his or her first visit to this page the user will be presented with a form. Once the form is submitted and the page recalls itself with the new variable information, only the thank you message will appear.

Form variables will also be accessible through either the $HTTP_POST_VARS or $HTTP_GET_VARS array, depending on the method used in your form. These are convenient if you have variables coming from both methods, if variables from forms could carry the same name as variables in your script, or if you have an undefined set of variables being passed and you need to check what's there.

If you are wondering when you might have to deal with variables from both GET and POST, consider a situation where a user gets to a page by clicking on a link with querystring information. The user may then end up at a page with a form. If the action of form is an empty string, the form will submit to itself and it will maintain the querystring If the method of the form is POST, variables will be coming from both GET and POST

You can access any individual element like any associative array ($HTTP_POST_VARS["e-mail"]). Or you can loop through all of the contents of the array as follows:

```
while (list($key, $value) = each($HTTP_POST_VARS))
{
    echo "variable = $key value = $value <br>";
}
```

Passing arrays

There are occasions when passing scalar variables won't work, and you'll need to pass arrays from your HTML page to your PHP script. This will come up when your user can choose one or more form elements on a page. Take, for example, multiple select boxes, which allow users to pass one or more items from a number of items. The form element is made with the HTML in the following code example. The "multiple" attribute indicates that the user can choose more than one element, as shown in Figure 4-1. To choose more than one element on the PC, hold down the Ctrl key while selecting additional values. On the Mac, use the Apple key, and you Gnome users can select and unselect individual elements with a click.

```
<form action ="mypage.php" method="post">
    <select name="j_names[]" size=4 multiple>
        <option value="2">John
        <option value="3">Jay
        <option value="4">Jackie
        <option value="5">Jordan
        <option value="6">Julia
    </select>
    <input type="submit" value="submit">
</form>
```

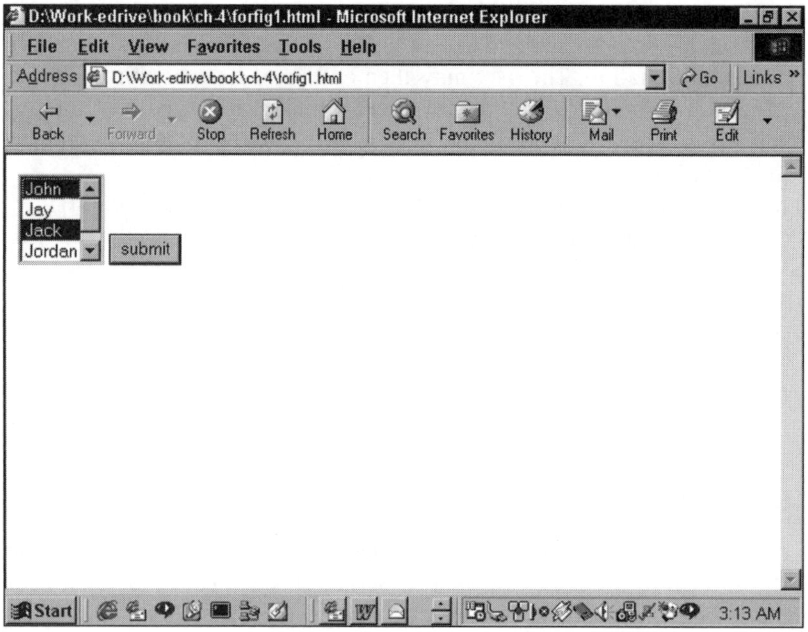

Figure 4-1: Multiple select box

Notice that in the select "name" attribute we've added opening and closing brackets ([ ]). This tells PHP to expect an array. If we didn't include the bracket, there could be two values fighting for the same variable name, and that's no good at all.

Once it has been submitted you can address this array like any other.

```
if (is_array($j_names))
{
    echo "<b>the select values are:<br> <br>";
    while(list($key, $value) = each($j_names))
    {
        echo $value . "<br>\n";
    }
}
```

Passing arrays can also be useful when you want to present a series of checkboxes that the user may or may not check before pressing the submit button. In Chapter 8, there is a code example for a page that allows the program's administrator to use checkboxes to select which entries should be deleted. Figure 4-2 shows a sample of this type of page. If we were to assign a different name to each checkbox, we would have to check each one individually. With arrays, we write a three-line loop to check them all.

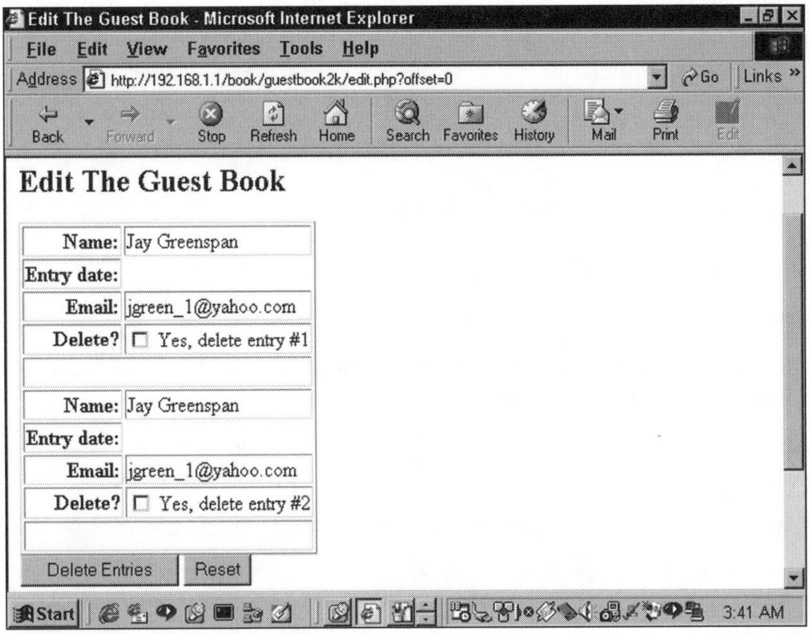

Figure 4-2: Series of checkboxes

Arrays passed from forms can also have associative keys, which can be multi-dimensional. The name of the form element should take the form name="array_name[element_name]". Or for a multi-dimensional array, array_name[element_name][subelement_name]".

Cookies

Cookies are small pieces of information that are stored on a user's hard drive. A cookie contains a bit of text that can be read by the Web server that put it there. Cookies provide the only way to keep track of users over the course of several visits. Remember that the Web is a stateless environment. Your Web server really has no idea who is requesting a page. Cookies help you keep track of users as they move around your site.

When they exist, cookies become part of the HTTP request sent to the Web server. But first you'll need to set a cookie. The developers have made this, like everything else in PHP, exceedingly simple. Use the setcookie() function. This function takes the following arguments:

```
setcookie(name, value, time_to_expire, path, domain, security
setting);
```

We will discuss this in more detail in Chapter 6, but for now, suffice it to say that the following statement

```
setcookie("mycookie",
"my_id",time()+(60*60*24*30),"/",".mydomain.com", 0)
```

would set a cookie with the following parameters:

◆ Stores a variable named my_cookie

◆ Value of mycookie "my_id"

◆ The cookie will expire 30 days from the time it is set (current time + the number of seconds in 30 days).

◆ The cookie will be available to every page in the domain. We could restrict it to a specific path within a domain by including a path.

◆ It will be available to every site with a mydomain.com address.

◆ There are no special security settings.

Once the cookie is set, the variables retrieved from the cookie behave precisely like the variables retrieved from form elements. They will automatically be available as global variables. After a PHP script places the cookie, additional scripts within the domain can access it directly.

If you wanted to be careful that $mycookie didn't conflict with another variable also named $mycookie, you could access it through the HTTP_COOKIE_VARS array, using HTTP_COOKIE_VARS["mycookie"].

You can also set cookies that are accessible as arrays:

```
setcookie("mycookie[first]",
"dddd",time()+2592000,"/","192.168.1.1", 0);
setcookie("mycookie[second]",
"my_second_id",time()+2592000,"/","192.168.1.1", 0);
```

These two variables would be accessible as an associative array.

The preceding code worked fine using Internet Explorer 5 on the PC. However, this may not work on other browsers. In any case, you are probably better off avoiding situations that require arrays within cookies.

Sessions

PHP 4, like ASP and ColdFusion, natively supports sessions, only it does a much better job. What's a session? Basically, it's another way of maintaining state between pages. Your script declares that a session should start with the `start_session()` function. At that point PHP registers a unique session ID, and usually that ID is sent to the user via a cookie. PHP then creates a corresponding file on the server that can then keep track of any number of variables. The file has the same name as the session ID.

Once the session is created, you can register any number of variables. The values of these variables are kept in the file on the server. As long as the session cookie lives, these variables will be available to any page within the same domain that wishes to access them. This is a much more convenient setup than sending variables from page to page through hidden form elements or bloated cookies.

Of course, there is the possibility that some users will not allow cookies. For this reason, PHP allows you to track the Session ID through the querystring. You can do this manually by appending the Session ID onto the querystring, or by changing a configuration option.

To add the session ID to the querystring manually, use <?= SID?>. This automatically prints out a string like this:

```
PHPSESSID=07d696c4fd787cd6c78b734fb4855520
```

Adding this to a link will pass the PHPSESSID variable via the querystring. Use something like this:

```
<a href="mypage.php?<?=SID?>">click to page</a>
```

 <?= is shorthand for echo. You can use it any time you like, not just with sessions.

If PHP is compiled with the `-enable-trans-id` option the session ID will automatically be added to every relative link.

Basically, it is pretty simple. The following script will register a session variable named `$my_var`, and will assign it a value of "hello world".

```
<?
session_start();
session_register("my_var");
$my_var = "hello world";
?>
```

On subsequent pages the variable $my_var will be available, but only after you run the session_start() function. That function tells PHP to look for a session and if the session exists, to make all the session variables accessible as globals.

It can take a little work with if statements to make your session variables properly accessible. Look at the following short script for an example.

```php
<?php
session_start();
session_register("your_name");
//check to see if $your name contains anything
if(!empty($your_name))
{
    echo "I already know your name, $your_name";
}
//this portion will probaby run the first time to
//this page.
elseif(empty($your_name) && !isset($submit))
{
    echo "<form name=myform method=post action=$PHP_SELF>
        <input type=text name=first_name> first name<br>
        <input type=text name=last_name> last name<br>
        <input type=submit name=submit value=submit>
        </form>";
//if the form has been submitted, this portion will
//run and make an assignment to $your_name.
} elseif (isset($submit) && empty($your_name))
{
    $your_name = $first_name . " " . $last_name;
    echo "Thank you, $your_name";
}
```

After running this code, hit refresh on your browser. You will see that the script remembers who you are.

TIP   Your setcookie() and session_start() functions should always be at the very top of your file. If you try sending anything to the browser prior to setting a cookie, you will get error messages.

Using Built-In Variables

There are a variety of variables set by your server and PHP environment. You can find a complete list of these by running `phpinfo()`. If you haven't done it yet, go to your keyboard, type in the following, and then run the following script:

```php
<?php
phpinfo();
?>
```

It will deliver a page that looks like what you see in Figure 4-3.

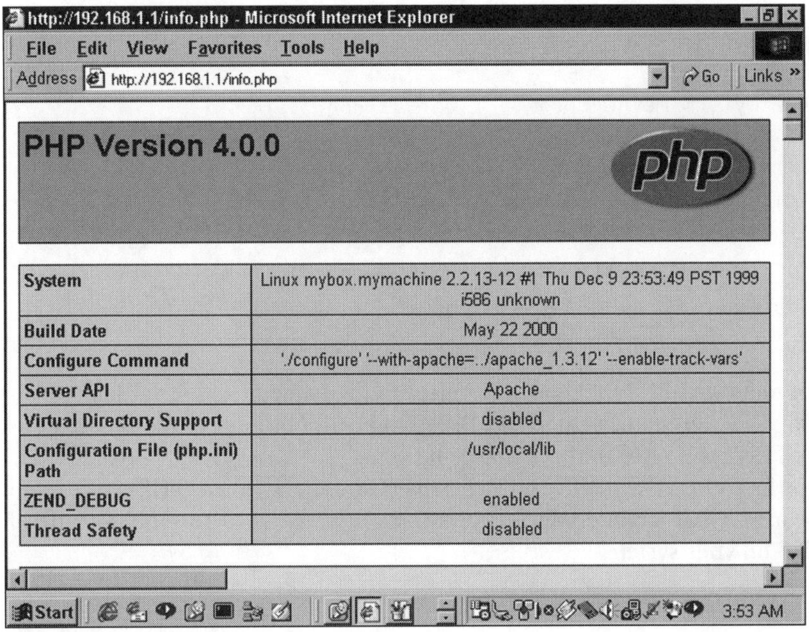

Figure 4-3: phpinfo();

It's a good idea to delete this page when you're done with it. No need to give crackers any more information than absolutely necessary.

You can use this variety of variables in a variety of ways. We'll take a look at some of these now, and show where and when you might use them. Some variables come from the PHP engine, while others originate from your Web server.

PHP variables

These are variables available through PHP.

PHP_SELF

This is the address of the file being run. Usually, the full path is given from the ServerRoot directory, which is very useful when a form is both presented and processed in the same PHP page.

```
<?
if(isset($submit))
{
  //do some form processing here
  echo "thanks for the submission";
} else {
?>
<form name=myform method=post action=<?=$PHP_SELF?>>
        <input type=text name=first_name> first name<br>
        <input type=text name=last_name> last name<br>
        <input type=submit name=submit value=submit>
 </form>
<?
}
?>
```

Keep in mind that PHP_SELF always refers to the name of the script being executed in the URL. So in an include file, PHP_SELF will not refer to the file that has been included. It will refer to the script being run.

It's worth noting that PHP_SELF behaves strangely when PHP is run on Windows or as a CGI module. Make sure to look at phpinfo() to see the value of $PHP_SELF on your system.

HTTP_POST_VARS

This is the array that contains all the variables sent through the POST method, usually through forms. You can access each individual variable as an element in an associative array (for example $PHP_POST_VARS["myname"]).

HTTP_GET_VARS

This is the array that contains all the variables sent through the GET method. You can access each individual variable as an element in an associative array (for example $PHP_GET_VARS["myname"]).

HTTP_COOKIE_VARS

All of the cookies sent to the browser will be readable in this associative array. This includes the session cookie. If you are wondering how your cookies are behaving, `phpinfo()` will give you a quick readout of what your browser is sending to the server.

Apache variables

Apache keeps track of dozens of variables. We can't include a complete list of variables here, as the variables you use will vary depending on your current setup. Here are some of the ones you might use frequently in your scripts.

As you look at this list and `phpinfo()`, keep in mind that if you are not getting what you want out of your Web server variables, you will need to make changes to your server configuration, not PHP. PHP just passes the information along and cannot alter these variables.

DOCUMENT_ROOT

This variable returns the full path to the root of your Web server. For most Apache users, this directory will be something like /path/to/htdocs. We use this variable throughout the book to make our applications portable. Take this include statement as an example:

```
include"$DOCUMENT_ROOT/book/functions/charset.php";
```

By using the `DOCUMENT_ROOT` variable instead of an absolute path, we can move the book directory and all its sub-folders to any other Apache server without worrying that the include statements will break. Keep in mind that if you are using a Web server other than Apache, DOCUMENT_ROOT may not be available.

 TIP If you set the include_path directive in your php.ini file, you will not need to worry about specifying any path in your include statement — PHP will look through all of the directories you specify and try to find the file you indicate.

HTTP_REFERER

This variable contains the URL of the page the user viewed prior to the one he or she is currently viewing. Keep in mind when using `HTTP_REFERER` that not every page request has a referer. If someone types the URL into a browser, or gets to your page via bookmarks, no referer will be sent. This variable can be used to present customized information. If you had a relationship with another site and wished to serve up a special, customized header for only those referred from that domain you might use a script like this.

```
//check if my user was referred from my_partners_domain.com
if(ereg ("http.*my_partners_domain.com.*" , $HTTP_REFERER))
{
```

```
   include'fancy_header.php';
}else{
   include'normal_header.php';
}
```

Keep in mind that HTTP_REFERER is notoriously unreliable. Different browsers serve up different HTTP_REFERERs in certain situations. It is also easily spoofed. So you wouldn't want to use a script like the preceding one to serve any secure information. I worked on a site where HTTP_REFERER was used to determine if a special GIF should be included in the header.

HTTP_USER_AGENT

Anyone who has built a Web page knows how important browser detection is. Some browsers will choke on fancy JavaScript, and others require very simple text. The user_agent string is your key to serving the right content to the right people. A typical user_agent string looks something like this:

```
Mozilla/4.0 (compatible; MSIE 5.01; Windows 98)
```

You can then parse this string to get what you are looking for.

You may be interested in PHP's get_browser() function. Theoretically, this function will determine the capabilities of your user's browser so you can find out if your script can safely serve out, for example, frames or JavaScript. The PHP manual has instructions for installation and use of get_browser(), but I do not recommend using it. Why? Using get_browser() you will be told that both Internet Explorer 5 for the PC and Netscape Navigator 4.01 for the Mac support CSS (cascading stylesheets) and JavaScript. But as anyone with client-side experience knows, writing DHTML that works on both of these browsers is a major task (and a major pain). The information you get from get_browser() can lead to a false sense of security. You're better off accessing HTTP_USER_AGENT and making decisions based on the specific browser and platform.

REMOTE_ADDR

This is the IP address of the user that sent the HTTP request. REMOTE_ADDR is easily spoofed and doesn't necessarily provide information unique to a user. You might want to use it for tracking, but it should not be used to enforce security.

REMOTE_HOST

This is the host machine sending the request. When I dial it up through my ISP (att.net), the REMOTE_HOST looks like this: 119.san-francisco-18-19rs.ca.dial-access.att.net. REMOTE_HOST is often not available.

REQUEST_URI

This is pretty much the same as PHP_SELF, except that it contains information in the querystring in addition to the script file name. It contains everything from the root path on. So if you were visiting `http://www.mydomain.com/info/products/index.php?id=6`, REQUEST_URI will equal /info/products/index.php?id=6.

SCRIPT_FILENAME

This variable contains the filesystem's complete path of the file.

Other Web server variables

As mentioned earlier, `phpinfo()` is your friend. We developed applications for this book on Unix systems running Apache Web servers. But, as PHP will run on a variety of operating systems and Web servers and MySQL does run on Windows as well as Unix, you should be aware of the different variables associated with whatever Web server and operating system you're running.

You'll see that include files in our applications make use of the DOCUMENT_ROOT Apache variable. If you were to attempt to move the application files to Windows, you would get an error in the include statements. The better choice when using Microsoft's Personal Web Server is the $APPL_PHYSICAL_PATH variable.

Figure 4-4 gives a glimpse of some of the variables you can access from Personal Web Server.

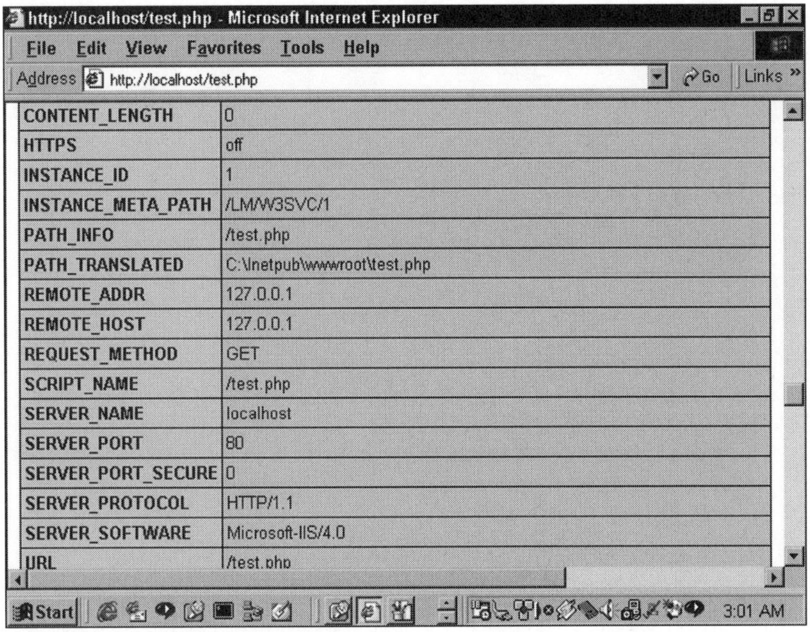

Figure 4-4: Personal Web Server variables

Testing Variables

At the start of this chapter, we showed that assigning data to a variable determines the variable type. The appearance of the variable gives no indication as to what the variable contains. If you see $var sitting in a script you'll have no idea if this contains a string, an integer, a floating-point number, or an array. In fact, many times in your scripts you won't be sure if the variable contains a value, or even if it exists at all. For all these reasons, you need to perform tests. The following sections describe the types of tests you can perform.

isset()

This function tests whether a variable has any value, including an empty string. It returns a value of either true or false. If the variable has not been initialized or has not been set, isset() will test false.

Consider the following script, which processes a MySQL query. You already know that database fields can contain both empty strings and null values. It's quite possible that in your script you would want to treat the two differently. To print out a special message when the query comes across null values, you would need to use isset(). In this code, $query is a select statement typed into a form element.

```
$result = mysql_query($query) or
    die (mysql_error());

$number_cols = mysql_num_fields($result);

echo "<b>query: $query</b><br>\n";
//layout table header
echo "<table border = 1>\n";
echo "<tr align=center>\n";
for ($i=0; $i<$number_cols; $i++)
{
    echo "<th>", mysql_field_name($result, $i), "</th>\n";
}
echo "</tr>\n";//end table header

//layout table body
while ($row = mysql_fetch_row($result))
{
    echo "<tr align=left>\n";
    for ($i=0; $i<$number_cols; $i++)
    {
        echo "<td>";
        if (!isset($row[$i])) //test for null value
            {echo "NULL";}
```

```
        else
            {echo $row[$i];}
        echo "</td>\n";
    }
   echo "</tr>\n";
}
echo "</table>";
```

Note that the exclamation point (!) means "not". So the phrase if(!isset ($var)) will test true if the variable is not set.

If you wish to destroy a variable, use the unset function.

empty()

The empty() function overlaps somewhat with the isset() function. It tests true if a variable is not set, contains an empty string, or has a value of 0. It is useful for, among other things, processing form data. If you want to determine if the user put something in a text field you could use something like this:

```
if(empty($first_name))
{
   echo "Please enter your first name. It is a required field";
   exit;
}
```

is_int()

This tests whether a variable is an integer. It has two synonyms: is_integer() and is_long(). You may need this function to troubleshoot a script when you're not sure if a variable is an integer or a string containing numerals.

```
$a = "222";
$b = 22;
```

Given these two variable assignments, is_int($a) would test false and is_int($b) would test true.

is_double()

This function tests whether a variable is a floating-point (or double) number. It has two synonyms: is_float() and is_real().

is_string()

This function tests whether a variable is a text string.

is_array()

This function tests whether a variable is an array. This is used frequently in the course of this book. A good example can be found in Chapter 6, in the discussion of the `implode()` function.

is_bool()

This tests whether a variable is boolean, (contains either TRUE or FALSE). Note that the following examples are not boolean.

```
$a = "TRUE";
$b = "FALSE";
```

In Chapter 6 you will see a variety of functions that return FALSE on failure. In these, FALSE is a boolean value.

is_object()

Returns true if the variable is an object. See Chapter 6 for a discussion of objects and object-oriented programming if you don't know what an object is.

gettype()

This function will tell you the type of variable you have. It will return the expected values (string, double, integer, array, or boolean), and it can also return types related to object-oriented programming (object, class). There will be more information on PHP object-oriented programming in Chapter 6.

Note that `gettype()` returns a string. So the following would test TRUE and print "Yes".

```
$str = "I am a string";
$type = gettype($str);
if ($type == "string")
{
    echo "Yes";
}
```

Changing Variable Types

There are three ways to change the type of any variable.

Type casting

By placing parentheses containing the variable type you require before the variable name, you will change the variable type.

```
$a = 1;
$b = (string) $a;
echo gettype($a), "<br>\n";
echo gettype($b), "<br>\n";
```

This code would print,

```
integer
string
```

Using this method you can cast a variable as an array, a double, an integer, an object, or, as in the preceding code, a string.

Using settype()

This function takes two arguments. The first is a variable name. The second specifies the variable type. The advantage of using this function over casting is that settype() will return a value of FALSE if the conversion fails. And there is no way to detect a failed casting. It can take the same types as listed in type casting.

```
$a = 1;
settype($a, "string");
```

intval(), doubleval(), and stringval()

Finally, if you don't have enough ways to evaluate variable types, use one of these functions. They do not actually change the type of the variable, but return a value of the specified type. So in the following, you can be sure, $a will be treated like an integer.

```
$a = "43";
$b = (intval($a) * 2);
```

Variable Variables

PHP includes variable variables, which, in the wrong hands, could be used to write the most incomprehensible code imaginable. It enables you to take the contents of a variable and use them as variable names. Two consecutive dollar signs let PHP know to take the value of the variable and use that as a variable name. The following creates a variable name $foo with the value of "bar":

```
$a = 'foo';
$$a = 'bar';
```

In the context of a database application, variable variables might be used to create a series of variables against which you compare other variables. In the following, $firstrow is an associative array.

```
$firstrow = array ("firstname"=>"jay", "lastname"=>"greenspan");

while (list($field,$value) = each($firstrow))
{
    $field = "first_$field";
    $$field = $value;
}

echo $first_firstname, " ", $first_lastname;
```

When run through the while loop, the following variables would be created and printed.

```
$first_firstname = "jay"
$first_lastname = "greenspan"
```

Summary

If you read this chapter attentively (or even if you didn't) you should have a pretty good idea of how to work with PHP variables.

PHP does a better job than any scripting language in making variables easy to access and process. If you want to get a feel of how PHP variables are used, take a look at Chapter 8, the first application in the book. There, many of the functions and concepts presented here are put to work. By flipping back and forth between this chapter and those scripts, you will see how variables are used and how scripts come together.

One very important point: This chapter did not discuss variable scope, which is a very important topic. See Chapter 7, when we discuss functions, for an explanation of this topic.

Chapter 5

Control Structures

IN THIS CHAPTER

♦ Understanding the syntax of if statements

♦ Determining true and false values with PHP

♦ Learning PHP loops

♦ Choosing loops to use in your scripts

CONTROL STRUCTURES ARE THE BUILDING blocks of programming languages. PHP has all of the control structures needed to make a language work. If you're familiar with C or Perl, none of the features we discuss in this chapter should come as much of a surprise. However, if you're approaching PHP from a background in VBScript or Visual Basic, the syntax will probably be different from what you're used to. If you find the syntax to be a little heavy at first, stick with it. You might find that the extra brackets and parentheses actually help you write readable code.

The if Statements

The if statement is pretty much the cornerstone of all programming languages. In PHP, an if statement typically takes this basic form:

```
if (condition)
{
    actions to perform if condition is true.
}
```

After the word "if" there is a set of parentheses. Within those parentheses is the single condition or set of conditions to be tested. If the condition is evaluated as being true, the code within the curly braces will be executed. The following will test true and print "I'm True!" to a Web page.

```
<?php
    $foo = 100;
    $bar = 10;
    if ($foo>$bar)
```

```
    {
    echo "I'm True!";
    }
?>
```

This is clear enough. But before we mention the complexities of the if statement, you should know how PHP determines whether a condition is true or false.

Determining true or false in PHP

The next section will show the operators commonly used in if statements. These are fairly intuitive. In the preceding code example, 100 is greater than 10, so it will test true. No problem. But there's a bit more to these tests in PHP.

The words TRUE and FALSE also carry the expected meaning.

```
if (TRUE)
{
    echo "Yup!"; //this will be printed
}
if (FALSE)
{
    echo "Nothing doing.";  //this will not be printed
}
```

But you're not limited to simple mathematical operators or the words TRUE and FALSE when testing a true or false condition. As you saw in Chapter 4, you will often test for the existence of a variable using isset() or empty(). These functions, like many others in PHP, will return a value of 0 if the condition is false, and a value of 1 if the condition is true. The following will actually print out "1".

```
$myvar = "I am setting a variable";
echo isset($myvar);
```

In PHP "0" is equivalent to false. As you can guess, "1" is equal to true. But it's not just "1" that is true—any non-zero, non-empty value tests as true. This gives you some flexibility in your tests.

When working with Web pages, you'll usually be doing some sort of text manipulation. Often you'll need to test whether the text string you're working with has a certain structure. For example, you might want to test if a string contains certain characters. You could use one of the regular expression functions for this, but you could also use the strstr() function. The strstr() function takes two arguments, both of them strings. It searches for the first occurrence of the string in the second argument in the first argument. It returns the string in the second argument plus all of the characters following that string. However, if the string isn't found, the function will return FALSE. In the example below strstr() returns the "text string".

```
$str = "my little text string";
strstr($str, "text");
```

Since the result of this function is not empty and not 0 it could be used in a test. The following would test True and print out "Yeah!"

```
$str = "my little text string";
if (strstr($str, "text"))
{
    echo "Yeah!";
}
```

But, in the example below, the string is not found, so the function will return FALSE and nothing will print.

```
$str = "my little text string";
$new_str = strstr($str, "nothing");
if($new_str)
{
    echo "nothing to print"; //this will not be printed
}
```

This is a good place to note that the functions you create in the course of your programming will often need to return a TRUE or FALSE value. You can make your functions do this by returning TRUE or FALSE, or, if you prefer, 1 or 0. See Chapter 6 for a rundown of functions if you don't know how to use them. Take a look at this example:

```
//tests whether a variable starts with "http://"
function url_test ($url)
{
    if (strtolower(substr($url,0,7))== "http://")
     {
     return TRUE; //this could also be 1
     }
else {
        return FALSE; //could be 0
}
}

$myurl = "http://www.theonion.com";
if (url_test ($myurl))
{
    echo "Thanks for entering a valid URL.";
}
```

Comparison operators

There aren't too many comparison operators in PHP. Table 5-1 lists them.

TABLE 5-1 PHP'S COMPARISON OPERATORS

Symbol	Operator	Description
== (2 equal signs)	equal to	Determines if two quantities are equal.
=== (3 equal signs)	identical to	Determines if the two values are of the same value and the same variable type.
!=	not equal	Determines if the values are not equal.
>	greater than	Determines if the value to the left of the symbol has a higher value than the one to the right of the symbol.
<	less than	Determines if the value to the left of the symbol has a lower value than the one to the right of the symbol.
>=	greater than or equal to	Determines if the value to the left has a higher or equal value to the one on the right.
<=	less than or equal to	Determines if the value to the left has a lower or equal value to the one on the right.

Logical operators

In addition to comparison operators, you will be using logical operators in your scripts. Table 5-2 lists the logical operators.

TABLE 5-2 PHP'S LOGICAL OPERATORS

Symbol	example	Description
and	if ($a ==0 and $b==1)	Checks both conditions.
&&	if ($a ==0 && $b==1)	Same as the previous row, but has a higher precedence (see Note below).

Symbol	example	Description
or	if ($a ==0 or $b ==1)	Determines if one or the other meets the condition.
||	if ($a ==0 || $b ==1)	Same as the previous row, but has a higher precedence (see Note below)
xor	if ($a ==0 xor $b==1)	This is known as "exclusive or". It determines if one of the two is true but not both. If both of these conditions are true, the overall test will be false.
!	if (!empty($a))	Determines if something is not the case. In this example the condition will be true if $a has a value.

 The difference between && and and is their order of precedence. PHP must determine which operators to compare first. It does this based on the list found at http://www.php.net/manual/language.operators. precedence.php.

Complex if statements

Using the operators in Table 5-1 and 5-2 you can create if statements that are a bit more complex than the basic one at the beginning of this chapter. Here are a few quick examples:

```
if ($var == 1 && $var2 <=5 && !empty($var3))
{
    //do some stuff
}
```

Since this is a book dealing with MySQL databases, we'll show some examples of if statements you can use when playing with database queries.

To test if a select query returned any rows, you could use either of the following:

```
$query = "select * from my_table";
$result = mysql_query($query)or
    die(mysql_error());
if (mysql_num_rows($result) >0)
{
```

```
    //do something here.
}
//this would also work...
if (!$row = mysql_fetch_array($result))
{
    echo "there were no rows to fetch, so the query must have
returned no rows.";
}
```

This will test if an update query actually changed anything. A similar construct would work for update and delete statements.

```
$query = "update mytable set col1='my text' where id = 1";
mysql_query($query) or
    die(mysql_error());
if (mysql_affected_rows() == 0)
{
    echo "query did nothing";
}
```

if ... else statements

If you're clear on the previous sections, there's nothing here that will surprise you. The else portion of an if ... else statement allows you to specify code that is executed if the condition specified is false.

```
$a = 2;
if ($a == 1)
{
    echo "it's equal";
} else {
    echo "it is not equal";
}
```

This code will print "it is not equal".

if ... elseif statements

You will often have to check a variable against more than one set of conditions. For instance, you might have a single page that will insert, edit, and delete records from a database. It would be fairly typical to indicate which portion of the script you wish to run by assigning different values to a submit button in an HTML form. When the form is submitted, the value of the submit button can be checked against several elseif statements.

```
if ($submit == "edit")
```

```
{
    // code for editing database
} elseif ($submit =="update")
{
    //code for updating records
}elseif ($submit == "delete")
{
    //code for deleting records
} else
{
    echo "I have no idea what I should be doing.";
}
```

TIP   "elseif" is not that same as "else if". If you have that space between the words, you will not get an error, but you may get some weird behavior.

Alternative if... structures

There are a couple of different ways to write if statements. The first simply substitutes a colon for the opening curly brace and the word endif with a semicolon for the closing curly brace.

This syntax is depreciated. You're better off not using it.

```
if ($a==1):
    echo "I knew a was equal to one.";
elseif ($a>1):
    echo "a is bigger than I thought.";
else:
    echo "a is a little number.";
endif;
```

The other alternative if structure we have is what's known as a *trinary operator*. It's essentially a shortened form of an if ... else statement and we'll use it in this book to save a few lines of code when there's a simple assignment of a variable to be done. It looks like this:

```
$a = ($x==1) ? "x was one" : "x wasn't one";
```

The portion before ? is the condition to be tested (here, is x equal to 1). If the condition is true, the portion between ? and : is carried out ($a is assigned the string "x was one"). If not, the expression in the third portion, between : and ; will be executed and $a will carry the string "x wasn't one".

switch ... case

The switch structure is an alternative to using multiple if ... elses. This won't work for everything, but in some situations switch will help you remove some ugly syntax.

Choose a variable against which you wish to run a comparison. Continuing the example given in the discussion of if... else, we may wish to execute different parts of script based on the value passed by a submit button.

```
switch ($submit)
{
    case "insert":
        // code to insert to database
        break;
    case "update":
        //code to update database
        break;
    case "display":
        //code to display
        break;
}
```

Here the code tests against the value in $submit. In the case that $submit is equal to "insert", that portion of code is run.

Note the use of break above. If break is not included the code will continue to run. For example, the if $submit was equal to "update" the following would run the code for both the update and display portions:

```
switch ($submit)
{
    case "insert":
        // code to insert to database
        break;
    case "update":
        //code to update database
```

```
case "display":
    //code to display
    break;
}
```

Loops

No matter what language you've used in the past, you'll know that loops are an essential part of programming. PHP has as rich set of loops that should satisfy your every programming need.

while...

This is probably the most common loop, therefore we'll discuss it first. You will give the while loop a condition to validate. As long as that condition is true, the code within the curly braces will be executed.

```
while (condition)
{
    code to execute here;
}
```

For a very basic example, the following would print all the numbers between 0 and 10:

```
$a = 0;
while ($a<=10)
{
    echo "$a <br> \n";
    $a++;
}
```

For something a bit more practical, you will use a while loop to iterate through every row returned by a database query. Since mysql_fetch_array() will return FALSE if there's no row to be fetched, it works quite nicely with a while... loop.

```
$query = "select fname, lname from people";
$result = mysql_query($query) or
    die(mysql_error());
while ($row = mysql_fetch_array($result))
{
    echo $row["fname"] , " " , $row["lname"] , "<br> \n";
}
```

USING WHILE WITH LIST() = EACH()

Another place while... often comes into play is with arrays, when using the `list()` = `each()` structure. This structure assigns elements in an array to named variables. It will iterate through the array, and when there are no more elements to pull from, it will test FALSE, and the while loop will stop. When pulling from an array, `list()` is expecting an associative array and will take two variables: the first for the key, the second for the value.

```
$knicks = array (center => "Ewing", point => "Childs",
shooting_guard => "Houston",
forward => "Sprewell", strong_forward => "Johnson"
        );
echo "<h2>The Knicks 1999 Starting Five Were</h2>";
while (list($key,$value) = each ($knicks))
{
    echo "$key: $value <br>\n";
}
```

After running the preceding code the array pointer will be at the end of the array. If you wish to loop through it again, you will have to move the pointer to the beginning of the array with reset. In the preceding example, `reset ($knicks)` would work.

Note that if you don't have an associative array and you wish to grab array values, you will need to account for it in your `list()`. Do this by including a comma within the list parentheses.

```
$names = array("John", "Jacob", "Jason", "Josh");
while (list ( , $value) = each ($names))
{
    echo "$value <br> \n";
}
```

If you didn't have the comma preceding `$value`, the ordinal placement of each element would be assigned to value and the code would print "0, 1, 2, 3".

If you want to just get the keys out of an associative array, your list statement should contain something like `list($key, )`.

List is also useful with `mysql_fetch_array()`. It can be kind of a pain to keep referring to values by their associative array reference (e.g., `$row["first_name"]`).

If you use `list() = each()`, you won't have to assign each record to a variable and then reference it as an associative array. The following works just fine:

```
$query = "select fname, lname from users";
$result = mysql_query($query) or
    die(mysql_error());
while (list ($fname, $lname) = mysql_fetch_array($result))
{
    echo $fname . " ". $lname . "<br>\n";
}
```

As you saw above, list() has a couple of uses. Though we're stressing its use with the each() statement, it can generally be thought of as an "array destructor". That is, it pulls elements out of an array. Similarly, `each()` is an "array iterator", it walks through all of the elements in an array, and it doesn't need to be used with `list()`, though that is by far the most common usage.

Continuing with the subject of while loops and `mysql` queries, you will probably need a quick piece of code that will print out the results of any query. For this, you can use a nested set of while loops. The outer loop fetches each individual record from the database. The inner one prints out the contents of each individual record.

```
while($row = mysql_fetch_array($result, MYSQL_ASSOC))
{
    while (list($key, $value) = each ($row))
    {
        echo "<b>$key:</b> $value <br>\n";
    }
}
```

Note the use of `MYSQL_ASSOC`. If you didn't use this, `mysql_fetch_array` would return every column twice, once with ordinal reference and once with the associative key.

ALTERNATIVE WHILE... SYNTAX
If you wish, you can write a while loop like this:

```
while (condition):
    //code here
endwhile;
```

 This is also deprecated. You are better off not using it.

do ...while

The do...while loop is nearly identical to the while loop discussed above. The only difference is that the condition is tested after the code in question has been run once.

```
do
{
    //code to be used here.
} while (condition);
```

This structure may be useful to you. It may even be vital to scripts you need to write. But in the course of writing seven applications for this book, we didn't need to use it once.

for

The for loop takes three expressions. The first is evaluated only the first time through the loop. The second argument is a condition that is evaluated each additional time through the loop; if the condition in the second argument tests false, the loop will end. The third expression will be executed in every loop after the first.

As an example, the following would iterate through every value in an array and print the value for each element.

```
$myarray = array (jay, brad, john, kristin);
for ($i = 0; $i < count($myarray); $i++)
{
    echo $myarray[$i] . "<br>\n";
}
```

The first time through, $i is assigned the value of 0, so the first element in the array will be printed. The next time and each subsequent time through, $i will be incremented by one. The loop will end as soon as $i is equal to the length of the array (which would be 4). Remember that the elements in the array start at 0, so the last element in the above array is $myarray[3].

You can also leave any of the three expressions in the for loop empty. If you leave the second expression empty, the if condition will evaluate to true, and you will need to make sure that your loop will eventually hit a break statement (break will be discussed soon). The following would be very bad: it would run indefinitely, using up your memory and CPU. You'd have to kill the Web server to get this script to stop. It could bring your entire machine down.

```
for ($i = 0;; $i++)
{
    echo "$I <br>\n";
}
```

There are occasions when leaving the second expression empty serves a purpose. But again, this is something that will not come up in the course of the applications presented in this book.

The following is an alternative structure for the for loop (this is probably starting to look a bit familiar). This is also deprecated and shouldn't be used:

```
for ($i=0; $i<100; $i++):
    //run code here
endfor;
```

foreach

The foreach structure is used exclusively with arrays. If you prefer, you can use it in place of list() = each() on most occasions. This structure will work from the beginning to the end of an array, assigning each element to a scalar variable you indicate with the word *as*. The following would print all the values in the array $names_array.

```
$names_array = array("jay", "brad", "ernie", "bert");
foreach ($names_array as $first_name)
{
    echo $first_name;
}
```

If you are working with an associative array, you will likely need to access both the key and the value of every array element. The following syntax will achieve this.

```
$jay_info = array (fname => "jay", lname => "greenspan", wife =>
"melissa", hobby =>"juggling");
foreach($jay_info as $key => $value)
{
    echo "<b>$key:</b> $value <br>\n";
}
```

There is no good reason to recommend either list() = each() or foreach(). They both do the same thing for arrays. Choose whichever you think looks best on your PHP page.

We used list()=each() in the applications in this book, mostly because it was available when we were writing code in PHP3 and foreach() wasn't available.

continue and break

Within loops you may need to either break out of the loop entirely or skip to the next item to be addressed in the loop. For these situations, you can use continue and break, respectively.

continue

Consider a situation when you're reading from the file system and you would like your script to address each file in a specific directory, but we have no need to address any subdirectories. When PHP reads names from the directory, you don't know if the item is a file or directory, so you need to run a test using the is_dir() function. We'd want to skip over listings that are directories. The script looks something like this:

```
$directory=opendir('/home/jay/');
echo "Files are:<br>\n";
while ($file = readdir($directory))
{
    if (is_dir($file)){continue;}

    echo "$file <br>\n";
    //process files here;
}
closedir($directory);
```

?>

Note that continue isn't necessary here. You could also code this script like this, and some feel this a better way of going about it.

```
$directory=opendir('/home/jay/');
echo "Files are:<br>\n";
while ($file = readdir($directory))
{
    if (!is_dir($file)){
        echo "$file <br>\n";
    }
}
closedir($directory);
```

break

Break will release the script from a control structure but will continue the execution of a script. It is almost always better to avoid using break. if statements can accomplish the same thing and make for cleaner code.

Including files

Including files in your PHP scripts is vital to writing good code. And technically, the functions for including files (`include` and `require`) are not control structures, they are language constructs. They are discussed in detail in Chapter 7.

Summary

In this chapter you saw the building blocks of the PHP language. You saw how to make use of loops and if blocks. If you read Chapter 4, where variables were discussed, you now know all of the basics needed for programming with PHP.

Coding is all about working with variables, loops, and if blocks. The various combinations of these will take care of everything you will need to accomplish in your applications. However, there is still one major portion you need to learn: functions. Chapter 6 shows how PHP's built-in functions operate on your scripts.

Chapter 6

PHP's Built-in Functions

IN THIS CHAPTER

- ◆ Using PHP's built-in variables
- ◆ Handling strings
- ◆ Working with arrays

PHP HAS AN AMAZING number of built-in functions. Many are only available to you if PHP is compiled with certain options. If, for example, you need to do some XML parsing, PHP has two function sets that can help you. (One uses a SAX approach, the other a DOM approach). If you need LDAP, IMAP, or PDF functions, there is a function set for you. Additionally, PHP has an API (application program interface) for about every relational database on the planet. But really, there's no need to cover most of these functions in this book.

Another thing to keep in mind is that the function set is changing almost daily. PHP 4 is internally structured in a way that makes it extremely easy for programmers to add additional functions. In fact, if you know your way around C, you could probably add a new function into PHP in a few hours. So you can expect regular additions to the core function set.

Your best friend, as always, is the online PHP manual: `http://www.php.net/manual`. It's is the only source where you can be sure that the list of functions will be more or less up to date. If you want to go directly to the explanation of a function, all you need to do is point your browser at `http://www.php.net/function_name`.

We want to point out one more thing before we get started here. There are seven applications in the final two portions of this book. In the course of creating these functions, we made use of a little over 100 of PHP's built-in functions. So while there are thousands of built-in functions, you will probably only make regular use of a relatively small number.

 A pretty neat resource is the function table at: `http://www.zugeschaut-und-mitgebaut.de/php/`.

Function Basics

Functions all take the same basic form.

```
return_type function_name(argument1, argument2, argument3)
```

First there is the function's name; note that the name of the function is not case-sensitive. However, we don't know of any programmer who ever uses uppercase letters to refer to a built-in function.

Next there is a set of parentheses. Every function will have a set of parentheses marking the beginning and end of the arguments.

Arguments

So what's an argument? An argument is simply a value that the function is expecting. Depending on the purpose of the function, it may expect zero, one, two, three, or more arguments, and any of the arguments may be any variable type – maybe a string, maybe an integer, or maybe an array. To give you a better idea of what arguments are, let's look at a very useful function for string handling.

The str_replace() function is extremely helpful. Let's say you had the following string:

```
$str = "My name is Jay.";
```

Say that in the $str variable you need to replace "Jay" with "John". Within $str you need to search for "Jay" and replace it with "John". Here, you would expect a function to take three arguments: the string to be searched for, the replacement string, and the string to be searched through. It so happens that in PHP, the arguments come in this order:

```
str_replace(string to search for, replacement string, string to be
searched through);
```

Or to put it in practice:

```
$str = "My name is Jay.";
$new_str = str_replace("Jay", "John", $str);
```

Keep in mind that certain functions will have optional arguments and a few will take no arguments at all. The substr() function, for example, has an optional third argument. This function returns a portion of a string by its ordinal references. To get everything from the second character to the next-to-last character, you would use the following:

```
//note, the first character in the string is 0
$new_str = substr ($str_var,1,-1);
```

However, to get everything from the second character on, you would use the following:

```
$str = substr ($str_var,1);
```

So in this function the third argument is optional. (We'll point out optional arguments as we move through the functions.) The details of working with substr() will be covered later in the chapter.

There are also a few occasions when a function will take no arguments at all. A good example of this is phpinfo(). It spits out everything you need to know about your PHP environment without taking any arguments. Another good example is time(), which returns the current Unix timestamp.

Return values

The final thing you should be aware of is what the function will return. In the above case, str_replace() will return a string. What you do with this string is your business. You could assign it a variable or print it out, or do whatever else seems appropriate.

```
//assign to variable
$new_str = str_replace("Jay", "John", $str);
//print directly
echo str_replace("Jay", "John", $str);
```

Note that functions may return arrays, integers, doubles (floating-point numbers), objects, or sometimes Boolean values. In Chapter 5, you saw a good example of a function that returns a Boolean value (that is, TRUE or FALSE). If you want to determine whether a variable is an array, you can use the is_array() function.

```
if (is_array($var))
{
    //process array
}
```

There are also functions that will return a value if there is a value to be returned, and that will return FALSE if there is no value to be returned. A good example of this is the mysql_fetch_array() function. This function will grab rows from a result set returned by a query as long as there are results to grab. When there are no more rows to be had, it returns FALSE. As you saw in Chapter 5, this is very helpful for looping through all rows returned by a query.

```
$result = mysql_query("select * from my_table") or
    die ( mysql_error() );
```

```
while($row = mysql_fetch_array($result))
{
 //process row
}
```

Finally, there are occasions where a function will return nothing. This will be common in functions that perform a specific action, like closing a connection to a database or the file system.

Function Documentation

As we say repeatedly throughout this book, the PHP online manual is your friend. The documentation team is amazing, and we really believe the quality of the online manual is one of the reasons for the success of the language. As there is no way we can cover every PHP function in this book, you will need to consult the manual. For that reason, we want to take a minute to go over how the functions are presented in the manual.

A typical manual reference will look something like this:

```
int mysql_affected_rows ([int link_identifier])
```

This function returns the number of rows affected by an update, insert, or delete query. Looking at this, you can see that the first portion (int) indicates the variable type that will be returned. This could be any of the variable types or void (meaning that the function will return nothing). Then within the parentheses there will be a list of arguments. The type of argument is listed as well as what it represents. Note that optional arguments are placed in brackets. So above, the function requires no arguments but has one optional argument: the connection identifier grabbed from mysql_connect(). In a case like phpinfo(), you will see that the argument list is void.

In the preceding example, if you pass an argument, it better be an integer. If you were to give it a string or an array, you will get an error.

Important PHP 4 Functions

In this section, we will attempt to break down PHP 4 functions into logical groupings. Along the way we will cover every function used in the applications presented in this book.

MySQL API

There are a total of 33 MySQL functions available in PHP. Only 17 of these are used in the applications in this book. You may find uses for some of the other MySQL functions in your applications, but you probably won't use all of them. For the sake of this listing, I'll break the functions into the set you might use the most, and then the ones that you're less likely to use extensively.

FREQUENTLY USED MYSQL FUNCTIONS

You will probably end up using the following functions frequently. You may want to dog-ear this page.

MYSQL_CONNECT()   You can't do anything with MySQL until you make the connection using the following function.

```
int mysql_connect(str host, str username, str password)
```

Most often you will be connecting to MySQL on localhost using a username and password assigned to you, the Web developer. The integer that this function returns to you is a connection identifier. You may need to track the connection identifier and use it with the `mysql_db_select()` function. It will typically look something like this:

```
$conn = mysql_connect("localhost", "username", "password") or
    die ("Could Not Connect to Database");
```

 If MySQL is not installed on a standard port or if the mysql socket is not located in /tmp/mysql.sock, you can specify the port of socket location in the host string. For example:

```
mysql_connect("localhost:/usr/local/mysql.sock",
"username", "password");
```

Or, if the MySQL database in sitting on another machine, you can access it with the following

```
mysql_connect("mymachine.mydomain.com", "username",
"password");
```

 You can also specify host, username, and password in the php.ini file. That way you could leave one or more of these arguments empty.

MYSQL_PCONNECT()   The `mysql_pconnect()` function works exactly like `mysql_connect()` but with one important difference: The link to MySQL will not close when the script finishes running.

```
int mysql_pconnect(str host, str username, str password)
```

When you use this function the connection remains open, and additional calls to `mysql_pconnect()` will attempt to use these open connections when they run. This could make your scripts quite a bit faster.

It is interesting to note what happens when `mysql_pconnect()` is run. The first time the script is run, PHP will ask for a connection, and MySQL will open a connection to the database. When that script finishes, the connection remains available. The next time a PHP page is requested, PHP will ask for a connection that is already open. If MySQL has one available, it will grant PHP the open connection. If there are no open connections available, a new connection will be opened.

Establishing a connection with the MySQL database will be about the slowest function in your scripts. If PHP can use a connection that has already been opened, there will be far less overhead in the application.

In order for `mysql_pconnect()` to work, set the following lines in your php.ini file:

```
mysql.allow_persistent    =    On
mysql.max_persistent    =    -1; maximum number of ;persistent
links. -1 means no limit
```

Note that these are the defaults. You will probably want to limit the number of persistent connections if you use this method.

MYSQL_SELECT_DB()   The `mysql_select_db()` function changes the focus to the database you wish to query.

```
int mysql_select_db (string database_name [, int link_identifier])
```

You can include the integer it returns in the `mysql_query()` function, but it is only really needed if you are connecting to more than one database. The second, optional argument is the link identifier retrieved from the `mysql_connect()`/`mysql_pconnect()` function. It typically looks like this:

```
$db = mysql_select_db("database_name") or
    die ("Could Not Select Database");
```

See the description of the `db_connect()` function in Chapter 8 to see how to handle connections to the MySQL server and a specific database in a single function.

MYSQL_QUERY()   This `mysql_query()` function is probably the MySQL function that you will use most frequently in your scripts.

```
int mysql_query (string query [, int link_identifier])
```

This function sends any query that you can put together to MySQL. It is important to understand that this function does not actually return the result of the query. It opens a cursor that points to the result set on MySQL. So if you were to do the following:

```
echo mysql_query("select * from table");
```

you would not get a meaningful answer, only the number that identifies the result set. Following `mysql_query()`, you will need to make use of one of the functions that actually retrieves the data from MySQL (`mysql_fetch_row()`, `mysql_fetch_array()`, `mysql_result()`).

The optional second argument would be the result of either `mysql_connect()` or `mysql_select_db()`. It is typically used as in the following code sample. Note that a query can fail for any number of reasons. It is best to use `mysql_error()` to find out why the query failed.

```
$result = mysql_query("select * from db") or
    die (mysql_error() );
```

See the discussion of the `safe_query()` function in Chapter 8 to see how to safely handle queries with a uniform function.

MYSQL_FETCH_ARRAY()   Once you have retrieved your result from a query, you will (more often than not) use `mysql_fetch_array()` to retrieve the rows from a query.

```
array mysql_fetch_array (int result [, int result_type])
```

This function returns an associative array, with names of the select columns as the key. By default, `mysql_fetch_array()` will return each column in a row twice: the first will have an associative key, the second will have a numeric key. To tell PHP to limit the results to numeric results use MYSQL_NUM as the second argument. To get only the associative keys, use MYSQL_ASSOC as the second argument.

This function returns FALSE when there are no rows left to fetch.

The following will print the results of a query as a table:

```
$query =("select * from table_name");
```

```
$result = mysql_query($query)
or die ( echo mysql_error()  );
echo "<table>";
//if I don't use MYSQL_ASSOC or MYSQL_NUM, each row will
//be retrieved twice, and I don't want that
while ($row = mysql_fetch_array($result, MYSQL_ASSOC))
{
echo "<tr>";
while( list ($key, $value) = each($row) )
{
    echo "<td>" . $value . "</td>";
}
echo"</tr>";
}
echo "</table>";
```

In Chapter 3 there is a script that prints any query to a table that includes the column names as table headers.

MYSQL_FETCH_ROW( )   The `mysql_fetch_row()` function works almost exactly like `mysql_fetch_array()`, but it only returns a numeric array of the fetched row.

```
array mysql_fetch_row (int result)
```

There's generally little reason to use `mysql_fetch_row()`, and we recommend that you use `mysql_fetch_array()` instead. However, you will see many scripts that use this function.

MYSQL_INSERT_ID()   Frequently the primary key of a MySQL table will be an auto_increment field. In such cases, after you do an insert query you may need to know the number MySQL assigned to the newly inserted row.

```
int mysql_insert_id ([int link_identifier])
```

We use this function used many times throughout the book; one example is in Chapter 12 in the discussion of the admin_user.php page.

You might think that the following method would work equally well for getting the row that was just inserted into the database.

```
mysql_query("insert into users (fname, lname) values ('jay',
'greenspan') or
    die (myslq_error());
mysql_query("select max(user_id) from users");
```

However, there is no guarantee that this script will return an accurate result. On a busy server, it is possible that an insert (perhaps run by another users accessing the script at nearly the same time) will occur between the time it took for these two queries to run. In such cases, your user will end up with bogus data.

mysql_insert_id() returns the value of the auto_increment field associated with the specific copy of the script, so you know the number that it returns is accurate.

MYSQL_NUM_ROWS() A query can execute successfully, but still return zero rows in the result. This function will tell you exactly how many rows have been returned by a select query.

```
int mysql_num_rows (int result)
```
   You might use it in a case like this:

```
$query = "select * from table_name";
$result = mysql_query($query) or
    die( mysql_error() );
if (mysql_num_rows($result) == 0)
{
    echo "Sorry, no results found.";
} else{
    //print results
}
```

MYSQL_AFFECTED_ROWS() This function is similar to the mysql_num_rows() function, but works for a different set of queries. It returns the number of rows in a table that are affected by an update, insert, or delete query.

```
int mysql_affected_rows ([int link_identifier])
```

This function is excellent for checking that a query you have run has actually accomplished something.

```
$query = "delete from table_name where unique_id = 1";
$result = mysql_query($query) or
    die (mysql_error());
$deleted_rows = mysql_affected_rows();
if ($deleted_rows == 0)
{
    echo "no rows removed from the table.";
```

```
} else {
    echo "You just removed $deleted_rows row/rows from the
database.";
}
```

MYSQL_ERRNO()   If there is a problem with a query, this function will spit out the error number registered with MySQL.

```
int mysql_errno ([int link_identifier])
```

On its own, this isn't terribly helpful. For the most part, you would only use this if you wished to use custom error handling. Better error messages come from mysql_error() which is discussed next.

MYSQL_ERROR()   This function should accompany every mysql_query() you run.

```
string mysql_error ([int link_identifier])
```

As you can see in code samples throughout the book we make use of mysql_error with the die statement.

```
mysql_query("select * from my_table") or
    die (mysql_error())
```

Without it, you will only know that your query has failed. You won't know if you're searching for a database that doesn't exist or if you're trying to insert a string into a numeric field, or have made some sort of syntactical blunder.

MYSQL_RESULT()   This function, which grabs the contents of a specific cell, should be used sparingly.

```
mixed mysql_result (int result, int row [, mixed field])
```

It's relatively slow and can almost always be replaced by mysql_fetch_array(). However, if you need to grab contents from a single cell it can be convenient. The second argument will always be the number of the row you are accessing. The third can either be the numeric offset of the column or the column name.

Here's an example of how you could use mysql_result(). In this case, we're running a simple count(), so there is only one value to be accessed. Using mysql_result() is a bit easier than mysql_fetch_array().

```
mysql_connect("localhost", "username", "password");
mysql_select_db("test");
$result = mysql_query("select count(*) from users") or
    die ( mysql_error() );
echo mysql_result($result,0,0);
```

If you have many rows, or even many columns, that need to be retrieved you should use `mysql_fetch_array()`.

LESS FREQUENTLY USED MYSQL FUNCTIONS

Given the title of this book, it wouldn't make too much sense if we didn't cover the entire API. There are many available functions that probably won't come into play too often. But if you're going to be writing applications with these tools, it's best to know what's available.

MYSQL_FETCH_OBJECT()   This function provides another way to access data retrieved from a query.

```
object mysql_fetch_object (int result [, int result_typ])
```

This grabs a row just like `mysql_fetch_array()`. The only difference is that you refer to values fetched from a row as object properties. It can also take the constants MYSQL_ASSOC, MYSQL_NUM, or MYSQL_BOTH.

```
$result = mysql_query("select distinct fname, lname from users where
id=1") or
    die (mysql_error());
$an_object = mysql_fetch_object($result);
echo "First name: " . $an_object->fname;
echo "Last name: " . $an_object->lname;
```

We discuss the object-oriented approach in Chapter 7.

There are two reasons you might want to use this function. First, you love working with OO syntax and wish to extend it to your database calls. The second reason may be relevant to the Perl hackers out there.

PHP 4, like Perl, allows for Here printing, which we discussed in Chapter 4 under the discussion of delimiting strings.

"Here" printing may not work on Windows installations.

When using Here printing, you can print only simple variables – no arrays. However, object properties are allowed. Thus, the following would work:

```
print <<<EOQ
field value is $an_object->fname;
EOQ;
```

MYSQL_FREE_RESULT()   This function frees result memory used by a query.

```
int mysql_free_result (int result)
```

Usually you won't need this function, as connections to MySQL are automatically closed after a script executes. If you run some sort of query that returns a slew of results and then the script continues to do some other work, you can clear up the memory used to store the initial query by using `mysql_free_result()`.

This is a good point to note PHP's impressive memory-handling capabilities. When a connection is closed (either implicitly at the end of the script or by using `mysql_close()`) PHP clears up all of the memory used by the query. When you are writing your applications this is one less thing you will need to worry about.

MYSQL_CLOSE()   This closes the link to MySQL.

```
int mysql_close ([int link_identifier])
```

You don't really need to use this function, as links opened with `mysql_connect` are closed automatically at the end of a script's execution, and it has no effect on `mysql_pconnect()`.

In the Content Management application we use this function because within the course of a script we add a user to the MySQL Grant tables (see Appendix D) and then reconnect to the database as that user. In a case like this we must first close the connection.

MYSQL_DATA_SEEK()   This function repositions the cursor to the row number you specify; the first row is 0.

```
int mysql_data_seek (int result_identifier, int row_number)
```

This function could be useful if for some reason you need to rewind the array and go through the result set a second time. If you find yourself using it frequently, however, it might be worth rethinking the logic in your pages. In most cases you should be able to get all the information you need from your array in a single pass.

MYSQL_CREATE_DB()   This function can only appear after a connection is made to MySQL with `mysql_connect()` or `mysql_pconnect()`. The user connected to MySQL

must have rights necessary to create tables. However, you could just as easily use
`mysql_query("create database db_name");`

int mysql_create_db (string database name [, int link_identifier])

TIP This function and the MySQL functions that follow are fine, but we find it easier to use normal SQL statements (create, alter, drop, etc.) and send them to MySQL through the `mysql_query()` function. They work just as well and can be used within scripts and in the command-line client. In the end, there are fewer functions that you need to remember.

MYSQL_DROP_DB()   This function removes a database from MySQL, which is something you probably don't want to be doing from your scripts too often.

int mysql_drop_db (string database_name [, int link_identifier])

MYSQL_LIST_DBS ()   This function lists databases available on a MySQL server.

int mysql_list_dbs ([int link_identifier])

You will have to use the `mysql_list_tables()` function to retrieve the exact tables. Since MySQL responds just fine to the following, it's best to avoid this function and use the `mysql_fetch_array()`.

```
mysql_connect("localhost", "username", "password");
mysql_query("show databases");
```

MYSQL_LIST_TABLES()   If given a database name this function will return a result identifier to a list of tables within a database.

int mysql_list_tables (string database [, int link_identifier])

Like `mysql_query()`, this function doesn't contain the results; those must be fetched with the `mysql_tablename()` function. The following example shows how you might use these functions to get a listing of tables from the database named "test".

```
$tables=mysql_list_tables("test");
for($i=0; $i<mysql_num_rows($tables); $i++)
{
    echo mysql_tablename($tables,$i), "<br>\n";
}
```

If you don't wish to commit these functions to memory, you could use the following code to achieve the same thing.

```
$result = mysql_query ("show tables from test") or
    die( mysql_error() );
while( $row = mysql_fetch_row($result) )
{
    echo $row[0], "<br>\n";
}
```

MYSQL_LIST_FIELDS()   This function returns a result identifier, which you can then use to grab information about the MySQL columns.

```
int mysql_list_fields (string database_name, string table_name
[, int link_identifier])
```

You must use a result identifier from this function to get information from the `mysql_field_flags()`, `mysql_field_len()`, `mysql_field_name()`, and `mysql_field_type()` functions. All of these functions take the same arguments: the first is the result identifier, the second is the numeric offset of the column, starting at 0. These columns return about what you'd expect, respectively name flags (such as NOT NULL, PRIMARY KEY), the length, the name of the field, and the type (such as int, text, enum, and so on).

As an example, take the table created with the following create statement:

```
create table show_stuff (
    stuff_id int not null primary key auto_increment,
    stuff_desc varchar(255) null,
    stuff_stuff text
);
```

The following script will return about everything you'd need to know about the columns. (The results of the script can be seen in Figure 6-1.)

```
$result= mysql_list_fields ("test", "show_stuff");
$i = 0;
while($i <mysql_num_fields($result))
{
    echo "<b>" . mysql_field_name ($result, $i) . "</b><br>";
    echo mysql_field_flags ($result,$i) . "</b><br>";
    echo mysql_field_len ($result, $i) . "</b><br>";
    echo mysql_field_type ($result, $i) . "<br>";
    $i++;
}
```

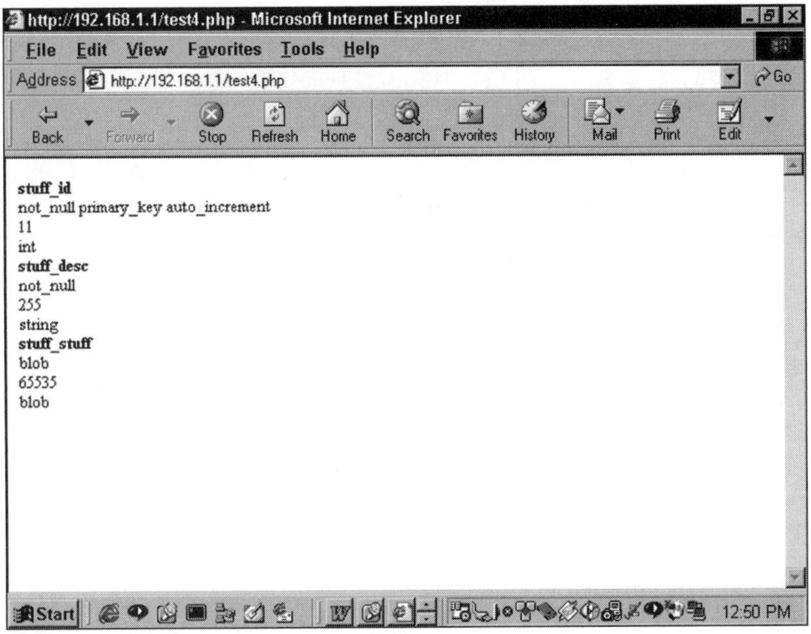

Figure 6-1: Results of field description script

Note once again that you can make use of MySQL's descriptive queries to achieve the same results. The queries "show columns from table_name" and "describe table_name" get all the information you need and keep you from having to use these functions.

String-handling functions

In creating Web-based applications, string handling and manipulation is one of the most critical tasks of the language you work with. Text cleanup and validation is extremely important, and good Web middleware will make working with text relatively easy. PHP excels in this department: It contains built-in functions that cover most anything you'd want to do to text.

In fact, there are far more functions than we could cover here. As of PHP 4.0.2, there were 70 string-handling functions listed on http://www.php.net/manual/ref.strings.html. In this book we can cover only a portion of these. We will cover all of the string-handling functions we used in the course of creating the applications in Sections III and IV, and we will cover some other notable functions that we didn't have the opportunity to use.

STRING FUNCTIONS USED IN THIS BOOK

I thought it would be nice to start with a function that clearly demonstrates why PHP is so cool.

STRIP_TAGS()   This function removes HTML and PHP tags.

```
string strip_tags (string str [, string allowable_tags])
```

One of the most important things that you will need to do with every Web-based application you write is make sure that the users of your Web pages haven't passed you malicious text. As we discuss in Chapter 8, if you're not careful, you might find your pages filled with HTML tags (`<img>`, `<div>`, etc.) or JavaScripts that you don't want. You could also find yourself in real trouble if some cracker decides to litter your form fields with something like `<script> alert("you stink");</script>`.

The `strip_tags()` function will remove all HTML and PHP tags, except for those explicitly allowed in the second argument. If you wanted to allow `<b>` and `<i>` tags, you might use this:

```
strip_tags($str, "<b><i>")
```

ADDSLASHES()   This function is intended to work with your database insert and update queries.

```
string addslashes (string str)
```

If you take a look at a typical insert query you can see a potential problem:

```
insert into table_name(char_field, numeric_field)
values ('$str', $num);
```

What if the value in $str contains a contraction such as "ain't"? You could get an error because the apostrophe is going to confuse MySQL. You will need to escape all occurrences of single quotes ('), double quotes ("), and NULLs in the string.

For example:

```
$str1 = "let's see";
$str2 = "you know";
$str1 = addslashes($str1);
$result = mysql_query("insert into show_stuff
    (stuff_desc, stuff_stuff) values('$str1', '$str2')");
echo mysql_affected_rows();
```

So, given this potential problem, do you need to put all of your form input information through `addslashes()`? Not necessarily. It depends on the `magic_quotes_gpc` setting in your php.ini file. If it is set to on, which is the default, data that come from Get, Post, or Cookies is automatically escaped, so you don't need to worry about putting the information through `addslashes()`.

Make sure to check your `magic_quotes` settings in your php.ini. Note that if set to yes, `magic_quotes_runtime` will automatically add slashes to data returned from queries and files. See Appendix B for more discussion on magic_quotes settings.

In addition to the characters listed here, there are a few other characters that you need to escape if you are going to put them in a MySQL database. You can see the full list at the following URL: `http://www.mysql.com/documentation/mysql/bychapter/manual_Reference.html`. If you'd like a little PHP function that will automatically escape these characters, see the `mysql_escape_string()` function in Appendix G.

STRIPSLASHES() This function will remove the slashes inserted by the `magic_quotes_gpc` or `addslashes()`.

```
string stripslashes (string str)
```

And why might this be necessary? Say you've put some form input through some validation and the validation fails. You are probably going to want to echo the values originally entered into forms back to the user. But if you do this with the `magic_quotes` on and the user enters text into the form that needs to be escaped, the escaping backslash will appear to the user. That is not a good thing. See Appendix B for more information on magic quotes.

STR_REPLACE() This function replaces all occurrences of the first argument and replaces them with the string in the second argument.

```
string str_replace (string to search for, string to replace with,
string to be affected)
```

For example, if we wanted to print out the names of both authors of this book, the following would work:

```
$str = "This book written by Brad. Brad wrote a nice book.";
$str = str_replace("Brad", "Brad and Jay", $str);
echo $str;
```

This would print: "This book written by Brad and Jay. Brad and Jay wrote a nice book."

SUBSTR_REPLACE()   This function operates on the string in the first argument. The portion of the string to be manipulated will be identified by the numbers in the third and fourth arguments.

```
string substr_replace (string string, string replacement, int start
[, int length])
```

The third argument should be the offset of the character you wish to start with. The fourth, which is optional, can have an integer representing the number of characters after the third argument. If the fourth argument is a negative number, the portion will determined from the end of the string.

For example:

```
echo substr_replace("this are my string", "this is", 0,8);
```

will print "This is my string". And:

```
echo substr_replace("this is my string", "new string!", 11,-1);
```

will print "This is my new string!".

STRCMP()   This function compares two strings.

```
int strcmp (string str1, string str2)
```

If the first string is greater than the second the function will return a number greater than 0. It will return a number less than 0 if string two is greater than string one.

STRLEN()   This function returns an integer that gives the number of characters in a string.

```
int strlen (string str)
```

For example:

```
echo strlen("My String");
```

will print "9".

STRPOS()   This function returns the position of the string in the second argument within the first argument. It will return FALSE if the string isn't found.

```
int strpos (string to search, string to find [, int offset])
```

For example:

```
$str = "Where is the first space";
echo strpos($str, " ");
```

This will return "5". If you wanted to get the first space after the fifth character you could make use of the optional third argument.

```
$str = "Where is the first space";
echo strpos($str, " ", 6);
```

This would return "8".

An interesting note: Suppose you want to test if a string contains a specific character, say a space. You might think the following would work since strpos() returns FALSE if the string in the second argument is not found.

```
if( strpos($str, " ") )
{
    echo "thank you for including a space";
} else
{
    echo "include a space, please";
}
```

But, if you remember back to Chapter 5, the value of zero will also test as FALSE. So in the preceding code, if $str starts with a space, the condition will evaluate as FALSE. Therefore, if you want to use a test like this, you will need to alter the condition. In PHP 4 you can run a test against the constant FALSE. For example,

```
$str = " Whereisthefirstspace";
if( strpos($str, " ")===FALSE )
{
    echo "you have not included a space.";
} else
{
    echo "thank you for the space.";
}
```

STRRPOS()   This is similar to the strpos() function except that it finds the final position of the character in the second argument.

```
int strrpos (string to search, char to find)
```

For example:

```
$str = "Where is the final space";
echo strrpos($str, " ");
```

will return "18".

SUBSTR()   This function returns a portion of a string based on numeric offsets.

```
string substr (string string, int start [, int length])
```

For example:

```
echo substr("this is my string", 5);
```

will return everything after the fifth character. In this case "is my string". The optional third argument can represent the number of characters to be returned, following the third argument. For example

```
echo substr("this is my string", 5,2);
```

will return "is". A negative number in the fourth argument specifies a character from the end of the string. For example,

```
echo substr("this is my string", 5,-7);
```

will print "is my".

The substr function works really well with functions like strpos() and strrpos().

STRREV()   This function reverses the order of a string.

```
string strrev (string string)
```

Use of strrev() may not come up too often in your programming life. In this book, it comes into use in the credit-card validation algorithm.

STRTOLOWER()   This function makes an entire string lower case.

```
string strtolower (string str)
```

It's particularly useful when you're dealing with something like file names. Since Unix file names are case-sensitive, you may want to be sure that all files that you write have all lowercase letters. We also make use of this function when dealing with passwords.

STRTR()   This function takes the string in the first argument and translates each character in the second argument to the corresponding character in the third argument.

```
string strtr (string str, string from, string to)
or
string strtr (string str, associative array)
```

So in the following, each *a* will be tuned into an *i* and each *o* will be turned into a *u*.

```
strtr ($str, "ao", "iu")
```

Note that it does all of the replacements at once. For example, given this code

```
$str = "i";
echo strtr($str, "iu", "uv");
```

you might think that this function would first turn "i" into "u", then "u" into "v". This is not the case. It will do the replacements in a batch, so the output of this operation is "u".

This function can also work with only two arguments. In such cases, the second argument should be an associative array. Then each key will be replaced by its corresponding value in the string.

```
$str = "this is my strings";
$replace_array = array("this"=>"these", "is"=>"are");
echo strtr($str, $replace_array);
```

This code prints "these are my strings".

Once again, the replacements are done in a batch. If you had a third element in the preceding array "these"=>"those", you wouldn't have to worry about the word "this" being changed to "these" and then being changed to "those".

UCFIRST()   This function makes the first character in the string upper case.

```
string ucfirst(string str);
```

Note that it leaves everything after the fist character untouched. So if you wanted to make sure that the first and only the first character of a string was capitalized, you would have to something like this.

```
$str = "this is My string";
echo ucfirst(strtolower($str));
```

This would print out "This is my string".

UCWORDS()   This function makes the first character in every word in the string upper case.

```
string ucwords(string str);
```

Like `ucfirst()`, `ucwords()` does not touch characters that do not start a work.

TRIM()   This function removes any white space from the beginning and end of a string including return characters, line feeds, spaces, and tabs.

```
string trim (string str)
```

PHP also has the `ltrim()` function to strip white space from only the start of a string or `chop()` to remove white space from only the end of a string.

HTMLSPECIALCHARS()   This function transforms <, >, &, and " into their proper HTML entities: <, >, &, and ".

```
string htmlspecialchars (string string)
```

This function is useful for printing HTML source code to the browser.

In addition to `htmlspecialchars()`, you can make use of `html entities()`. `htmlentities()` transforms every character that has an HTML entity. For example the copyright symbol is turned into ©.

GET_HTML_TRANSLATION_TABLE()   This function gets a full list of characters that have HTML entities, or just those used by `htmlspecialchars()`. You can indicate which you need access to by including HTML_ENTITIES or HTML_SPECIALCHARS within the function. For example `get_html_translation_table(HTML_ENTITIES)`, gets a full list of characters and their entities.

Each character and its entity are available as key=>value pairs in an associative array. The resulting array can be of use with the `strtr()` function.

NUMBER_FORMAT()   This function formats a number to your specifications.

```
string number_format (float number, int decimals, [[string dec_
point], [string thousands_sep)]]
```

The fist argument will be the number you wish to format. The second argument will state the number of digits you would like after the decimal point. You can use this function with just these two arguments. For example,

```
echo number_format( (10/3), 2 );
```

will print "3.33", and

```
echo number_format(1000,2);
```

will print "1,000". Note that if there are two arguments, `number_format()` includes a comma as a thousands separator.

In the third and fourth arguments you can include a decimal point separator and a thousands separator, respectively. For example,

```
echo number_format( 10000.67, 2, "&", "R");
```

will print, 10R000&67.

If `number_format()` doesn't cut it for you, you can make use of PHP's `sprintf()`,`printf()`,and `scanf()` functions. If you have a background in Perl or C you probably know how these functions work. They're powerful, complex, and take a good deal of time to get used to. If you want to familiarize yourself with these functions, take a look at the PHP manual (http://www.php.net/manual/function.sprintf.php) and this tutorial: http://wdvl.com/Authoring/Scripting/Tutorial/perl_printf.html.

HELPFUL STRING FUNCTIONS NOT USED IN THIS BOOK

Just because we didn't use them doesn't mean you won't. And again, it's entirely possible that something we didn't cover will suit your needs perfectly. Please look over the PHP manual for a complete list.

NL2BR()   This function adds an HTML break (`<br>`) after each newline (`\n`) in a string.

```
string nl2br (string string)
```

Note that the newline characters will remain after going through this function. For example, this code

```
$str = "jay
john
bob
stan";

echo nl2br($str);
```

will print the following (note that this is the HTML source of the resulting page):

```
jay
<br>
john
<br>
bob
<br>
stan
```

STRTOUPPER ()   This function makes an entire string upper case.

```
string strtoupper (string string)
```

MD5()   `md5()` is a one-way algorithm that encrypts information.

```
string md5 (string str)
```

This function is often used for passwords. If you were to put a password in a text file, it is possible that someone who had (legitimate) access to your system could view the passwords. However, if you pass it through `md5()`, the correct password is unknowable. For example, `md5("jay")` is `baba327d241746ee0829e7e88117d4d5`. If this is what is entered in the text file, those who have rights to view the database will not know what the correct password is.

TIP   A safe password will be a lot more complex than "jay". A cracker could (and will) run an entire dictionary through `md5()` to see if something allows entry to the system.

md5() is one-way only. There is no way to un-encrypt it. If you are interested in two-way encryption look to the mycrpt functions in the PHP manual: http://www.php.net/manual/ref.mcrypt.php.

Regular expression functions

Regular expressions offer a method for complex pattern matching. If you're new to the concept of regular expressions, consider this: Given the string handling functions you have seen so far, how could you insert a newline and a break (\n
) after every 45 characters? Or how could you find out if a string contains at least one uppercase letter? You may be able to pull it off, but it won't be pretty.

By the way, the following code will solve the previous two questions.

```
//insert \n<br> after each 45 characters
$new_str = ereg_replace("(.{45})", "\\1\n<br>", $str);

//check if string contains uppercase letter
if (ereg("[A-Z]", $str))
{
    echo "yes it does.";
}
```

Statements like these may seem a bit opaque at first, but after working with them for a while, you will grow to love the convenience they offer.

 See Appendix F for a rundown on how regular expressions work.

Note that regular expressions are a good deal slower than string-handling functions. So if you have, for example, a simple replace that doesn't require regular expressions, use str_replace() and not ereg_replace().

REGULAR EXPRESSION FUNCTIONS USED IN THIS BOOK
The following regular expression functions are used in the application in this book.

EREG()   Tests whether a string matches a regular expression.

```
int ereg (string pattern, string string [, array regs])
```

You can use this function in two ways. First, you can place a regular expression in the first argument and search for its existence in the second argument. The function will return TRUE or FALSE, depending on the outcome of the search. For example:

```
if ( ereg("^http://.*", $str) )
{
    echo "This is a URL";
}
```

The optional third argument is an array that is created from the regular expression. The portions of the regular expression that will become elements in the array are indicated by parentheses in the regular expression.

```
ereg("(....)-(..)-(..)", $publish_date, $date_array);
```

This example, which was taken from the Content Manager application, creates an array named $date_array, wherein the first element will be the complete string matched by the regular expression. The next three elements in the array will be the portions indicated by the parentheses. So $date_array[1] will contain 4 characters, and $date_array[2] and date_array[3] will contain 2 characters each.

Note that arrays created by the third argument in ereg() will always contain 11 elements. Even if you have more than ten substrings within parentheses, only the first 10 will be put in the array. If you have fewer than 10 substrings, the array will still contain 11 elements. If you want to test whether anything exists in the array element, you have to test against an empty string (""). An isset() will always test TRUE.

So, after running this code:

```
$publish_date = "2000-10-02";
ereg("(....)-(..)-(..)", $publish_date, $date_array);
```

$date_array would contain the following:

```
[0] => 2000-10-02
[1] => 2000
[2] => 10
[3] => 02
[4] =>
[5] =>
[6] =>
[7] =>
[8] =>
[9] =>
```

Note that ereg() performs a case-sensitive match.

EREGI()   This function is a case-insensitive version of `ereg()`.

```
int eregi (string pattern, string string [, array regs])
```

EREG_REPLACE()   You can use this function for string replacement based on complex string patterns.

```
string ereg_replace (string pattern, string replacement, string string)
```

For example, if you wanted to delete the querystring from a URL, you could use this:

```
$url= "http://www.phpmysqlbook.com/index.php?var=hello";
$parsed_url = ereg_replace("\?.*\$", "",$url);
echo $parsed_url;
```

This would print `http://www.phpmysqlbook.com/index.php`. This regular expression matches a question mark, and all characters that occur after it until the end of the line. The question mark must be escaped with a backslash because it has a specific meaning to the regular expression. Following the question mark we match any number of characters until the dollar sign, which is the endline character. It needs to be escaped with a backslash because without the backslash, PHP will think the character represents a variable.

But often you will need a bit more functionality than this. What if you want to preserve the string you are searching for in the replacement string? Or what if your search contains distinct portions offset by sets of parentheses? Here's a simple example. We want to replace the current querystring by placing an additional `name=value` pair between the two `name=value` pairs currently in the string. That is, we want to put "newvar=here" after "var=hello" and before "var2=yup".

```
$url= "http://www.phpmysqlbook.com/index.php?var=hello&var2=yup";
$parsed_url = ereg_replace("(\?.*&)", "\\1newvar=here&",$url);
echo $parsed_url;
```

This creates the following string:

```
http://www.phpmysqlbook.com/index.php?var=hello&newvar=here&var2=yup
```

Here the single set of parentheses indicates portion 1. Then, by using the notation \\1, we can include that portion in the newly created string. If more than one portion is indicated by additional parentheses, you can echo the others back into the result by noting which portion you need.

```
$url= "this is a test ";
$parsed_url = ereg_replace("(this.*a).*(test)", "\\1 regular
```

```
expression \\2",$url);
echo $parsed_url;
```

The result of these commands is: "this is a regular expression test".

The regular expression matches everything between "this" and "test". We use parentheses to indicate a substring that starts with "this" and moves to the letter "a". The next .* portion matches any number of characters. Finally, "test" is another substring. These substrings are echoed back in the second argument, with \\1 echoing the first substring and \\2 echoing the second substring.

The regular expression match is case-sensitive.

EREGI_REPLACE() This is the same as `ereg_replace()`, except that the match is case-insensitive.

REGULAR EXPRESSION FUNCTIONS NOT USED IN THIS BOOK

The following regular expression functions, while not used in the examples in this book, are still useful to know.

SQL_REGCASE() This nifty little function will alter strings so that you can use them in case-insensitive regular expressions.

```
string sql_regcase (string string)
```

This might be of use if you are doing a regular expression search in a database server that doesn't support case-insensitive regular expressions. It will save you from having to type in every character in a string as both an uppercase and lowercase letter. For example:

```
echo sql_regcase("this string");
```

produces:

```
[Tt][Hh][Ii][Ss] [Ss][Tt][Rr][Ii][Nn][Gg]
```

PERL-COMPATIBLE REGULAR EXPRESSIONS (PCRE)

For years, the Perl programmers of the world have had regular expressions unlike any others. If you have some experience with Perl, it's likely that you've come to love the additional power these regular expressions give you. If you don't come from a Perl background, you might enjoy learning a bit about the features.

PCREs are, however, a fairly large topic, one that Appendix F explains only briefly. However, if you're looking to get a good jump on learning about Perl's regular expressions and how they can work for you, the information at the following URL is a good read: `http://www.perl.com/pub/doc/manual/html/pod/perlre.html`. There is also a decent description of Perl regular expressions in the PHP4 manual: `http://www.php.net/manual/pcre.pattern.syntax.html`.

The major reason for using PCRE functions is that they give you choice between "greedy" and "non-greedy" matching. For a quick example, take the following string.

```
$str = "I want to match to here. But end up matching to here"
```

Using `ereg()` or `ereg_replace()` there is no way to match from "I" to the first occurrence of "here". The following will not work as you might expect:

```
$str = "I want to match to here. But end up matching to here";
$new_str = ereg_replace("I.*here", "Where", $str);
echo $new_str;
```

This will print "Where" and nothing else. The entire string will be replaced. Using `ereg_replace()` there is no way to indicate that you want to match to the first occurrence of "here". However, using `preg_replace()`, you could do the following:

```
$str = "I want to match to here. But end up matching to here";
$new_str = preg_replace("/I.*?here/", "Where", $str);
echo $new_str;
```

In this instance, .*? means "match all characters until the first occurrence".

PCRE FUNCTIONS USED IN THIS BOOK

PREG_MATCH()   This is similar to the `ereg()` function in that you can assign the optional third argument an array of matched subpatterns, if any are found in the regular expression. `preg_match` returns the number of pattern matches found or False, if none are found.

```
int preg_match (string pattern, string subject [, array matches])
```

PREG_REPLACE()   This makes replacements based on Perl regular expressions.

```
mixed preg_replace (mixed pattern, mixed replacement, mixed subject
[, int limit])
```

This is similar to `ereg_replace()`, though the pattern here must be a Perl regular expression. It can also make use of \\digit to echo the matched substring into the result. The optional fourth argument will limit the number of replaces that `preg_replace` makes.

```
preg_replace("/[<br> \s]*$/i","",$body);
```

This example, taken from the content management system application, will remove all occurrences where breaks (<br>), non-breaking spaces ($nbsp;), or white space (spaces, tabs, new lines) appear consecutively. This replacement is not case-sensitive (the "i" flag determines that) to ensure that both <BR> and <br> are matched.

The brackets indicate that anything within the brackets will start the match. The asterisk indicates that if the character following the first match is also one of the characters within the brackets, the pattern is matched and a replace should occur.

PCRE FUNCTIONS NOT USED IN THIS BOOK

There are a few PCRE functions that we did not use to create these applications. They are: `preg_match_all`, `preg_quote()`, and `preg_grep()`. See the online manual for their usage. Note that we will discuss `preg_split()` in the next section.

Type-conversion functions

This is a category of my own making. In the manual, these functions will fall under other headings. However, we feel that the specialized nature of these functions demands a unique category.

Chapter 4 discusses PHP variables in detail, including PHP's flexible variable typing. If you recall, if you need to evaluate a string as if it were an integer, you can make use of the `intval()` function. See Chapter 4 for similar variable conversion functions.

But at times the variable conversion will be a bit more extreme, turning strings into arrays and arrays into strings. Why, you ask, might you want to do this? Consider a string like the following:

```
24,16,9,54,21,88,17
```

So you have this string of integers, maybe retrieved from a text file. How would you go about sorting it in ascending order? If you have to deal with it as a string the code is going to get very nasty. However, if you can make use of myriad array functions, life gets quite a bit easier. You could simply use the `sort()` function. Take a look:

```
$str = "24,16,9,54,21,88,17";
//turn $str into an array
$array = explode(",", $str);
//sort the array in ascending order
sort($array, SORT_NUMERIC);
//turn the array back into a string and print
$new_str = implode(",", $array);
echo $new_str;
```

This will print:

9,16,17,21,24,54,88

More on the sort() function a bit later.

TYPE CONVERSION FUNCTIONS USED IN THIS BOOK

The following type conversion functions are used in the examples in this book.

EXPLODE()   This function transforms a string into an array.

```
array explode (string separator, string string [, int limit])
```

The second argument is the string you wish to break into an array. The first is the character or characters that separate the different elements. In the example immediately above, the string is separated on a comma.

The third argument limits the number of elements in the resulting array. If you were to use the following code

```
$str = "24,16,9,54,21,88,17";
//turn $str into an array
$my_array = explode(",", $str, 3);
```

$my_array would have three elements: $my_array[0] => 24 $my_array[1] => 16 $my_array[2] => 9,54,21,88,17. You can see that the last element contains what's left of the original string. If you wanted to sort only the first three elements in a string and discard the rest you might do this:

```
$str = "24,16,9,54,21,88,17";
//turn $str into an array
$array = explode(",", $str, 4);
unset($array[3]);
sort($array, SORT_NUMERIC);
echo implode(",", $array);
```

If the string separator does not exist, the entire string will be placed in array element zero. If the string does not exist, an empty string will be placed in the first element.

IMPLODE()   As you might expect, implode() is the opposite of explode(): it turns an array into a string.

```
string implode (string glue, array pieces)
```

The first argument is the string that will separate the string elements. The second is the array to be separated.

A good example of when you might use `implode()` is in a page that runs an SQL delete command. Say that in a page you have presented a series of checkboxes to indicate the rows you wish to delete from the database. You are probably going to want to pass the elements you wish to delete within an array. In the page that does the deletes, you could then run a script like this:

```
//say $deleted_comes from an HTML page and
//contains (1,3,7)
if( is_array($delete_items) )
{
    $str = implode("," , $delete_items);
    $query = "delete from table where item_id in ($str)";
    mysql_query($query);
}
```

SPLIT()   The `split` function does the same thing as `explode`, but it allows you to specify a regular expression as the separation string.

```
array split (string pattern, string string [, int limit])
```

This could come into play if you want to separate a string based on more than one element. Say you had a string you needed as an array, the elements of which could be separated by either a new line or a tab. The following would do the trick:

```
//note there is a tab between 524 and 879
//and a tab between 879 and 321
$items = "524    879    321
444
221";
$array = split("[\n\t]", "$items");
```

 `split()` is more flexible than `explode()`, but it's also slower.

PREG_SPLIT()   This works like `split()`, only it uses a Perl regular expression as the pattern.

```
array preg_split (string pattern, string subject [, int limit [, int flags]])
```

Note that if the flag is PREG_SPLIT_NO_EMPTY, empty items will not be placed in the array.

Again, if `explode()` can do it, make sure to use it.

TYPE CONVERSION FUNCTIONS NOT USED IN THIS BOOK
In addition to the functions in the previous section, you can make use of `spliti()`, which uses a case-insensitive pattern match.

Array functions

I am a big fan of the array functions available in PHP 4. Just about anything you'd like to do to an array you can do with a built-in function. The developers of PHP have done a good job of making sure you have to loop though arrays very infrequently.

In the PHP 4.0.2 manual there are exactly 47 listed array functions. It's likely that by the time you read this chapter, there will be several more. So make sure you scan the manual to see the full range of available array functions.

See Chapter 5 for a discussion of how to create, add to, and walk through an array.

ARRAY FUNCTIONS USED IN THIS BOOK
When you're dealing with database applications, much of your logic should come within your SQL statements. Thus, in the applications presented in this book fairly few array functions were necessary. Here's a rundown of the ones we used.

ARRAY_FLIP()   This function, which is useful with associative arrays, exchanges the keys and values. That is, the keys become the values and the values become the keys.

```
array array_flip (array trans)
```

This comes up once in the course of the book, in the following code:

```
$trans = array_flip(get_html_translation_table(HTML_ENTITIES));
$title = strtr($title, $trans);
```

Before the `array_flip()` function, the array will return many elements. Here are a couple of examples:

```
[(c)] => &copy
[(r)] => &reg
```

Once the array is flipped, these entries will look like this:

```
[$copy] => (c)
[&reg] => (r)
```

Then `strtr()` replaces each value to its key. So in the end this code will make sure that any character that needs to be represented by an HTML entity will be.

Note that if an array has two identical values before being flipped, only one can survive in the flipped array. You can't have two array elements with same key. If there is a conflict the element in the right-most position will be maintained.

ARRAY_MERGE()   As you can probably guess, this function merges, or concatenates, two or more arrays.

```
array array_merge (array array1, array array2 [, array ...])
```

If any of the arrays contain the same associative keys, the elements in the right-most array will be preserved.

ARRAY_SPLICE()   This function takes the array indicated in the first argument and removes all elements following the offset specified in the second argument. It can then insert additional elements.

```
array array_splice (array input, int offset [, int length [, array replacement]])
```

If the offset is a positive number, the elements will be counted from the left; if the offset is a negative number, all items to the left of the indicated number will be deleted. The optional third argument can indicate how many elements after the offset you wish to delete. For example:

```
$knicks_array = array ("Childs", "Sprewell", "Ewing",
"Johnson","Houston");
array_splice($knicks_array, 2,1);
```

will remove elements starting at offset 2 and remove only one element. So "Ewing" will be deleted from this array. `array_splice()` also gives you the ability replace the deleted portion with another array. So, to account for trades, you can do this.

```
$knicks_array = array ("Childs", "Sprewell", "Ewing",
"Johnson","Houston");
$new_knicks = array ( "Longley","Rice");

array_splice($knicks_array, 2,1,$new_knicks);
```

Following this code, $knicks_array would contain six elements: Childs, Sprewell, Longley, Rice, Johnson, Houston.

Note that the value returned by this function is an array of the deleted items. In the code that follows, $traded_knicks will be an array with one element, "Ewing".

```
$traded_knicks = array_splice($knicks_array, 2,1);
```

COUNT()   This returns the number of elements in an array, and is frequently used with loops.

```
int count (mixed var)
```

For example:

```
$array = array(1,2,3,4,5);
for($i=0; $i<count($array); $i++)
{
    echo $array[$i] . "<br>\n";
}
```

Note that sizeof() is a synonym for count().

ARRAY FUNCTIONS NOT USED IN THIS BOOK
Again, there are many great array functions in PHP 4. Here are some of the highlights (from my point of view, anyway).

ARRAY_COUNT_VALUES()   This nifty function will return an associative array, the keys of which will be all of the unique values within the array.

```
array array_count_values (array input)
```

The values of the resulting array will be an integer representing the number of times the value appears within the array.

```
$array = array("yes","no","no","yes","why");
$result = array_count_values($array);
```

After this $result will contain:

```
[yes] =>, 2, [no] => 2, [why] => 1
```

ARRAY_DIFF()   If given two arrays, this function will return all of the elements that are in the first array, but not in the second array.

```
array array_diff (array array1, array array2 [, array ...])
```

For example:

```
$knicks = array("sprewell", "houston", "Ewing", "childs");
$all_stars = array("mourning", "houston", "carter", "davis",
"miller");
$non_knick_allstars = array_diff($all_stars, $knicks);
```

Note that in the returned array, the elements maintain the keys they had in the array from which they were taken. So after running this code, $non_knicks_array will contain the following:

```
[0] => mourning, [2] => carter, [3] => davis, [4] => miller
```

Additional arrays can be added to the function. For example,

```
$knicks = array("sprewell", "houston", "Ewing", "childs");
$all_stars = array("mourning", "houston", "carter", "davis",
"miller");
$non_knick_allstars = array_diff($all_stars, $knicks,
array("carter"));
```

Given this, "carter" will also be removed from the returned array.

ARRAY_INTERSECT() This returns the array elements that two (or more) arrays have in common.

```
array array_intersect (array array1, array array2 [, array ...])
```

ARRAY_POP() The array_pop() function returns the last element in an array, and removes that element from the original array.

```
mixed array_pop (array array)
For example,$array = array(1,2,3,4,5);
$int = array_pop($array);
```

After this runs, $array will contain (1,2,3,4), and $int will contain 5.

ARRAY_PUSH() This function will add elements to the array indicated in the first argument.

```
array_push (array array, mixed var [, mixed ...])
```

The additional arguments will be values you wish to tack onto the array.

```
$array = array (1,2,3);
array_push($array,4,5,6);
```

The resulting array will contain 1,2,3,4,5,6.

ARRAY_RAND()   This function will pick one or more random elements from an array.

```
mixed array_rand (array input [, int num_req])
```

Note that it does not pick the value; rather it picks the key of the chosen elements. For instance, given the following,

```
srand ((double) microtime() * 1000000);
$names = array("jay", "brad", "john", "Jeff");
$rand_keys = array_rand ($names, 2);
```

`$rand_keys` will contain an array with two numbers. To get the values from the $names array, you will first need to get to the key value extracted by array_rand(), and so you will need to use something like this:

```
echo $names[$rand_keys[0]];
```

 Seed the random number generator only once per script.

SHUFFLE()   This function randomizes the elements in an array.

```
void shuffle (array array)
```

You will need to seed the random number generator before using it. For instance:

```
srand ((double) microtime() * 1000000)
shuffle ($array);
```

IN_ARRAY()   This very convenient function will search all of the values of an array, and return TRUE if the value in the first argument is found in the array in the second argument.

```
bool in_array (mixed needle, array haystack)
```

You might be wondering if there is an in_keys() function. Actually, there is no need for such a function, because the following will serve the same purpose.

```
if(isset($array["key"]))
```

SORT()   If there is no second argument, this function will sort an array in ascending or alphabetical order.

```
void sort (array array [, int sort_flags])
```

The flags can be:

- ◆ SORT_NUMERIC – compare items numerically
- ◆ SORT_STRING – compare items as strings

If the array you wish to sort has only numbers, PHP will sort the array numerically; if the array contains only strings, it will be sorted alphabetically. If the array has a mix of strings and numbers, it defaults to sorting by a string.

 PHP4 offers many other ways to sort arrays. Please look at the manual entries for arsort(), ksort(), rsort(), and usort().

Print functions

There are a few functions that you can use to print information to the screen. Only two pop up in this book, but you should be aware of all the functions listed in this section.

PRINT FUNCTIONS USED IN THIS BOOK

In this case the word "functions" may be something of a misnomer. For instance, print() is probably better described as a language construct. In any case, you will use all of these very much like you will use functions; thus, they are included here.

PRINT   As you would expect, this prints what you specify.

```
print
```

ECHO   This also isn't a function, but a language construct. We use it constantly throughout this book, so at this point you probably know what it does.

```
echo
```

Keep in mind that you can mix variables and code within double quotes.

```
$var = "this string";
echo "Please print $var";
```

However, within single quotes the string will be treated literally:

```
$var = "this string";
echo 'Please print $var';
```

The preceding code will print "Please print $var". This concept is discussed in greater detail in Chapter 4.

print versus echo. Which should you use? This is very much a matter of personal preference: use whichever you think looks better on the page. There's only one major difference between the two, and this may influence your decision. echo can take multiple arguments. That is, with echo, different portions can be separated by commas. This will work:

```
echo "this is part 1", "this is part 2";
```

But this will not:

```
print "this is part 1", "this is part 2";
```

PRINT FUNCTIONS NOT USED IN THIS BOOK
They didn't come up here, but these are really important to know about.

PRINTF()   This function outputs a string using the format specified in the description of the sprintf() function.

PRINT_R()   This function is great for putting to productive use the time you'd otherwise spend pulling your hair out. It prints the entire contents of any variable – most notably arrays and objects – to the screen.

```
void print_r (mixed expression)
```

We use it frequently when we're not getting the results we expect from arrays or objects.

Do not do print_r($GLOBALS). You will create an infinitely recursive loop.

VAR_DUMP()   This function behaves like `print_r`, but gives you a bit more information.

```
void var_dump (mixed expression)
```

In addition to printing out the contents of a variable, it includes the data type — including the data type for each element in an array or object. The same caution given for print_r applies to `var_dump()`.

Date/time functions

In point of fact, dealing with PHP and MySQL as a team, you will have to get to know two sets of date/time functions — and they are quite different. This isn't the time or place to go into MySQL's functions (see Appendix I for that). PHP's time/date functions are very well designed.

DATE/TIME FUNCTIONS USED IN THE BOOK

The following are some date/time functions used in the applications in this book.

DATE()   You can use this function and the indicators outlined next to return the date and time.

```
string date (string format [, int timestamp])
```

If you include a second argument, that value will be formatted as you prescribe. Otherwise, the current time and date will be used.

The time and date the functions return are based on the time on the server. You will need to make use of JavaScript to get an idea of the time on the client's computer.

Often the second argument will be the result of the `mktime()` function, which we discuss next.

You can format the date using any of the indicators in Table 6-1.

TABLE 6-1 INDICATORS FOR THE DATE( ) FUNCTION

Indicator	Meaning
a	am or pm
A	AM or PM
B	Swatch Internet time
d	Day of the month, 2 digits with leading zeros; 01 to 31
D	Day of the week, textual, 3 letters; e.g. Fri
F	Month, textual, long; e.g. January
g	Hour, 12-hour format without leading zeros; 1 to 12
G	Hour, 24-hour format without leading zeros; 0 to 23
h	Hour, 12-hour format; 01 to 12
H	Hour, 24-hour format; 00 to 23
i	Minutes; 00 to 59
I [capital *i*]	1 if Daylight Savings Time, 0 otherwise
j	Day of the month without leading zeros; 1 to 31
l (lowercase *l*)	Day of the week, textual, long; e.g. Friday
L	Boolean for whether it is a leap year; 0 or 1
m	Month; 01 to 12
M	Month, textual, 3 letters; e.g. Jan
n	Month without leading zeros; 1 to 12
s	Seconds; 00 to 59
S	English ordinal suffix, textual, two characters; e.g. th, nd
t	Number of days in the given month; 28 to 31
T	Time-zone setting of this machine; e.g. MDT
U	Seconds since the epoch (midnight, January 1, 1970)
w	Day of the week, numeric, 0 (Sunday) to 6 (Saturday)

Continued

TABLE 6-1 INDICATORS FOR THE DATE( ) FUNCTION *(Continued)*

Indicator	Meaning
Y	Year, four digits; e.g. 1999
y	Year, two digits; e.g. 99
z	Day of the year; 0 to 365
Z	Time-zone offset in seconds (-43200 to 43200)

For example, if you want to print the date in the format, "September 14, 2000 7:21 pm," this would do the trick:

```
echo date("F d, Y g:i a");
```

In case you're wondering about the significance of the above date: it was the exact time we wrote this portion of this chapter.

MKTIME()   This function is most useful for calculating valid dates.

```
int mktime (int hour, int minute, int second, int month, int day,
int year [, int is_dst])
```

For example, say that you have a form that collects a date, maybe the current month, day, and year. You want to calculate and set a due date exactly 30 days from the date submitted.

```
$year = 2000;
$month = 5;
$day = 24;
echo date("l F d, Y", mktime(0,0,0,$month,$day+30, $year) );
```

This will output 30 days from May 24, 2000 and will print out "Friday June 23, 2000."

Keep in mind that this function allows you to add or subtract dates without worrying that PHP will return a fictitious result. In the previous example, you could subtract 6 from the month value of 5, and PHP would return a meaningful date. You can add or subtract any number of years, months, or days without worrying that PHP will return a bad result. For instance, this is a perfectly acceptable way to get date information on the last day of 1999.

```
$year = 2000;
$month = 1;
$day = 1;
echo date("l F d, Y", mktime(0,0,0,$month,$day-1, $year) );
```

This code will let you know that December 31, 1999 was a Friday.

Notice that the preceding code first calculates the timestamp of the date indicated by mktime() and then prints that out using the date function.

If you exclude arguments from the right, those parameters will be retrieved from the current timestamp. So, to print what the date and time will be in five hours, this will do the trick:

```
echo date("l F d, Y g:i a", mktime( date(H)+5) );
```

Note the nesting of functions here. Starting at the innermost function, first date(H) returns the current hour, in 24-hour format. Then five is added to that, and the timestamp is calculated for five hours in the future. The timestamp is then formatted using the string indicated.

TIME()   This function returns the current time measured in the number of seconds since the Unix Epoch (January 1 1970 00:00:00 GMT).

```
int time(void);
```

MICROTIME()   This function returns the string "msec sec" where *sec* is the current time measured in the number of seconds since the Unix Epoch (0:00:00 January 1, 1970 GMT), and *msec* is the microseconds part.

```
string microtime(void);
```

This function is only available on operating systems that support the gettime ofday() system call.

The returned string will look something like 0.12082400 969034581. With this function you can be reasonably sure that it will never return the same number twice. It is often used to seed the random number generator.

DATE/TIME FUNCTIONS NOT USED IN THE BOOK

There a few other time/date functions that you might find useful. They include several for printing the current date and time. If you need to know about something specific that isn't discussed here, take a look at the manual: http://www.php.net/manual/ref.datetime.html.

Filesystem functions

PHP has a whole range of functions that enable you to manipulate files and directories on the host computer. In the course of creating applications for this book, there was only one occasion when files needed to be written to or taken from the filesystem: in the Catalog (and Shopping Cart) when we needed to store images that have been uploaded.

But if you work with PHP frequently there's little doubt that you will need to become familiar with these functions. By way of introduction, we will say that the directory and filesystem functions in PHP are simply terrific. The programmers have really done a great job of making working with files, either on the local system or elsewhere on the Internet, a piece of cake. Just to give a quick example, it took about two minutes to write this script, which will grab a stock quote from a site we will not specify for legal reasons.

```
$farray = file("http://domain.com/stockquote?symbols=ORCL", "r");
foreach ($farray as $value)
{
        if( ereg("last:.*$", $value) )
        {
                $value = strip_tags($value);
                break;
        }


}
```

This brief script slurps up an entire page and assigns each line to an element in the $farray. We then loop through the array looking for the string "last". On the site we played with, the word "last" indicates the most recent quote. All we had to do was strip the HTML tags, and we had all the information we needed. If we wanted to, we could have done some more string processing to format the information in a way we liked.

FILESYSTEM FUNCTIONS USED IN THIS BOOK
If you would like to see these in use, check out Chapters 10 and 14.

FOPEN()   This opens a file pointer to the indicated file or URL in the first argument. (The pointer is very much like the result identifier returned by mysql_connect().)

```
int fopen (string filename, string mode [, int use_include_path])
```

The mode will determine what you can do with the file. Table 6-2 shows the available modes.

TABLE 6-2 MODES FOR THE FOPEN( ) FUNCTION

Mode	Meaning
r	Open for reading only; place the file pointer at the beginning of the file.
r+	Open for reading and writing; place the file pointer at the beginning of the file.
w	Open for writing only; place the file pointer at the beginning of the file and truncate the file to zero length. If the file does not exist, attempt to create it.
w+	Open for reading and writing; place the file pointer at the beginning of the file and truncate the file to zero length. If the file does not exist, attempt to create it.
a	Open for writing only; place the file pointer at the end of the file. If the file does not exist, attempt to create it.
a+	Open for reading and writing; place the file pointer at the end of the file. If the file does not exist, attempt to create it.

Note that this function returns a resource identifier. If you wish to read from or write to a file you will need to do something like this:

```
//open a file and read contents into a variable
$filename="test99.txt";
$fp = fopen($filename, "r+") or
    die("could not open file");
$contents = fread ($fp, filesize($filename));
//replace all occurrences of Jayso
$new_contents = str_replace("Jayson", "Jay", $contents);
//write out new file contents.
rewind($fp);
fwrite($fp, $new_contents);
//ftruncate assures there wont be extra
//characters if the resulting file is shorter
//than the original.
ftruncate($fp,ftell($fp));
fclose($fp);
```

FCLOSE( )   This function closes the pointer to a file.

```
int fclose (int fp)
```

Make sure to use it when you are done with a file. If you don't PHP will do it for you, just like `mysql_close()`.

FEOF()   This function tests whether a file pointer has reached the end of a file.

```
int feof (int fp)
```

See the `fgets()` function for an example of `feof()`.

FGETS()   This function returns a single line from the file indicated by the file pointer (usually taken from `fopen`).

```
string fgets (int fp, int length)
```

If you are working with a large file, it's easier on the system to load files into memory one line at a time, rather than in one big chunk as is done with `fread()`.

This function will read a line up until a newline character. Optionally, you can specify the maximum number of bytes to read within a line in the second argument. The number 2048 is traditionally used in the second argument because on many filesystems that was the maximum line length. These days, you're safe using something larger. You shouldn't use this function with binary files.

```
$fp = fopen("/path/to/file","r");
while ($fp && !feof($fp))
{
        print fgets($fp,2048);
}
fclose($fp);
```

FILE()   This function reads a file line by line, each line becoming an element in an array.

```
array file (string filename [, int use_include_path])
```

UMASK()   This function sets the umask value (see your Unix man page if you don't know what this is).

```
int umask (int mask)
```

`umask()` sets PHP's umask to mask & 0777 and returns the old umask.

COPY()   This function makes a copy of the file in argument one and copies it to the location in argument two.

```
int copy (string source, string dest)
```

If the copy works, the function returns True. If not, it returns False. This function is used in Chapter 10.

TMPNAME()   This creates a unique file name in the directory indicated in the first argument.

```
string tempname (string dir, string prefix)
```

The string prefix in argument two will be placed before each file name. This could help you keep track of what files belong to what scripts.

 On Windows, the behavior of this function can be a bit unpredictable.

DIRNAME()   This function will return the directory name of the supplied string.

```
string dirname (string path)
```

For example:

```
echo dirname("/www/htdocs/teswrite.txt");
```

will return /www/htdocs.

FILESYSTEM FUNCTIONS NOT USED IN THIS BOOK
This is an important topic, and one you should spend some time learning. Most of the more popular files system commands are available through PHP, and there are many commands for opening, reading, writing and displaying files. But, as this book deals with a relational database for data storage, we will not cover them here.

Random number generator functions

Every now and then you will need to pick something at random. It may be an individual element, or it may have to do with randomizing an array with shuffle() or getting a random element from an array with array_rand(). In any case you will need to make use of PHP's random number generator functions.

Note that the random number generator needs to be seeded before use. That is, it has to be given a number that is reasonably unique to begin with. For this, as you will see, the microtime() function will be of great use.

Keep in mind that there are really two sets of random number generators, There are the standard rand() and srand(), which you need in order to seed the generator for shuffle() and array_rand(). However, if you just want to get a random number and not use it with any other functions, use the `mt` functions described below – they're faster and more random

RANDOM NUMBER GENERATOR FUNCTIONS USED IN THIS BOOK
Now we will examine some important random number generator functions not used in the applications in this book.

MT_SRAND()   This function seeds your random number generator.

```
void mt_srand (int seed)
```

Use the following line and you can be sure your numbers are plenty random:

```
mt_srand ((double) microtime() * 1000000);
```

Seed the random number generator only once per script.

MT_RAND()   This function returns a random number. You can specify a minimum value and/or a maximum value.

```
int mt_rand ([int min [, int max]])
```

So to get a random number between 1 and 100, do the following:

```
mt_srand((double)microtime() * 1000000);
$number = mt_rand(1,100);
echo $number;
```

cURL functions

These are explained in detail in Chapter 14. cURL is a library that allows for communication between servers using a variety of protocols. For the sake of the applications in this book, cURL was most useful for its ability to communicate with HTTPS. This is a secure protocol used in the shopping cart to do credit card transactions.

Session functions

These are explained in detail in Chapter 14. Sessions are means of maintaining state between pages. Remember that HTTP, the language of the Web, does not allow servers to remember much of anything between requests for pages from a specific user. Sessions allow the server to keep track of activities by a single user.

HTTP header functions

There are two vital HTTP header functions, both of which you will need to get to know.

HEADER()

If you are going to be communicating with the browser or with other HTTP servers, this is the function to use.

```
int header (string string)
```

Essentially, you can send any header that would be expected under RFC 2616 (ftp://ftp.isi.edu/in-notes/rfc2616.txt). The RFC itself is a handful (and perhaps the sleepiest reading you'll do all year). Here is a common header you are likely to send.

```
header("Location:http://www.php.net");
```

This is nothing more than a redirect: it sends the browser to a page you specify. If you have been working with straight HTML and the <META type=refresh> tag or JavaScript to do your redirects, you should switch to this type of header whenever possible. It will work for all browsers and the redirection will be totally transparent to the user.

 IMPORTANT: No, make that **VERY IMPORTANT**. You cannot send a header after anything — ANYTHING — has been sent to the browser. If you send a header after even a hard return, there will be an error. If there is a hard return before your opening <?php tag, you will get error. If there is a hard return in an included file that precedes your header() function, you will get an error. This should not be a problem you encounter frequently; your pages should be designed so that most of the logic is handled prior to the display. However, if you have a situation you just can't work around, take a look at the output buffering functions.

SETCOOKIE()

This is basically a specialized header function, because a cookie is set by nothing more than a specific HTTP header.

```
int setcookie (string name [, string value [, int expire [, string
path [, string domain [, int secure]]]]])
```

The first argument will be the name of the cookie. The second will be the value. The expire value should be set with the time function. The following is a pretty typical use of setcookie():

```
setcookie("id",$id_val,time()+(24*60*60),"/",".domain.com",0);
```

This will set a cookie that will expire in 24 hours ($24 \times 60 \times 60$). The cookie will be available to every directory within `domain.com`. It you want to restrict it to a specific directory, you could change the / to a directory name.

You can find more on cookies in Chapter 4, in the discussion of variables.

In some versions of Internet Explorer, you must either give both time and path values or neither.

HEADER_SENT( )

This function can keep you from sending headers after some text has been sent to the browser.

```
boolean header_sent(void)
```

If you are relying heavily on this function, you are probably not coding your pages properly.

Mail function

If you have Sendmail or another suitable email program installed on your system, this function will take all of the fuss out of sending e-mail from your PHP pages.

Sendmail is the program most commonly used with PHP's Mail function, but qmail with Sendmail wrappers will work, and on Windows, apparently Pegasus (`http://pegasus.usa.com/`) can work (though we haven't tested it).

MAIL( )

This sends an e-mail from your PHP script.

```
bool mail (string to, string subject, string message [, string
additional_headers])
```

Your basic e-mail will look like this:

```
mail("name@domain.com","Subject Text", "The  Complete message goes
here");
```

And if you want to get a little fancier and include a From and a Cc, use the following:

```
mail("jay@trans-city.com","Test Message", "Here I am",
"From: Jay G\r\nCc: webmonkey@trans-city.com\r\nReply-to:
myname@mydomain.com");
```

Additional headers have been added in the fourth argument, and the different headers are separated by line feeds and newlines (\r\n).

If you want to set up a large e-mail system, don't use PHP. There are better tools out there. This function is intended for sending an occasional e-mail from within PHP scripts.

If you'd like to send attachments in your PHP e-mail, check out this excellent article at PHPbuilder.com:http://phpbuilder.com/columns/kartic 20000807.php3.

URL functions

If you've even looked at a querystring, you may have noticed that the text you entered into your form fields has been changed. For examples, spaces are turned into plus signs (+) and ampersands (&) are turned into %26. There are many other characters that are encoded. (All non-alphanumeric characters other than hyphen (-), underscore (_) and dot (.) are replaced by a percentage sign and two characters).

There will be occasions when you need to encode or decode text. For that you will use the functions below.

URLENCODE()

This function will encode a string so that it's URL ready. Most often you will use this if you want to send variable information to another page.

```
string urlencode(string)
```

For example:

```
$myvar="this string with weird &* stuff";
$encoded = urlencode($myvar);
header("Location: http://www.mydomain.com?var=$encoded");
```

Notice that this code snippet has only encoded the values of a querystring element. If you were to urlencode the entire URL, you would not be happy with the results. The result of this code

```
urlencode("http://www.mydomain.com");
```

is "http%3A%2F%2Fwww.mydomain.com".

URLDECODE()
This function undoes the encoding process. It's usually unnecessary because the variable created from your GET or POST data is decoded in your variables.

```
string urldecode(string)
```

RAWURLENCODE()
Returns a string in which all non-alphanumeric characters except hyphen, underscore and period have been replaced with a percent (%) sign followed by two characters.

```
string rawurlencode(string);
```

This is the encoding described in RFC1738 for protecting literal characters from being interpreted as special URL delimiters, and for protecting URL's from being mangled by transmission media with character conversions (like some e-mail systems).

RAWURLDECODE()
Unencodes according to the same provisions as rawurlencode().

```
string rawurlencode(string);
```

Output buffering

Output buffering is the process of writing the results of your script to a temporary buffer. Instead of being sent out over the Web it will gather in a buffer, where you can manipulate it if you wish.

Probably the most common use of output buffering is to ensure you don't get errors caused by sending headers after text has been sent to the browser. To prevent this, you could start a buffer, write some of an HTML page to the buffer, and then, given a specific condition, write a header (maybe a cookie), and then output the rest of the page. When you flush the buffer, the contents will be written to the browser without error.

 TIP If you are frequently using buffering to prevent headers from causing errors, rethink your page logic. Decisions first, output second.

People have also been playing with using output buffering to gzip page contents. Then, in browsers that are capable of unzipping, the page could be downloaded a lot faster. However, given browser craziness, we wouldn't recommend this.

BUFFERING FUNCTIONS USED IN THE BOOK
There are quite a few object buffering functions. We used very few of them.

OB_START()   This starts the buffer.

```
void ob_start(void)
```

FLUSH()   This clears the buffer.

```
void flush(void)
```

BUFFERING FUNCTIONS NOT USED IN THE BOOK
Check the manual for some more sophisticated buffering functions.

INFORMATION FUNCTIONS
These functions will give you information about the environment in which you are working.

PHPINFO()   Your guide to all that is available in your PHP environment. Use it. Use it. Use it. And then take it off your system. No point in letting crackers get a look at the specifics of your system.

PHPVERSION()   Returns only the version of PHP you are using.

Summary

As you've seen, PHP has more functions than you will be able to commit to memory any time soon. It can seem intimidating, but the quantity and quality of these functions are what make PHP such a great language. Most anything you need to do can be done quickly and painlessly.

At first, you may need to study and play with the functions in order to get them to work. But in time, it will get a lot easier. You'll be making use of more and more functions, and keeping your scripts more compact and easier to read.

Chapter 7

Writing Organized and Readable Code

IN THIS CHAPTER

◆ Keeping your code tidy

◆ Understanding the power and convenience of functions

◆ Using object-oriented code

◆ Learning the importance of comments

THIS CHAPTER PRESENTS A run-through of the preferred ways to present and organize your code. Along the way you will see how to construct functions and classes in PHP. By the end of this chapter, you should have a good idea of how write efficient, readable applications in PHP. And you should be ready to dive into the applications in Parts III and IV of this book.

Indenting

If you have done coding in any language, this point should be pretty obvious. But it is an important point, and therefore deserves some mention. In the type of coding needed for Web applications, following a few indenting rules could help make your life a little easier.

How far should you indent? Some feel that each level of code should be indented by three spaces. Others, like us, think a single tab is the way to go. If you use spaces, it is possible that your code will look terrible in another text editor (maybe the one used by your co-worker). We really believe tabs are a better choice anyway.

Code blocks

The most obvious use of indenting comes in differentiating blocks of code. For instance, it is fairly typical to have an if block within a while loop.

```
$i = 0;
while ($i < 100)
{
    $i++;
    if ($i  < 50 )
    {
        echo "Within the first 49.";
    }
    else
{
        echo "Between 50 and 99.";
    }
}
```

As you can see in this PHP code, each block is delimited by curly braces ({ }); this goes for both loops and if blocks. When a block is entered with an opening curly brace, the next line should indented. Each line following at the same level of execution should be indented at the same level. Additional nested blocks should be indented another level.

Looking at the preceding brief snippet of code, it is easy enough to see that there are three distinct blocks. This may not seem like such a big deal with a small bit of code like this, but as scripts get longer, and levels of nesting get deeper, you will see how important this is. We're not going to belabor this point, because it should be pretty clear. But, for a quick example, we will re-present the previous code without indents. Note that it will work just fine – PHP doesn't care if you don't write your code neatly. But imagine coming back to this a month after you wrote it and having to troubleshoot or add code. Life would be a lot easier if you could easily find the block that needs work.

```
$i=0
while ($i < 100)
{
$i++;
if ($i  < 50 )
{
echo "Within the first 49.";
}
else
```

```
{
echo "Between 50 and 99.";
}
}
```

Are you getting a parse error you can't identify? Make sure you have an identical number of opening and closing curly braces and parentheses. If you have, say, five closing curly braces in a page and only three opening, you haven't closed one of your code blocks.

Function calls

Indenting code should not stop at code blocks. Often you will need to use nested function calls or complex variables that take up several lines. You will be much happier in your coding life if you use indents in these situations. Take a look at the following, which is borrowed from the Catalog application.

```
$file_ext = strtolower(
    substr($file
        , strrpos($file,".")
    )
);
```

The purpose of this code is pretty simple: it takes the name of a file and assigns its extension (the characters following the final dot (".")) to $file_ext. It takes three separate built-in PHP functions to get this done. PHP will execute the innermost level first. There, strrpos() finds the numeric position of the final dot. For instance, in the stringmyfile.jpg, it would return 6. Then the substr() function would return only the characters following the dot. Finally, that string would be set to lower case characters.

This could be written on one line, but as you can see, it becomes rather difficult to read.

```
$file_ext = strtolower(substr($file, strrpos($file,".")));
```

Or maybe you find this easier to read. A lot of things we'll talk about in this chapter are matters of personal preference. The important thing is that you spend a lot of time considering how to make your code as readable as possible.

In the first example of this code, it's much easier to see what each of the closing parentheses relate to, and you can more quickly get an idea of what this code accomplishes and how.

 TIP   You might be tempted to write the code above using temporary assignments to variables. Something like:

```
$file_ext = strr_pos($file, ".");
$ ext_letters = substr($file, $file_ext);
$lower_ext_letters = strtolower($file_ext);
```

But this is a good deal slower. Variable assignments do take time, and in a short piece of code where they aren't necessary, stay away from temporary variable assignment. That said, you should never sacrifice readability. In some places temporary variables can help make code much easier to read.

SQL statements

In Web database applications, SQL statements will be interspersed throughout PHP code. Usually PHP variables will be included within SQL statements to get specific results based on variable data. Indenting SQL statements will help keep the code readable and maintainable. In the following, we show a few examples of SQL statements of various types. You will see many examples of these in the applications in Parts III and IV of this book.

```
//2 table select
$query ="select n.fname, n.lname, c.co_name, c. co_address,
              c.co_zip
       from names n, companies c
      where n.name_id = $name_id
          and n.co_id = $c.co_id
";

//update query
$query="update products
     set product = '$product'
         , description = '$cleandsc'
         , price = $nullprice
         , image_src = $nullimage_src
     where product_id = $product_id
");

//insert query
$query="insert into products
```

```
      (category_id, product)
    values ($category_id, '$product')
");
```

 We've heard stories of database engines refusing to process queries, like the ones above, that have newlines in them. This is not a problem with MySQL and won't be a problem with most databases. However, there are other perfectly acceptable ways to write queries. Here are a couple of examples:

```
$query = "select col_1, col2 ";
$query .="from table_1, table_2 ";
$query .="where col_1 = $var";
```

or:

```
$query = "select col_1, col_2 "
          ."from table_1, table_2 "
          ."where col_1 = $var";
```

Choose whichever you like best.

Includes

Every language has a facility for including external files. PHP has four commands that accomplish this. Before we get to those, we will briefly discuss why includes are so critical for writing organized and readable code. We'll start with a very common example.

In most Web sites, header information will vary very little from page to page. There are opening tags (<HTML>, <HEAD>, etc), and perhaps some navigation information. The following is a typical header to an HTML page.

```
<HTML>
<HEAD>
  <TITLE>My Page Name</TITLE>
</HEAD>
<body bgcolor="#FFFFF" link="#8e0402" vlink="#20297c">
```

It would be an absolute waste to type this text into every file within a Web site. Moreover, it could be a real pain. Say you wanted to change the bgcolor attribute of the <body> tag throughout the site. If this information were hard-coded in every file, you would have no choice but to go into each file individually and make the change, or write a script that would do it for you.

You are far better off keeping all of this information in a single file (maybe called header.php) and then using a command that will spit the contents of that into the file being accessed. For this, you would use one of the PHP functions discussed in the following section. For this example we will use `include()`.

 If you have access to your Apache httpd.conf file you will probably want to give your include files a distinct extension; .inc is a typical choice. Additionally, if possible, you will want to keep your includes out of the htdocs directory, so that they can not be accessed by a URL. We did not use either of these techniques in this book because most who use ISPs to host their PHP/MySQL applications will not be able to alter their setups in this way.

Let's say we have two files, header.php and index.php. Notice that we have made an important change in header.php: the `<title>` tags now contain a PHP variable

```
<HTML>
<HEAD>
   <TITLE> <?php echo $page_title; ?> </TITLE>
</HEAD>
<body bgcolor="#FFFFF" link="#8e0402" vlink="#20297c">
```

Now for the index.php file.

```
<?php

$page_title = "Welcome to My Site";
include('header.php');

echo "Here are the contents of my PHP pages. Anything could be here.";

?>
```

Notice that the variable `$page_title` will be picked up in the include. So when the index.php is served, the source code of the PHP page will be as follows:

```
<HTML>
<HEAD>
   <TITLE> Welcome to My Site </TITLE>
</HEAD>
<body bgcolor="#FFFFF" link="#8e0402" vlink="#20297c">
```

Any code, whether HMTL or PHP, that is needed in a variety of pages should be kept within include files. Header and footer information, database connection code, and pages that contain functions or classes are all good candidates for includes.

At the start of an include, PHP reverts to HTML mode. If code within your include needs to be parsed as PHP, you must first indicate that with the `<?php` marker.

Once again, PHP4 contains a variety of commands that do slightly different things with includes. We will look at these commands in the following sections.

include() and require()

These commands are very similar and can usually be used interchangeably. However, you should know what distinguishes the two, as at times using the wrong one can cause problems.

The `require()` command imports the content of the specified file even if the file is not used. This means, for starters, that even if the `require()` is within an if block that tests false, the outside file will still be included. You can probably deduce that this isn't such a big deal because code within a block that tests false won't be executed. However, it does take time for PHP to do the import, and there's no need to add execution time to your script by placing a require within an if block that could test false.

There are other differences between include and require listed in the PHP manual, but these are more relevant to PHP 3. PHP 4 is pretty smart about handling includes and decides for which is the best for you when it interprets your script. It is very difficult to write a script that will behave differently using include and require.

The `include()` command will work better in a situation like the one above. An `include()` command will be executed each time it is encountered within a script.

include_once() and require_once()

In addition to `include()` and `require()`, PHP provides `include_once()` and `require_once()`. These are provided to keep you, the developer, from stepping on your own toes. As you might expect, they keep you from including the same file twice, which could cause some problems when it comes to calling user-defined functions.

For example, say you had a file that contained a function, but that the function relied on another function from an outside file. You'd do something like this:

```
require'helpful_file.php';
another_function();
{
    function_from_helpful_file();
}
```

Say we name this file short_function.php. If we needed both short_function.php and helpful_file.php in a third file, we could have a problem. All functions in helpful_file.php would in fact be included twice. If we called one of the twice-included functions, PHP would not be able to resolve the ambiguity and would spit out an error. So in cases like this, use include_once() or require_once(). Note that if files are included more than once we might also have a problem dealing with variables that inadvertently overwrite each other.

Note that include_once() and require_once() inherit behavior from include() and require(): require_once() will only be processed once, and include_once() can be executed multiple times within loops.

User-Defined Functions

In Chapter 6 you saw many of the functions built into the PHP processing engine. If you are a humble person and look at Appendix E or visit the online PHP manual, you should be duly impressed by the quantity and power of PHP's built-in functions. But it isn't enough — and no matter how much work the able developers put into the language, it never will be enough. That is because every developer on the planet has unique needs. We need to accomplish specific tasks, and we need to do it in ways that fit our own styles and predilections.

User-defined functions allow us developers to create blocks of code that achieve specific tasks. The great thing about user-defined functions is that the code becomes reusable. Any piece of code that you find yourself writing over and over should be committed to a function. There's little doubt that it will save you time in the long run.

In the applications presented in this book nearly all of the code is within functions. The files that you see in your browser are very much an assemblage of function calls. As you will see, this helps to keep things readable.

Function basics

We'll start by writing a simple function that writes out the start of an HTML table.

```
function start_table()
{
    echo "<table border=1>\n";
}
```

To call this function within my PHP page, we would access it just like a built-in PHP function:

```
start_table();
```

That's easy enough. But what if we want the border to vary in given situations? We could make the border a variable, and then in the function call specify the value for border.

```
function start_table($border)
{
    echo "<table border=$border>\n";
}

start_table(1);
```

Now say that most of the time we want the border to be 1, but would like to be able to change the border within the function call. The following would do the trick:

```
function start_table($border=1)
{
    echo "<table border=$border>\n";
}
```

Here $border has been given a default value of 1. But we can overwrite that value by specifying a different value when calling the function. For example, if we were to call the function with the following command, the table would have a border of 2:

```
start_table(2);
```

Once again, 1 is the default value, so if this function is called with the following code, the table border will be 1:

```
start_table();
```

If you know your HTML, you know that the table tag can have multiple attributes: cellspacing and cellpadding are two others. We could add those to the function, along with default values.

```
function start_table($border=1, $cellspacing=2, $cellpadding=2)
{
echo "<table border=$border cellspacing=$cellspacing
 cellpadding=$cellpadding>\n";
}
```

Then, in the call to this function you could alter any of these:

```
start_table(4,2,5);
```

The table created with this command would have a border of 4, cellspacing of 2, and cellpadding of 5.

 The values that the function will accept are known as arguments. So the `start_table` function shown here will take three arguments.

When constructing functions you should be aware that if you wish to change one of the default values in your function call, you must specify all the arguments that precede it (to the left). For instance, the first command in the following code will produce an error. However, the second one will work and will create a table tag with a border of 4, cellspacing of 3, and cellpadding of 2.

```
//this will cause an error
start_table( ,5,5);
//this will work
start_table(4,3);
```

Functions can accept more than simple variables; you can pass any of the scalar types (string, integer, double), any array (numeric, associative, or multi-dimensional), or objects. You might want to make use of a function that turns an array into HTML unordered list, using <ul> and <li>.

```
function create_ul($array)
{
    echo "<ul>\n";
    while(list( , $value) = each ($array))
```

```
    {
        echo "<li>$value</li>\n";
    }
    echo "</ul>\n";
}
```

Returning values

Of course your functions will do more than print HTML. Functions may perform database calls or mathematical computations or do some string handling. They can do just about anything, and often you will want to make the rest of the script aware of the results of your function. You can do this by using the keyword *return*. When a function hits the word *return* it leaves the function, and it will return whatever you specify – a variable, a boolean value (TRUE or FALSE), or nothing at all, if that's what you prefer.

```
function basic_math($val_1, $val_2)
{
    $added = $val_1 + $val_2;
    return $added;
}
```

You could then call this function and print the results.

```
$added_value = basic_math(5,4);
echo $added_value;
```

If fact, the following would work equally well:

```
echo basic_math(5,4);
```

Functions can return any variable type (strings, object, arrays, and the like), or, in the case of database calls, they can return result identifiers. Additionally, functions can return FALSE. If you read Chapter 5, you may remember that in PHP, any non-zero, non-false value will be evaluated in an if statement as true. So we might want to improve the previous function by making sure the values passed can be added.

```
function basic_math($val_1, $val_2)
{
    if (!is_int($val_1) || !is_int($val_2))
    {
        return FALSE;
    }
    $added = $val_1 + $val_2;
    return $added;
}
```

If either of the arguments in the call to this function is not an integer, the function will return FALSE and stop. A call to this improved function might look like this.

```
if(!($added_value = basic_math(7, 5)))
{
    echo "What exactly are you doing?";
}
else
{
    echo $added_value;
}
```

If the function returns a value (any value), that value will be added. If not, a special message will be printed. Notice how this mimics the behavior of many of the PHP built-in functions. Its purpose is to perform a task, and if it fails to do so, it returns false.

Actually, there's something else that needs to be pointed out in this function. What will happen if the sum of the arguments sent to the function equal zero, say −1 and 1. In a case like that, your function will return 0. And, as we discussed in Chapter 5, 0 is evaluated as FALSE in PHP. So you need to be careful about situations like this. You may run into situations like this with some of PHP's string handling functions, strpos(), for example. You might be better off evaluating a call to the previous function like this:

```
if (!is_int($added_value = basic_math(-1,1)))
```

Take a quick look at the following function. We think it's a good example of how functions can really save you time, headaches, and keystrokes. The mysql_query function is fine; it sends a query from PHP to MySQL and, if it succeeds, returns a result identifier. If it fails, however, it does not automatically return any error information. Unless you do a bit of digging, you won't know what the problem was with the query. So for every query in your applications (and there will be plenty) you tack on an or die phrase:

```
mysql_query("select * from table_name") or die
    ("Query failed:" . mysql_error());
```

But life gets quite a bit easier if you create a function like the following, and then send all of your queries through that function.

```
function safe_query ($query = "")
{
    if (empty($query)) { return FALSE; }
    $result = mysql_query($query)
        or die("ack! query failed: "
```

```
             ."<li>errorno=".mysql_errno()
             ."<li>error=".mysql_error()
             ."<li>query=".$query
        );
    return $result;
}
```

So your applications might include a file with this function on every page, and then use `safe_query()` in place of `mysql_query()`.

Using a variable number of arguments

One nice feature of PHP 4 is that you can pass an indefinite number of arguments to a function and then assign the list of arguments to an array. Consider the following code:

```
function print_input_fields()
{
    $fields = func_get_args();
    while (list($index,$field) = each($fields))
    {
        print " <tr>\n";
        print "  <td valign=top
align=right><b>".ucfirst($field).":</b></td>\n";
        print "  <td valign=top align=left><input type=text
name=$field size=40 value=\"".$GLOBALS[$field]."\"></td>\n";
        print " </tr>\n\n";
    }
}
start_table();
print_input_fields("name","location","email","url");
end_table();
```

The GLOBALS array is discussed later in this chapter in the "Variable Scope" section.

This function prints out form fields within a table. First, using `func_get_args()` creates an associative array, with the name of the argument as the key. Then each form field is printed out. This is pretty convenient because we can call a function in a number of situations and vary the output by including as many arguments as needed.

If you're wondering how this would work if your function contained some required parameters prior to the set of arguments that might vary, good for you: it's an excellent question.

There are two other PHP functions that will work in such situations: `func_num_args()`, which returns the number of arguments sent to a function, and `func_get_arg()`, which returns a specific argument based on its numeric index, starting at 0. So, for example, you might have a function that prints an HTML form with a variable number of input fields.

```
function print_form($action="", $method="POST")
{
    if (empty($action)){return FALSE;}
    echo "<form action=$action method=$method>";
    $numargs = func_num_args();
    for ($i = 2; $i < $numargs; $i++)
    {
        echo "<input type=text name=" . func_get_arg($i). ">";
    }
    echo "</form>";
}

print_form("myurl.php", "", "myfield1", "myfiels2");
```

Variable scope

To work with functions you need to understand how PHP handles variable scope. Scope is an important topic in any programming language, and PHP is no different.

In PHP, variables assigned outside of functions are known as *global variables*. These can be variables that you create, they can come from HTML form elements through either GET or POST, or they may be any of the variables inherited from the Apache environment. All globals are accessible from an array known as $GLOBALS. You can add to and delete from this array.

 TIP We've said it before, and we'll say it again: use `phpinfo()` to get information about variables in your environment or your configuration.

In PHP a global variable is not automatically available within a function. If you want to use a global within a function, you must indicate within the function that the variable you are accessing is a global.

Here is an example of using a global within a function:

```
function add_numbers($val_2)
{
```

```
    global $number;
    echo $number + $val_2;


}
$number = 10;
add_numbers(5);
```

This code will print "15". Here $number is a global because it was assigned outside of a function. Using the keyword global tells PHP that we want to fetch the specified number from the $GLOBALS array. This code could also be written like this:

```
function add_numbers($val_2)
{
    echo $GLOBALS["number"] + $val_2;
}
$number = 10;
add_numbers(5);
```

In the applications in this book we will be using the technique shown in the first example, because it seems a little cleaner. It's nice to see where your variable is coming from at the top of the function.

Within your functions, you may wish to make variables available as globals. That way they will be available in the body of your script and in other functions. To accomplish this, you must explicitly assign the variable to the $GLOBALS array. Here's a quick example:

```
function assign_to_global($val_1, $val_2)
{
    global $sum;
    $sum = $val_1 + $val_2;
}

assign_to_global(5,6);
echo $sum;
```

This script will print "11". For something a bit more complicated, we'll borrow a function from the applications section of the book.

```
function set_result_variables ($result)
{
    if (!$result) { return; }
    $row = mysql_fetch_array($result,MYSQL_ASSOC);
    while (list($key,$value) = each($row))
```

```
    {
        global $$key;
        $$key = $value;
    }
}
```

This function expects a result identifier gathered from `mysql_query()`. Assume that the query run prior to this function call will return a single row. That row is then assigned to an associative array named $row. Then each column taken from the query (which is now the key in the associative array) and its value will be available as a global. This could be useful if the values retrieved from the query are needed in many other functions. Note the use of variables in this code. See Chapter 5 for an explanation of this concept.

TIP All of the Apache variables ($DOCROOT, $REQUEST_URI, and so forth) are available as globals. To use them within functions you will need to make the function aware of them.

USING GLOBAL VARIABLES

Throughout the applications in this book you will see that global variables are used sparingly within functions. This is because it is just easier to keep track of your variables if you are passing them through arguments and retrieving them through return values. If you start using globals extensively, you may find that your variables are returning unexpected values in different places — and finding the functions that are causing the error can be a major pain.

Here's another reason to avoid globals when possible: You will be using the same variable name over and over and over again. We don't know how many times in these applications the variable names $query, $result, $row, or $i are used, but trust us when we say they are used frequently. All kinds of hassle would be introduced into my life if we had to keep track of each time we used one of these variable names.

At times you will have little choice but to use global variables, but before you do, make sure that you can't accomplish the same thing using variables of local scope.

Object-Oriented Programming

A few years back there was a large move toward object-oriented programming. Some people just thought that the procedural approach — that is, coding strictly with functions — just wasn't enough. Therefore, the folks working on languages like C++ and Java popularized an approach that allows a developer to think about code in a different way.

The idea behind object-oriented programming is to think of portions of your application as objects. What is an object? Well, it's an amorphous thing, a kind of black box — a superstructure of variables and functions. But if you are new to the concept, this description may not be so clear.

To make things clearer conceptually, we'll give an example that comes up later in the book. Chapter 10 presents a catalog, a place where your business could post a listing of goods. In this application, there is an organizational breakdown. At the highest level there is a list of categories, and each category will contain one or more products. Knowing this, you could think about a category as an object.

As this is a catalog, you might expect certain things in a category. A category would probably have a name and a caption; it might also have a unique ID number. There might also be other parameters that further describe the category object.

In addition to these descriptive items, there are certain actions you will want to perform on a category. Actions include things such as saving a new category, deleting an existing category, or maybe just printing out a specific category.

Now all you need is the correct nomenclature. These descriptions of the object (such as name and unique ID) are called *properties*, and the actions (save, delete, print) are known as *methods*.

Before we get to using objects, we want to explain a couple of advantages to this object-oriented approach. Say some programmer has created an object for categories and tells you about the methods and properties. You don't really need to know *how* any of it works; you just need to know that it does. You can make use of the methods and properties of the object in your scripts with little effort.

Of course, the same could be said of a well-designed procedural approach. A well-documented collection of functions could work equally well. In fact, many programmers dislike object-oriented programming, feeling it is unnecessary. There is no doubt, you should be able to write good procedural code before you move on to objects.

Using objects, not only can you make use of methods and properties in the heart of your scripts, you can extend the functionality of a class by making use of a concept called *inheritance*. Going back to the catalog example, a category will have one or more products. Thus every product will belong to a category. So a product will have its own set of properties and methods, but in addition, it will inherit the properties and methods from its category.

 If you are coming from a language like Java, you will need to be aware of some of PHP's shortcomings in this department. There is no way to designate methods as "private" and there are no deconstructors.

Classes

In object-oriented programming, you will be working with classes. A class is a structure that encompasses your methods and properties. Within a class, properties (items that describe the object) are variables. And methods (actions to be take on the object) are functions. Let's start with a simple class called Category.

This is NOT the same set of classes used in the catalog application in Chapter 10. For instructive purposes, the code here has been simplified.

```
class Category
{
    //here are the properties
    var $category_name;
    var $category_desc;
    var $category_id;
```

Here, at the start of this class, we defined the properties. Notice the use of var to declare each of the properties. You don't need to declare properties elsewhere in PHP, but in classes you must. Now we're going to create the first method.

```
class Category
{
    //here are the properties
    var $category_name;
    var $category_desc;
    var $category_id;

    //gets all the properties for a give category_id
    function Category($category_id=0)
    {
        //expecting a category id when the object is
        //instantiated
        if ($category_id == 0)
        {
            return;
        }

        $query = "select category_name, category_desc from
          categories where category_id = $category_id";
        $result = mysql_query($query) or
          die(mysql_error());

        list($category_name, $category_desc) =
        mysql_fetch_array($result);
```

```
    $this->category_name=$category_name;
    $this->category_desc=$category_desc;
    $this->category_id=$category_id;
  }
}
```

There are a few things here that require explanation. First, notice that the method (i.e., the function) has exactly the same name as the class. That tells PHP that this is the *constructor*. A constructor is automatically run as soon as a class is instantiated. The other thing to note is the use of $this->. It indicates a property or method within the current class. Above, we are assigning values to the properties: category_id, category_name, and category_description. If we wanted to call a method, we would indicate that with parenthesis: $this->method_call() or $this->method_call($value)

To continue with this example, we will add a method for deleting a category. Note that the method below assumes that the database contains two tables — one named categories and one named products — and that there is a one-to-many relationship between categories and products. Therefore, you would want to make sure that a category isn't deleted if it contains products.

```
class Category
{
//all the stuff you saw above goes here

    function delete_category($category_id=0)
    {
        //make sure a category_id was defined in the
        //constructor or is indicated explicitly
        if($category_id == 0 && empty($this->category_id))
        {
            $this->error = "Nothing to delete";
            return FALSE;
        }
        //create where clause with the category_id
        //retrieved from the proper place
        if ($category_id !=0)
        {
            $where_clause = "where category_id =
             $category_id";
        }
        else
        {
            $where_clause = "where category_id =
            $this->category_id";
        }
```

```
        //make sure there are no products left for this
        //category
        $query = "select * from products  $where_clause";
        $result = mysql_query($query) or
          die(mysql_error());
        if (mysql_num_rows($result)>0)
        {
            $this->error = "There are
still products for this category";
            return FALSE;
        }
        $query="delete from categories $where_clause";
        $result = mysql_query($query) or
          die(mysql_error());
        if(mysql_affected_rows() == 0)
        {
            $this->error = "There were no rows to delete";
            return FALSE;
        }
        return TRUE;
    }
}
```

We now have a class with two methods, the constructor and `delete_category`, and three properties. Now it is time to put this class to work.

Instantiating an object

Instantiating basically means "creating." Let's say we have a PHP page that is intended to delete categories. To make this work with the above class, we need to do a few things. First, we need to include the file containing the class.

```
require "classes.php;"
```

Next we have to create an instance of the object. We can do this with the keyword new:

```
$c = new Category;
```

Now, using the object $c, we can access any of the properties or methods using the same syntax seen in the previous example: $c-> property or $c->method().

Now we want to put together a page that actually removes a record from the database. For the sake of this example, assume that a single $category_id has been passed via the querystring.

```
<?

require classes.php;

$c = new Category($category_id);


if(!$c->delete_category())
{
    echo "Deletion Failed: $c->error";
}
else
{
    echo "Deletion Succeeded for:";
    echo "<ul>
            <li>$c->category_name
            <li>$c->category_description
            <li>$c->category_id
        </ul>
    ";
}

?>
```

As you can see this makes for a pretty clean page, which everyone is looking for ultimately.

Inheritance

So far, we have worked with only one class. But one of the great advantages of object-oriented programming is that methods and properties from one class are inherited by another. We'll show a very quick example of this by writing a class called Product. Here's the shell:

```
class Product extends Category
{
    var $product_id;
    var $product_name;
    var $product_price;

}
```

Notice the use of the word *extends*. This tells PHP that all of the products and methods available in Category should be available in Product. If we wanted to call the delete_category() method from within the Product class, we could call it with $this->delete_category($category_id).

> **TIP** In PHP, constructor methods of parent classes are not automatically run when the child class is called. For example, calling $p = new Product will not run the Category() method.

Now we'll add a quick constructor method:

```
class Product extends Category
{
    var $product_id;
    var $product_name;
    var $product_price;

    function Product($product_id=0)
    {
        //expecting a product_id to be passed
    if ($product_id ==0)
        {
            return FALSE;
        }

        $query = "select product_name, product_desc,
product_price, category_id from
products where product_id = $product_id";

        $result = mysql_query($query);
        list($this->product_name, $this->product_desc,
$this->product_price) =
mysql_fetch_array($result)
;
    $this->Category($category_id);

    }
}
```

Notice that this method not only assigns values to the properties for this product, it also calls the constructor of the Category class, which then assigns values to those properties. Note that because of inheritance, we could write a script as follows:

```
require 'classes.php';

$p = new Product($product_id);
echo $p->category_name;
```

You see that the properties of Category are available to the Product object.

Object-Oriented Code versus Procedural Code

Here's the million-dollar question: In your applications, should you use object-oriented code or procedural code? This is another topic that inspires religious debate. But really there is no need for that because there is a correct answer: It depends. If you have an extensive background in object-oriented programming, and you are more comfortable coding classes, do that. However, if you dislike the way object-oriented code works, use only functions.

 There are a few large class libraries on the included CD-ROM, including some taken from Manual Lemos' impressive site `http://phpclasses.upperdesign.com`. His form creation and validation class is truly epic, but it may be a bit unwieldy for some.

Object-oriented code comes with a couple of advantages and disadvantages. Weigh them and decide for yourself if you should use classes or just functions.

Advantages:

- You can save time using the object-oriented approach.
- You can make highly reusable pieces of code.
- You can make use of extensive class libraries available for free on the Web.

Disadvantages:

- It's slower than the procedural approach.
- The syntax can be confusing at first.
- Web programming does not make use of many of the advantages of object-oriented code.
- If you're using very large class libraries, there may be a performance hit.

Comments

In any programming language, comments are essential – not only to you as you're writing the code, but to those who come to the code after you. What may be crystal-clear to you may be absolutely unreadable to others. Or, if you've had to do something particularly complex, you might find that you don't even understand what you were thinking if you come back to the code a couple of months after you wrote it.

In PHP, you can indicate comments with two slashes (//), with a hash (#), or by surrounding commented code with /* and */. This last method is particularly helpful for multi-line comments.

Comment all of your functions, what they do, what they are expecting, and what they return. Make sure to make note of any variables that could be tough to track.

As you look through the /functions directory of the CD, you will see that every function has an initial comment that mimics the style used in the PHP manual. For example,

```
int fetch_record (string table name [, mixed key [, mixed value]])
```

Then we provide some description as to what these arguments mean and the significance of the return value. When writing the body of the function, you should comment on anything that would not be intuitive to someone coming to the script at a later date. If you have a series of functions that perform some complex string handling or use lengthy regular expressions, make sure to note exactly what those functions are intended to accomplish. For example, we will reprise this line of code:

```
$file_ext = strtolower(substr($file, strrpos($file,".")));
```

This isn't especially difficult to figure out, but you could sure help the next person coming to this line with a simple comment.

```
//get characters following the final dot
//and make lowercase
$file_ext = strtolower(substr($file, strrpos($file,".")));
```

The other important thing to comment is the overall logic of pages, especially long pages. Often a script will behave differently in varying circumstances. Variables passed from forms, errors, and other factors will effect what portions of script will run. At the top of the page, you can indicate what factors will affect the page's logic and then as you reach different if blocks, explain where the conditions are coming from and what they mean.

For a brief example, take the confirm_delete.php page from Chapter 8, Guestbook2k:

```
/*
his script will only run if the user is logged in.
It will be accessed in two circumstances:
    -- The "Delete Entries" button was pressed on
       the edit.php page. (Normally this will be the
       first time to this script). The ids of the
       records to be deleted are passed in the entry_id
```

```
       array.
    -- The "Confirm Delete" button was pressed on this
       page. This will comfirm the deletion and run the
       delete queries.
*/
include("header.php");
include("authenticate.php");

$page_title = "Confirm Changes";
include("start_page.php");

//if coming from edit_page.php. The first time to
//this script. Print a form with checkboxes that
//the user must check in order to confirm deletion.
if ($submit == "Delete Entries")
{
    //the form contains no action, so it will submit
    //to the same page, and the value of submit will be
    //"Confirm Delete"
    print "<form method=post>\n";
    if (is_array($entry_id))
    {
        while (list($key,$value) = each($entry_id))
        {
            print "<li>Delete entry #$value?\n";
            print "<input type=hidden name=\"entry_id[]\"
value=\"$value\">\n";
        }
    }
    print "<br><input type=submit name=submit value=\"Confirm
Delete\">\n";
    print "<input type=hidden name=offset value=\"$offset\">\n";
    print "</form>\n";
}

//if the page has been submitted to itself,
//to confim that the deletion should happen.
elseif ($submit == "Confirm Delete")
{
    //loop through each element in the entry_id array
    //and run a delete query for each item.
    while (list($key,$value) = each($entry_id))
    {
        print "<li>Deleting entry #$value\n";
        $q = "delete from guestbook where entry_id = $value";
```

```
        mysql_query($q) or die("Invalid query:$q");
    }
}
else
{
    print "No action to confirm\n";
}
```

We will end this section on a word of caution: don't over comment. Commenting every single line, or making the obvious even more obvious is annoying. For example, the following comments are completely unnecessary and will only make your scripts difficult to read.

```
//make string lowercase
$str = strtolower($str);
//increase $i by 1
$i++
```

Commenting calls for good judgement. You don't want to comment too much, you don't want to comment too little. My best advice is to take a look at how many programmers comment their code and pick a style that you like. We use one method for the applications in this book; others have different styles.

The PEAR directory of your PHP installation is a great place to look for tips on good coding style. PEAR stands for PHP Extension and Application Repository. It is a growing set of scripts that contains a series of best practices for programming with PHP. The folks working on PEAR are real pros who write terrific code. We recommend looking through the scripts in that directory to glean some tips on writing quality code.

Summary

In this chapter we have presented some ways to write clean and organized code. When you look at your scripts, you should ask yourself a few questions. *Are there blocks of code that are common to every page?* Maybe those blocks should be moved into an include. *Are there chunks of code that I'm writing over and over again?* Perhaps writing a function would save time. *Is the next person who comes to this script going to be able to figure out what I've been doing?* If not, make sure that you add enough comments to make things clear.

You will need to decide whether or not an object-oriented approach is good for you and the application you're writing. The fact is that if you're not immediately sure, the answer if probably *no*. Make sure you are comfortable writing clean procedural code before you jump into classes.

Now that you've done all the required reading, it is time to move into Part III, where we put PHP and MySQL to work.

Part III

Simple Applications

Chapter 8

Guestbook 2000, the (Semi-)Bulletproof Guestbook

IN THIS CHAPTER

- ◆ Learning the power of guestbook 2000
- ◆ Organizing your code in a reasonable way
- ◆ Writing good, reusable functions

IN THIS CHAPTER WE WILL develop the first of our applications – a guestbook. Guestbooks aren't complex and they aren't very exciting. However, this application does give us the chance to introduce some concepts such as validation and put many of the practices discussed earlier in this book to work.

In the Introduction of this book we introduced some code that could be used for the most basic guestbook possible. However, using that code for your guestbook is not a good idea. It's got all kinds of holes that will allow malicious people out there to mess with your pages. There is another problem with the ultra-basic guestbook: given the way the code is just dumped into one page, there's not a line that's reusable. One of the top goals of developing any application is to create chunks of reusable code.

Determining the Scope and Goals of the Application

The easiest way to get yourself into trouble when coming at an application is to not know exactly what you are trying to achieve. A vital part of the developer's job is to figure out exactly what is needed in the application. Usually this will involve extensive discussion with the people for whom the application is being developed. During these discussions, it is important to think a step ahead and ask questions that may not have been considered. What if the scope increases in a certain way?

What if additional information but related information needs to be tracked? All of these things will affect the way you design your database and your scripts, and that is why it is best to know the exact scope and goals of your application. Depending on whom you're working with, you may want to get some sketches of pages that need to be developed.

The scope of this application is small and the goals are minimal. The guestbook stores names, addresses and the like. (But, to tell the truth, the goal of this chapter is not so much to show you how to write a guestbook as it to show you how to write good, reusable, organized code for your applications.) In any case, you should know what guestbook2k looks like before you proceed.

 In this chapter, we're not going to take the notion of creating good functions as far as it can go. In the next chapter we'll present a more extensive set of functions that we'll use throughout the rest of the book.

Necessary Pages

There are three basic pages: one for signing the guestbook, one for viewing the guestbook, and one for administering the guestbook.

Figure 8-1 shows the page that gives the user the opportunity to sign the guestbook. It's pretty simple, a form with four text fields and one textarea field. Additionally, there is a submit button and a reset button.

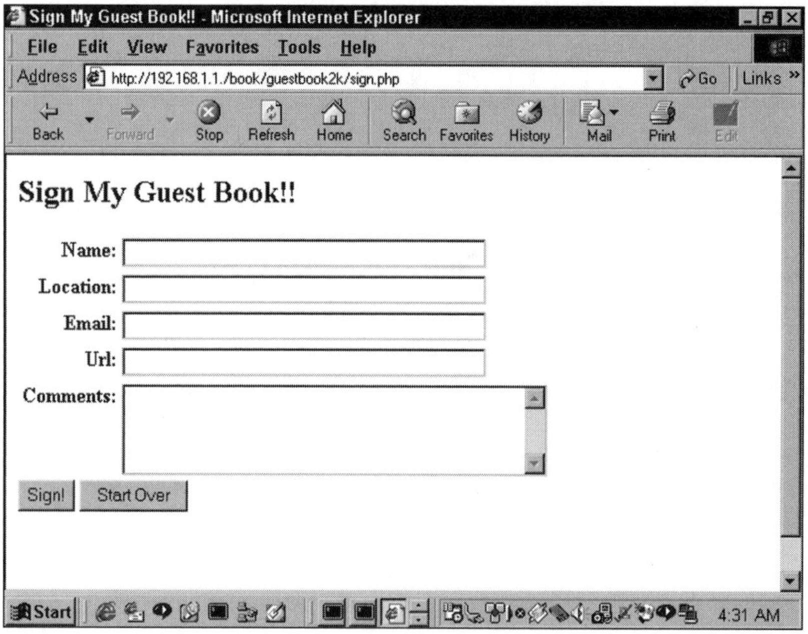

Figure 8-1: Page for signing the guestbook

Next, there must be a way to see who has signed the guestbook. For the sake of having readable Web pages, we created a page, shown in Figure 8-2, where only two entries are printed on each page. At the bottom of the page are navigational elements that indicate whether there are previous or additional entries. These should be conditional and should disappear appropriately when you are at the beginning or end of the guestbook.

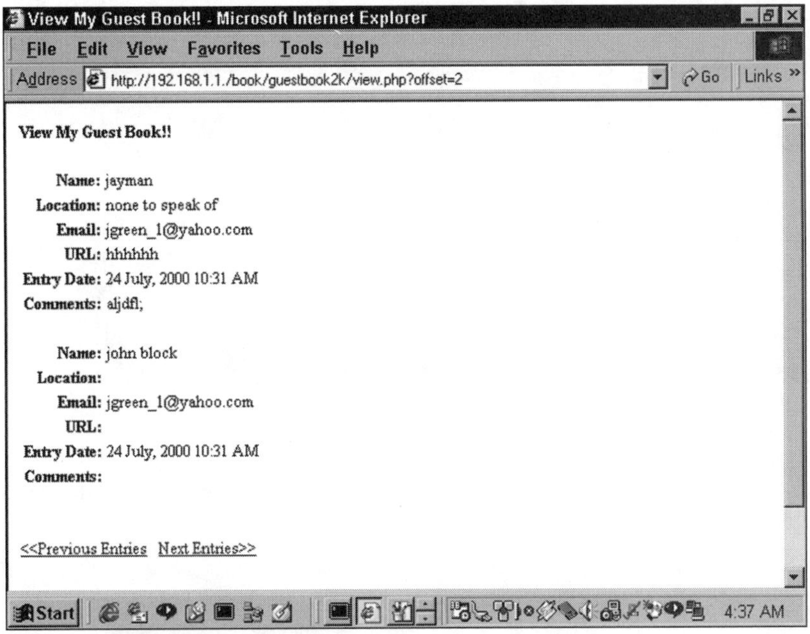

Figure 8-2: Page for viewing the guestbook

Finally, we need a page that enables you to delete entries you don't want. The page in Figure 8-3 seems to do the trick. Access to this page needs to be limited to authorized users. You don't want any old schmo going in and cleaning out your guestbook.

What do we need to prevent?

The major problem that we need to tackle here is one that is common to any application with form input. It is possible for vandals to input nasty code into your forms that will screw up the pages for everyone else who comes along. If you used the guestbook application in the Introduction you could be in serious trouble. Consider what would happen if someone inserted the following code into a text field:

```
<script>alert("boo");</script>
```

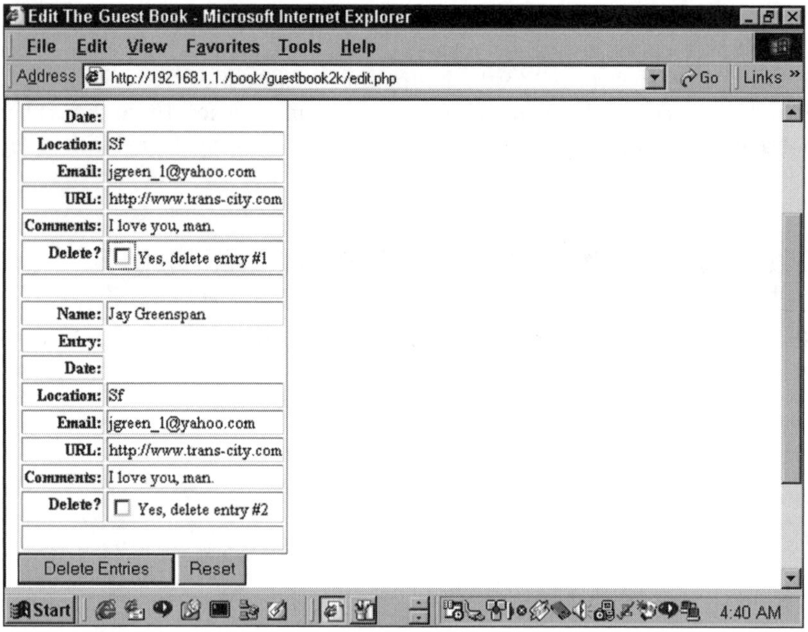

Figure 8-3: Page for administering the guestbook

The next time the page loaded, the viewer would be greeted with the little treat seen in Figure 8-4.

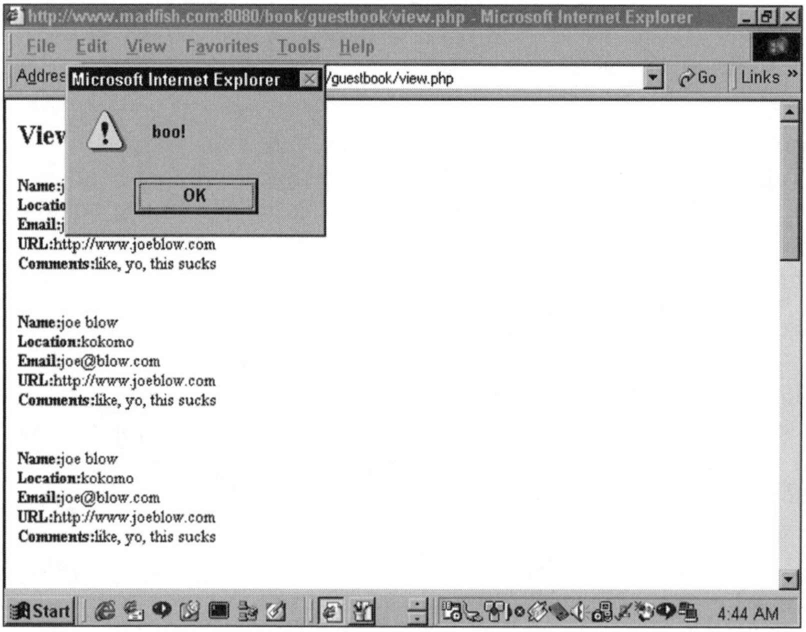

Figure 8-4: Results of a problem entry

If some jerk felt like it, he could screw up your page with all sorts of tags. This code, for instance, would create the disaster seen in Figure 8-5.

```
<img src=http://www.britney-spears.fsnet.co.uk/britney4.jpg>
```

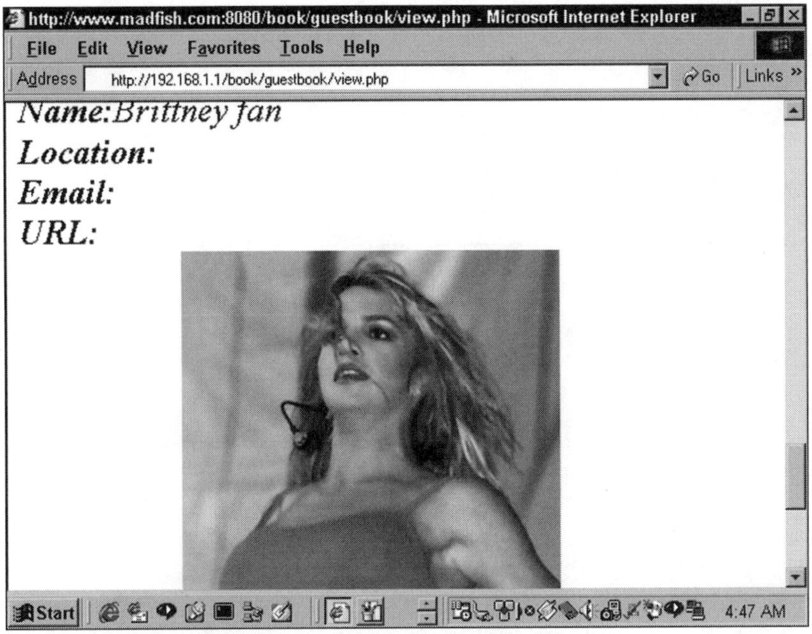

Figure 8-5: Another problem entry

Additionally, this application requires some validation. When the user enters information, this application is going to see that it makes sense. The application will check for the following:

◆ E-mail addresses should contain an at symbol (@), one or more characters before the @, and a dot somewhere after the @. E-mail validation can get more complex (and will in later chapters).

◆ URLs should look like URLs, complete with an `http://` prefix and at least one dot.

◆ There must be some text entered in the name field. There's little point in a guestbook entry without a name.

◆ No e-mail address should appear more than once in the database.

Once the application has checked all of this, the user will need to be made aware of any errors. Figures 8-6 and 8-7 show how we will indicate these errors.

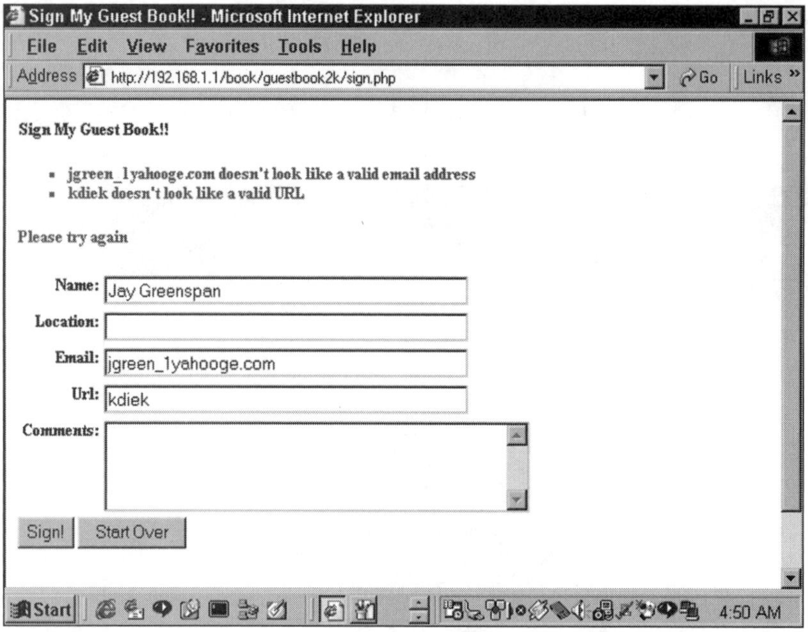

Figure 8-6: Reporting bad information

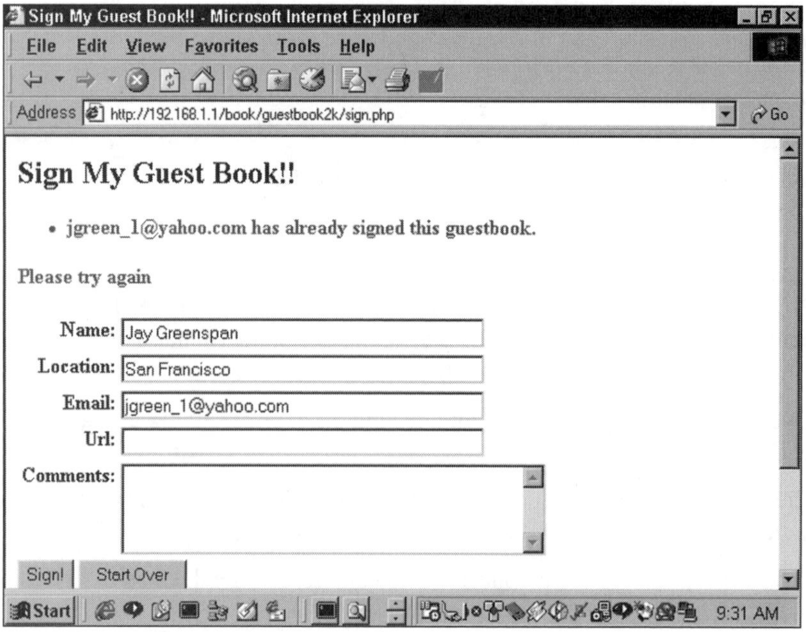

Figure 8-7: Reporting duplicate entry

Designing the Database

We covered the normalization process in Chapter 1 and before long we'll put these normalization skills to work. For this application the set of information is pretty simple. So simple, in fact, that a single table will do the job. Actually, this isn't quite true. For administrative purposes, you should create a table against which user names and passwords can be authenticated. Here are the create statements that will make the tables.

```
create table guestbook
(
        entry_id        integer not null auto_increment,
        name            varchar(40) null,
        location        varchar(40) null,
        email           varchar(40) null,
        url             varchar(40) null,
        comments        text null,
        created         timestamp,
        remote_addr     varchar(20) null
, key guestbook_key (entry_id)
);




create table guestbook_admin
(
        username        varchar(50) not null,
        password        varchar(255) not null
);
```

When adding a user to the guestbook_admin table, it would be best to encrypt the password. The easiest way to do this is by using MySQL's password function.

```
insert into guestbook_admin (username, password)
    values ('jay', password('rules'));
```

After you've run this command, the actual value stored in the password column is 065cb7f12ad99fe3. When you need to find out whether a user knows the password, you can use the password function again.

```
select * from guestbook_admin where
username = 'jay' and
password = (password('rules'));
```

Code Overview

In this, the first of your applications, you need to look at the architecture you will use in constructing your applications. The applications on the CD have been constructed so that they are as reusable and portable as possible.

To start with, there is a folder named book, which should be copied to the root directory of your Web server. On Apache this folder is named htdocs by default. The book folder contains all the applications documented in this book. If you need for some reason to copy the book folder to a spot other than the root directory, you'll need to make sure to change the include commands at the top of header.php. Figure 8-8 shows the folder structure.

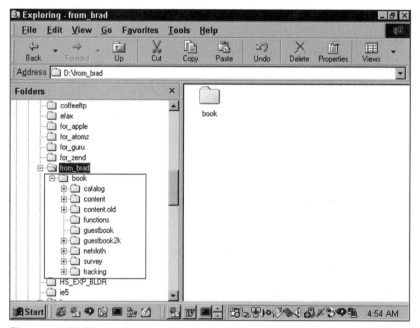

Figure 8-8: Application folder structure

Within the book folder, there is a series of folders, one for each of the applications presented here and one labeled functions. In this application we will concern ourselves with basic.php. This file will contain some functions that you will use in a variety of applications. We'll discuss the functions in basic.php that are used in guestbook2k in the section entitled "Code Breakdown." The code that is relevant only to guestbook2k is kept in the guestbook2k folder. Here, the functions that will need to be addressed across a number of pages are kept in the header.php file. We will also explain these functions in detail in the "Code Breakdown" section.

The pages that are called from the browser are named intuitively: view.php, sign.php, and edit.php. Each of these pages calls start_page.php and end_page.php. These contain standard header and footer information and are easy enough to read, so they we won't discuss them here.

You may find the view.php, sign.php, and edit.php files surprisingly short. They only contain a couple of dozen lines of code each. This is because just about everything is written in reusable functions.

So once again the important thing is to understand the functions that are kept in /book/functions/basic.php and /book/guestbook2k/header.php.

Code Breakdown

As mentioned in the previous section, the vast majority of the work is done in functions, and these functions are kept in files that will be included in the pages called from the browser.

Reusable functions

Here we will cover the contents of function/basic.php and guestbook/header.php

FROM FUNCTIONS/BASIC.PHP

We can address these in any order—alphabetical seems as good as any.

AUTHENTICATE()   This little function sends a 401 HTTP response code. This header forces your browser to open the username and password box shown in Figure 8-9.

```
function authenticate ($realm="Secure Area"
    ,$errmsg="Please enter a username and password"
)
{
    Header("WWW-Authenticate: Basic realm=\"$realm\"");
    Header("HTTP/1.0 401 Unauthorized");
    die($errmsg);
}
```

The values entered into these text fields are set to PHP variables $PHP_AUTH_USER and $PHP_AUTH_PW. PHP can then query MySQL to check if the values are stored in the database. Note that this function merely sends the header. It does nothing to check the values entered in the text boxes. They are checked in the guestbook2k/authenticate.php file. This function is called if either no values have been entered or the values match nothing in the database.

If the user hits the Cancel button the string stored in $errmsg is printed.

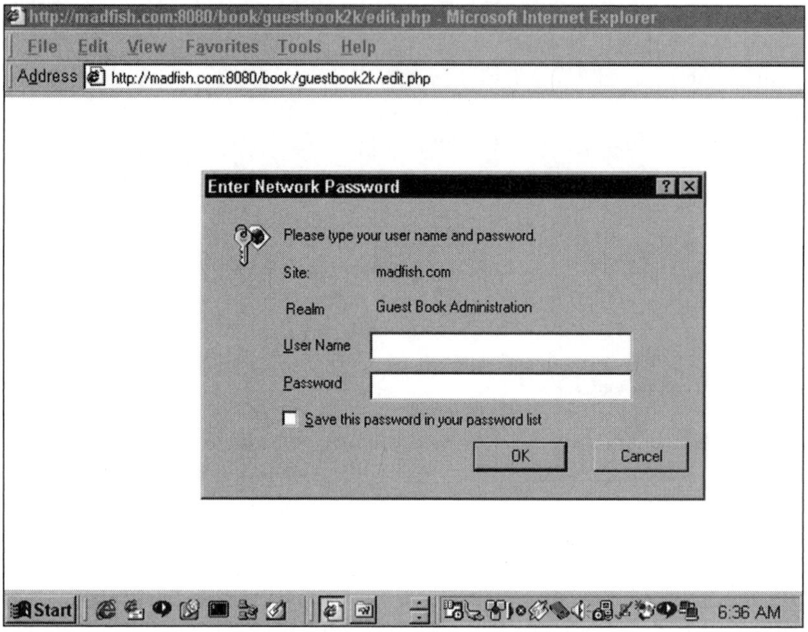

![Screenshot of Internet Explorer showing an "Enter Network Password" dialog box at http://madfish.com:8080/book/guestbook2k/edit.php. The dialog reads "Please type your user name and password." Site: madfish.com, Realm: Guest Book Administration, with User Name and Password fields, a "Save this password in your password list" checkbox, and OK/Cancel buttons. Taskbar shows Start button and 6:36 AM.]

Figure 8-9: Results of a 401 unauthorized header

TIP This type of authentication is available only if PHP is installed as an Apache module. If you are using PHP as a CGI, which is the only way to run it under Windows, this will not work. If you are doing some development work on Windows, go into the applications comment out the calls to authenticate() and create an include for win_authenticate.php file.

CLENUP_TEXT() This function goes a long way toward making sure we don't insert malicious text in our database.

```
function cleanup_text ($value = "", $preserve="", $allowed_tags="")
{
    if (empty($preserve))
    {
        $value = strip_tags($value, $allowed_tags);
    }
    $value = htmlspecialchars($value);
    return $value;
}
```

This function accomplishes two things. First, it removes all HTML tags. The `strip_tags()` function takes care of that. No need to worry about malicious Britney Spears pictures here — unless you want them. You can indicate tags you want to keep with the second argument ($allowed_tag). For instance if you wanted to allow bold and italic tags, the second argument to strip_tags() could be a string like this: "<b><i>".

Then html_specialchars() changes ampersands and double quotes to their proper HTML entities (& and "). After being run through this little function, your text is ready to be inserted in the database.

SAFE_QUERY()   This function will save you from pulling your hair out when you're trying to get your queries right.

```
function safe_query ($query = "")
{
        if (empty($query)) { return FALSE; }
        $result = mysql_query($query)
                or die("ack! query failed: "
                        ."<li>errorno=".mysql_errno()
                        ."<li>error=".mysql_error()
                        ."<li>query=".$query
                );
        return $result;
}
```

Throughout the application, you will run our queries through this function. This way, if the query fails for some reason, you will get a pretty good idea of what happened. This is another example of safe coding. After troubleshooting your code, you won't run into these problems often, but if a change is made somewhere (perhaps without your knowledge) you'll get a pretty good idea of what's going on.

TIP   For a site that is publicly available, there is a danger in running every query through this function. If a query fails, a hacker is likely to see more about your setup than you'd like. To prevent this from happening you could define a constant (discussed shortly) that prevents the function from printing out descriptive errors. Something like this:

```
function safe_query ($query = "")
{
    if (empty($query)) { return FALSE; }

    if(QUERY_DEBUG == "Off")
    {
        $result = mysql_query($query) or
```

```
                        die ("Query failed: please
                            conatact the Webmaster");
                }
                else
                {
                $result = mysql_query($query)
                        or die("ack! query failed: "
                                ."<li>errorno=".mysql_errno()
                                ."<li>error=".mysql_error()
                                ."<li>query=".$query
                            );
                }
                  return $result;
        }
```

FROM /GUESTBOOK2K/HEADER.PHP

Once again, this file will be included in every page in this application. It will keep
all of the functions specific to this application. In addition, there are a few details
that the first few lines of this application will see to. Notice the use of the variable
$DOCUMENT_ROOT. This is an Apache variable, accessible through PHP, which indi-
cates the default root folder. By making use of this variable, our entire application
becomes portable. If we move the entire book folder and all of its sub-folders, these
files will be found and accessed properly. Keep in mind that this is an Apache variable; your operating system and Web server may require a different variable. Check
phpinfo() to make sure.

```
include("$DOCUMENT_ROOT/book/functions/charset.php");
include("$DOCUMENT_ROOT/book/functions/basic.php");
$conn = mysql_connect("localhost", "username","password") or
    die("could not connect to database");
mysql_select_db("guestbook2k", $conn)
    die("could not select guestbook2k");
```

```
define("PAGE_LIMIT", 2);
```

The first line includes our default character set. The charset.php file contains just
one line:

```
header("Content-Type: text/html; charset=ISO-8859-1");
```

This function will help prevent people from sending you values encoded in a different character set. If they did send text in a different character set, the functions in `cleanup_text()` would fail, and you would still be open to some cross-site scripting hacks. This is a difficult problem. If you want more details check out these articles:

```
http://www.cert.org/tech_tips/malicious_code_mitigation.html
http://www.apache.org/info/css-security/encoding_examples.html
```

Here we've included something interesting: a constant, here named PAGE_LIMIT. A constant is like a variable in that it contains a value (in this instance, 2). However, that value cannot be changed by a simple assignment or by functions other than `define()`. Constants do not run into the same scope problems that are encountered with variables, so they can be used within functions without having to pass them is arguments or worry about declaring globals. After running the `define()` function, the constant PAGE_LIMIT will be available everywhere in my script.

PAGE_LIMIT decides the number of entries that will be viewable on each page. You are welcome to change this if you would like to see a larger number.

If you are putting together a query using a constant, you will have to end your quoted string in order to make use of the constant value. For example,

```
query = "select * from db_name limit PAGE_LIMIT"
```

will confuse MySQL, because PHP has not replaced the name of the constant with its value. However, this will work:

```
query = "select * from db_name limit " .  PAGE_LIMIT
```

PHP has many built-in constants you can use within your scripts. A list of constants is included in the PHP manual: http://www.php.net/manual/language.constants.php

PRINT_ENTRY()   This prints the results of a query within a table.

```
function print_entry($row,$preserve="")
{
    $numargs = func_num_args();
    for ($i = 2; $i < $numargs; $i++)
    {
        $field = func_get_arg($i);
        $dbfield = str_replace(" ", "_", strtolower($field));
```

```
        $dbvalue = cleanup_text($row[$dbfield],$preserve);
        $name = ucwords($field);
        print " <tr>\n";
        print "  <td valign=top align=right><b>$name:</b></td>\n";
        print "  <td valign=top align=left>$dbvalue</td>\n";
        print " </tr>\n\n";
    }
}
```

The easiest way to see how this function works is to take a look at the line of code that calls a function. This snippet was taken from the view.php file:

```
print_entry($row,$preserve,"name","location","email","URL","entry
date","comments");
```

Notice that the function itself has only two default arguments ($row and $preserve), while the call to the function has nine arguments. The first argument, $row, is a row from a database call. It is expecting that a row was taken from a query using mysql_fetch_array() so that the contents of row are an associative array, the keys of which are equal to the column names of the database table. The second argument, $preserve, is needed for the cleanup_text function, which we have discussed previously. The rest of the arguments are equivalent to associative keys in $row.

The arguments sent to any user-defined function make up an array. The number of the final element in the array can be retrieved with func_num_args(). Using the call to print_entry() seen above, the previous paragraph, func_num_args() would return 8. (There are 9 arguments, the first of which is 0.)

The value of each argument can then be accessed with func_get_arg(). This allows for a structure like the one used here, where a loop accesses and then processes each argument sent to the function. The first time through the for loop, $field is assigned the third element in the array, "name". You can use the value in $field to access an element in the associative array $row ($row["name"]).

After you make sure the argument contains no capital letters or spaces, the value is sent to the cleanup_text function and printed.

It's nice to structure a function this way because it allows an arbitrary number of arguments to be sent to the function. You could include one or many fields to print.

PRINT_INPUT_FIELDS()   This function works much like print_entry(). func_get_args() makes $field an array, each element of which is an argument sent to the function. The list structure moves through all elements in the array and prints a text field for each. The name of the field will be in one table cell, and the input box will be in an adjoining cell.

```
function print_input_fields()
{
```

```
    $fields =func_get_args();
    while (list($index,$field) = each($fields))
    {
        print " <tr>\n";
        print "  <td valign=top
align=right><b>".ucfirst($field).":</b></td>\n";
        print "  <td valign=top align=left><input type=text
name=$field size=40 value=\"".$GLOBALS["last_$field"]."\"></td>\n";
        print " </tr>\n\n";
    }
}
```

Notice the use of a global variable for the default value of the text field. This is here in the event that the user enters bad information and the information needs to be re-presented with the values he or she entered. Why would information need to be printed a second time? That should make perfect sense after you read about the next function, create_entry().

CREATE_ENTRY   We are not going to simply dump user information into the database. First it needs to be verified.

```
function create_entry($name,$location,$email,$url,$comments)
{
    // remove all HTML tags, and escape any
    //other special characters
    $name = cleanup_text($name);
    $location = cleanup_text($location);
    $email = cleanup_text($email);
    $url = cleanup_text($url);
    $comments = cleanup_text($comments);

    // start out with an empty
    //error message. as validation tests fail,
    // add errors to it.
    $errmsg = "";
    if (empty($name))
    {
        $errmsg .= "<li>you have to put in a name, at least!\n";
    }

    // do a very simple check on the format of the email address
    // supplied by the user. an email address is required.
    if (empty($email) || !eregi("^[A-Za-z0-9\_-]+@[A-Za-z0-9\_
-]+.[A-Za-z0-9\_-]+.*", $email))
    {
```

```
            $errmsg .= "<li>$email doesn't look like a valid email
address\n";
    }
    else
    {
    // if the format is OK, check to see if this user has already
    // signed the guestbook. multiple entries are not allowed.
        $query = "select * from guestbook where email = '$email'";
        $result = safe_query($query);
        if (mysql_num_rows($result) > 0)
        {
            $errmsg .=
            "<li>$email has already signed this guestbook.\n";
        }
    }

    // perform a very simple check on the format of the url supplied
    // by the user (if any)
    if (!empty($url) && !eregi("^http://[A-Za-z0-9\%\?\_\:\~\/\.
-]+$",$url))
    {
        $errmsg .= "<li>$url doesn't look like a valid URL\n";
    }

    if (empty($errmsg))
    {
        $query = "insert into guestbook "
        ." (name,location,email,url,comments,remote_addr) values "
        ."('$name', '$location', '$email', '$url',
'$comments','$REMOTE_ADDR')"
        ;
        safe_query($query);

        print "<h2>Thanks, $name!!</h2>\n";
    }
    else
    {
        print <<<EOQ
<p>
<font color=red>
<b>
<ul>
$errmsg
</ul>
Please try again
```

```
</p>
EOQ;
    }
    return $errmsg;
}
```

This function is going to make sure that the information entered is moderately useful. If there are problems with the information, a text string describing the problem will be assigned to the variable $errmsg. If, after the function is executed, $errmsg is empty, the values will be inserted into the database. Otherwise the error message will be printed, and the values the user entered will be assigned to globals so that they can be printed as the default values in the text fields the next time through.

In order, this function checks for the following:

◆ That the name field contains something

◆ That the e-mail address is potentially a proper address (contains text, an @, and a period (.)) Note that this is not very strong validation of e-mail. It takes a very long and complicated script to thoroughly validate an email, as you will see in later chapters.

◆ If the e-mail looks okay, that this e-mail address hasn't been entered in the database already

◆ That the URL is potentially valid

Check Appendix F for more detail on regular expressions.

SELECT_ENTRIES()   This function's sole purpose is to put together your database call.

```
function select_entries ($offset=0)
{
    if (empty($offset)) { $offset = 0; }

    $query = "select *
        , date_format(created,'%e %M, %Y %h:%i %p') as entry_date
        from guestbook
        order by created desc
        limit $offset, " . PAGE_LIMIT
        ;
    $result = safe_query($query);

    return $result;
```

You already know that PAGE_LIMIT sets the number of records displayed per page. As the second argument in the limit clause, the $offset variable indicates which records will be returned from the query. If you are having problems understanding $offset, take a look at the explanation of the limit clause in Chapter 3. A value for $offset will be passed through the navigational elements. We'll examine this in detail when we discuss the next function.

To retrieve the date value in a readable way, this query makes use of MySQL's date functions. MySQL stores the date and time as a 14-digit number (YYYY:MM:DD:HH:SS), but it's nicer to return the date information in a way that's easier for humans to read. The MySQL date_format function retrieves the information in the way we want to use it. This function and many other MySQL functions are discussed in Appendix I.

NAV()   This function's sole purpose is to create navigational elements.

```
function nav ($offset=0,$this_script="")
{

    global $PHP_SELF;

    if (empty($this_script)) { $this_script = $PHP_SELF; }
    if (empty($offset)) { $offset = 0; }

    // get the total number of entries in the guest book -
    // we need this to know if we can go forward from where we are
    $result = safe_query("select count(*) from guestbook");
    list($total_rows) = mysql_fetch_array($result);

    print "<p>\n";
    if ($offset > 0)
    {
        // if we're not on the first record, we can always go
        backwards
        print "<a href=\"$this_script?offset=".($offset-PAGE_
LIMIT)."\">&lt;&lt;Previous Entries</a>   ";
    }
    if ($offset+PAGE_LIMIT < $total_rows)
    {
        // offset + limit gives us the maximum record number
        // that we could have displayed on this page. if it's
        // less than the total number of entries, that means
        // there are more entries to see, and we can go forward
        print "<a
href=\"$this_script?offset=".($offset+PAGE_LIMIT)."\">Next
Entries&gt;&gt;</a>   ";
```

```
    }
    print "</p>\n";
}
```

When appropriate, this function will insert links that will enable the user to view the next set of entries, the previous entries, or both. It is all determined by the `$offset` variable and the PAGE_LIMIT constant.

The first time through there will be no value for $offset, and therefore there will be no previous entries link (because `$offset` will not be greater than 0). But if there are more rows to be displayed, a link will be created that creates a value for `$offset` to be accessed if that link is followed.

Say it's the first time we're executing this function, so $offset has no value, and there are 10 rows in the database. When it reaches the last if..., the script will see that there are more rows to be displayed ($offset + PAGE_LIMIT = 2, which is less than 10), and so the following link will be printed.

```
<a href="/book/guestbook2k/view.php?offset=2">
Next Entries&gt;&gt;</a>
```

Interesting code flow

Once you understand how the functions presented thus far work, you should have no problem figuring out how guestbook2k works. For the most part, very, very little work is done in the pages called by the browser. These pages are pretty much an assemblage of function calls.

We will break down one file in detail so you can get the feel of how this structure works. Most of the rest you should be able to figure out by flipping between the files and the explanations of the functions. In the following sections we will walk through the view.php file.

VIEWING ENTRIES

Here is the logical flow of the code.

```
<?php
include "header.php";

$page_title = "View My Guest Book!!";
include "start_page.php";
?>
```

The first thing you need to do in every page is include the header.php file. This will allow access to all of the functions we outlined previously. After that you should include standard header information from start_page.php. You have to declare $page_title prior to including start_page.php, so that the title can be printed in a standard way across every page.

```
<table border=0>

<?php

if (empty($offset)) { $offset = 0; }

$result = select_entries($offset);
$preserve = "";
while ($row = mysql_fetch_array($result))
{

    print_entry($row,$preserve,"name","location","email","URL","entry
    date","comments");
    print "<tr><td colspan=2> </td></tr>\n";
}
mysql_free_result($result);
?>

</table>
<?php
nav($offset);

include "end_page.php";
?>
```

This is it. You determine a value for $offset, run the query with the select_
entries() function, and then print the results by running the print_entry()
function within a while loop. Navigational elements are determined by the nav()
function.

DELETING ENTRIES

The most complex portion of this application involves deleting entries from the
guestbook. This stands to reason because you don't want your guestbook being
fooled by anonymous users. So the first thing you need to do before deleting
an entry is authenticate users. When discussing the authenticate() function, we
showed how an HTTP 401 header will bring up the browser's username and
password dialog box. The values entered then need to be checked against the
guestbook_admin database table. The authenticate.php file takes care of this for
you, which is why this file is included in the edit.php file.

The heart of authenticate.php is this:

```
if (empty($PHP_AUTH_USER))
{
    authenticate($realm,$errmsg,"header");
}
```

```
else
{
    $query = "select username from guestbook_admin where password =
password(lower('$PHP_AUTH_PW')) and username =
lower('$PHP_AUTH_USER')";
    $result = mysql_query($query);
    if ($result) { list($valid_user) = mysql_fetch_row($result); }
    if (!$result || empty($valid_user))
    {
        authenticate($realm,$errmsg,"query");
    }
}
print "<p><b>Editing as $PHP_AUTH_USER</b></p>\n";
```

If no username has been entered the header is sent through your `authenticate()` function. If the username does exist, a query is sent to the database to validate the user. If a row is returned, the user is validated and can continue working; otherwise the header is sent again.

Once a valid username and password have been entered, the remainder of the edit.php file will be sent. But this time, in addition to all the other information, the checkbox will be included, so the user can decide which entries should be deleted. The value of the checkbox will be the primary key of the guestbook table.

```
while ($row = mysql_fetch_array($result))
{
    print_entry($row,$preserve,"name","entry
date","location";"email","URL","comments");

    print " <tr>\n";
    print "  <td valign=top align=right><b>Delete?</b></td>\n";
    print "  <td valign=top align=left><input type=checkbox
name=\"entry_id[]\" value=\"".$row["entry_id"]."\"> Yes, delete
entry #".$row["entry_id"]."</td>\n";
    print " </tr>\n\n";

    print "<tr><td colspan=2> </td></tr>\n";
}
```

This form is then submitted to the confirm_delete.php file. Notice how you're passing an array here. The name of the form element is entry_id[], which means that when this form is passed to PHP, entry_id will become an array. The number of values in the array depends on the number of boxes checked. HTTP will not send the unchecked boxes at all.

The first time through the confirm_delete.php file, we will print out the entries. This will make the person deleting these entries make sure he or she isn't doing something stupid.

```
while (list($key,$value) = each($entry_id))
{
    print "<li>Delete entry #$value?\n";
    print "<input type=hidden name=\"entry_id[]\"
value=\"$value\">\n";
}
```

If any of these entries are to be deleted, this page will submit to itself, with a different value (Confirm Delete) sent with the submit button. This will make the following code run:

```
while (list($key,$value) = each($entry_id))
{
        print "<li>Deleting entry #$value\n";
        $q = "delete from guestbook where entry_id = $value";
        safe_query($q);
}
```

We loop through the $entry_id array, deleting records for each member.

Scripts

There are a few more scripts, but these don't warrant much discussion. sign.php, start_page.php, end_page.php, and confirm_delete.php, are included on the CD. We suggest you look at them and the comments to get a feel for how they fit into the application.

Summary

The skills you learned here may not get you the big bucks as a programmer, but there if you understand everything that is being done here, you should be in pretty good shape as you move forward in your PHP programming life.

In particular, you should see the priority that is put on creating reusable code. Nearly everything we have is in functions. This makes it much more likely that the code we write will be usable in some future application.

Additionally, you got to see some basic validation. Validation is an important concept and one you will need to take very seriously when your application allows for user input. If you'd like to see how seriously some people take validation, check out Manual Lemos' form validation class, which is included on the CD.

Chapter 9

Survey

IN THIS CHAPTER

♦ Learning functions for creating HTML tags

♦ Understanding data that use a relational structure

♦ Putting MySQL's date functions to work

IF A GUESTBOOK IS the most common application on the Web, a survey isn't far behind. Many sites have some sort of widget that lets you choose you favorite color or sports hero, or whatever, to see what percentage of voters take what stance. So let's go forth and create a survey.

In this application there will be a bit more complexity than you saw in Chapter 8. The programming will get a bit trickier, and the administration of the application will require more work. Unlike the guestbook, this application will require some knowledge of database theory. There are related tables, complete with the primary and foreign keys discussed in Section 1 of this book. This means that your SQL queries will include joins.

Determining the Scope and Goals of the Application

A survey application could be ultra-simple. If you wanted only to gather responses from a single question and return basic statistical information on the responses (how many votes for choice A, B, and so on), you wouldn't need a whole lot of code (or a chapter explaining it). A single table that stored answers would do the trick. The question could even be hard-coded into the HTML. But that would not make for very interesting learning experience, would it?

It gets more interesting if there can be any number of questions. Instead of just one, this application will allow for two, five, ten, or more – whatever you want. Not only that, this survey will record demographic information (such as age and country of origin) and allow for sorting on the basis of this information. We also decided to add the ability to pick a winner from those who filled out the personal information – this might encourage people to give real rather than fictitious answers.

There is one more wrinkle to discuss here. There is really no way to create a survey application that records perfect data. Even if you go to extreme lengths, there will always be an opportunity for the shrewd and persistent to submit multiple entries. But in all likelihood your survey will not have to pass muster with the Federal Elections Commission. A small step to weed out those ruining your survey should do the trick, and you will see one way to accomplish this later on.

Necessary Pages

Entering and viewing information will require three pages. The first is where the questions will be presented and where the user will enter name, address, and geographic and demographic information. A second page will show the basic survey results. A third will give a detailed breakdown. Figures 9-1, 9-2, and 9-3 show these pages respectively.

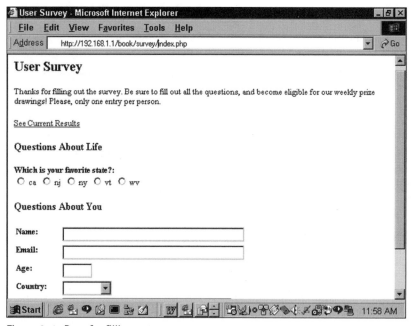

Figure 9-1: Page for filling out survey

Note that for this application you will use a .gif file for your chart. The script will change the size attributes of the gif in the <img> tag to give a representation of the information. This works, but isn't necessarily ideal. You could install the gd libraries and compile PHP with the -with-gd flag. These functions are beyond the scope of this book.

This application, like all others, needs some administrative tools. For starters, you will need to be able to add, delete, and edit questions. Additionally, there is a page that selects a winner at random from the database. Figures 9-4 and 9-5 show the administrative page and the select winner page, respectively.

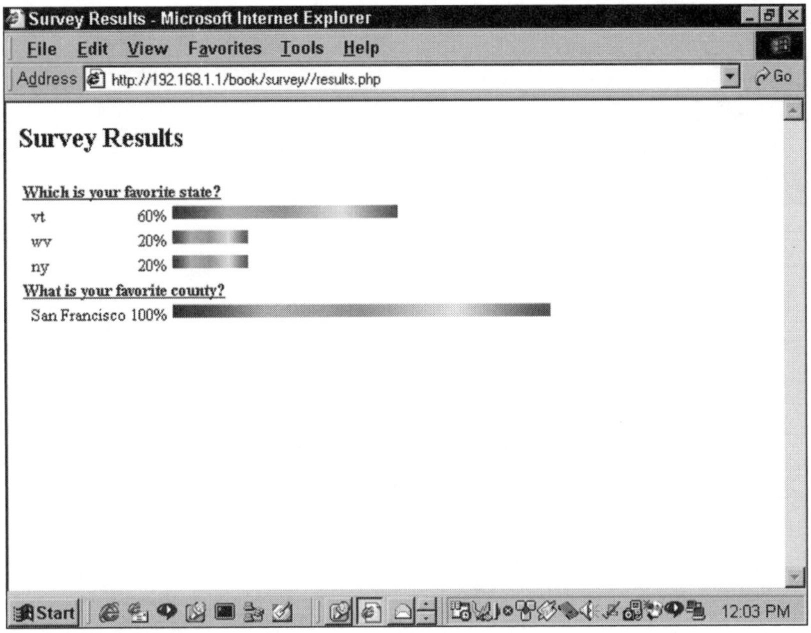

Figure 9-2: Basic survey results

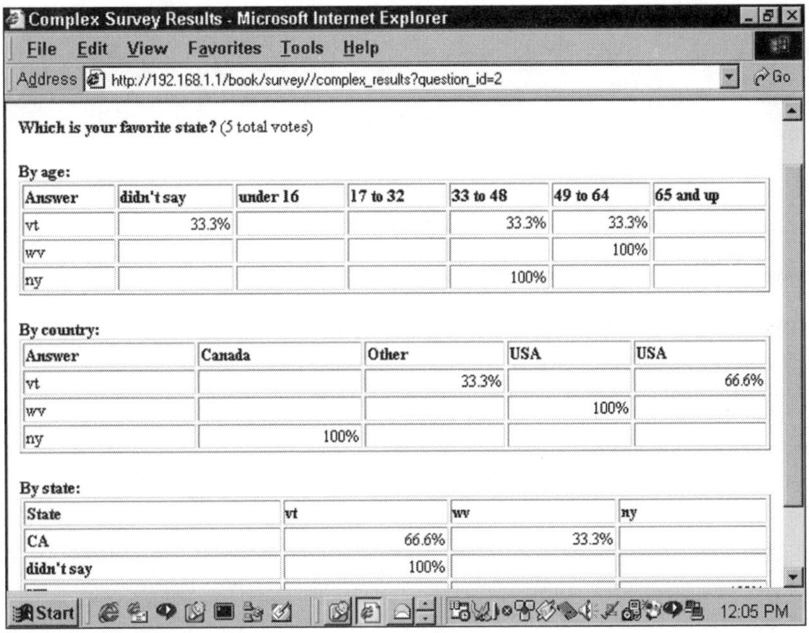

Figure 9-3: Detailed survey results

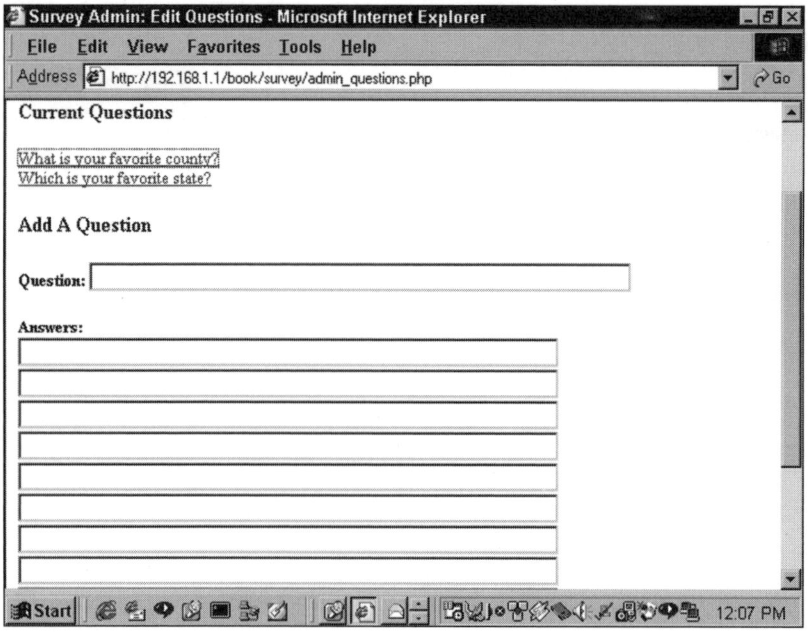

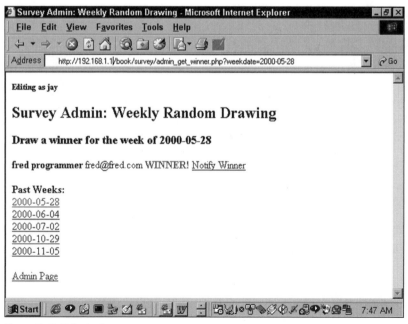

Figure 9-4: Survey administration page

Figure 9-5: Select winner page

Winners will be notified via e-mail and sent a URL that they will need to travel to in order to claim their prize. This page will look like the one in Figure 9-6. Once there they will need to confirm who they are, just so you have an extra level of security.

```
Claim Your Prize In Our Weekly Drawing - Microsoft Internet Explorer    _ 8 X
 File   Edit   View   Favorites   Tools   Help
Address  http://madfish.com:8080/book/survey/claim.php                  Go

Claim Your Prize In Our Weekly Drawing

Welcome! To claim your prize, please enter the email address where you received your notification message, and
then click on the button that says "I accept!"

Your Email Address: [                                          ]
 I accept!




Start                                                          12:13 PM
```

Figure 9-6: Claim prize page

What do we need to prevent?

In the previous chapter we discussed methods for removing junk information that people attempt to send through the form elements. We will continue to use these functions here. This application will also do some e-mail address validation.

Want to see what it really takes to verify that an email is in the proper format? It takes a lot of work. Take a look at the CheckEmail.php file in /functions directory on the CD. You can see that it takes multiple regular expressions to make sure the e-mail is just right. Given that regular expressions are fairly slow, you may be wondering if it is even worth running a script like that, especially if you are running a site with very heavy traffic. You will need to decide that for yourself. Do you need to make sure e-mails are perfect, or will a simpler, less-robust form of validation be good enough? Even if you make sure the address is in the proper format, there's almost no way to know if the address is attached to an actual mailbox.

This application will provide you with a simple means for blocking some people from entering information at your site. It's nothing terribly sophisticated; a savvy Internet user would be able to work around it in a minute. Using the form shown in Figure 9-6 you will be able to enter a domain of origin that will be blocked from the site. All users who enter data will have their REMOTE_HOST variable checked against a table in the database. If that host is found, the application will refuse that user access. Again, this isn't perfect. Depending on the ISP used, some clients won't even identify the REMOTE_HOST in the HTTP header. If you really have sensitive information and need effective means of blocking users, you should work with some sort of login scheme. This is just an example of what you could do with a database and HTTP header information.

You'll also need to take some steps to make sure that the wrong people won't be claiming prizes. You'll need to make sure that the people coming to claim prizes are who they say they are.

Designing the Database

This survey application allows for any number of questions. Each question can have any number of answers. To create this relationship you'll need two tables, one named questions and one named responses, that have a one-to-many relationship. (Each (1) question can have (n) any number of answers.)

User information is best represented with multiple tables as well. A table named users will store the relevant user information. Two tables, named states and countries, serve as lookup tables and have one-to-many relationships with the users table.

Finally, there are two tables with relationships to no others. They store other information this application needs to track. They are aptly named blocked_domains and survey_admin.

Figure 9-7 shows a visual representation of the structure of the database. The create statements for making these tables are shown in Listing 9-1. Note that these table definitions were copied from the mysqldump utility. If you're not aware of mysqldump, or the other mysql utilities, make sure to check up on Appendix C.

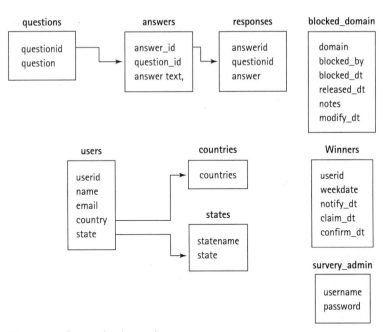

Figure 9-7: Survey database schema

Listing 9-1: Create Statements for Survey

```
# Table structure for table 'age_ranges'
#

CREATE TABLE age_ranges (
   min_age int(11) NOT NULL,
   max_age int(11) NOT NULL,
   age_range varchar(10)
);


# ---------------------------------------------------------
#
# Table structure for table 'answers'
#

CREATE TABLE answers (
   answer_id int(11) NOT NULL auto_increment,
   question_id int(11),
   answer text,
   PRIMARY KEY (answer_id)
);
```

```
# --------------------------------------------------------
#
# Table structure for table 'blocked_domains'
#

CREATE TABLE blocked_domains (
    domain varchar(30) NOT NULL,
    block_by varchar(10) NOT NULL,
    block_dt datetime DEFAULT '0000-00-00 00:00:00' NOT NULL,
    release_dt datetime,
    notes text,
    modify_dt timestamp(14)
);



# --------------------------------------------------------
#
# Table structure for table 'countries'
#

CREATE TABLE countries (
    country varchar(30) NOT NULL
);



# --------------------------------------------------------
#
# Table structure for table 'questions'
#

CREATE TABLE questions (
    question_id int(11) NOT NULL auto_increment,
    question text NOT NULL,
    KEY question_key (question_id)
);



# --------------------------------------------------------
#
# Table structure for table 'responses'
#

CREATE TABLE responses (
    user_id int(11) NOT NULL,
    answer_id int(11) NOT NULL
);
```

```
# -------------------------------------------------------
#
# Table structure for table 'states'
#

CREATE TABLE states (
   statename varchar(30) NOT NULL,
   state char(2) NOT NULL
);


# -------------------------------------------------------
#
# Table structure for table 'survey_admin'
#

CREATE TABLE survey_admin (
   username varchar(50) NOT NULL,
   password varchar(255) NOT NULL
);


# -------------------------------------------------------
#
# Table structure for table 'users'
#

CREATE TABLE users (
   user_id int(11) NOT NULL auto_increment,
   name varchar(50),
   email varchar(50),
   country varchar(20),
   state char(2),
   age int(11),
   remote_addr varchar(15),
   remote_host varchar(80),
   create_dt timestamp(14),
   KEY user_key (user_id)
);


# -------------------------------------------------------
#
# Table structure for table 'winners'
#
```

```
CREATE TABLE winners (
    user_id int(11) NOT NULL,
    weekdate datetime DEFAULT '0000-00-00 00:00:00' NOT NULL,
    notify_dt datetime,
    claim_dt datetime,
    confirm_dt datetime
);
```

Code Overview

If you already read the section by the same name in Chapter 8, the structure we use here should be familiar to you. Items in the /functions folder are included and ready for reuse.

It's obvious that this survey application requires several more pages than the guest-book: there's more that needs to be done. Though you can include several actions in a single page, and sort through the ones you need by passing variables and using if state-ments, it can make code difficult to keep track of. Better to have several intuitively named files that perform specific tasks. That said, there are pages in this application that make use of variables in order to decide what action to take on a given page.

If you've done any Web work at all you know how tedious it can be to deal with HTML tables and forms. For that reason, in this and most of the other applications in this book, we will try to ease the pain involved in dealing with tables and forms. In the following sections you will see several functions that will make life, in the long run at least, a lot easier. The functions in the coming sections will make a lot more sense if you see what they accomplish first. Here's some code that will work just fine if used with the following functions.

```
print start_table();
print table_row(
    table_cell("Cell text")
);
print end_table();
```

 If you don't like the functions we've created for tables, forms, and other HTML elements, don't use them. It is perfectly acceptable (and perhaps even more common) to type out HTML elements, rather than create them through func-tions. Like many things in programming, it comes down to a matter of prefer-ence. In a case like this there's no right answer: Do what you prefer.

This will create a table with one cell. You could build on the complexity of this by adding additional table_cell() calls within the table_row function call. You can do this because of PHP's ability to deal with a variable number of arguments. You can design the table_row function to loop through all of the arguments (some of which are calls to the table_cell() function). You may be wondering how these functions deal with table attributes, like width, align, and others. How could you alter those for particular tables? These attributes and their values must be included in the function call, so the attributes must be another argument in the function call. The function will identify the attributes by variable type. That is, the function will check the variable type of the argument, and if it is an array (an associative array), the function will assume it contains attribute information, and will turn the key/value pairs from the array into name=value attribute pairs in a string. A more complex function call would look like this:

```
print (table_row (array("bgcolor" => $bgcolor),
        table_cell("New entry"),
        table_cell(text_field("entered_by", "", "10")),
        table_cell(submit_field("submit", "insert"))
        )
    );
```

Here the first argument, (array ("bgcolor"=> $bgcolor)), identifies the row's background color; the remaining arguments create table cells. As an added bonus, these table cells contain form elements.

Keep in mind that the methods for achieving nested function calls will be explained later. The application will also be using more of MySQL. Throughout this application, there is more extensive use of MySQL functions than seen in Chapter 8.

Code Breakdown

As with the guestbook application, the code here is divided for convenience. The functions used exclusively by this application are in the /book/survery/header.php file. This will be included in every file. The start_page.php and end_page.php will contain header and footer information, respectively.

Since we covered the functions sitting in the /book/functions/functions.php file in Chapter 8, we're not going to go over it again here. But we did add a little bonus this time around.

Reusable functions

As your applications get more complex, you're going to need to continually use some HTML ingredients – forms, tables, paragraph tags, anchors, and the like. For this reason we've added a series of functions that make it easier to create those repetitive HTML elements. We've also moved some of the commonly used database functions into their own file.

FUNCTIONS FROM /BOOK/FUNCTIONS/DB.PHP

Some of this will look familiar if you've gone through the guestbook application in Chapter 8. But know that for the rest of the applications, you can find these functions in this file. We're not going to cover every function, just those that require some explanation.

SET_RESULT_VARIABLE()   This function turns results of a query into global variables.

```
function set_result_variables ($result)
{
    if (!$result || !mysql_num_rows($result)) { return; }
    $row = mysql_fetch_array($result,MYSQL_ASSOC);
    if (!is_array($row))
    {
    print $query."<li>no array returned : result=$result row=$row";
        return $result;
    }
    while (list($key,$value) = each($row))
    {
        global $$key;
        $$key = $value;
    }
}
```

If you remember our discussion about variable scope in Chapter 7, you'll remember that variables passed through either GET or POST or declared outside of a function are globals, and they are available within the GLOBAL's array.

Frequently, you are going to want to use the column names used in your query as variables. It's nice to be able to use them without having to go through the associative array returned by `mysql_fetch_array()`. This function will turn the variables used in a query into globals throughout your script.

```
$query = "select distinct fname, lname from table_1 where id=1";
$result=safe_query($query);
set_result_variables($result);
```

So this code will make the variables $fname and $lname, along with their values, available as globals. If a result set with multiple rows is sent to the query, only the first row is used by this function.

Note the use of variable variables in this function.

```
while (list($key,$value) = each($row))
{
    global $$key;
```

```
    $$key = $value;
}
```

Each element is taken from the array retrieved from mysql_fetch_array(). The key (the column name) is declared as a global variable. Then that global is assigned the contents of $value. Variable variables are discussed in Chapter 7.

This function is intended to work with the fetch_record() function documented next.

FETCH_RECORD()   This function helps create simple queries.

```
function fetch_record ($table, $key="", $value="")
{
    $query = "select * from $table ";
    if (!empty($key) && !empty($value))
    {
        if (is_array($key) && is_array($value))
        {
            $query .= " where ";
            $and = "";
            while (list($i,$v) = each($key))
            {
                $query .= "$and $v = ".$value[$i];
                $and = " and";
            }
        }
        else
        {
            $query .= " where $key = $value ";
        }
    }
    $result = safe_query($query);
    if (!empty($key) && !empty($value) &&
mysql_num_rows($result) == 1)
    {
        set_result_variables($result);
    }
    return $result;
}
```

It won't be of much use if you need to use MySQL's functions or if you need to use fancy predicates (LIKE, GROUP BY HAVING). It doesn't take a list of columns to be selected from the database, but it can take multiple parameters and values in the where clause.

First, check whether one value or multiple values have been sent in the $key and $value variables. If scalar variables are sent, only one item will be added to the where clause. If arrays are sent, they will be looped through and added to the where clause.

If there is only one row returned by the query, it calls the set_result_variables() function to set the columns and their values as global variables. In all cases, the function then returns the entire result identifier from the query.

DB_VALUES_ARRAY()   This function is extremely useful for creating drop-down boxes and other form elements from a database table.

```
function db_values_array ($table="", $value_field="",
$label_field=""
    , $sort_field=""
    , $where=""
)
{
    $values = array();

    if (empty($table) || empty($value_field)) { return $values; }

    if (empty($label_field)) { $label_field = $value_field; }
    if (empty($sort_field)) { $sort_field = $label_field; }
    if (empty($where)) { $where = "1=1"; }

    $query = "select $value_field as value_field
        , $label_field as label_field
        from $table
        where $where
        order by $sort_field
    ";
    $result = safe_query($query);
    if ($result)
    {
        while (list($value,$label) = mysql_fetch_array($result))
        {
            $values[$value] = $label;
        }
    }
    return $values;
}
```

In this application, and many others that you'll come across, there will be tables in your database that will serve as "look up" tables. These are tables whose sole purpose is to ensure that good information ends up as other tables. Take a look at the diagram in Figure 9-6, and you will see that the countries and states tables serve this purpose.

A query is carefully crafted. Aliases are set (using "as") so that the column names will match the attributes you wish to have in the forms. An associative array is then created; the $value will serve as the key in this associative array and will probably become the value attribute in the HTML form.

FUNCTIONS FROM /BOOK/FUNCTIONS/HTML.PHP

These functions make it easier to create common HTML tags. Most of the functions in this file are very similar. But before we get to these, you will need to understand the get_attlist() function, which has been added to the basic.php file.

GET_ATTLIST()   This function takes an associative array and creates name="value" pairs suitable for HTML tags.

```
function get_attlist ($atts="",$defaults="")
{
    $localatts = array();
    $attlist = "";

    if (is_array($defaults)) { $localatts = $defaults; }
    if (is_array($atts)) { $localatts = array_merge($localatts,
$atts); }

    while (list($name,$value) = each($localatts))
    {
        if ($value == "") { $attlist .= "$name "; }
        else { $attlist .= "$name=\"$value\" "; }
    }
    return $attlist;
}
```

No matter the base tag, all HTML tags take attributes in the form name="value". This function will build an attribute list for any tag. The function will be called by other functions that write out individual HTML tags. As you can see, this function takes two arguments. The second is an array with a set of attributes required by a specific tag. For instance, an <img> tag isn't much good without an src attribute. So if the function is called from another function that creates images, the second argument should be an array with one element, something like $myarray = array("src" =>"myimage.gif").

The first argument will take another array containing other attributes. For the <img> tag, that first array might contain alt text, width, and height — $myarray = array("alt" =>"My Image", "width"=>"20", "height"=>"25".

If appropriate, these two arrays will be merged into one. Then, from this merged array, a string is created that has the "name"= value pairs. If a value is empty, the name will exist without a value.

Note that elements passed in the second array will overwrite those in the first, enabling you to overcome default values easily. This occurs because in the array_ merge() function, if there are two elements with the same associative key, the last one will overwrite the previous one. This allows other functions that create HTML tags to keep a set of defaults in the first argument and values for the specific call in the second.

Take a look at the following functions to get a better idea of how this works.

ANCHOR_TAG()   This function creates an anchor tag.

```
function anchor_tag($href="",$text="",$atts="")
{
    $attlist = get_attlist($atts,array("href"=>$href));
    $output = "<a $attlist>$text</a>";
    return $output;
}
```

For an anchor tag, there are only two things you could really expect every time: an href attribute and some text to go between the opening enclosing <a> tags. However, it is possible that a name attribute might be helpful. But more often than not, the call to this function will be something like this:

```
anchor_tag("myurl.com/index.html", "this is a great link");
```

Note that if there were a third argument, it would have to be in the form of an array. These arguments are then sent to the get_attlist() function and turned into a usable string, which is put together in the $output variable.

IMAGE_TAG()   This creates an <img> tag

```
function image_tag($src="",$atts="")
{
    $attlist = get_attlist($atts,array("src"=>$src));
    $output = "<img $attlist>";
    return $output;
}
```

This function works just like the anchor_tag() function described above.

PARAGRAPH()   This function will print out opening and closing <p> tags and everything between them.

```
function paragraph ($atts="")
{
    $output = "<p";
    $i = 0;
    $attlist = get_attlist($atts);
    if ($attlist > "")
    {
        $output .= " $attlist";
        $i++;
    }
    $output .= ">\n";
    $args = func_num_args();
    while ($i < $args)
    {
        $x = func_get_arg($i);
        $output .= $x."\n";
        $i++;
    }
    $output .= "</p>\n";
    return $output;
}
```

The first thing to understand about this function is that it will print not only the opening <p> tag along with its attributes, it will also print the closing </p> tag and everything that could occur between the two. This could include anchor tags, image tags, or just about anything else. The following function call would work just fine, and in fact is used within the survey application:

```
print paragraph(anchor_tag("admin_block.php",
                "Return to Domain List"));
```

There is one argument in this function call, which is another function call with two arguments. In effect, when one function call is nested inside another, PHP executes the internal one first. So first the anchor_tag() function is called and creates a string like <a href="admin_block.php">. Then the outer function is executed, so the call to the paragraph function will actually be something like this:

```
print paragraph("<a href=\"admin_block.php\">Return to Domain List</a>");
```

Note how flexible this becomes. By looping through the number of arguments, you can send any number of additional function calls to the paragraph function. And you can happily mix text and function calls together. In the while... loop, $x can be set to a text string or the output of the function call. So the following is a perfectly fine call to the paragraph function:

```
print paragraph(
    "<b>Blocked by:</b> $block_by <br>"
```

```
    , "<b>Date blocked:</b> $block_dt <br>"
    , "<b>Date released:</b> $release_dt <br>"
    , "<b>Last Modified:</b> $modify_dt <br>"
    , hidden_field("old_domain",$domain)
);
```

UL_LIST()   This function turns an array or a string into an unordered HTML list.

```
function ul_list ($values="")
{
    $output .= "<ul>\n";
    if (is_array($values))
    {
        while (list(,$value) = each($values))
        {
            $output .= " <li>$value</li>\n";
        }
    }
    else
    {
        $output .= " <li>$values</li>\n";
    }
    $output .= "</ul>\n";
    return $output;
}
```

With this function you can create a bulleted list. Most frequently, an array will be passed to the function, each member of which will be prepended with a <li> tag. The function also prepends a string with <li> if the contents of $values is a string.

FUNCTIONS FROM /BOOK/FUNCTIONS/FORMS.PHP
Most of these functions are fairly straightforward and don't require any explanation. We will show a couple just for examples.

TEXT_FIELD()   This prints out an HTML text field.

```
function text_field ($name="", $value="", $size=10, $maxlen="")
{
    $output = <<<EOQ
<input type=text name="$name" value="$value" size="$size"
maxlength="$maxlen">
EOQ;
    return $output;
}
```

All the expected attributes should be passed to the function. Most of the other functions look similar to this one, the only real exceptions being the checkbox and radio button.

CHECKBOX_FIELD()   This function creates an HTML checkbox.

```
function checkbox_field ($name="", $value="", $label="", $match="")
{
    $checked = ($value == $match || $label == $match) ? "checked" :
"";
    $output = <<<EOQ
<nobr><input type=checkbox name="$name" value="$value" $checked>
$label</nobr>
EOQ;
    return $output;
}
```

The only thing that may be of interest in this function is how you should note in your function call if a checkbox is to be checked by default. You do this by adding an argument called $match. If $match equals either $label or $value it will be checked by default. The radio_field function works in the same way.

FUNCTIONS FROM /BOOK/FUNCTIONS/TABLES.PHP
Until style sheets are a reliable means for positioning pieces of a Web page, it is likely that you'll be using tables extensively. These functions make creating tables easier.

START_TABLE()   This function creates an opening <table> tag.

```
function start_table ($atts="")
{
    $attlist = get_attlist($atts);
    $output = <<<EOQ
<p>
<table $attlist>
EOQ;
    return $output;
}
```

Again, this function calls the get_attlist() function to add attributes to the opening table tag. Add an array of attributes to the function call to have attributes added to the resulting tag.

END_TABLE()   This function creates the closing </table> tag.

```
function end_table ()
{
    $output = <<<EOQ
</table>
</p>
EOQ;
    return $output;
}
```

This function does pretty much what you would expect. It is not really necessary, but it supplies nice symmetry with the start_table() function.

TABLE_ROW()   This function not only prints out the opening `<tr>` tag and its attributes; it also prints the table cells that will be nested within the `<tr>` tags.

```
function table_row ()
{
    $attlist = "";
    $cellstring = "";

    $cells = func_get_args();
    while (list(,$cell) = each($cells))
    {
        if (is_array($cell))
        {
            $attlist .= get_attlist($cell);
        }
        else
        {
            if (!eregi("<td",$cell))
            {
                $cell = table_cell($cell);
            }
            $cellstring .= "  ".trim($cell)."\n";
        }
    }
    $output = <<<EOQ
<tr $attlist>
$cellstring
</tr>
EOQ;
    return $output;
}
```

This function works by taking nested function calls.

```
print table_row(
    table_cell("hello world", array("align"=>"right"))
);
```

The `table_row()` call in the preceding code has one argument, which is itself another function call. Since all the arguments sent to a function can be extracted using the `func_get_args()` command, you can set an array that contains all of the arguments. In the preceding code, that array is $cells.

Remember when we said earlier that inner function calls are executed prior to outer ones? In the preceding example the `table_cell` call is executed first. Thus, the call to table row will actually be something like:

```
print table_row("<td align="right">hello world</td>")
```

So when this function call becomes the active argument, the regular expression will test false and the `table_cell` function will not be called. This makes sense: Since you already have a table cell string, there is no need to call the `table_cell` function.

You may be wondering why the function contains that regular expression and the `table_cell()` function call. That's for a case like the function call in the following code, where table cell isn't called explicitly.

```
print table_row("Cell text");
```

FUNCTIONS AND CODE FROM /BOOK/SURVEY/HEADER.PHP
This file is included in every file in the survey application, so every one of these functions will be available.

START OF PAGE   Before we get to the functions in this file, there is some code that does a bit of housekeeping.

```
if (!defined("LOADED_HEADER"))
{
    include "../functions/charset.php";
    include "../functions/basic.php";
    dbconnect("survey");
    include "functions.php";
    define("LOADED_HEADER", "yes");
}


$result = safe_query("select 1 from blocked_domains
    where '$REMOTE_HOST' like concat('%',domain)
    and release_dt is null
");
```

```
if (mysql_result($result,0) > 0)
{
    print "<h2>sorry - your domain has been blocked from this
page</h2>\n";
    exit;
}
```

This preceding code contains information you're going to need before working with the heart of the application. The includes are clear enough. The includes have been put inside an if statement as a precaution. There is no need to reload the header once it has been loaded once. We can make sure that doesn't happen by creating a constant named LOADED_HEADER. If by chance, this page were loaded a second time, you wouldn't have to worry that includes would be imported more than once.

Remember that PHP 4 has the include_once construct, which will ensure that no files are included multiple time.

As we mentioned earlier, there is a facility here to block domains, and this application will be doing that off the $REMOTE_HOST variable. This is hardly necessary, and it is easy enough to comment out this code. In order to understand this code, look more closely at the query, particularly the like predicate. When we dial in to the net from my ISP (att.net), my REMOTE_HOST is something like this: 119.san-francisco-18-19rs.ca.dial-access.att.net. When you block domains, you'll be doing it on the top-level domain — in this case, att.net. And this top-level domain is what will reside in the database. So the query will have checked on any number of wildcard characters prior to the top-level domain name.

To achieve this you will need to concatenate the domain names with the % wild-card character. So, for instance, the query will work against %att.net. This may seem somewhat different from your typical like predicate. It's another powerful technique to use with your SQL.

Also note that the start of the select statement doesn't contain a select count(*), instead opting for select 1. This is a good way of testing if any rows meet the condition of the where clause. If the where clause matches any number of rows, the query will return a single column with the value of 1, which in the programming world means TRUE. If there are no rows returned you know the where portion of the query had no matches.

WEEKSTART() This function creates a MySQL function to grab the day that starts the week. You use this in the application to pick a winner for the current week.

```
function weekstart ($when="")
{
    if (empty($when)) { $when = "now()"; }
    elseif ($when != "create_dt") { $when = "'$when'"; }
    return "from_days(to_days($when)-dayofweek($when) + 1)";
}
```

It works like this: the MySQL to_days() function returns an integer of the number of days since January 1, 0000. dayofweek() returns an integer representing the day of the week (Sunday equals 1, Saturday equals 7). So the portion (to_days($now)-dayofweek($when) + 1) will return an integer representing the Sunday of the week in question. The from_days() function then turns that number into a date. Here is the result of this query run on Thursday July 27, 2000 (the day this chapter was written):

```
mysql> select from_days(to_days(now())-dayofweek(now()) + 1);
+------------------------------------------------+
| from_days(to_days(now())-dayofweek(now()) + 1) |
+------------------------------------------------+
| 2000-07-23                                     |
+------------------------------------------------+
1 row in set (0.00 sec)
```

Note that the value passed here can be a string representing a date, it can be empty, or it can be a field from the users table — namely the create_dt field.

COUNTRYLIST() This function creates a drop-down list of country names.

```
function country_list ()
{
    $countries[""] = "";
    $countries = array_merge($countries
        ,db_values_array("countries","country")
    );
    return $countries;
}
```

Uses the db_values_array() function (discussed earlier in this chapter, in the section "Reusable functions") to get an array of countries and their abbreviations.

STATE_LIST() This creates a drop-down list of state names.

```
function state_list ()
{
    $states[""] = "";
```

```
    $states = array_merge($states
        ,db_values_array("states","state","statename","state")
    );
    return $states;
}
```

Uses the `db_values_array()` function (discussed earlier in this chapter, in the section "Reusable functions") to get an array of countries and their abbreviations.

FETCH_QUESTION()   This function grabs the contents of a row in the questions table and assigns the columns to global variables.

```
function fetch_question ($question_id="")
{
    if (empty($question_id)) { $question_id = 0; }
    $result = fetch_record("questions","question_id",$question_id);
    return $result;
}
```

This will run the `fetch_record()` function and return from the database all the information regarding a particular question, based on the questionid.

FETCH_USER()   This function grabs the contents of a row in the users table and assigns the columns to global variables.

```
function fetch_user ($user_id="")
{
    if (empty($user_id)) { $user_id = 0; }
    $result = fetch_record("users","user_id",$user_id);
    return $result;
}
```

Returns the result set based on a `user_id`.

Interesting Code Flow

There are a few pages in this application that could stand some explanation. However, you should be able to follow most of them if you understand the functions in the previous section.

admin_question.php

This is a fairly lengthy page, and for good reason: it is used for adding, editing, and deleting questions in the database. The portion of the page that will be run will be determined by the values passed by forms or links. The first time through there will be no variables passed, so a list of the current questions will be presented along with a form for entering a new question. Each of the links to questions that already exist in the database look like this:

```
<a href="admin_questions.php?what=edit&question_id=2" >
```

When a link like this is clicked, and the admin_questions.php script is run again, the very bottom of the script will run, as shown here:

```
else
{
    $qform_title = "Edit A Question : $question_id";
    fetch_question($question_id);
}

print subtitle($qform_title);

print start_form("admin_questions.php");

print paragraph("<b>Question:</b>",
text_field("question",$question,60));
```

Notice how you can get all the information associated with $question_id with one function call (fetch_question()). Because of the way the functions have been created, this automatically gives you a global variable for $question.

Next, go into this loop:

```
$acount = 0;
if ($question_id > 0)
{
    $result = safe_query("select answer_id, answer
        from answers
        where question_id=$question_id
        order by answer_id
    ");
    while (list($aid,$atxt) = mysql_fetch_array($result))
    {
        $acount++;
        print text_field("answer_text[$acount]","$atxt",60);
        print hidden_field("answer_id[$acount]","$aid");
        print " ($aid)<br>\n";
    }
}
```

The number 10 here limits the number of answers to each question to 10. This block gets the answers for the selected question and prints them out inside text fields. Additional information is put inside hidden fields. When printed out the result for one answer will look like this:

```
<input type="text" name="answer_text[1]" value="Answer"
size="60" >
<input type="hidden" name="answer_id[1]" value="10">
```

When this form is submitted, $answer_text will be an array. $acount will see that the key of the array is incremented by 1 for each additional form field. Note that we need to make use of a hidden form element here. That is because each answer requires three pieces of information: what the answer number is (1-10), the answer text, and if the answer came from the database, we need to know the primary key of the row the answer came from. The hidden field will create an array named $answer_id. The value in each element of that array will be the primary key of the row storing the answer. The index of that array will be the match with the index of $answer_text. So in code it looks like this,

```
$i = 1;
$answer_text[$i];
$answer_id[$i];
```

You'd know that $answer_id[$i] contains the primary key of a row, and $answer_text[$i] is the answer text that belongs in that row.

The previous section of code will print out form elements only where there is an answer. But you should offer blank form elements so the administrator can enter new answers.

```
while ($acount < 10)
{
    $acount++;
    print text_field("answer_text[$acount]","",60);
    print hidden_field("answer_id[$acount]",0);
    print "<br>\n";
}
```

This will complete the form, giving all the blank elements you need. For these blank answers, the form will contain the following:

```
<input type="text" name="answer_text[8]" value="" size="60" >
<input type="hidden" name="answer_id[8]" value="0"><br>
```

In these form elements, the value of the hidden field is set to 0. That way, when it comes time to process these form elements, the script will have something to evaluate: if $answer_id[$i] is equal to zero or empty ($answer_id[$i]), this is a new element.

When the form is submitted this chunk of code will run.

There will always be 10 elements to be looped through, so a for loop works nicely.

```
for ($i = 1; $i <= 10; $i++)
{
    if (!empty($answer_text[$i]))
```

First we make sure there is available answer text.

```
    {
        $answer = cleanup_text($answer_text[$i]);
        if (empty($answer_id[$i]))
        {
            $query = "insert into answers
                (question_id, answer)
                values
                ($question_id, '$answer')
                ";
        }
```

If the element of $answer_id is not empty (which means it can't be equal to zero) an insert statement is run.

```
        else
        {
            $query = "update answers
                set question_id = $question_id
                , answer = '$answer'
                where answer_id = ".$answer_id[$i]
                ;
        }
        safe_query($query);
    }
}
```

Otherwise, if there was an existing answer, an update query will do the trick.

admin_get_winner.php

Most of this file is readable. Your goal is to draw a qualified winner at random from the database. First you use the `weekstart` function (discussed earlier in this chapter in the section "Functions and code from /book/survey/header.php") to get the date that the current week begins.

```
$qweekdt = weekstart($weekdate);
list($thisweek) = mysql_fetch_array(safe_query("select $qweekdt"));
print subtitle("Draw a winner for the week of $thisweek");
```

You then create a query that will determine who is qualified. As you can see, we've decided that in addition to signing in the last week, they need to have entered a name and an e-mail address, and a legitimate age.

```
$query = "select name, email, user_id from users
        where week(create_dt) = week('$thisweek')
                and year(create_dt) = year('$thisweek')
                and name is not null and name != ''
                and email is not null and email != '' and email like
                  '%@%.%'
                and age > 0
                and country is not null and country != ''
";
$result = safe_query($query);
$tot = mysql_num_rows($result);
```

With the total number of qualified entrants in hand, the script makes a couple of decisions to determine a winner. First it needs to account for occasions when there are no possible winners.

```
if($tot ==0)
{
    echo "There were no entrants this week";
}
```

We already ran a select query that has the potential winners. The first row in the result set is row number zero. So if there's only one possible winner, row 0 is the only row returned.

```
    else
    {
        if ($tot == 1)
        {
                // if there's only one entry, they win.
```

```
        $winner = 0;
}
```

However, if more than one possibility exists, the random number generator is seeded, and a row number is pulled. Note that the total number of rows will be one greater than the final row number (because the first row is numbered 0). This is why the top range of the random number must by $tot-1.

```
else
{
    mt_srand((double)microtime()*1000000);
    $winner = mt_rand(0,$tot-1);
}


mysql_data_seek($result, $winner);
list($name, $email, $user_id) = mysql_fetch_array($result);
$urlthisweek = rawurlencode($thisweek)
print paragraph(
    "<b>$name</b> $email "
    , "<b><font color=red>WINNER!</font></b> "
    ,anchor_tag("admin_winners.php?weekdate=$urlthisweek"
      ."&what=notify&user_id=$user_id"
      , "Notify Winner"
    )
);
```

This last chunk of code gets the information needed about the winner and provides a link to the admin_winners.php page that contains the correct user_id, the week associated with this prize, and the variable $what, which will identify which portion of the admin_winners.php page we want to run.

There's more to this file, but you should be able to follow the comments included with the code.

admin_winners.php

We created a few pages to ensure that the winner selected is notified of the exciting news and that we give the notification in a way that gives some security. This isn't much, but to make reasonably sure that the person who claimed the prize was the person you intended, you would need to make use of a login system, and users of a silly little survey may not be interested in keeping track of yet another password.

The best we can do here is try to make sure that if some immoral person sees the claim information one week, that person will not be able to easily spoof our system in future weeks. When we send the winner notification, we will include an eight-character claim code. This prize can only be claimed with knowledge of the code.

To make things as secure as possible, we want to make sure this code is unique and very difficult to guess.

```
mt_srand ((double) microtime() * 1000000);
$claim_code = substr(md5(uniqid(rand())),0,8);
```

This uses the uniqueid() and md5() functions to create string that is very random. There's little for a hacker to latch onto when trying to figure out how the string is constructed. md5() will create a string that is 32 characters, but that can be a bit unwieldy. So we're using substr() to limit the string to 8 characters.

The user_id, the claim code, and the week of interest are inserted into the winners table.

```
$query = "replace into winners
    (weekdate, user_id, claim_code, notify_dt)
        values
    ('$weekdate', $user_id, '$claim_code', now())
";
```

The winner is sent an email that is something like, where the claim code matches what has been entered in the database: http://mydomain.com/claim.php?claim_code=ki5g4ju9.

If the user is interested, she will go to this page.

CLAIM.PHP

If the winner comes to claim.php, we first need to check that the claim code exists in the database. The query in the following code grabs queries the database to see if the claim code exists, and if it does, the query performs a join and returns the user information associated with the claim code.

```
$user_id = 0;
if (!empty($claim_code))
{
        $query = "select u.user_id, u.email, w.weekdate
                from users u, winners w
                where w.claim_code = '$claim_code'
                        and w.user_id = u.user_id
        ";
        $result = safe_query($query);
```

If the query returns data, the pertinent information will be assigned to variables.

```
if ($result)
{
```

```
                list($user_id, $winner_email, $weekdate)
                    = mysql_fetch_array($result);
        }
}
```

If nothing was assigned to $user_id, we know that this is not a valid claim code.

```
if ($user_id == 0)
{
        // we couldn't find a record corresponding to the claim_code
        // submitted (if any). print out an error and exit.
        print <<<EOQ
<p>
I'm sorry, that doesn't appear to be a valid claim code.
The URL may not have registered properly.
Make sure to copy the complete link into your browser and try again,
or forward your original prize notification to $admin_email.
</p>
EOQ;
        exit;
}
```

Once it is established that a claim code is valid, we want to do a bit of double-checking and make sure that the person who submitted this claim code knows the e-mail address that the notification was sent to. The application accomplishes this by sending a form asking the user to input the correct e-mail. That form is sent and processed by this page. When the form is submitted, the following code will execute.

```
if(!empty($user_id)
{
    if ($user_email != $winner_email)
    {
$notice = <<<EOQ
I'm sorry, that email address doesn't match our records.
Please try again, or forward your original prize notification
to $admin_email.
EOQ;
```

This comparison $user_email != $winner_email will work because the query that ran at the top of the page retried the correct winner's e-mail, and the form submitted by the user creates $user_email. If that comparison fails, an error message prints. However, if it does not fail, the following code updates the winners database, recording the time the prize was claimed and sends an e-mail to the winner letting them know that the claim was successful.

```
    }
    else
    {
        $claimquery = "update winners set claim_dt = now()
            where user_id = $user_id
            and claim_code = '$claim_code'
            and weekdate = '$weekdate'
        ";
        $result = safe_query($claimquery);
        if ($result && mysql_affected_rows() > 0)
        {
$msgtext = <<<EOQ
The prize for $weekdate has been claimed by $email.
Confirm the prize at

http://$HTTP_HOST/book/survey/admin_winners.php

EOQ;
            mail($admin_email,"Prize Claim",$msgtext);
print <<<EOQ
<p>
Thanks! Your claim has been accepted. Your prize should be on its
way soon!
EOQ;
exit;
```

The final portion of this page simply prints the form where the user will enter the e-mail. There's really no need to show that here.

Summary

There's quite a bit more code in the application, but there isn't anything that you shouldn't be able to figure out with some close scrutiny of the files and reading of the comments. Take a look at the complex_results.php page and its includes (age_results.php, state_results.php, and country_results.php) for a look at how MySQL aggregate functions can come in handy.

This application contains quite a bit more complexity than the guestbook. In this application, we have a real database schema complete with related tables. In the course of the application we need to make use of queries that contain MySQL functions. (See Appendix I for more information on MySQL functions).

The other notable thing seen in this chapter is the function set we've created for creating common HTML elements. Whether you want to make use of these or something similar is up to you. You may prefer typing out the individual form elements, tables, and the like. But you will be seeing these functions used in the remainder of this book.

Part IV

Not So Simple Applications

Chapter 10

Catalog

IN THIS CHAPTER

◆ Working with object-oriented code

◆ Looking at database schemas

◆ Working around MySQL limitations

◆ Running shell commands from within PHP

IN THE COURSE OF THIS chapter we are going to show one way of creating an on-line catalog. You'll see how to present and administer an application that presents some typical retail items.

We, the authors of this book, feel that you are an intelligent person, as well as someone with great taste in technical literature. We also believe that you picked up this book because you want to learn as much as you can about applications development with PHP and MySQL. That's why we're not wasting any time. Each chapter introduces additional challenges, or at least presents something new and different. This chapter will be no exception.

If this chapter were to use the functions presented in the survey application in Chapter 9, there would be little new material to present here. All the application would need is a simple database schema, a few queries with some joins, and calls to the HTML functions in the /functions/ folder.

To keep things interesting, this application uses a completely different way of organizing code. This survey makes use of object-oriented, or OO programming. However, we're not giving up on all of those functions. Some of them are just way too convenient (safe_query() comes to mind).

 Chapter 7 covers the concepts and nomenclature associated with object-oriented programming. In this chapter we assume that you read and understood that information.

Determining the Scope and Goals of the Application

The goals we have in mind for this application are pretty modest. Imagine for a moment that you own some sort of retail establishment that has goods you wish to hawk. Further, assume that you have no interest in actually conducting transactions over the Web. Maybe you are just paranoid about this new-fangled method of processing credit cards. Or perhaps you are running an elaborate tax-fraud scheme that requires you to deal solely in unmarked twenties.

The code used in this catalogue will be re-used in the shopping cart application, where we will show how to process credit-card transactions.

Whatever the circumstance, all this site needs to do is show your wares in logical categories and breakdowns. You will hear more about the breakdown of the information when we discuss the database schema.

The chief goal of this chapter is to create code that makes the best use of the object-oriented approach. The classes must make use of inheritance and encapsulation, and should make the task of writing individual scripts a whole lot easier. It's also important to think about modularity. The code created here will be reused in Chapter 14, so we want to write code in a way that it becomes easily reusable elsewhere.

We also wanted to throw in something really cool. One day on the PHP mailing list some guy named Rasmus mentioned a set of free software utilities that run on Unix that can be used to resize and otherwise manipulate all sorts of images. The PHP scripts in this application will interface with these utilities (called PBMplus) to automatically create thumbnails of the images of the catalogue items. We think you'll have to admit that this is pretty cool.

Rasmus Lerdorf started the language that would evolve into PHP. He is one of the core developers, an active member of the mailing list, and an effective advocate of PHP software. The history of PHP is actually pretty interesting. If you have an MP3 player you can hear all about it from Rasmus and other core developers at: `http://hotwired.lycos.com/webmonkey/radio/php.html`.

PBMplus can be found on the CD.

Subscribe to the PHP mailing list. You'll learn about all sorts of groovy things you never would have guessed existed. If you are going to subscribe, be ready for the volume. The list can generate over 100 emails on a given day. Check Appendix H for a list of some of the other mailing lists.

Necessary Pages

The pages that display the catalogue aren't very extravagant. For navigational purposes there is a simple page that displays a list of categories. Figure 10-1 shows the category list.

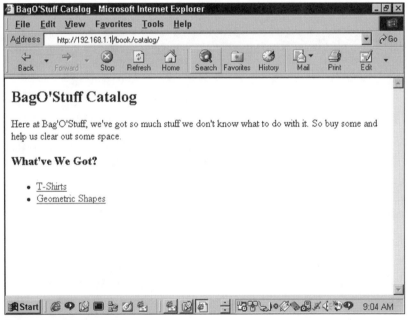

Figure 10-1: Category list page

From the list of categories, the viewer of the page will click through to see a listing of products within that category. Figure 10-2 shows this rather underwhelming page.

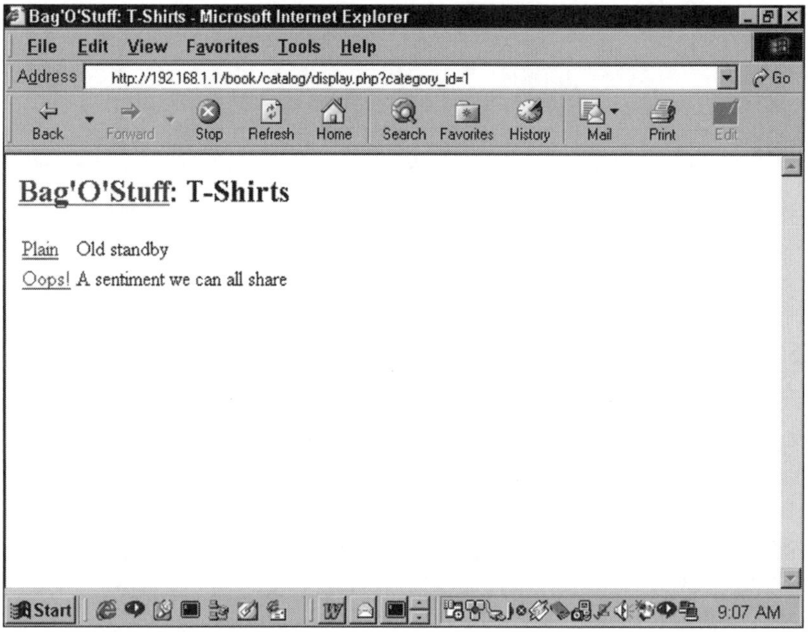

Figure 10-2: Products list page

Finally, there is a page that lists the actual items for sale. Notice that a thumbnail of each item is shown, and that alongside each item is a listing of variants of the item. In Figure 10-3, the items are t-shirts, and specific sizes are listed.

Like all the applications in this book, this one has a series of administrative pages. Given what you have seen in the previous paragraphs and figures, it should be no surprise that the administrative pages create, delete, and alter information on the following levels: categories, products, items, and sub-items, the pages for which are shown in Figures 10-4, 10-5, and 10-6 respectively.

> **NOTE** *Sub-items* is the term that is applied to, for example, the sizes in which a specific t-shirt is available. Sub-items represent slight variations of specific items.

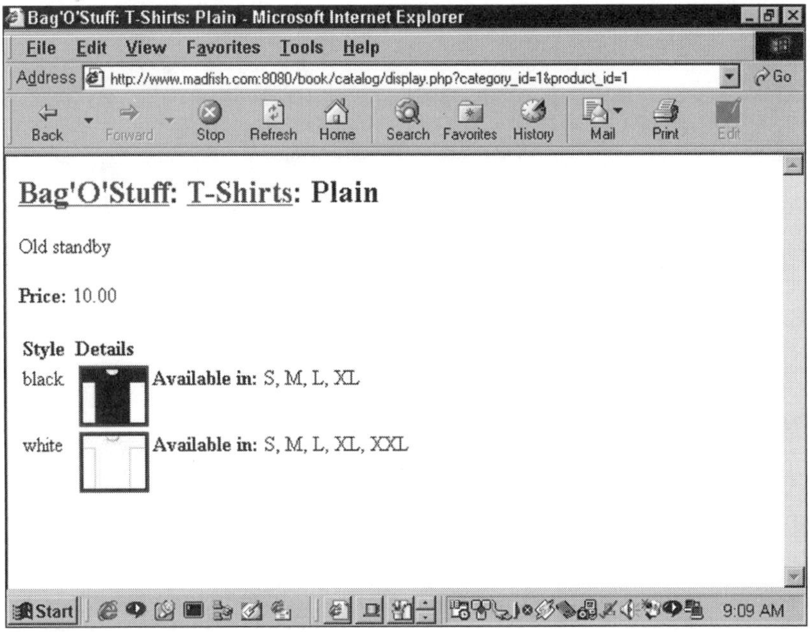

Figure 10-3: Items list

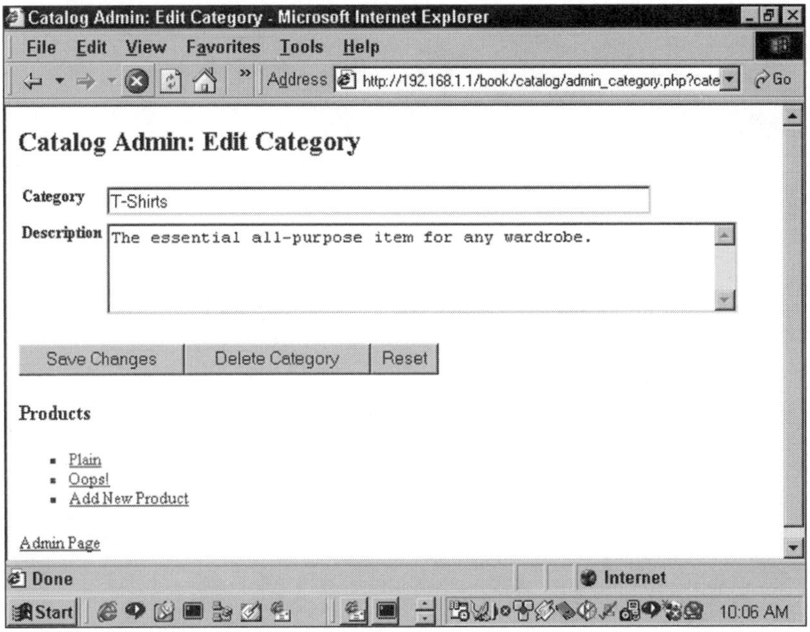

Figure 10-4: Category administration page

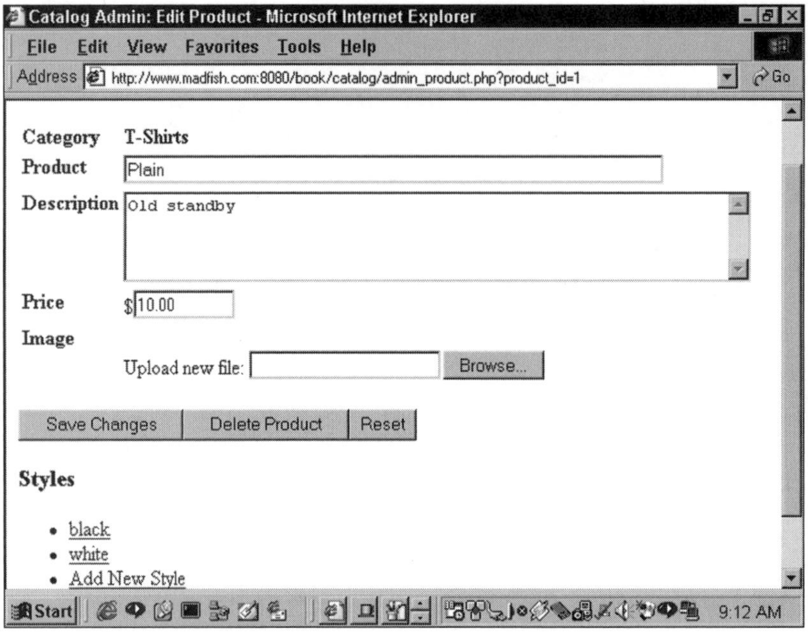

Figure 10-5: Products administration page

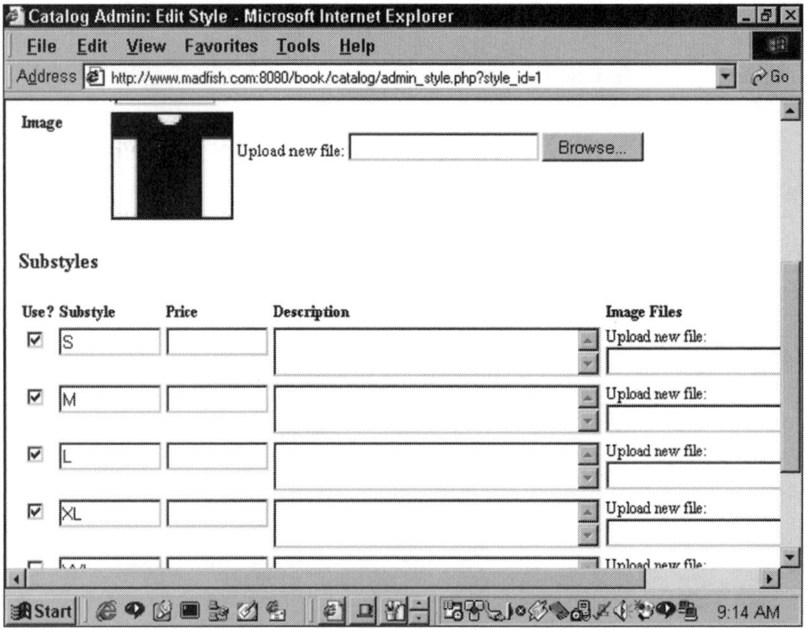

Figure 10-6: Item and sub-item administration page

What Do We Need to Prevent?

Unlike in the survey and the guestbook, there is no user interaction in this application. To the world at large the catalog is read-only. So we don't need to be quite as concerned with bored people adding unwanted tags and scripts to our pages.

In this application there are more general concerns, the type of things that come up in every application: are there bugs, is the code efficient, are our data normalized properly, and other questions of that ilk.

The Data

For this application, we think it is useful to spend a few paragraphs discussing why we did not use what might seem to be the easiest and most obvious schema.

A flawed data design

If you were attentive in reading the previous pages, you will remember the breakdown of the data. There are one or more categories, and each category will contain many products. Each product will have many styles, and each style can have a number of substyles.

This might lead you to believe that a simple hierarchical structure of our tables would work just fine. Figure 10-7 shows the one-to-many relationships that would create this hierarchical effect.

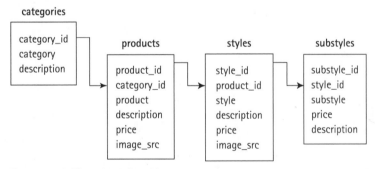

Figure 10-7: Flawed catalog schema

Now consider what would happen if we were to add data to these tables. Let's take the example of t-shirts. There is a category for t-shirts, and a number of products (different clever phrases stenciled on the t-shirts) for this category. Each product will come in a number of styles (colors), and each color will come in a number of substyles (sizes). Figure 10-8 shows what data in the hierarchical table form might look like. (Note that the tables have been simplified).

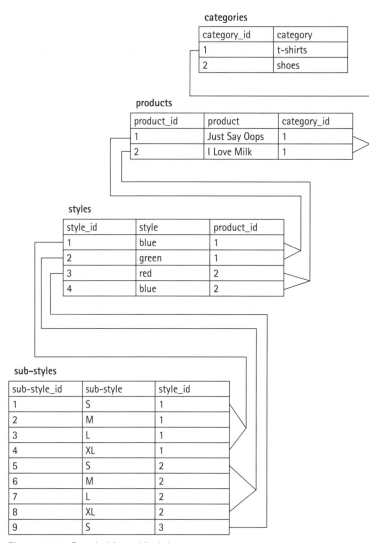

Figure 10-8: Sample hierarchical data

Take a look at the substyles table in Figure 10-8. It is already starting to get a bit messy. Even with just a couple of t-shirts there is some repeating data. As you can see, size small (S) appears several times, and as we add to the catalog, more rows will be inserted and this table will get even messier.

Thinking about the data a bit more carefully, you might notice something interesting: In the case of the t-shirts, the sizes are not dependent on the color of the t-shirts at all. If you remember back to Chapter 1, you will remember that a lack of a dependency is a bad thing. So the above data really aren't properly normalized.

In fact, the sizes in which a t-shirt is available are not dependent on the color (style table) or the phrase on the t-shirt (products table). Size is, in fact, dependent on the category. All t-shirts (category_id=1) will come in S, M, L, or XL. Therefore, in the final schema there will be a relationship between the category table and the substyle table.

 Test your schemas. Before you go live with your own applications use some test data and see what happens. What seems right in theory could have some serious flaws in practice.

 Before you make a single table in your database, work with pencil and paper to draw out your tables and relationships. Erasing a line there is a lot less trouble than deleting a column.

MySQL oddities

Before we get to the final schema, this is a good time to point out one of the weirdnesses of MySQL. In Part I, we noted that MySQL doesn't support unions or subselects. Given these limitations, take a look at Tables 10-1 and 10-2, and tell me how you could find all the names in Table 10-1 that are NOT in Table 10-2.

TABLE 10-1 NAMES

first_name
brad
jay
john

TABLE 10-2 OTHER_NAMES

first_name
brad
jay
William

If MySQL supported sub-selects, this would work:

```
select name from Names where first_name not in (select first_name
from Other_names)
```

However, in MySQL the best way to go about this is to perform an outer join. Something like this:

```
select N.first_name
from Names N
left join Other_names Otn on
    N.first_name = Otn.first_name
where Otn.first_name is null
```

With an outer join we can be sure that the Names table will be preserved in its entirety. Then, in the joined table, there will be non-null results where there are matching values. For instance, since 'Jay' is in both tables, that string will exist in both columns of the resulting query. But if there is no matching value, there will be a null value in the joined table.

You will also see sub-selects used for statements such as this:

```
select first_name from Names where first_name in (select first_name
from Other_names)
```

In a case like this a straight join would produce the same result.

```
select N.first_name
from Names N, Other_names Otn
where N.first_name = Otn.first_name
```

MySQL will not support unions until version 3.24. However, there is a way to work around this without too much difficulty in version 3.23. You can create a temporary table into which you can insert different select statements. For instance in other database packages you might do something like this:

```
select first_name, last_name from table_1
union
select first_name, last_name from table_2
```

In MySQL 3.23 you would create a temporary table and then insert the results of the select statements into that table. The preceding code would be re-created like this:

```
create temporary table name_union
select first_name, last_name from table_1;
```

```
insert into name_union
select first_name, last name from table_2;
```

Now that you have a table holding the union, you could perform a select on that table. The temporary table created will be very fast because it is not written to the disk; it is only stored in memory.

Note that this syntax was not available in version 3.22.

A better schema

Now that we're done with that little digression, we'll get back to the structure for this application. Figure 10-9 shows the preferred schema, the one that we actually use.

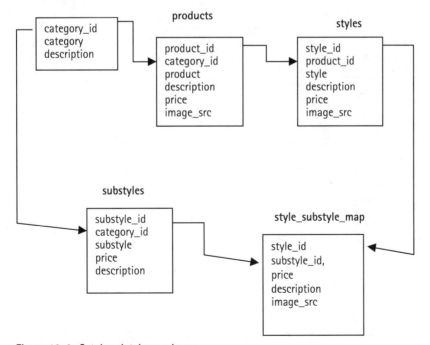

Figure 10-9: Catalog database schema

For starters, notice that there is a direct relationship between the categories and the substyles tables. The reason for this was explained earlier. The tables in the top half of the figure should make sense. They are the part of the hierarchy that still made sense.

The neat and different thing in this application is the style_substyle_map table. If you are going through this book in order, this will be the first time that you encounter a many-to-many relationship. In this application a category can have many substyles (e.g., t-shirts come in S, M, L, and XL). And any style of shirt (e.g, "I Love Milk" in red) can come in zero, one, or more than one substyle (size). The style_substyle_map tracks that intersection. Figure 10-10 illustrates how the data come together.

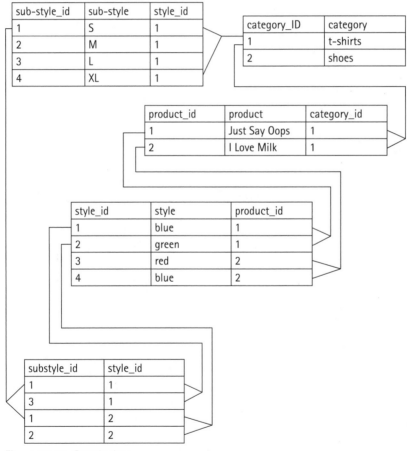

Figure 10-10: Sample data

In Figure 10-10 the "Just Say Oops" t-shirt in blue comes in two sizes: S and M. Listing 10-1 shows the statements that will create these tables.

Listing 10-1: Create Statements for Catalog Application

```
# ---------------------------------------------------------
#
# Table structure for table 'catalog_admin'
#
CREATE TABLE catalog_admin (
    username varchar(50) NOT NULL,
    password varchar(255) NOT NULL
);
# ---------------------------------------------------------
#
# Table structure for table 'categories'
#
CREATE TABLE categories (
    category_id int(11) NOT NULL auto_increment,
    category varchar(255) NOT NULL,
    description text,
    PRIMARY KEY (category_id)
);
# ---------------------------------------------------------
#
# Table structure for table 'products'
CREATE TABLE products (
    product_id int(11) NOT NULL auto_increment,
    category_id int(11) NOT NULL,
    product varchar(255) NOT NULL,
    description text,
    price decimal(10,2),
    image_src varchar(255),
    PRIMARY KEY (product_id),
    KEY product_category_id (category_id)
);
# ---------------------------------------------------------
#
# Table structure for table 'styles'
#
CREATE TABLE styles (
    style_id int(11) NOT NULL auto_increment,
    product_id int(11) NOT NULL,
    style varchar(255) NOT NULL,
    description text,
    price decimal(10,2),
    image_src varchar(255),
    PRIMARY KEY (style_id),
    KEY style_product_key (product_id)
```

```
);
# ----------------------------------------------------
#
# Table structure for table 'substyles'
#
CREATE TABLE substyles (
    substyle_id int(11) NOT NULL auto_increment,
    category_id int(11) NOT NULL,
    substyle varchar(255) NOT NULL,
    price decimal(10,2),
    description text,
    PRIMARY KEY (substyle_id),
    KEY substyle_category_key (category_id)
);
# ----------------------------------------------------
#
# Table structure for table 'style_substyle_map'
#
CREATE TABLE style_substyle_map (
style_id int(11) NOT NULL,
substyle_id int(11) NOT NULL,
price decimal(10,2),
description text,
image_src varchar(255),
KEY map_style_key (style_id),
KEY map_substyle_key (substyle_id)
);
```

Code Overview

The code in this section is going to look substantially different from the chapters you have seen so far. Only the shopping cart (which, in fact, builds on this application) uses a similar method of organizing and accessing code. The other major differences are the use of utilities outside of PHP and accessing the file system.

The object-oriented approach

In the preceding applications, and the ones that follow, we make use of a procedural approach. That is, there is a series of functions, and each function performs a fairly specific procedure. In the actual application, there is little to do but call these functions. But in an application such as this, where the data are largely hierarchical, it's helpful to make use of OO programming's inheritance. After all, a Style is really an extension of a product. The style may be red, but "red" means very little without the inherited property of t-shirt, which comes from the Category table.

If you use objects, the contents within the files called by URLs will be even sparser. Almost all of the work will be performed within the classes. Once you understand what actions the class files perform, there will be little else for you to do.

To advocates of OO programming, this is a major advantage. You, the programmer, can get a class file and not really know what happens inside of it. All you need to know is what attributes it has and what its methods do. Then you can just include it in your application and painlessly make use of its sophisticated functionality.

We said it in Chapter 7 but it's worth repeating here: You can write procedural code that encompasses all of the benefits discussed here. If you're not careful with OO programming, your code can end up being much more difficult to maintain and use.

Accessing the filesystem

You have probably noticed by now that in this book, almost all of our data are stored within the MySQL database. But even when you're using MySQL, there are times when you are better off using the filesystem for storage. Images (jpegs, gifs, pngs) are a perfect example. Even if your database supports binary data, there's little advantage in putting an image in a database. You need a database for storing and querying normalized data. In your database you are much better off storing the path to the image stored in your filesystem. That way it will be easy enough to fill in the src attribute in your <img> tag.

Do not store images in a database. Put them on the filesystem.

Uploading files

This is the first application that lets users upload files; specifically, the administrators of the catalog will need to be able to upload images of their products. Uploading files is easy enough in PHP, but before you understand how the upload works, you will need to know how PHP handles uploaded files.

In your HMTL page you will have a form, like the following.

```
<form action="admin_product.php" method="post"
enctype="multipart/form-data" >
<input type=file name="imagefile">
</form>
```

When you allow file uploads, you open yourself up for denial of service (DoS) attacks. If you're not careful, someone could send many multi-megabyte files to your system simultaneously, which could bring your machine to a crashing halt. There are two things you can do about this. First is to put a hidden form field prior to your <input type="file"> tag. The hidden field should look like this:

```
<INPUT TYPE="hidden" name="MAX_FILE_SIZE" value="1000">
```

where value is the maximum size allowed, in bytes. This is a reasonable first step, and could be of help in stopping someone who didn't know you had a size limit. However, this will not stop anyone with malicious intent. All they would have to do is look at the source code of your page and make the needed changes. The php.ini file contains the upload_max_filesize item. If you have access to your php.ini, you can set this to a number that you think is reasonable. By default, php.ini will allow 2 MB uploads.

When a file is specified and this form is submitted, PHP automatically creates a few variables. They would be:

♦ $imagefile: the name of the file as stored in the temporary directory on the server

♦ $imagefile_name: the name of the file as it was on the user's machine

♦ $imagefile_size: the size of the file, in bytes

♦ $imagefile_type: the mime type, in this case image/gif, image/png, or image/jpg

The image will be stored in the temp directory specified in the php.ini file; if no temp directory is specified in php.ini, the operating system's default temporary directory will be used.

The Paths and Directories category of the php.ini controls many of the file upload options.

Accessing outside utilities

For this application, we need thumbnails for each of the images. The application could require the user to include both a full-size image and a thumbnail. But that's really not necessary, because the open-source world has provided all of us developers with a utility that powerfully and easily manipulates images. It's called PBMplus.

You can find the PBMplus package on the CD-ROM that accompanies this book.

PBMplus contains several utilities that come in two basic flavors. One set of utilities transfers images to and from an intermediary format. So, whether you have a gif, a jpg, or a png, it must first be converted to the intermediary format, pbm. Another set of utilities alters the pbm files. These utilities do a variety of things: check the README file and the man pages that come with PBMplus to learn about them. Once you have made the .pbm file, you can convert it to whatever format you need.

To use these utilities, you need to run shell commands from within your PHP script. For the purposes of this application, the `system()` function will be the best choice. More on that when we get to it in the code.

There is potential danger when using functions that run shell commands. If and information supplied from the user is transported to the shell commands, you should take great care to ensure that damaging commands cannot be executed. The escapeshellcmd() function will help http://www.php.net/manual/function.escapeshellcmd.php examine shell commands. In this application only people who are logged in will reach commands that access the shell.

If you wish to output the results of PBMplus utilities directly to the browser, use the `passthrough()` function.

Code Breakdown

In OO coding, good documentation is your best friend because, as already stated, it almost shouldn't matter how the classes you are using accomplish their tasks. You just need to know that they work.

TIP PHPbuider has an excellent article on software that can help document classes: `http://www.phpbuilder.com/columns/stefano20000824.php3`.

Objects in theory

For instance, if we were to tell you about a class named Category, we could just tell you the following:

Class Category:
Inherits Base
Properties:

- products

Methods:

- `LoadCategory`: Loads all of the columns for the categories table into object properties, based on a unique category_id. Products belonging to the category will be available as sub-objects.

- `SaveCategory`: Writes a new or updated category to the database.

- `FetchCategory`: Based on a unique category_id, assigns all columns for a row to properties.

- `DeleteCategory`: Removes a Category from the database based on a unique category_id.

- `PrintCategory`: Writes out a category to the browser.

Knowing this, and really nothing else, you could write a new script that displayed a category. The script below assumes that a category_id was passed through the querystring, or via a POST.

```php
<?php
$c = new Category;
$c -> LoadCategory($category_id);
$c -> PrintCategory();
```

But if we left it at this, the learning experience would only be a fraction of what it should be. Of course we will go over the code in depth. But before we do, you should see how objects are constructed.

Objects in practice

So far in this book you have seen variables of all shapes and sizes. There have been strings, integers, arrays, associative arrays, and all other kinds of fun stuff. However, here our variables are going to be quite a bit more complex. Take a look at these two lines, which we have already explained:

```
$c = new Category;
$c -> LoadCategory($category_id);
```

If you read the previous section, you know that this creates an object with sub-objects. It will be easier to understand with a visual representation. Figure 10-11 shows a sample Category object.

```
category Object (
    ([whatami] => Category
    [category_id] => 1
    [category] => T-Shirts
    [description] => The essential all-purpose item for any wardrobe.
    [products] => Array (
        [0] => product Object (
                            [product_id] => 1
                            [category_id] => 1
                            [product] => Plain
                            [description] => Old standby
                            [price] => 10.00
        )
        [1] => product Object (
                            [product_id] => 2
                            [category_id] => 1
                            [product] => Oops!
                            [desription] => A sentiment we can all share
                            [price] => 10.00
        )
    )
)
```

Figure 10-11: Sample category object

In Figure 10-11 you can see that the object contains not only properties. One of its properties (products) contains an array of other objects. Just to make this is clear, the following code will print, "You Bet".

```
$c = new Category;
$c -> LoadCategory($category_id);
if(is_array($c->products))
{
```

```
if(is_object($c->products[0]))
{
    echo "You Bet";
}
}
```

The methods within the classes will be constructed so as to get these sub-objects. Functions that perform administrative tasks will need to account for this structure.

Keep this in mind as you look at the other classes as well. A Products object might have an array of sub-objects for styles and a Styles object will have an array of sub-objects for sub-styles.

Classes

We designed the classes in this application so that most of them look and behave similarly. As you look at the classes, you should notice that all but the Base class have methods with similar names. Our hope is that once you understand one class, the workings of the others will be pretty clear. For this reason, we're only going to break down two classes in this chapter. Note that the each method in each class is extensively commented on the CD. So if you have a specific question as to the working of a snippet of code, you will likely find the explanation within the comments.

In the following pages, we will break down code in the following classes: Base and Product. For the other classes, we will only describe how to use the methods and properties. But once you understand the Product class, the other classes (Product, Style, and Sub-style) should be easy enough to figure out.

The classes are pretty extensive; dumping them all into one file would make life unnecessarily difficult. It is a better idea to create a file called classes.php, which includes the actual classes. Here are the contents of classes.php

```
include "base_class.php";
include "category_class.php";
include "product_class.php";
include "style_class.php";
include "substyle_class.php";
```

TIP   Please be sure that you have mastered the concepts in Chapter 7 before reading this section.

Breaking the classes into includes also allows us to selectively reuse specific classes when we need them. This becomes important in Chapter 14, when we reuse some of these classes in creating the shopping cart.

BASE

There is always a base class on which the inherited classes are built (though it's not always named Base). In this application, Base will contain a set of utilities that all of the other classes will make use of. The class is declared with the following statement:

```
class Base
{
```

Now on to the properties. There are only three default properties. The following three come into play when dealing with images and thumbnails.

- $image_src;

- $thumb_src;

- $thumb_width

Other properties will be created dynamically in course of the methods.

METHOD SQL_FORMAT()   This method helps build update and insert queries.

```
function sql_format ($field)
{
    if (empty($this->$field))
    {
        return "null";
    }
    elseif (is_numeric($this->$field))
    {
        return $this->$field;
    }
    else
    {
        return "'".$this->$field."'";
    }
}
```

For the sake of a query, a variable may be null, a numeric quantity, or text string. Each of the data types requires a slightly different format within a query. Strings must be surrounded by single quotes. Numeric files can have no quotes, and for nulls, this method will return the string "null" – with no single quotes surrounding it.

METHOD SET_IMAGE_SRC()   This method both saves the uploaded image to the filesystem and creates the thumbnail.

It is complex enough to break down section by section. First remember that the $file_src is the sole argument of the method call. $file_src is a string that will contain the path to the image. Most often, $file_src will be a string like "images/image_product_8_style_7".

```
function set_image_src ($file_src="")
{
    if (!empty($this->imagefile) && $this->imagefile != "none")
    {
        if ($file_src === "")
        {
            $file_src = "images/".uniqid("image_");
        }
        umask(2);
        $sizearr = GetImageSize($this->imagefile);
```

Here, imagefile is a file that has been uploaded by a user. If a file itself exists but no file name is indicted by the $file_src argument, a variable called $file_src is created. Using the uniqueid() function, we create a file name that starts with "image_" and then contains some random characters. We want to make sure file names are unique, so we don't end up accidentally overwriting existing files. After that the umask is set (see your Unix man page for a description of umask), and then we use the getimagesize() function. This function returns an array with four elements: the first is the image height, the second is width, the third is the image type (1 = GIF, 2 = JPG, 3 = PNG, 4 = SWF), and the fourth is the height and width in a string that is ready for the <img> tag. This information is really helpful in that the script will be able to assign a correct extension, even if the supplied filename had a faulty extension, or none at all.

```
if ($sizearr[2] == 1) { $file_ext = ".gif"; }
elseif ($sizearr[2] == 2) { $file_ext = ".jpg"; }
elseif ($sizearr[2] == 3) { $file_ext = ".png"; }
else {
    $file_ext = strtolower(
    substr($this->imagefile_name
        , strrpos($this->imagefile_name,".")
            )
    );
}
```

Using the information in the third element of the array, we determine the appropriate extension. If the file type doesn't match any of the possible values returned by getimagesize(), we parse the string containing the uploaded file's name. We take the characters from the final dot on, make them lowercase, and assign them to $file_ext.

```
$thumb_src = $file_src."_thumb".$file_ext;
$file_src .= $file_ext;
copy($this->imagefile, $file_src);
```

Now that we have a unique filename and the proper extension, we can put together filenames for both the main file and the thumbnail that we're going to make. Then the source file is copied from its temporary home to the full path on the filesystem, as indicated in $file_src.

```
if ($file_ext == ".jpg")
{
$cmd = "../catalog/makeimagethumb $file_src $thumb_src $this->thumb_width";
                $out = system($cmd,$err);
```

If the image is a jpg, we call a shell script, using the system() function. Here it is:

```
#!/bin/sh
PATH=/usr/local/bin:/usr/new/pbmplus:$PATH
export PATH
rm ./$2
djpeg ./$1 | pnmscale -xysize $3 $3 | pnmmargin -black 1 | cjpeg >
./$2
```

This script will be passed two text strings ($file_src and $thumb_src), which are assigned to variables $1 and $2. The shell script first removes the existing thumbnail (if it exists), and then goes about creating a new one. djped converts the jpg to the pbm format. The output of that is piped to pnmscale, which reduces the picture to a 50×50 px image; the output of that is piped to pnmmargin, which adds a black border. Finally, the resulting image is redirected to a file, as indicated by $2 (or $thumb_src).

 The previous shell script could have been kept within PHP. It could have been written more like this:

```
$path = "/path/to/pbmplus/";
$djpeg = $path . "djpeg";
$pnmscale = $path . "pnmscale";
$pnmmargin = $path . "pnmmargin";
$cjpeg = $path."cjpeg";
$cmd = " $djpeg $file_src | $pnmscale -xysize 50 50 |
$pnmmargin -black 1 | $cjpeg > $thumb_src";
$out = system($cmd,$err);
```

If this shell script had produced an error, it would have been returned to the system function as the second argument, $err.

```
if ($err) { print "<h4><li>cmd=$cmd <li>err=$err
    <li>out=$out</h4>\n"; }
}
else
{
    copy($file_src, $thumb_src);
}
    $this->image_src = $file_src;
    $this->thumb_src = $thumb_src;
}
else
{
    $this->set_thumb_src();
}
```

If the file wasn't a jpeg, the uploaded file is copied to the place where the thumbnail would be kept. Following that, we place the full path location of the file and the thumbnail to the image_src and thumb_src attributes.

Note the final if block. This portion will run if a file has not been uploaded.

METHOD SET_THUMB_SRC()   This method sets a thumb_src property. It determines this property based on the image_src property stored in the database. We are not storing the thumb_src property in the database, so when we need access to the thumbnail, we will need to run this method.

The last period image_src is replaced with "_thumb.". If no period is found in image_src, thumb_src is set to image_src plus "_thumb".

```
function set_thumb_src()
{
    $last_period = strrpos($this->image_src,".");
    if ($last_period === false)
    {
        $this->thumb_src = $this->image_src."_thumb";
    }
    else
    {
        $this->thumb_src = substr_replace(
                $this->image_src
                , "_thumb."
            , $last_period
            , 1
```

```
        );
    }
}
```

METHOD BASE   This is the constructor method for this class. As you can see it does little but make calls to a method called Construct.

```
function Base ($parent="",$atts="")
{
    $this->Construct(get_object_vars($parent));
    $this->Construct($atts);
}
```

Notice the use of get_object_vars(). It's a handy function that turns all of the object properties into elements in an associative array. So if an object is passed to this method (through the first argument), it can be passed to Construct as an array.

METHOD CONFIRM_DELETE_FORM()   This method prints a form that forces the administrator of the catalog to confirm that they want to continue with a delete. This comes into play when a deletion is indicated for an item that contains related child elements. For example, if the administrator indicates that a category should be deleted but the category still contains products, this form will print.

```
confirm_delete_form($message="", $label="")
{
    $warning = "<b>Please confirm your delete request</b>";
    if (!empty($message))
    {
        $warning .= "- $message";
    }
    $output = <<<EOQ
<p>
<form method="post">
$warning
<input type="hidden" name="confirm" value="Confirm Delete">
<input type="submit" name="submit" value="$label">
</form>
</p>
EOQ;
        return $output;
}
```

METHOD CONSTRUCT() This method is expecting an associative array. Most often, in the course of the application, the associative array will be the result of mysql_fetch_array(). Each of the keys in the array will become properties of the current object. Note that we have to run the set_thumb_src() property because the thumb_src is not stored in the database.

```
function Construct ($atts="")
{
    if (is_array($atts))
    {
        while (list($name,$value) = each($atts))
        {
            if (!empty($value) && !is_array($value))
            {
                $this->$name = $value;
            }
        }
    }
    if (!empty($this->image_src))
    {
        $this->set_thumb_src();
    }
}
```

METHOD BASE() This is the constructor of the Base class. Its major job is to call the Contruct() method. If it receives an object in the first argument, the properties of the object are turned into an associative array with the get_object_vars() function before it is sent to Construct. The thumb_width property is set here because a value of a default property cannot accompany the property's declaration.

```
function Base ($parent="",$atts="")
{
    $this->thumb_width = 50;
    if (is_object($parent))
    {
        $this->Construct(get_object_vars($parent));
    }
    $this->Construct($atts);
}
```

PRODUCTS

Before we get started in explaining this class, let us re-state that this class is very similar to the other classes in this application. If you understand how this works, the rest of the classes should be relatively easy to figure out.

In Figure 10-11, a few pages back, you saw what a Catalog object looked like. Now, we'll show what a typical Product object looks like (Figure 10-12).

```
product Object
(
    [product_id] => 1
    [category_id] => 1
    [product] => Plain
    [description] => Old standby
    [price] => 10.00
    [style_count] => 9
    [substyle_count] => 9

    [styles] => Array
      (
        [0] => style Object
          (
              [substyles] => Array ()
              [product_id] => 1
              [category_id] => 1
              [product] => Plain
              [description] => Old standby
              [price] => 10.00
              [style_count] => 9
              [substyle_count] => 9
              [style_id] => 1
              [style] => black
              [image_src] => images/product_1_style_1.jpg
              [thumb_src] => images/product_1_style_1_thumb.jpg
          )

        [1] => style Object
          (
              [substyles] => Array ()
              [product_id] => 1
              [category_id] => 1
              [product] => Plain
              [description] => Old standby
              [price] => 10.00
              [style_count] => 9
              [substyle_count] => 9
              [style_id] => 2
              [style] => white
              [image_src] => images/product_1_style_2.jpg
              [thumb_src] => images/product_1_style_2_thumb.jpg
          )
      )
)
```

Figure 10-12: Sample Product object

Notice that the Product object contains and array of related styles. That array, named styles, contains Style objects. So at some point in this class, you can expect some code that will manufacture this structure. Specifically, somewhere in this class, we can expect the Product class to make calls to the Style class, in order to create these sub-objects.

Additionally, if you look at Figure 10-11, you will notice that the Catalog object contains an array of Product objects. You can probably now see the parallel structure we had mentioned. This is particularly important because as you look through the product object you should expect to see places where the Catalog class would be making calls to the Product class in order to create this structure. In fact, you will see that in the constructor of the Product class.

METHOD PRODUCT()   This is the constructor of the class. It is very brief.

```
function Product ($parent="",$atts="")
{
    $this->styles = array();
    $this->Base($parent,$atts);
}
```

Remember that we said that this will be called from the Category class. The $parent variable will contain the name of the parent, and $atts will be a row retrieved from the database. Though it's not important to show all of the code that will call to this method at this time, you should have an idea of what is needed to create the data structure seen in Figure 10-12.

Somewhere in the Category class, a query to the database will retrieve a list of all of the products associated with a category_id, something like select * from products where categorey_id = $category_id. The result set of this query will be looped through and each time through the loop a row will be assigned to the second argument in the call to the Product object. You will see an example of this later in the chapter, when the Product class makes calls to the Styles class.

The call to Base() will take each of the elements in the associative array and assign them to object properties.

Note that this constructor will also run if a product object is instantiated within a script. But after being instantiated, the information associated with the product_id will not be automatically loaded. The FetchProduct() or LoadProduct() methods will be needed for that. It is the LoadProduct() method that will make the Style class. But before we break that down, you need to see the FetchProduct() method.

METHOD FETCHPRODUCT()   This method grabs the row form the products table associated with the given product_id. It includes some error handling, for the event that no product_id or a bad product_id was given. Then, using the Construct method from the Base class, each of the returned fields is turned into a property of the Product object.

```
function FetchProduct ($product_id=0)
{
    if (!empty($product_id))
    {
        $this->product_id = $product_id;
    }
    if (empty($this->product_id))
    {
        $this->error = "no product_id specified for fetch";
        return FALSE;
    }
    $result = safe_query("select * from products
        where product_id = $this->product_id
    ");
    if (!$result)
    {
        return FALSE;
    }
    $row = mysql_fetch_array($result,MYSQL_ASSOC);
    $this->Construct($row);
    return TRUE;
}
```

Notice the use of $this->error. By using defining an error in this way, in our scripts we can do the following:

```
$p = new Product;
if (!$p->FetchProduct(1))
{
    echo $p->error;
} else{
    echo "The product name is: $p->product";
}
```

if the fetch didn't work out. The method will return FALSE, and you will have access to a meaningful error message.

METHOD LOADPRODUCT()   As mentioned earlier, this is the method that will create the structure seen in Figure 10-12. If you look at that figure, you will see there is quite a bit of information: the number of associated styles, the number of associated sub-styles. Then there is the array that contains Style objects.

```
function LoadProduct ($product_id=0)
{
    $this->FetchProduct($product_id);
```

Before doing anything, we will need to have access to all of the information associated with the product_id. As you saw, FetchProduct() will take care of that, and will assign all of the columns to object properties.

```
$result = safe_query("select count(s.style) as style_count
    , count(s.price) as style_price_count
    , count(m.substyle_id) as substyle_count
    , count(m.price) as substyle_price_count
    from products p
    left join styles s on s.product_id=p.product_id
    left join style_substyle_map m on m.style_id=s.style_id
    where p.product_id = $this->product_id
    group by p.product_id
");
$row = mysql_fetch_array($result,MYSQL_ASSOC);
$this->Construct($row);
```

In the preceding code, the query will retrieve the number of associated styles and substyles, as well as a number of prices for styles and substyles. After the query is run and the row is fetched, the Construct() method assigns each of the columns in the result to object properties.

```
if ($this->style_count > 0)
{
    $squery = "select * from styles where product_id = "
        .$this->product_id
    ;
    $sresult = safe_query($squery);
    while ($srow = mysql_fetch_array($sresult,MYSQL_ASSOC))
    {
        $this->AddStyle($this,$srow);
    }
}
}
```

If there are styles for this Product, as indicated by style_count, a query is run to get all of the information from the styles table. Each row returned will be sent to the AddStyle() Method. There is only one line in the AddStyle() Method:

```
$this->styles[] = new Style($parent,$atts);
```

Here a new Style object is created, and is placed in the styles array. This creates the structure seen in the previous two figures.

In case you're wondering, the AddStyle() method isn't really necessary here – this code could easily be in the LoadProduct() method. We will show the reasoning for this in Chapter 14.

METHOD SAVEPRODUCT()   In the administration of the catalog, you will need to update existing products and save new products.

```
function SaveProduct()
{
    if (empty($this->product_id))
    {
        safe_query("insert into products
            (category_id, product)
             values ($this->category_id, '$this->product')
        ");
        $this->product_id = mysql_insert_id();
    }
```

If there is no existing product_id, we have MySQL assign one. By doing an insert into the products table, mysql_insert_id() will return the primary key of the new row. Now that we have the row, we need to format the fields that were uploaded. Then we can run the query.

```
    $cleandsc = cleanup_text($this->description);
    $this->set_image_src("images/product_image_$this->product_id");
    $nullprice = $this->sql_format("price");
    $nullimage_src = $this->sql_format("image_src");
    return safe_query("update products
        set product = '$this->product'
        , description = '$cleandsc'
        , price = $nullprice
        , image_src = $nullimage_src
        where product_id = $this->product_id
    ");
}
```

METHOD DELETEPRODUCT()   Finally, there needs to be a way to purge an existing product. Note the single argument to this method. For safety reasons, this method forces the administrator to confirm any delete. To accomplish this, we make use of the confirmation form seen in the Base class.

```
function DeleteProduct ($confirm="")
{
    if (empty($this->product_id))
```

```
    {
        $this->error = "no product_id to delete";
        return FALSE;
    }
    $result = safe_query("select style_id from styles
        where product_id = $this->product_id
    ");
```

As an added measure of safety, we are checking that the product intended for deletion does not have any child styles. If it does, the form in the base class will be printed with an appropriate error message.

```
    if (mysql_num_rows($result) > 0)
    {
        if (empty($confirm))
        {
            $this->error = $this->confirm_delete_form(
            "The product $this->product ($this->product_id) still
contains styles."
.hidden_field("category_id",$this->category_id)
.hidden_field("product_id",$this->product_id)
            , "Delete Product"
            );
            return FALSE;
        }
```

We now loop through each of the styles_ids returned from the previous queries and run queries that delete the style_ids from the style_substyle_map table, the styles table, and the products table. Note that in other relational databases we could delete rows from many tables at once by using a join. MySQL, however, does not allow for joins when performing deletes.

```
        while ($row = mysql_fetch_object($result))
        {
            safe_query("delete from style_substyle_map
                where style_id = $row->style_id
            ");
        }
        safe_query("delete from styles
            where product_id = $this->product_id
        ");
    }
        return safe_query("delete from products
        where product_id = $this->product_id
    ");
    }
```

OTHER CLASSES

Now that you have seen one class in its entirety, and have a feel for how the data structures are created, it would be a waste of paper, as well as your time, to lay out all of the other classes here. As we've said (about the 5 times now) they're designed to work similarly. If you understand one, you really understand all of them.

If you'd like more detail on any of the remaining classes, see the comments within the files on the CD. In this section, we're going to tell you all you need to know to make use of the remaining classes. (Note that the Catalog class was described earlier.)

Class Name: Style
Extends Product
Default Properties:

- ◆ $substyle_count;

- ◆ $substyle_price_count;

- ◆ $substyles;

Methods:

- ◆ Style. The class constructor. Takes two arguments: $parent and $atts. If $atts is an array, the Base() method will be called, assigning each of the array elements to Object properties. (Note, this method is similar to the Product method).

- ◆ FetchStyle. Takes one argument, $style_id. Creates object properties for every row in the style table associated with the $style_id. (Note, this method is similar to the FetchProduct method).

- ◆ LoadStyles. Takes one argument, $style_id. First runs FetchStyle and the creates an array, each element of which is a object containing sub-style information. (Note, this method is similar to the LoadProduct method).

- ◆ SaveStyle. Takes no arguments, assumes a $this->style_id exists. Will both update existing styles and create new ones. (Note, this method is similar to the SaveProduct method).

- ◆ DeleteStyle. Takes no arguments. Removes a style from the database. It will force confirmation if there are related substyles. It will delete that style after if confirmation is provided. (Note, this method is similar to the DeleteProduct method).

- ◆ PrintStyleRow. Takes two arguments: $product_price, $product_dsc. Prints product information within a table row. If the arguments are equal to the equivalent fields in the Style, then those style fields are not printed.

Class Name: SubStyle
Extends Style

Default Properties:
None.
Methods:

◆ SubStyle. The class constructor. Takes two arguments: $parent and $atts. If $atts is an array, the Base() method will be called, assigning each of the array elements to Object properties. (Note, this is nearly identical in function to the Product method).

◆ FetchSubStyle. Takes one argument, $substyle_id. Creates object properties for every row in the substyle table associated with the $substyle_id. (Note, this is nearly identical in function to the FetchProduct method).

◆ SaveSubStyle. Takes no arguments, assumes a $this->substyle_id exists. Will both update existing styles and create new ones. (Note, this is nearly identical in function to the DeleteProduct method).

◆ PrintSubStyle. Takes two arguments: $product_price,$product_dsc. Prints product information within a table row. If either of the arguments contain information, the values of those arguments will overwrite the information from the database in the printed row.

Sample Script

Now that you have understanding of the classes available, we'll show how they are put to work in one of the scripts. We'll look at display.php. This page is expecting at least a category_id to be passed via the querystring. If there is a category_id and a product_id, all of the product information will be printed. If only a category_id exits, a list of products is printed.

```php
<?php
if (empty($category_id))
{
    header("Location: index.php");
    exit;
}
```

The above code is just some error handling. We need to have a category_id.

```php
include "header.php";
$page_title = anchor_tag("index.php", "Bag'O'Stuff");
```

We are going to be using breadcrumbs for navigation. This is the fist link, which takes the user to the home page. Since we already know that there is a category_id, we can instantiate a Category object, which we're calling $c. Note that at this point the $c really doesn't contain much, because we haven't used either FetchCategory or LoadCategory.

```
$c = new Category;


if (empty($product_id))
{
    $c->LoadCategory($category_id);

    $page_title .= ": $c->category";
    include("start_page.php");

    // print out a description of this category and a list of its
    // products
    $c->PrintCategory();
```

If there is no product_id, we know that we are only concerned with the category, so we call the LoadCategory() method. This creates a structure like the one seen in Figure 10-11. Then to print the category, all we have to do is call the Print Category() method.

```
}
else
{
```

This portion will run if there is a product_id. A product object is instantiated, and then LoadProduct() loads all of the associated style objects. See Figure 10-12 to see the data structure it creates. Then the LoadStyles() method grabs all the substyles associated with each of the styles.

```
    $p = new Product;
    $p->LoadProduct($product_id);
    $p->LoadStyles();

    $c->FetchCategory($p->category_id);

    $page_title .= ": "
        .anchor_tag("display.php?category_id=$c->category_id", $c-
>category)
        .": $p->product"
    ;
    include("start_page.php");

    $p->PrintProduct();
```

```
}

include("end_page.php");
```

Then all we need is another Method call and the page is ready to go.

Summary

You might have found this chapter to be quite a handful. In addition to adding code for file uploads and accessing utilities outside of PHP, we've used a completely different method for the organization of the code.

The object-oriented approach used here may not be your cup of tea. And if it's not, you're in good company. Many people who work with PHP feel that object-oriented programming makes little sense in a Web development environment. But there are advantages.

As you can see in this application, once the classes are created, there's very little you need to do get great functionality within your scripts. You will see in Chapter 14 that we can take the code created here and build on it.

Chapter 11

Content Management System

IN THIS CHAPTER

◆ Creating an affordable content-management system.

◆ Maintaining security in your databases

◆ Anticipating shortcomings in MySQL's privilege scheme

WELCOME TO OUR FAVORITE application in this book. Don't get me wrong, we love the guestbook, we love the shopping cart, and we adore the problem tracker. But, as we spent our formative years dealing with Web sites that produced a steady stream of prose, we know the importance of having some sort of content-management system in place.

Content-management systems come in all shapes, sizes, and costs. Depending on your needs or your company's, you might be inclined to make a five-figure investment in something like Vignette or a six- to seven-figure investment in Broadvision. But your choices don't end there. Zope (http://www.zope.org) and Midgard (http://www.midgard-project.org/) and eGrail (http://www.egrail.com/) are just three of the open-source options for content management.

Given all of these options, you might wonder why you should consider using the application presented here – why not just run off one of the aforementioned applications? There is, in fact, an excellent reason. Content management is a field in which a high degree of customization is necessary. Your company's concerns are going to be distinct from any other's, and no matter what system you end up using, you are going to need to do a lot of coding to get your systems working just the way you want.

If you decide on Vignette, you'll need to learn a nasty little language called Tcl (pronounced "tickle"). If you want to use Zope, you will have to add Python to your repertoire. Midgard is a PHP-based solution, and there's no question that there's a lot of good code in there. It's open source, and presents a nice opportunity to contribute to the development of an increasingly sophisticated piece of software.

But you may just want something you can call your own, a solution that you know inside out, something that is built to solve the problems specific to your organization. So take a look at what's available, see if your challenges, budget, and temperament make one of the ready-made solutions a good fit. If not, you can look at the framework and code presented here and adapt them to your needs, or maybe just re-code from scratch.

Determining the Scope and Goals of the Application

First off, you are going to need a site that presents content. For the sake of presenting this content-management application, we've created a fairly basic site (which is in the book/netsloth/ directory on the CD-ROM). But whatever site you create is going to require all the design and editorial resources you can muster, and we're not going to worry about that too much here.

Your content-management system is going to need to do several things. Its most obvious purpose is to offer an environment where writers, editors, and administrators can create new stories. Additionally, it must offer a flexible series of stages through which a story moves. For example, if originally implemented with a single editorial stage, the application must be flexible enough to accommodate an additional editorial stage (or several of them) if needed.

Additionally, this application must meet the various demands of a staff. There will be a series of writers, and some by-line information will be presented with each story. Further, in the editorial process staff members will be assigned specific functions. Various levels of permission will ensure that not everyone will have the authority to edit, proofread, or make a story available to the world at large.

Finally, there must be a sort of super-user authority. A few select people will have the authority to add users and authorities to the editorial staff.

Necessary pages

First off, you need a site, a place where the articles will be displayed. As this isn't really the focus of this application, we've dealt with it very briefly. You will obviously need to code a site that fits your needs. Figures 11-1 and 11-2 show the Netsloth site in all its glory.

This application manages content and the creators of the content. You will need a series of editorial stages and a series of users. Users will have access only to the stages that involve them. Figure 11-3 shows a page that lists sample stages and users. Figures 11-4 and 11-5 show pages that administer these rights and stages, respectively.

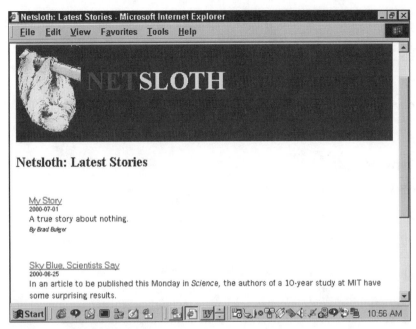

Figure 11-1: Netsloth index page

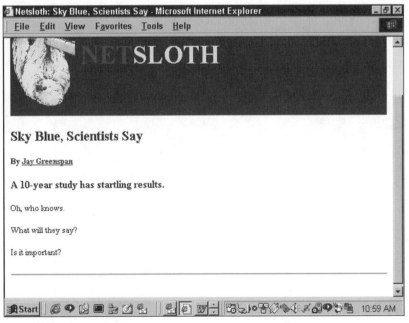

Figure 11-2: View story page

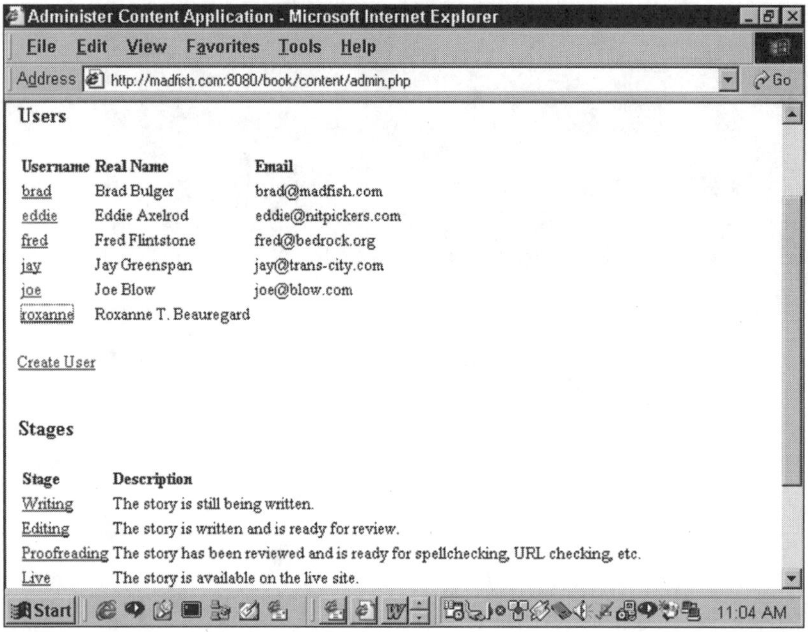

Figure 11-3: Rights and stages page

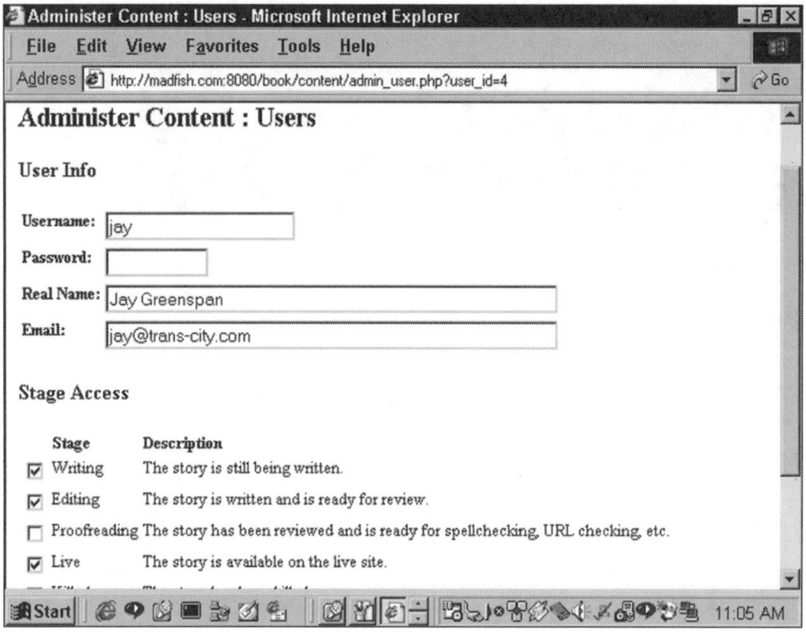

Figure 11-4: Rights administration page

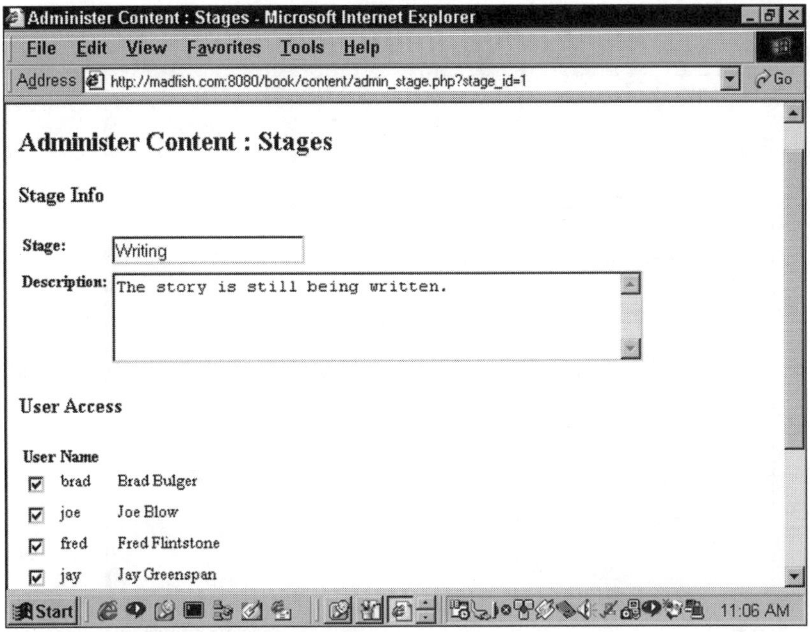

Figure 11-5: Stages administration page

This application also needs a workspace, a page where writers and editors can create stories, and where stories can work their way through the editorial process. The workspace will contain a few fields that identify the author, the date, the body of text, and other necessary information. Additionally, the stage of the editorial process that the story is in is indicated. This page is shown in Figure 11-6.

Another important aspect of an editorial environment is versioning. It's very important to be able to track pieces as they work through the process. You'll want to know who is making bad changes. Remember: good project management is all about keeping your hands clean and assigning blame. (Note: be completely arbitrary in your assignations — it will keep your staff off balance). Figure 11-7 shows the page that tracks versions, or the story history page.

This application performs a few more tasks, but they are minor enough to overlook here. Anyway, now that we're well into the "Not-So-Simple" portion of the book, you should be able to figure this stuff out. Right?

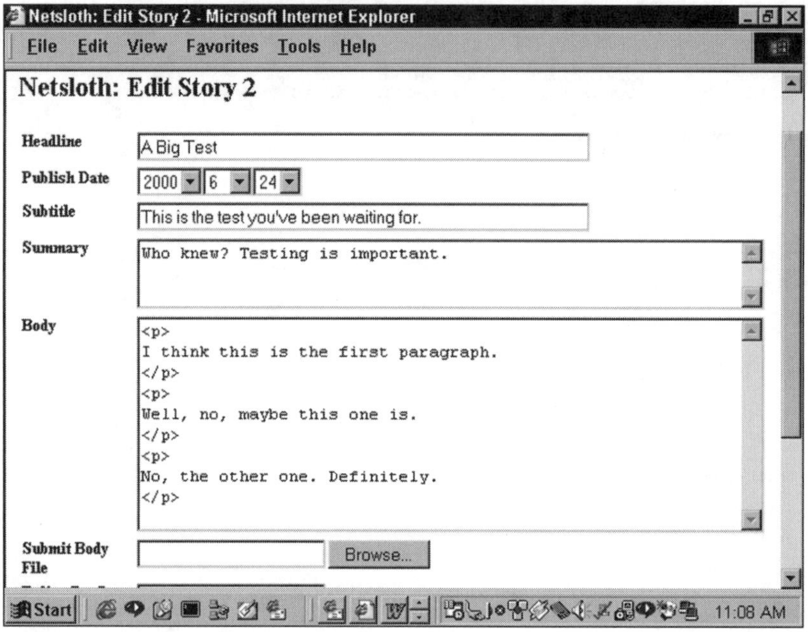

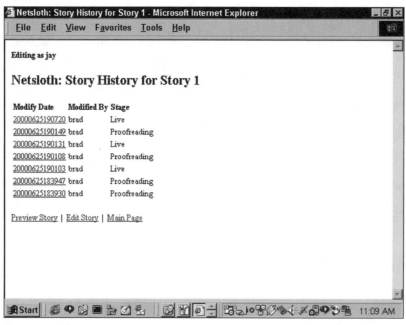

Figure 11-6: Editorial workplace

Figure 11-7: Story history page

What do you need to prevent?

The major issue in this application is ensuring that users do only what they are permitted to do, and absolutely no more. To do this, the application makes use of MySQL administrative privileges.

In all of the previous applications, there was a simple header file that called a function to log into the database. Each file ended up using the same `dbconnect()` call, with the same username and password. But that won't work here because different users need different levels of access.

Moreover, in this application some users are going to need the ability to grant access to others. Workers will come and go and their responsibilities will change. An administrator will need to be able to change these rights. Since we don't want everybody who logs into the database to have the same rights, this application will need the facility to have different people log in using different names and passwords.

Privileges in MySQL are granted and revoked with the aptly named grant statement. It's fairly painless and is described in Appendix D. So before you move forward with this application, it might be worth taking a quick look at that appendix.

It's worth mentioning here that in this application you will run into some of the weirder aspects of MySQL. If some of the design of this application seems a little strange, that's because it is. But that proverbial bridge will be crossed in due time.

Designing the Database

The schema represented in Figure 11-8 shows how this application divides its data. Keep in mind as you look at this that in database-development land there is usually more than one decent way to go about things. You might find a different way to arrange this type of data that works equally well. In fact, you may even prefer another way. That's fine with the writers of this book. We encourage independent thought and creativity, as long as it does not result in immoral or ungodly behavior. So normalize your data as you see fit, but in the process please don't violate any natural laws.

Start by looking at the story_author_map table. Notice how it is on the many end of one-to-many relationships with two tables: the story table and the author table. This is a classic many-to-many relationship. The reason for this is as follows: It is possible that a single story will have more than one author, and it's more than likely that an author will contribute to more than one story. The forms as set up in the application do not at this point have a facility for adding multiple authors, but that's easy enough to change if you wish. It's best to start with this flexibility, even if you don't need it right away.

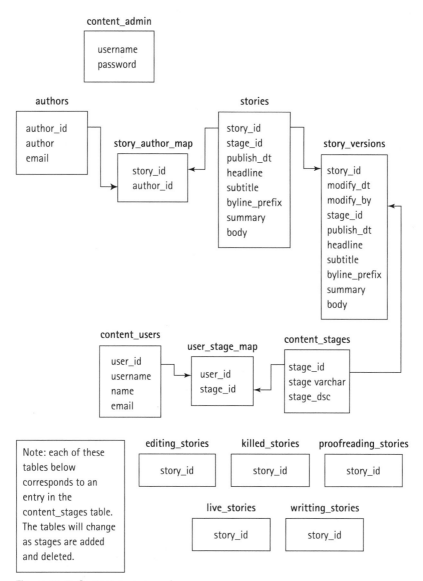

Figure 11-8: Content manager schema

The table story_author_map makes it possible for simple SQL statements with a couple of joins to get either a listing of specific authors and the stories they're involved with or specific stories and the authors who have worked them. For example, the following would get all the stories in the database written by Jay Greenspan.

```
select s.headline, s.byline_prefix, a.author
from stories s, story_author_map m, authors a
```

```
where s.story_id = m.story_id and
    m.author_id = a.author_id and
    a.author = 'Jay Greenspan'
```

The next thing to be aware of is the relationship between the stories table and the story_versions table. As we already mentioned, versioning is very important to a content-management system. In this case, it means that you must have access to old versions of articles. The way this schema is set up, the most current version of an article is always kept in the stories table. Additionally, every version of a story, including the most recent, is kept in the story_versions table.

Now on to the tables that define the stages in the editorial process and the users who will have access to those stages: content_users, content_stages, and user_stage_map. Once again, a many-to-many relationship ensures that the application will track the users and stages and the intersections of the two easily enough. Want to find all the users that have the rights to make content publicly available? This will work:

```
select c.user_id
from content_users c, user_stage_map m, content_stages s
where s.stage='Live' and
    s.stage_id = m.stage_id and
    m.user_id = c.user_id
```

This setup enforces some of the security needed in this application. If a user does not have a listing in the user_stage_map for a particular item, he will not be able to perform that task.

You might be wondering who has the rights to grant these privileges. Those people are listed in the content_admin table.

If you decide to tweak this application for your own purposes, you may find that using these tables may be all the security you need. If your users don't have access to the Unix box storing the database server, these tables should be enough. However, if your users are able to get at the data in others ways — perhaps by logging into the server and launching the MySQL command line client and running queries directly — you may need a bit more.

In a case such as this, you want to grant users privileges to log into the database. So you have to give them usernames and passwords using the grant statement discussed in Appendix D. Then no matter where the users are accessing the data from they will only have access to the appropriate data.

Sounds great, right? Well, it would be great, but when you try to do this your application runs into some of the limitations of MySQL, and working around these limitations makes for some weird solutions.

As of the writing of this book, MySQL is missing two things you could have made great use of here. First is a feature known as Views. A view is pretty easy concept to understand. When creating a view, an administrator defines a virtual table that may be a join of many tables and may only show some of the columns in the used tables. By restricting the user to a view of the data, the administrator can restrict what the user is permitted to see. Note that in most SQL servers, views are read only.

> **TIP** There isn't a development tool on the planet that doesn't have its quirks. Every language and every database presents it own challenges. The more of these that you are aware of before you start writing your application, the better off you will be.

The second thing missing from MySQL that would have been nice to use here is a more restrictive grant statement (please see Appendix D). As it stands, MySQL can grant authorities on several levels: for an entire installation, for a specific database, for tables within a database, or for columns within a table. While this may sound quite extensive, it is really not as complete as it could be.

Consider this problem: in MySQL, using table- or column-level grants, how could you prevent user john, who needs to have only editorial privileges, from updating stories that are already live? The best way to go about it would be to have very specific privileges in the stories table. If the stage_id for Live is 4, you'd want a grant to john that gave him access to alter any of the rows in the stories table, except those where stage_id = 4. Other databases allow this, but MySQL does not.

The best you could do with MySQL is provide backup security to the content_users, content_stages, and user_stage_map tables. This backup plan will only work within the PHP scripts that access the database. If you grant users permission, they will be able to log into the database via avenues other than the Web. And, as we already mentioned, the rights you can grant may not be as restrictive as you like. Grant rights at your own discretion.

Here's how the secondary security works within the PHP scripts. When the administrator creates a stage, a row is added to the content_stages table. In addition, a `create` query makes a table with a single column to store the story_ids. For the proofreading stage, there is a table called proofreading_stories.

When new users are created, rights to these tables will be granted when appropriate. As a story works its way through the editorial process, the story_id is written to the corresponding stage table, such as proofreading_stories. If the user does not have rights for that table, the update is rejected.

Here's a quick example of how this would work. Say that you, the administrator of this content management system, decided that you needed to add another stage to your editorial process, called format_review. If you are logged into the application as a user listed in the content_admin table, you will have the rights to create this stage. The stage will first be added to the content_stages table. When you create the stage, you will indicate which of the users should have the authority to use this stage. Those users will be added to the user_stage_map table with a different row for each user_id/stage_id combination. This is our primary security, and if you're adapting this application for use in your system, you would probably leave it at this.

However, using MySQL grants we're taking another step. MySQL grants won't allow us to say "grant all authority to user on stories table where stage_id=4". Instead we create an additional table named format_review_stories. Rights to this table will be granted to only those who need format review capability. As a story makes its way through the editorial process, the story_id will be copied to the appropriate stage table. When it reaches format_review, the story_id will be copied to the format_review_stories table. Because we can enforce grants on a table, we know that unauthorized users will not be able to access the format_review_stories table. If an unauthorized user tries to update the format_review_stories table, the query will be refused.

This is hardly ideal. In fact, it's pretty sloppy. If we were to deploy this application in the real world it is doubtful that we'd actually try to make this work with grant statements. We'd probably just make sure that the user had no direct access to the database whatsoever and let the user_stage_map table make sure the users were properly restricted. However, we thought it would be useful to show an example of how to work with MySQLs grant statements from a PHP interface.

Listing 11-1 shows the tables in the content administration application.

Listing 11-1: Create Statements for the Content Management System

```
# Table structure for table 'authors'
#
CREATE TABLE authors (
  author_id int(11) DEFAULT '0' NOT NULL auto_increment,
  author varchar(50),
  email varchar(255),
  bio text,
  PRIMARY KEY (author_id)
);


#
# Table structure for table 'content_admin'
#
CREATE TABLE content_admin (
  username varchar(50) DEFAULT '' NOT NULL,
  password varchar(255) DEFAULT '' NOT NULL
);


#
# Table structure for table 'content_stages'
#
CREATE TABLE content_stages (
  stage_id int(11) DEFAULT '0' NOT NULL auto_increment,
  stage varchar(20) DEFAULT '' NOT NULL,
```

```
    stage_dsc text,
    PRIMARY KEY (stage_id)
);


# Table structure for table 'content_users'
#
CREATE TABLE content_users (
    user_id int(11) DEFAULT '0' NOT NULL auto_increment,
    username varchar(20) DEFAULT '' NOT NULL,
    name varchar(50),
    email varchar(255),
    PRIMARY KEY (user_id)
);


#
# Table structure for table 'editing_stories'
#
CREATE TABLE editing_stories (
    story_id int(11) DEFAULT '0' NOT NULL,
    UNIQUE story_id (story_id)
);


#
# Table structure for table 'killed_stories'
#
CREATE TABLE killed_stories (
    story_id int(11) DEFAULT '0' NOT NULL,
    UNIQUE story_id (story_id)
);


#
# Table structure for table 'live_stories'
#
CREATE TABLE live_stories (
    story_id int(11) DEFAULT '0' NOT NULL,
    UNIQUE story_id (story_id)
);


#
# Table structure for table 'proofreading_stories'
#
CREATE TABLE proofreading_stories (
    story_id int(11) DEFAULT '0' NOT NULL,
    UNIQUE story_id (story_id)
```

```
);

#
# Table structure for table 'stories'
#
CREATE TABLE stories (
  story_id int(11) DEFAULT '0' NOT NULL auto_increment,
  stage_id int(11) DEFAULT '0' NOT NULL,
  publish_dt date,
  headline varchar(255),
  subtitle varchar(255),
  byline_prefix varchar(20),
  summary text,
  body text,
  PRIMARY KEY (story_id),
  KEY story_stage_key (stage_id)
);

#
# Table structure for table 'story_author_map'
#
CREATE TABLE story_author_map (
  story_id int(11) DEFAULT '0' NOT NULL,
  author_id int(11) DEFAULT '0' NOT NULL,
  PRIMARY KEY (story_id),
  KEY author_story_map_key (author_id)
);

#
# Table structure for table 'story_versions'
#
CREATE TABLE story_versions (
  story_id int(11) DEFAULT '0' NOT NULL,
  modify_dt timestamp(14),
  modify_by varchar(20) DEFAULT '' NOT NULL,
  stage_id int(11) DEFAULT '0' NOT NULL,
  publish_dt date,
  headline varchar(255),
  subtitle varchar(255),
  byline_prefix varchar(20),
  summary text,
  body text,
  KEY story_version_key (story_id,modify_dt)
);
```

```
#
# Table structure for table 'user_stage_map'
#
CREATE TABLE user_stage_map (
  user_id int(11) DEFAULT '0' NOT NULL,
  stage_id int(11) DEFAULT '0' NOT NULL,
  PRIMARY KEY (user_id,stage_id),
  KEY stage_user_map_key (stage_id)
);

#
# Table structure for table 'writing_stories'
#
CREATE TABLE writing_stories (
  story_id int(11) DEFAULT '0' NOT NULL,
  UNIQUE story_id (story_id)
);
```

Code Overview

At this point, we assume that you are getting comfortable with the way the applications in this book have been constructed. You should be familiar with the functions introduced in Chapter 8, and the way PHP embeds MySQL commands within the scripts.

As you work through, less and less of the code should require explanation. Thus, the descriptions of the code will deal only with those parts that are really new or tricky.

Here, most of the newer-looking code will come from assigning the privileges discussed in the previous section. The application sends queries that you haven't used before.

Code Breakdown

Once again, the code in this application will make heavy use of the functions in the /functions/ folder. A lot of the code presented here will make calls to those functions.

Reusable functions

In this application, there is only one file with application-specific functions: /content/ functions.php.

FUNCTIONS FROM /CONTENT/FUNCTIONS.PHP

These will be used throughout the application. There will be many references to Chapter 9 in this section.

LIST_STORIES() As mentioned in Chapter 10, in MySQL version 3.23 you can work MySQL's lack of support for unions by creating temporary tables. However, we developed all of the applications on this book using MySQL version 3.22, which does not support the create temporary table feature. This gets to be a problem when you need to print out the contents of two queries within a single table. If you look at the source code on the CD-ROM, you will see that the pages start by printing all of the stories currently within the workflow that the current user has access to. Following that, if the user has access to live stories, the live stories should be printed within the same table.

To create this table, we need to call this function twice, passing the result identifier of the query as the first argument. If the query has at least one row, the table header will be printed, and $in_table will be set to 1. The next time the function is called, the value of $in_table will be passed as the second argument. If the value of $in_table is 1 the header will not print.

Again, if you are using MySQL version 3.23, use the create temporary table feature.

```
function list_stories($result, $in_table="")
{
        if (empty($in_table)) { $in_table = 0; }

        while ($row = mysql_fetch_array($result))
        {
                if ($in_table == 0)
                {
                        print subtitle("Edit Stories");
                        print start_table();
                        print table_row("<b>Stage</b>"
                                , "<b>Story</b>"
                                , "<b>Publish Date</b>"
                        );
                        $in_table = 1;
                }
            print table_row($row["stage"],

anchor_tag("edit_story.php?story_id=".$row["story_id"]
                , $row["headline"]
                )
                , $row["publish_dt"]
        );
        }
        return $in_table;
}
```

FETCH_STORY() This function, like most of those in this section, makes use of the `fetch_record()` function, which is discussed in Chapter 9. In the call to the `fetch_record()`, a story_id, which is the primary key of the table, is specified. Therefore, you can be sure that the query created by fetch_record will have only one row. The query in fetch_record will get all columns for the story_id.

```
function fetch_story ($story_id="")
{
    $result = fetch_record("stories","story_id",$story_id);
    return $result;
}
```

Because there is only one row, the fetch_record will call the `set_result_variable()` function (also discussed in Chapter 9). That function will make all of the columns for that story_id available as globals. From the schema in Figure 11-7, you can see that those columns are story_id int, stage_id, publish_dt, headline, subtitle, byline_prefix, summary, and body.

So after running `fetch_story` you can access any of the columns as global variables.

```
fetch_story(1);
echo $headline;
```

The `fetch_record()` function is discussing in Chapter 9.

FETCH_STORY_VERSION() This function works almost identically to the `fetch_story()` function just described, the only difference being that multiple attributes are being passed to the `fetch_record` function. These are added to the SQL statement. Note that the modify_dt column is 14 digits (YYYYMMDDHHMMSS). The combination of a story_id and the second at which it was modified makes for a pretty good two-column primary key, so any query here should only return one row.

```
function fetch_story_version ($story_id="",$modify_dt="")
{
    $result = fetch_record("story_versions"
        ,array("story_id","modify_dt")
        ,array($story_id,"'$modify_dt'")
    );
    return $result;
}
```

FUNCTION FETCH_AUTHOR() This function works similarly to the `fetch_story` function. It creates global variables from row retrieved from the author table.

```
function fetch_author ($author_id="")
{
    $result = fetch_record("authors","author_id",$author_id);
    return $result;
}
```

FUNCTION FETCH_CONTENT_USER() This function also works identically to the `fetch_story` function. It creates global variables from the row retrieved from the content_user table.

```
function fetch_content_user ($user_id="")
{
    $result = fetch_record("content_users","user_id",$user_id);
    return $result;
}
```

FUNCTION FETCH_CONTENT_STAGE() Once again, this function works identically to `fetch_story`. It creates global variables from a row retrieved from the content_stages table.

```
function fetch_content_stage ($stage_id="")
{
    $result = fetch_record("content_stages","stage_id",$stage_id);
    return $result;
}
```

Interesting Code Flow

Since most of the more complicated stuff in this application has to do with maintaining users and stages, we will start the breakdown of code with the pages that take care of these stages. Later we will move on to the other features performed by this application.

content/authenticate.php

As we already mentioned, this application differs from the previous ones in that each user will be logging into the database with his or her own username and password. The script that performs this login will need to be just a touch more flexible than the one you used in the other applications.

This application is going to use the same 401-type authentication used in the previous examples, but here the values for $PHP_AUTH_USER and $PHP_AUTH_PW will also be the values used to log into the database.

 $PHP_AUTH_USER and $PHP_AUTH_PW are only available if PHP is installed as an Apache module. If you are working on Windows, you will not be able to use this type of authentication.

The header.php file, which is included in every page in the content management system, contains the following code:

```
if ($authentication == "admin")
{
    include "admin_authenticate.php";
}
else
{
    include "authenticate.php";
}
$this_username = $PHP_AUTH_USER;
```

This if ... else block determines which authentication script will run. In pages that require administrative access you will see a variable assignment like the following prior to the include of header.php.

```
$authentication = "admin";
```

If this does not exist, the authenticate.php will be included.
Here are the contents of the authenticate.php file.

```
$realm = "Netsloth Content";
$errmsg = "You must enter a valid name & password to access this
function";
if (empty($PHP_AUTH_USER)
    || ( !empty($newuser) && $olduser == $PHP_AUTH_USER )
)
{
        $what = empty($PHP_AUTH_USER) ? "login" :
            "newuser($newuser,$olduser)";
            authenticate($realm,$errmsg.":$what");
}
```

```
$mylink = @mysql_connect("localhost", $PHP_AUTH_USER, $PHP_AUTH_PW)
        or authenticate
        ($realm,"Could not login to db as $PHP_AUTH_USER");

mysql_select_db("netsloth");
```

As you look at the preceding code, keep in mind that in this script people using the application need to be able to change the usernames and passwords that they are using to log into the application – i.e., log in as a different user. If you go through the script step by step, you should see how to do it. We'll go through it line-by-line after one quick explanation.

Within the index.php page, there is a submit button that, when pressed, will indicate that the user wants to login in under a different username and password. The following creates the form with the submit button.

```
print paragraph(
    start_form("index.php")
    , hidden_field("olduser",$PHP_AUTH_USER)
    , submit_field("newuser","Log In As New User")
    , end_form()
);
```

Using the functions described in chapter Chapter 9, this code creates a form, that, if submitted, sends the variables $olduser and $newuser back to the index.php page. When the form is submitted and the variables are sent, they will hit this portion of the authenticate.php page.

```
if (empty($PHP_AUTH_USER)
    || ( !empty($newuser) && $olduser == $PHP_AUTH_USER )
)
```

The preceding if block will test true under two conditions. First, if the user has not yet logged in, because in that case $PHP_AUTH_USER will be empty. The other condition comes from the form we just discussed. If that submit button is pressed, $newuser will not be empty and $olduser will contain the value of $PHP_AUTH_USER, meaning the user wishes to change her login name and password. If either of these is true, the following code will run:

```
{
        $what = empty($PHP_AUTH_USER) ? "login" :
            "newuser($newuser,$olduser)";
            authenticate($realm,$errmsg.":$what");
}
```

The preceding code is a trinary operator that will determine the value of $what. If $PHP_AUTH_USER is empty (meaning the user is not yet logged in) $what will be assigned a value of "login". Otherwise, what will be assigned is a string of "newuser()" along with the values in $newuser and $olduser. The value of what is appended to the error message, which is sent to the authenticate() function, which is discussed in Chapter 9. If the user cancels the login an error message like one of the following will appear:

```
You must enter a valid name & password to access this function:login

You must enter a valid name & password to access this
function:newuser(Log In As New User,tater)
```

At this point all that's left to do is connect to MySQL and select the database.

```
$mylink = @mysql_connect("localhost", $PHP_AUTH_USER, $PHP_AUTH_PW)
        or authenticate
        ($realm,"Could not login to db as $PHP_AUTH_USER");
mysql_select_db("netsloth");
```

content/admin_user.php

This page, like many you have seen before, has many purposes. The exact portion of the script that will run will depends on the variables that are sent to the page. It will do the following:

◆ Enable an administrator to create new users.

◆ The information specific to a single user_id will be displayed, including the stages associated with that user.

◆ Additional stages can be granted to an exiting user.

◆ Rights to a stage can be revoked from a user.

If the page is accessed without any variable information in the querystring or from POST, the form elements for user information will be blank. This information must be filled in before the form is submitted. When the form is submitted the admin_user.php page will be called again, this time holding the entered form data and with the $submit variable equal to "Save Changes".

When submitted, the condition in the if statement at the top of the page will test true:

```
if (!empty($submit) && $submit == "Save Changes")
```

As the same form updates an existing user's information and creates a new user, there is a second condition that must be tested. If the user's information must be updated, the form passes a user_id from a hidden form element; otherwise the $user_id variable is empty. The result of this statement decides whether the script is to perform an update or insert query.

```
if (empty($user_id))
{
    safe_query("insert into content_users (username, name, email)
        values ('$username', '$name', '$email')
    ");
    $user_id = mysql_insert_id();
}
else
{
    safe_query("update content_users set
        username='$username',
            name='$name', email='$email'
        where user_id = $user_id
    ");

}
");
```

Note that when this section of the script is completed, the user_id is known: either it was passed from the form or it was retrieved with the mysql_insert_id() function.

That brings this script to a series of MySQL grant statements that are sent via the safe_query() function. Notice the first two queries, which are within if blocks. These test whether this is a new user who has previously been granted rights. If it is a user whose rights are being updated, she will already have an entry in the user table in the mysql database. If not, she will need to be placed in that table. Note that the "grant usage" query enters the person in the mysql table but gives no specific rights to any databases or tables.

```
$result = safe_query("select 1 from mysql.user
    where User = '$username'
");
$rows = mysql_num_rows($result);
if ($rows == 0)    {
    safe_query("grant usage on netsloth.* to $username");
}
if (!empty($password))
{
    safe_query("set password for $username
```

```
            = password('$password')
    ");
}
```

Now that the user has an entry in the mysql table, the script removes all rights to the netsloth database. You do this in order to start fresh, and grant only the needed privileges. If you didn't delete every entry, you would need to go through and test whether each privilege already existed, and revoke those that didn't belong. In the end, wiping away privileges and granting only those indicated by the checkboxes is the easiest way to go. But before granting user-specific rights, the following code cleans out the mysql.tables_priv table and grants rights needed by every user of the application.

```
safe_query("delete from mysql.tables_priv
       where Db = 'netsloth' and User = '$username'
    ");
safe_query("flush privileges");

safe_query("grant select,insert,update,delete
       on netsloth.stories to $username
    ");
safe_query("grant select,insert,update,delete
       on netsloth.story_versions to $username
    ");
safe_query("grant select,insert,update,delete
       on netsloth.authors to $username
    ");
safe_query("grant select,insert,update,delete
       on netsloth.story_author_map to $username
    ");
safe_query("grant select on netsloth.content_admin
       to $username");
safe_query("grant select on netsloth.content_users
       to $username");
safe_query("grant select on netsloth.content_stages
       to $username");
safe_query("grant select on netsloth.user_stage_map
       to $username");
```

Now the script removes entries from user_stage_map (which is the primary source of security here) because again we want to start fresh. The stages were presented in a series of checkboxes, and the ones that are checked when the form is submitted are passed as an array named $stages. The script loops through the array granting rights to the appropriate stage table (for example, proofreading_table) and making the needed inserts into the user_stage_map table.

```
safe_query("delete from user_stage_map where user_id = $user_id");
if (is_array($stages))
{
    while (list(,$stage) = each($stages))
    {
        $stage_table = strtolower(trim($stage))."_stories";
        safe_query("grant select,insert,update,delete
        on $stage_table to $username
        ");
        $pquery = "insert into user_stage_map
            (user_id, stage_id)
            select $user_id, stage_id
            from content_stages
            where stage = '$stage'
        ";
        safe_query($pquery);
    }
}
```

Finally this script prints out the appropriate user information (if existing user information exists) and the stages as a series of checkboxes. The checkboxes are checked if the user has rights for that stage.

The following query is intended to work with the checkbox_field() function you created earlier. That function takes three arguments (for name, value, and matchvalue). If the second and third match, the checkbox will be marked as checked.

```
$query = "select distinct
                if(m.user_id is null,'-',s.stage) as matchvalue
                , s.stage_id, s.stage, s.stage_dsc
                from content_stages s, content_users u
                left join user_stage_map m
                        on s.stage_id = m.stage_id
                        and m.user_id = u.user_id
                where u.user_id=$user_id
        ";
```

This query gathers all of the stages and does an outer join on the content_users table. If the user has been granted access to a stage, that stage name appears in the returned record set, in the matchvalue field. If not, a dash is returned in the field. When the checkbox_field() function is run later in the loop, the third argument will either be a dash or will have the same value as the stage field. The results of this query might look like this:

```
+------------+----------+--------------+----------------------+
| matchvalue | stage_id | stage        | stage_dsc            |
+------------+----------+--------------+----------------------+
| Writing    |        1 | Writing      | Being written.       |
| Editing    |        2 | Editing      | Ready for review.    |
| -          |        3 | Proofreading | Spellchecking, etc.  |
| Live       |        4 | Live         | Story is available.  |
| Killed     |        5 | Killed       | Dead.                |
+------------+----------+--------------+----------------------+
```

This knowledge should allow you to read the rest of this script. And, of course, there are further comments included with the application on the CD-ROM.

content/edit_story.php

At almost 500 lines, this script is long, but it isn't especially complicated. Given the data structure we discussed earlier, it needs to create new stories and update existing stories after they have been through an editorial pass. Along the way the script will need to check if the user has the rights to do the work on the story, and clean up text that a users put into the forms.

The file should be readable by examining the comments within the page, which are supplied on the accompanying CD-ROM. There are quite a few decisions that need to be made in order to get this page to work correctly, and that adds to the length. But decisions that are made within the file are pretty straight forward. Additionally, there are quite a few insert and update statements. If you keep figure 11-8 close by while you're reading through the code, this shouldn't be too tough to get through.

This chapter has spent a fair amount of space discussing how to assign rights to a user using MySQL's grant statements. Hopefully at this point you see how those rights are assigned. The short piece of script following tests whether the current user has the rights to work on a story, based on the rights in the grants tables.

It first gets the stage name, based on a stage_id, then creates the string of the table name by appending the stage name with "_table". Then a select statement runs that includes the table name you have just created. If that query is not allowed, the query will fail and return false. Also within the query, we are involving the user_stage_map table. That table provides our primary security, and the user must have rights for the current stage in the user_stage_map table. If the user does not have rights defined in that table, the query will return no rows. If the query fails or returns nothing, an error will print and the script will exit.

```
$result = safe_query("select stage from content_stages
    where stage_id = $stage_id
    $result = safe_query("select stage from content_stages
        where stage_id = $stage_id
");
$stage = mysql_result($result,0);
if (!empty($stage))
{
    $stage_table = strtolower(trim($stage))."_stories";
    $result = mysql_query("select a.story_id
        from $stage_table a, content_users u, user_stage_map m
        where a.story_id = $story_id
            and u.username = '$this_username'
            and u.user_id = m.user_id
            and m.stage_id = $stage_id
    ");
if ($result === false || mysql_num_rows($result) == 0)
{
        print subtitle("You do not have the ability to edit
            stories in the $stage stage.
        ");
        print paragraph(anchor_tag("index.php","Main Page"));
        exit;

    }

}
```

The other item of particular interest is the extensive text processing done in this script. This is an example of the type of processing you might need to do if your users are working with some sort of text processing tool (HTML editor, word processor). Every tool has its own little quirks that you will need to account for. The only way you are going to find out exactly what type of cleanup you need to do is examine the code created be the text editor in your workplace.

For instance, you are not going to want to have <body> tags in the body of an article.

```
$body = eregi_replace("^.*<body[^>]*>","",$body);
$body = eregi_replace("</body.*$","",$body);
```

Of course, PHP's strip_tags() function could work for you, if you want to allow a limited tag set and remove all others tags.

It's very important to run the stripslashes function on text that has been uploaded by a form and is being re-presented on an HTML page. In all likelihood, your magic_quotes_gpc setting (see Appendix B) will automatically escape and quotes or hyphens with backslashes in uploaded text. If you then send it out to the browser at that point, the user will see the backslashes on the screen. Furthermore, if the text is uploaded again, another set of backslashes will be added.

```
$body = stripslashes($body);
$headline = stripslashes($headline);
$subtitle = stripslashes($subtitle);
$summary = stripslashes($summary);
```

Starting at line 300 of the edit_story.php file there is a nice block of code that will do a couple of neat things. If it appears the user input the story without using <p> tags, the script will add them where it seems appropriate, assuming the user indicated paragraphs with newlines (hard returns). If the user did use <p> tags, the script examines the text, making sure that there are no funky spaces or malformed tags. We recommend that you look at the code and comments provided on the CD-ROM to get a good feel for how to do complex text handling.

Summary

In this chapter you saw some of the nifty things that can go into creating a content management system. Of course an application such as this can be far, far more complex than this. But this is a good start and presents a reasonable way to organize your code and database tables.

We also made use of MySQL's grant statements when creating this application. As we've said throughout this application, the grant scheme that we've used here may not be terribly practical. However, it does provide a good example of how you could go about setting up a system where one login name and password for the entire application isn't enough.

Also, make sure to take a look at some of the text handling code in edit_story.php. Some of the code provides an excellent example of what you can do with PHP's string handling functions and regular expressions.

Chapter 12

Threaded Discussion

IN THIS CHAPTER

◆ Adding community to your Web site

◆ Using an advanced technique to write functions

◆ Looking at other criteria to use when designing a database

IF YOU'VE CREATED A Web site or are looking to create one, it's probably safe to assume that you would like people to return frequently to your pages. But as everyone in the Web industry knows, loyalty is fleeting, and people are always looking for something better, more engaging, or closer to their interests. After all, there's always someone with a better collection of Britney Spears photos. One way to keep the anonymous masses involved with your site is to offer your visitors a way to contribute to its content. If someone has accessed your site, it's likely that he or she has an opinion on the topic you are presenting. And, if my conclusions from 30-plus years of observation are correct, people love to share their opinions. Using the threaded discussion application in this chapter, you can create an area on your Web site where your users can share their opinions and interact with you and each other.

Once you have this piece of your site up and running, you will be well on your way to creating your own Web community. I make special mention of the word *community* for two reasons. First, it is a huge buzzword within the industry. Everyone is looking to create a sense of familiarity and inclusion that will tempt users to return. The second – and perhaps more important – reason is that you, the webmaster, should know what you're getting yourself into. From personal experience, I can tell you that "community" can be a real pain in the butt. On the Web, everyone is pretty much anonymous, and there is little consequence associated with antisocial behavior. Thus, in many discussion groups, opinionated windbags have a way of ruining a promising discussion.

Before too long, you will undoubtedly see things that are mean or distasteful, and you must be prepared to deal with it. I'm not trying to scare you away from including a discussion list on your site. I'm just letting you know that you'll need to put some effort into administering it. Whether you monitor the list yourself or appoint someone to do it for you, somebody will need to make sure your users behave if you want it to be orderly and functional.

Determining the Scope and Goals of the Application

The purpose of any discussion board is reasonably simple. Any visitor to the site should be able to post a new topic to the board or reply to any of the existing topics. Furthermore, the board must be flexible enough to deal with any number of replies to an existing topic, or replies to replies, or replies to replies to replies, and so on and so forth. Put another way, this board must be able to deal with an indefinite level of depth. The script needs to react appropriately whether the discussion goes one level deep, five levels deep, or ten levels deep. This will require some new techniques, both in your data design and our scripts.

What do you need?

You will need only two files to generate all the views needed for this application. But these two files will have very different looks depending on what information is displayed.

The first file will display topics and their replies. The first time users come to the message board they will not know what threads they wish to read. Therefore a list of topics will be displayed. Figure 12-1 shows the list of top-level topics.

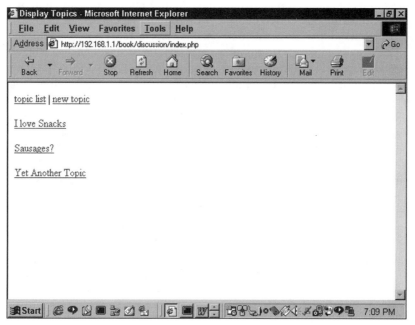

Figure 12-1: List of top-level topics

Once a user chooses a topic, the page will list all of the posts within that topic. As you can see in Figure 12-2, the top of the page shows the text and subject of the post being read. Below that, immediate replies to that post are indicated with a colored border, and the text of the immediate replies is also printed. Figure 12-2 also shows that the application provides a subject, name, and a link to posts that are more than a level deep in the thread. You can see that it is rather easy to see who has replied to what.

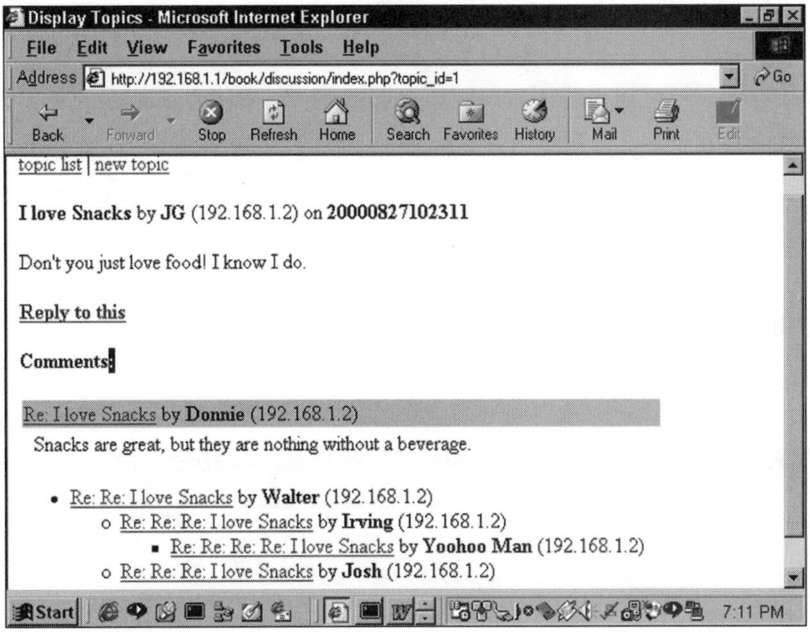

Figure 12-2: Display of a thread

This same page provides another view. If a user clicks through to a post that does not start a topic, the page will show all threads beneath. At the top of the page the script will print the top-level post (or root) and the post immediately prior to the one being viewed (or parent). Figure 12-3 shows an example of this view.

Everything you saw in the previous figures was handled by one page. The second page will post threads to the board. This requires only a simple form that contains form elements for a subject, a name, and room for the comment. The form will need to be aware of where in the thread the message belongs. For new top-level topics a form without any context will be fine (see Figure 12-4), but for replies within an existing thread some context will be helpful (see Figure 12-5).

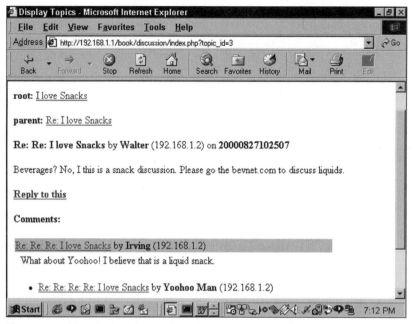

Figure 12-3: View further down a thread

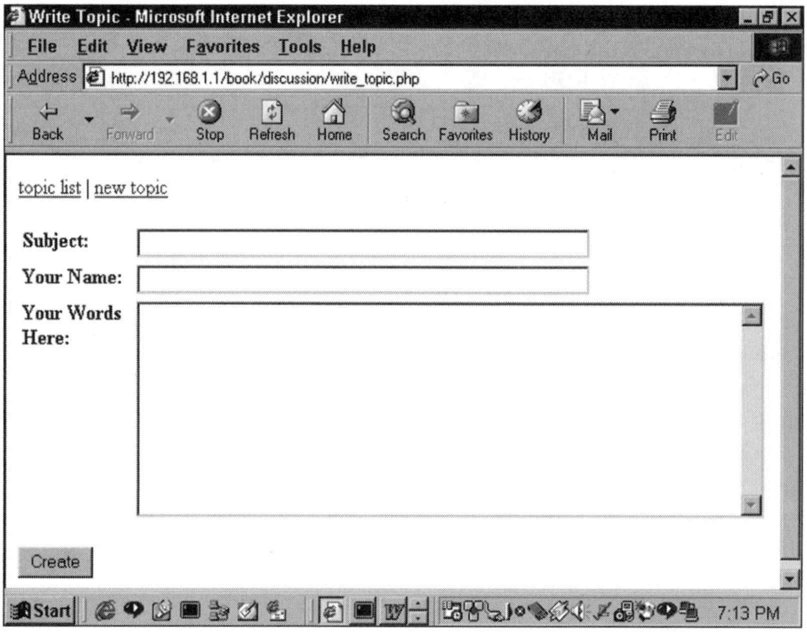

Figure 12-4: Form for posting a top-level topic

Write Topic - Microsoft Internet Explorer

File   Edit   View   Favorites   Tools   Help

Back   Forward   Stop   Refresh   Home   Search   Favorites   History   Mail   Print   Edit

root: I love Snacks

parent: Re: I love Snacks

Re: Re: I love Snacks by **Walter** (192.168.1.2) on **20000827102507**

Beverages? No, I this is a snack discussion. Please go the bevnet.com to discuss liquids.

Care to comment?

Subject: Re: Re: Re: I love Snacks

Your Name:

Your Words Here:

Start   7:14 PM

Figure 12-5: Form for posting a lower-level topic

What do you need to prevent?

As you've seen in previous chapters, you need to spend quite a bit of time making sure things work properly. We've talked before about the cross-site scripting bug. You'll surely want to prevent that from happening here.

Unless every post is reviewed before it becomes available on the site, there is no good way of preventing users from posting nonsense and then replying to their own meaningless posts. This kind of thing can get pretty distracting – and again, there is no foolproof way of preventing it. However, you can make it a bit more obvious to other users that the nefarious poster is a jerk. For that reason, this application collects the IP of origin and displays it for every post. This isn't great protection, but it is better than nothing.

As one of the reviewers of the book pointed out, all users behind the same firewall will have the same IP, and users who dial-up through an ISP will get a different IP every time. Furthermore, the reviewer felt including the IP address of someone who actually had a static IP was bad etiquette. After thinking about it, I tend to agree. However, we kept this code in the application just to keep the example. You could remove it from your code in a matter of seconds if you wish.

The Data

Of all the applications discussed in this book, this one has what I believe is the most unexpected data structure. In fact when I (Jay) saw what Brad had come up with for this section I broke down crying, unable to deal with the beauty of it.

I'll take a moment right here to tell you a little secret about database development: Though you can usually figure out the structure of a database by going through the normalization process, sometimes you're better off concentrating more on the hoped-for end result. You'll see what I mean as you read the rest of this section.

But before I show you what he created and why it works so well, let me give you an indication of what I was expecting — and why that would have been so problematic. You might think that this application would start with a table looking something like Table 12-1.

TABLE 12-1 PROBLEMATIC ROOT_TOPICS

root_topic_id	root_topic_date	root_topic_name	root_topic_subject	root_topic_text
1	08/20/2000	Jack	Snacks Rule	I love em.
2	08/20/2000	Edith	More Cheetos	I want my fingers orange.
3	9/1/2000	Archie	M&Ms	Mmmmore.

This table, as you can probably guess, would list the root topics. A simple SELECT * FROM root_topics would return a recordset of all the root topics. This table doesn't allow for any data below the root level. To take care of this, I envisioned a structure where each root_topic_id would be associated with another table. Whenever I inserted a row into the RootTopics table, I'd also run a CREATE TABLE statement to make a table that would store the replies to the root topic.

For instance, all the replies to the "Snacks Rule" post would be stored in a table that looked like Table 12-2. This would work. There would be a one-to-many relationship between the tables, and information would be available pretty readily. But now consider what would happen when somebody wanted to reply to one of these posts. I'd have to create yet another table. And what if I were to go another level or two deeper? I think it's easy to see that before long this would get completely out of control. With just a couple of active threads I could end up with dozens of tables that needed to be managed and joined. This would be no fun at all.

TABLE 12-2 PROBLEMATIC TOPICS

topic_id	topic_date	topic_author	topic_subject	topic_text
1	08/20/2000	Ellen	Re: Snacks Rule	You betcha
2	08/20/2000	Erners	Re: Snacks Rule	Indeed

Now let's move away from this ill-considered idea and move toward Brad's sound plan. Think about what information needs to be stored for each post to the mailing list. Start with the obvious stuff. You need a column that stores the subject of the thread (for instance, "Nachos, food of the gods"), one that stores the author's name, and one that records the date the item was posted. So the table starts with these columns – I've thrown in some sample information in Table 12-3 and an `auto_increment` primary key just to keep it clear.

TABLE 12-3 START OF A USEABLE TABLE

post_id	Subject	Author	Date
1	Nachos rule	Jay	3/12/2000
2	Cheetos are the best	Brad	3/12/2000

But of course this isn't enough. Somehow there needs to be a way to track the ancestry and lineage of any specific post. (Look again at Figure 12-1 if you are not sure what I mean.) So how are you going to be able to do this? If you are looking to track the ancestry of any particular thread, it would probably make sense to add a field that indicated the post that started the thread, which we're calling the root.

Take a close look at Table 12-4. Start with the first row. Here the root_id is the same as the post_id. Now look at the third row. Here the root_id (1) matches the post_id of the first row. So you know that the thread to which row three belongs started with post_id 1 – "Nachos Rule." Similarly, row 6 must be a reply to row 2.

TABLE 12-4 A MORE COMPLETE TABLE

post_ID	Root_ID	Subject	Author	Date
1	1	Nachos rule	Jay	3/12/2000
2	2	Cheetos are the best	Ed	3/12/2000
3	1	Re: Nachos rule	Don	3/12/2000
4	1	Re: Nachos rule	Bill	3/13/2000
5	5	What about cookies	Evany	3/14/2000
6	2	Re: Cheetos are the best	Ed	3/13/2000

Now look at rows 1, 2, and 5. Notice that in these rows the post_id and root_id are identical. At this point you can probably guess that whenever these two are the same, it indicates a root-level subject. Easy enough, right? The following SQL statement that would retrieve all of the root-level posts

```
select * from topics where root_id=post_id.
```

However, in this application, you will see us using a self join to get root-level topics.

```
select distinct current.topic_id, current.parent_id,
    current.root_id, current.name, current.description,
    current.author, current.author_host, current.create_dt,
    current.modify_dt
from topics current, topics child
where current.topic_id = child.root_id
```

This join will have the same effect, finding rows where the topic_id and root_id columns are the same. We use it here because, even though it's a little slower, it's more flexible, and is easier to adapt in the event there are changes to the system.

Now that you've added a root_id field to the table you should know the beginning of a thread. But how can you get all the posts that came between the original post and the one you're interested in? Initially you may think that it would be prudent to add a column that lists the ancestors. You could call the column ancestors and in it you'd have a listing of topic_ids. It might contain a string like "1, 6, 9, 12". This would be a very, very bad idea. Why, you ask? Well, the most important reason worth mentioning is that you should never put multiple values in a single field – you'll open yourself up to all kinds of hassles.

MySQL does have a column type that takes multiple values. It is called set. It is not used anywhere in this book because Dr. Codd would not approve. Do you remember Dr. Codd from Chapter 1? He's the guy who originally developed relational database theory in the first place.

So what options are you left with? Create another table to keep track of a post's lineage? I'm not sure how that would work, and as it turns out, it isn't necessary. The easiest thing to do is add a single column to the previous table that tracks the parent of the current post, as shown in Table 12-5.

TABLE 12-5 AN EVEN BETTER TABLE

post_id	root_id	parent_id	Subject	Author	Date
1	1	0	Nachos rule	Jay	3/12/2000
2	2	0	Cheetos are the best	Ed	3/12/2000
3	1	1	Re: Nachos rule	Don	3/12/2000
4	1	3	Re: Nachos rule	Bill	3/13/2000
5	5	0	What about cookies	Evany	3/13/2000
6	2	2	Re: Cheetos are the best	Ed	3/14/2000
7	1	4	Cheetos, are you kidding	Jeff	3/15/2000
8	5	5	Re: What about cookies	Jay	3/15/2000

When you look at the first couple of rows in Table 12-5, you might see little difference between the fields. And that sort of makes sense: if the post_id and the parent_id are the same, you already know it's a root level and that therefore the parent is irrelevant. Move your attention to row 7. Here you can see that root is row 1, "Nachos rule." That's easy enough. Now look at the parent_id, which is row 4. If you look at the parent of number 4, you will find that it's number 3 – and further that the parent of that row is row 1, which is also the root. So with just this information you can follow a thread to its origin. A very simple script that traces a post to its origin would look something like this:

```
Select all fields from current topic
If parent_id is not equal to 0 and parent_id does not equal root_id
    Make parent ID current topic
    Go to line 1
```

So that will about do it. Using this data structure, you can get all the information you are going to need. Throw in a couple of timestamps for safekeeping and it's all set. Here's the SQL statement that will create the table:

```
create table topics (
    topic_id integer default 0 not null auto_increment,
    parent_id integer default 0,
    root_id integer default 0,
    name varchar(255),
    description text,
    create_dt timestamp(14),
    modify_dt timestamp(14),
    author varchar(255),
    author_host varchar(255)
, primary key topics_key (topic_id)
);
```

Code Overview

As we mentioned earlier, there are two main functions involved in this application: displaying a listing of posts and inserting a new post to the database. Thus, it should come as little surprise that at the base level there are only two files: display_topic.php and write_topic.php. In addition to these files, you'll have a separate file that stores all of your functions (functions.php). If you read the previous section, you probably won't be surprised to find that most of the effort involved in developing this application, and therefore most of the code we'll be introducing, relates to displaying the ancestors and children of a particular post. Keep in mind that a post can have any number of ancestors and any number of children. So your script will have to be flexible enough to deal with a post with one reply or twenty.

The portion that writes a topic to the database should be pretty easy to deal with. In your form you'll need to have hidden fields that mark the root_id and parent_id, and you'll want to validate the contents of the forms, but other than that it should be pretty easy. Let's break it down.

Code Breakdown

As per usual, most of the fun occurs in the functions. In fact, in this application the only two files actually referenced by URLs are practically empty.

Reusable functions

Again, this application will make use of the functions described in Chapter 8. There are just a few other functions, one of which uses a technique that requires some explanation.

FUNCTIONS FROM /BOOK/DISCUSSION/FUNCTIONS.PHP

The concept that is new to this application is called *recursion*. It comes up in the display_kids() function.

DISPLAY_KIDS ()   Usually, in this part of the book, a function is displayed and then described. However, this function must be treated a bit differently because recursion can be somewhat difficult conceptually. So before I display the function, let's take a look at recursion. (If you already know your way around recursive functions, feel free to skim.)

The important thing to keep in mind is that you have no idea how deep any thread will be: there may be one level of replies, or there may be twenty. So to properly lay out all the children of any one thread you need a very, very flexible script. It will need to do something like this:

```
print current topic
while the current topic has unprocessed child topics
    set current topic to next unprocessed child
    go to line 1
end while
if current topic has a parent
   set current topic to that parent and go to line 2
else
   exit
end if
```

This must be repeated indefinitely until there are no other answers. But how do you tell a script to do something until it runs out of answers? The looping mechanisms we've discussed so far won't really work. The for.., while..., and do...while loops that we talked about in Chapter 2, and that we've used in the previous chapters, are of no help.

If that isn't clear take a look at Table 12-6 and the code that follows.

TABLE 12-6 SAMPLE TABLE

post_ID	root_ID	parent_ID	Subject	Name	Date
1	1	0	Nachos rule	Jay	3/12/2000
2	2	0	Cheetos are the best	Ed	3/12/2000
3	1	1	Re: Nachos rule	Don	3/12/2000
4	1	3	Re: Nachos rule	Bill	3/13/2000
5	5	0	What about cookies	Evany	3/13/2000
6	2	2	Re: Cheetos are the best	Ed	3/14/2000
7	1	4	Cheetos, are you kidding	Jeff	3/15/2000
8	5	5	Re: What about cookies	Jay	3/15/2000

Say you want each level to be indented a little further than the previous one, with the HTML blockquote tag. Now assume that you're calling the below function by passing the topic_id of 7.

```
function RecurForMe($topic_id)
{
    $query = "SELECT * from topics  WHERE topic_id =  $topic_id;
    $result = mysql_query($query) or
        die("Query failed");
    $row = mysql_fetch_array($result);
    echo "<blockquote>";
    echo $row["name"], "\n";
    RecurForMe($row["parent_id"]);
}
```

You know by now not to actually run a script like this — there's no error check-ing, and eventually, when there are no responses to the query, it will cause an error. I wrote this function so you can look at the last line. You see what it does: the func-tion calls itself. If you're not clear about the impact this will have, let's walk through it.

The first time through, given the $topic_id of 7, the query will return (surprise, surprise) row number 7. Then a blockquote tag and the name (Jeff) will be printed out. Then the function will call itself, this time passing the parent_id of 4. The next time through, the query will return row 4, the next time through it will return row 3, and finally it will call row 1. When done, the script output (before the error) will look like this.

```
<blockquote>Jeff
<blockquote>Bill
<blockquote>Don
<blockquote>Jay
```

The DisplayKids function will work in pretty much the same way. It will call itself for as long as necessary. But in the final script you will have to take a lot more into consideration. For instance, the description field of immediate children will be printed out, but further down the ancestral path you'll show only subject and name. Before you get caught up in the larger script, let's look at how to change layout based on ancestry in your simplified script.

```
function RecurForMe($topic_id, $level = 1)
{
    $query = "SELECT * from topics  WHERE topic_id = $topic_id";
    $result = mysql_query($query);
    $row = mysql_fetch_array($result);
    echo "<blockquote>";
    echo $row["name"], "\n";
    if($level == 1) {echo $row["subject"];}
    RecurForMe($row["parent_id"], $level + 1);
}
```

I've added another variable ($level) to this function to keep track of the level. The default value is 1, and it will be incremented each time through. The first time through the subject will be printed, but in iterations after the first, the subject will not be printed.

Recursion is an expensive process; it takes up quite a bit of processor time. To prevent a system from being overwhelmed, you might want to limit the depth of any topic

Armed with this information, you should be able to get through the DiplayKids function. There's a lot of info in there to assure good layout, but other than that, it's all pretty readable. There are some comments here to help you get through.

```
function display_kids ($topic_id=0, $level=0)
{
    $child_count = 0;
    if (empty($topic_id)) { $topic_id = 0; }

    // retrieve topic records from the MySQL database having
    // this topic_id value in their parent_id column (i.e. those
    // for whom this topic is the parent_topic
    $query = "select topic_id, name, author, author_host, create_dt
            , description
        from topics where
        parent_id = $topic_id
        order by create_dt, topic_id
    ";
    $result = safe_query($query);
    while
(list($r_topic_id,$r_name,$r_author,$r_author_host,$r_create_dt
        ,$r_description
        ) = mysql_fetch_row($result)
    )
    {
        if ($level)
        {
            // non-zero level - use unordered list format
            if (!$child_count)
            {
                // this is the first child record
                // - begin the list
                print "<ul>\n";
            }
            // begin the list item tag
            print "<li>";
        }
        else
        {
            // zero (first) level - print inside a table
            if (!$child_count)
            {
                // this is the first child record:
                // - print out a header
                print "<b>Comments:</b><br>\n";
            }
            print start_table();
            print " <tr bgcolor=skyblue>\n";
            print "  <td colspan=2 width=500>\n";
```

```php
    }
    $child_count++;

    if ($r_author == "") { $r_author = "[no name]"; }

    if ($r_topic_id != $topic_id)
    {
        print anchor_tag(
            "index.php?topic_id=$r_topic_id"
            , $r_name
        );
        print " by <b>$r_author</b>";
    }
    else
    {
        // this should never happen, but just in case -
        // don't print a link back to this topic
        print "$r_name by <b>$r_author</b>";
            }

    print " ($r_author_host)";
    if ($level)
    {
        // not the first level - close the list item
        print "</li>\n";
    }
    else
    {
        // first level - close the table cell & row containing
        // the topic name & author, then print out the text
        // of the topic and close the table
        print "  </td>\n";
        print " </tr>\n";
        print table_row(
            table_cell(" ", array("width"=>2))
            , table_cell($r_description,array("width"=>498))
        );
        print end_table();
    }
    // display any child topics of this child, at the next
    // higher level
    display_kids($r_topic_id, $level+1);
}
if ($level && $child_count)
{
```

```
        // if not the first level and at least one child was found,
        // an unordered list was begun - close it.
        print "</ul>\n";
    }
}
```

DISPLAY_TOPIC()   This function displays information about a given topic. If no topic_id is indicated, a list of the root-level topics is displayed.

```
function display_topic ($topic_id=0, $show_kids=1, $level=0)
{
    if (empty($topic_id)) { $topic_id = 0; }

    $fields = array("topic_id", "parent_id", "root_id", "name"
        , "description", "author", "author_host", "create_dt"
        , "modify_dt"
    );
    $query = "select distinct current.".implode(", current.",
$fields);
```

The next query that this script will send is a self join that uses aliases for the two copies of the table. One copy is named "current", the other "child". The implode function in the previous line will place the string ", current." between each array element. After this line of code runs, $query will be ready for the alias and will contain "select distinct current.topic_id, current.parent_id, current.root_id, current. name, current.description, current.author, current.author_host, current.create_dt, current.modify_dt".

The following portion executes if no topic_id is indicated. It will display the root-level topics.

```
    if (!$topic_id)
    {
        $query .= " from topics current, topics child
            where current.topic_id = child.root_id
        ";
        $result = safe_query($query);
        if (!$result)
        {
            print subtitle("Damn! result = $result");
        }
        else
        {
```

The query in the preceding snippet gets all of the root-level topics. The while...
loop directly below prints each topic as an HTML anchor, something like `<a
href="index.php?topic_id=1">Topic   name</a>`. Finally, the portion below
returns an empty array.

```
        while ($row = mysql_fetch_array($result))
        {
            print paragraph(anchor_tag(
                "index.php?topic_id=".$row["topic_id"]
                , $row["name"]
            ));
        }
    }
    return array();
}
```

If a topic_id is available, the following query gets the parent and root of the
indicated topic_id. An outer join assures that the information regarding the current
topic is returned by the query.

```
$query .= ", parent.name as parent_name
        , root.name as root_name
    from topics current
    left join topics as parent
        on current.parent_id = parent.topic_id
    left join topics as root
        on current.root_id = root.topic_id
    where current.topic_id = $topic_id
";
$result = safe_query($query);
if (!$result)
{
    print subtitle("Damn! result = $result");
    return array();
}
list($topic_id, $parent_id, $root_id, $name
    , $description , $author, $author_host
    , $create_dt, $modify_dt, $parent_name
    , $root_name
) = mysql_fetch_row($result);
```

```
if ($author == "") { $author = "[no name]"; }

if ($root_id != $topic_id && $root_id != $parent_id)
{
    if ($root_name == "") { $root_name = "[no topic name]"; }
    print paragraph(
        "<b>root:</b>"
        , anchor_tag("index.php?topic_id=$root_id"
            , $root_name
            )
        );
}
```

If there is a parent topic, the name of the topic is printed, along with a link to it.

```
if (!empty($parent_name))
{
    print paragraph(
        "<b>parent:</b>"
        , anchor_tag("index.php?topic_id=$parent_id"
            , $parent_name
            )
        );
}

// print out the current topic
print paragraph("<b>$name</b> by <b>$author</b> ($author_host)
    on <b>$create_dt</b>
");
print paragraph($description);

if ($show_kids)
{
    // print out a link to where the user can reply to
    // the current topic
    print paragraph(
        anchor_tag("write_topic.php?topic_id=$topic_id"
            , "<b>Reply to this</b>"
            )
        );

    // now display any children of the current topic
    print paragraph(display_kids($topic_id, $level));
}
```

```
        // return information retrieved about the current topic
        return array($root_id, $parent_id, $name);


}
```

CREATE_TOPIC()   This function inserts the data taken form a form and inserts it into the database. As mentioned earlier, we are taking the IP address from the Apache $REMOTE_ADDR variable, which will also be inserted in the database. Many of the fields (for instance, $root_id) will be coming from hidden form fields. And root_id will be set to 0 if the user is attempting to create a new top-level topic. In those cases the parent_id will need to be set to the same value as the topic_id.

```
function create_topic ($name="[no name]", $author="[no author]"
    , $description="[no comments]", $parent_id=0, $root_id=0
)
{
    global $REMOTE_ADDR;

    $name = cleanup_text($name);
    $description = cleanup_text($description);
    $author = cleanup_text($author);

    $query = "insert into topics
        (name,description, parent_id, root_id, author, author_host)
        values
        ('$name', '$description', $parent_id
            , $root_id, '$author', '$REMOTE_ADDR'
        )
    ";
    $result = safe_query($query);
    if (!$result)
    {
        print subtitle("hey! insert failed, dammit.");
    }
    $topic_id = mysql_insert_id();

    if (!empty($topic_id))
    {
        if ($root_id == 0)
        {
            safe_query("update topics set root_id = $topic_id
                where topic_id = $topic_id and root_id = 0
            ");
        }
    }
```

```
    else
    {
        print subtitle("Hey! that didn't work.");
    }
    return $topic_id;
}
```

This function simply inserts the data into the database. All the information will be coming from an HTML form.

Other Files

If you understand the functions in the preceding section, the other files will be a piece of cake. In fact, they're so easy we'll only look at one.

index.php

As you can see, this file contains almost nothing. The `display_topic()` function does all the heavy lifting.

```
<?php
include "header.php";
include "start_page.php";

display_topic($topic_id);

include "end_page.php";
?>
```

Summary

If you would like to see how the rest of the code comes together, take a look at the accompanying CD. The other files are well-commented and should be relatively easy to follow.

You should come away from this chapter with the understanding of two concepts. The first is recursion. Recursion is a nifty tool that can be very helpful at times. If you'd like to see another example of recursion at work, check out the `recurse_directory()` function in Appendix G, which will display all of the contents on a Web server.

The other key thing is the way we went about organizing the data. We didn't follow a strict normalization procedure, like the one described in Chapter 1. Here we were more concerned with what gets the job done. In the end that's what all us application developers are trying to do, right?

Chapter 13

Problem Tracking System

IN THIS CHAPTER

◆ Designing a tracking system

◆ Protecting yourself from redundant data.

◆ Creating a site that has both publicly available and private portions.

GOT PROBLEMS? Don't worry, we've all got problems. Relationships falter, bosses make capricious demands, and family – oh, we all know about family. Sadly, in the crazy lives that we all live, PHP and MySQL can do nothing to make your girl/boyfriend love you more or make your dealings with your parents or in-laws any easier. But it must be said that no scripting language or relational database is better equipped in these areas.

But if you're working for a company that sells or otherwise dispenses goods, it is a virtual guarantee that someone somewhere is going to be unhappy with what he or she has received. When that person complains you are going to want to have a place where you can record the problems and the steps required for resolution.

The problem-tracking application in this chapter can be used for that purpose. What we have here is fairly generic, and depending on the goods involved with your business, it is likely that you are going to want some fields that apply to your specific products. Anyhow, this application should get you moving in the right direction.

Determining the Scope and Goals of the Application

This problem-tracking system should have aspects that are publicly available and others that only someone with the proper authorization can view. It makes sense to have a form that users can access over the Web to report their problems. Alternatively, someone on the support staff should be able to report problems – for example, while taking a phone call from a dissatisfied customer.

Once the problem is entered, it should be tracked by the staff. Each action made in the attempt to solve the problem should be noted. And the tracking should have a public and a private realm – actions that you want the user to see must be differentiated from those that you do not want the user to see.

Those with issues should be able to keep track of their problems in two ways. They should be e-mailed whenever an update is made to their case that should be publicly viewable, and – it should go without saying – a Web page detailing their problem should be available.

What do you need?

The first thing you need is a form into which people can enter their complaints. What we present in Figure 13-1 is fairly generic; remember that for your own applications you will probably want to add information regarding specific products.

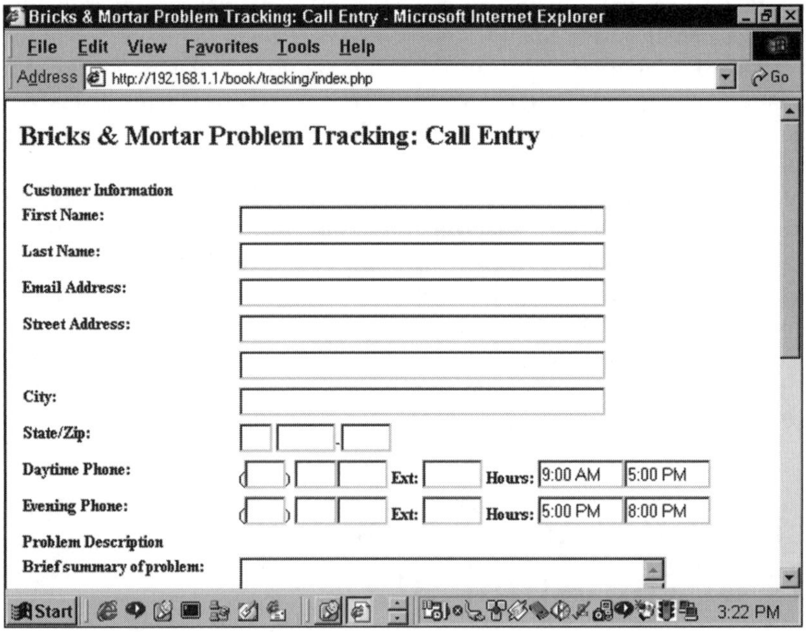

Figure 13-1: Problem entry form

Once a problem is entered, there must be a place for the staff to work on the complaint. It should include all of the information about the user, the history of the complaint, and a place to enter new information. This problem update form would look something like the one in Figure 13-2.

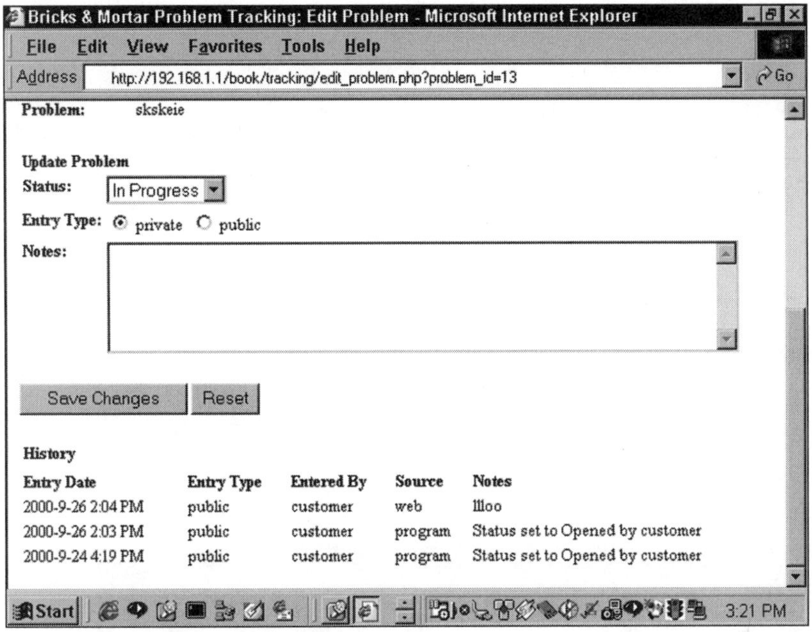

Figure 13-2: Problem update form

The support staff members need a home, a place where they can log in and see both the unassigned tasks and those that are assigned to them and are still open. The staff page would look something like the one in Figure 13-3.

If you want to see if any of your users are hypochondriacs, you can use the user history page in Figure 13-4, which lists all problems associated with a user.

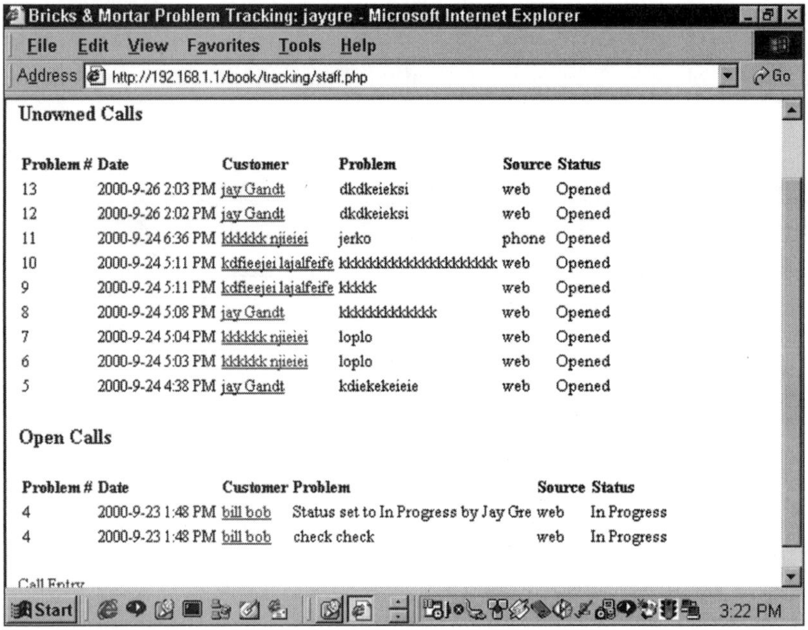

Figure 13-3: Staff page

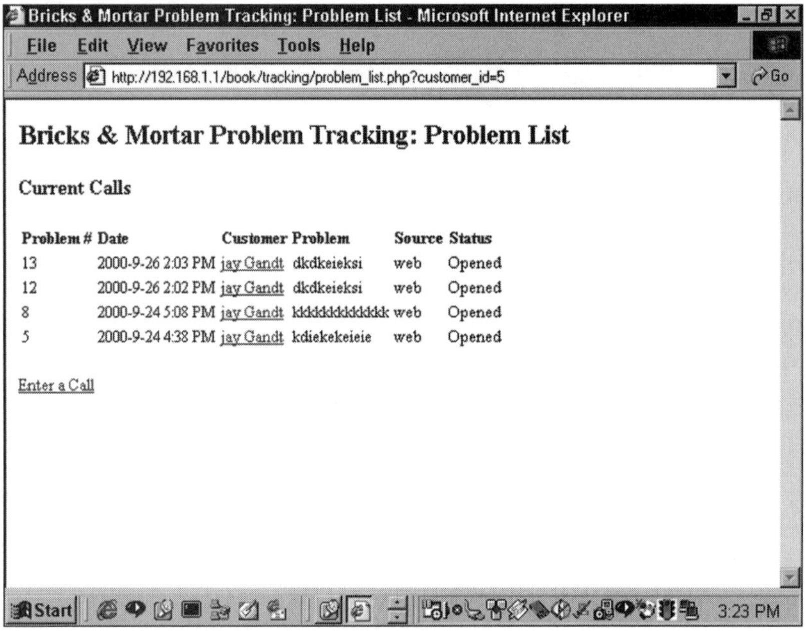

Figure 13-4: User history page

What do you need to prevent?

There is nothing terribly unique about what you need to prevent here. In fact, if you decide to put an application like this into production, you might want to take more safeguards than we show here. We'll make some suggestions along the way.

Designing the Database

As you can see from Figure 13-5 the problems table is at the center of the schema.

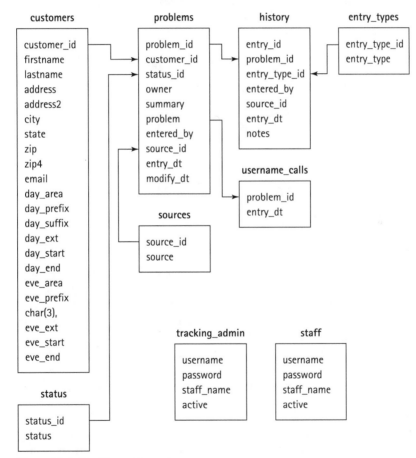

Figure 13-5: Tracking system schema

Each customer can have one or many problems. The history table records the steps taken to remedy the problem or problems.

The status table is a lookup table, containing the possible states of a problem; notably "open," "closed," "in processing," etc. The sources table is another lookup table that records where the problem was originally recorded. If a user enters a complaint over the Web, the sources table will record that; complaints received by the support staff might originate from a phone call, e-mail, or flaming arrow.

The entry_types table notes whether a specific item in the history table should be public or private. If it is private it will not be available on the Web page when the user comes to view the progress of the problem and an e-mail will not be sent to the user when there is an update. The "public" updates will be viewable and the user will receive e-mail notification.

There is something a bit strange in this schema; namely, the calls table. The purpose of the calls table is to store the most recent entry for each call that has an owner. If you look at this schema, you might wonder why this is necessary. After all, there are relationships between staff, problems, and history. Therefore, there should be a way to join these three tables to get the information you are after. Normally you would use sub-selects for something like this.

```
select problem.*, history.*, staff.*
from problem , history, staff
where problem.owner = '$PHP_AUTH_USER'
and history.entry_dt in (
select max(n.entry_dt) from history)
```

If we were using MySQL version 3.23, we would make use of temporary tables.

```
create temporary table calls
select  max(entry_dt) from history
```

Then you could join the problem and history table onto this temporary table. However, since this isn't available in version 3.22, which we used when creating these applications, we had to use a make shift temporary table. Each time it is accessed, the calls table will be emptied out and repopulated with information we need to complete the joins. See the staff.php page for the specific SQL we used.

Now for a couple of notes on this schema and the create statements that follow. Depending on how you plan on running your site, you may wish to add a table or change a column definition or two. First off, you might want to add a password column to the user table, so that you can ensure that the people looking at the site should be there.

Notice that we have a problem_code column in the problems table. However, if you will be e-mailing users regarding the status of problems, you may want something a little less transparent than the following: http://yoursite.com/tracking/problems.php?problem_id=7.

If you remember back to Chapter 9, we took some precautions when we ran into a similar situation. We didn't want people to be able to access to restricted parts of our data by simply guessing at variable names in the URL. Here we will adopt the same technique we used in the survey application, creating a random 8-character alpha-numeric string from the md5() and uniqueid() functions.

Listing 13-1 shows the create statements for the tables we used in this application. In addition to the create statements, this listing includes some of the default data you will need to start the application. Note that if you install this application from the CD-ROM you will have a full set of dummy data you can play with.

Listing 13-1: Create statements used in the problem tracking system

```
CREATE TABLE customers (
    customer_id int(11) NOT NULL auto_increment,
    firstname varchar(40),
    lastname varchar(40),
    address varchar(40),
    address2 varchar(40),
    city varchar(20),
    state char(2),
    zip varchar(5),
    zip4 varchar(5),
    email varchar(255),
    day_area char(3),
    day_prefix char(3),
    day_suffix varchar(4),
    day_ext varchar(5),
    day_start varchar(8),
    day_end varchar(8),
    eve_area char(3),
    eve_prefix char(3),
    eve_suffix varchar(4),
    eve_ext varchar(5),
    eve_start varchar(8),
    eve_end varchar(8),
    PRIMARY KEY (customer_id)
);

# ----------------------------------------------------------
#
# Table structure for table 'entry_types'
#

CREATE TABLE entry_types (
    entry_type_id tinyint(4) NOT NULL auto_increment,
    entry_type varchar(10) NOT NULL,
    PRIMARY KEY (entry_type_id)
);
INSERT INTO entry_types VALUES (1,'private');
```

```
    INSERT INTO entry_types VALUES (2,'public');


    # --------------------------------------------------------
    #
    # Table structure for table 'history'
    #

    CREATE TABLE history (
        entry_id int(11) NOT NULL auto_increment,
        problem_id char(32) NOT NULL,
        entry_type_id tinyint(4) NOT NULL,
        entered_by varchar(20),
        source_id tinyint(4) NOT NULL,
        entry_dt timestamp(14),
        notes text,
        PRIMARY KEY (entry_id),
        KEY history_problem_id (problem_id)
    );


    # --------------------------------------------------------
    #
    # Table structure for table 'problems'
    #

    CREATE TABLE problems (
        problem_id char(32) NOT NULL,
        customer_id int(11) NOT NULL,
        status_id tinyint(4) NOT NULL,
        owner varchar(20),
        summary text,
        problem text,
        entered_by varchar(20),
        source_id tinyint(4) NOT NULL,
        entry_dt datetime,
        modify_dt timestamp(14),
        problem_code char(8) not null
        PRIMARY KEY (problem_id),
        KEY problem_customer_id (customer_id)
        KEY problem_code_key (problem_code)
    );


    # --------------------------------------------------------
    #
    # Table structure for table 'sources'
```

```
#

CREATE TABLE sources (
   source_id tinyint(4) NOT NULL auto_increment,
   source varchar(10) NOT NULL,
   PRIMARY KEY (source_id)
);
INSERT INTO sources VALUES (1,'web');
INSERT INTO sources VALUES (2,'email');
INSERT INTO sources VALUES (3,'phone');
INSERT INTO sources VALUES (4,'in-store');
INSERT INTO sources VALUES (5,'staff');
INSERT INTO sources VALUES (6,'program');
# ---------------------------------------------------------
#
# Table structure for table 'staff'
#

CREATE TABLE staff (
   username varchar(20) NOT NULL,
   password varchar(255) NOT NULL,
   staff_name varchar(50) NOT NULL,
   active tinyint(4) DEFAULT '1',
   PRIMARY KEY (username)
);

# ---------------------------------------------------------
#
# Table structure for table 'status'
#

CREATE TABLE status (
   status_id tinyint(4) NOT NULL auto_increment,
   status varchar(20) NOT NULL,
   PRIMARY KEY (status_id)
);

INSERT INTO status VALUES (1,'Opened');
INSERT INTO status VALUES (2,'In Progress');
INSERT INTO status VALUES (3,'Closed');
INSERT INTO status VALUES (4,'Re-opened');
# ---------------------------------------------------------
#
# Table structure for table 'tracking_admin'
#
```

```
CREATE TABLE tracking_admin (
    username varchar(50) NOT NULL,
    password varchar(255) NOT NULL
);
```

Code Overview

There's nothing terribly new and exciting in the code presented in this chapter. Some of the queries are lengthier than in previous chapters. But it's really nothing major.

Code Breakdown

This application makes more liberal use of includes then some of the previous ones you have seen. There are a couple of very long forms that could really clutter up a page. They have been pushed off to includes.

Reusable functions

The base function set, described in Chapter 9, will be used here once again.

FUNCTIONS FROM /BOOK/TRACKING/FUNCTIONS.PHP
The first few of these are for convenience. The ones a little further down do some pretty heavy and cool work.

DB_AUTHENTICATE() This calls our standard authentication function, first described in Chapter 9.

```
function staff_authenticate()
{
        db_authenticate("staff", "Bricks and Mortar Support");
}
```

PRINT_ROW() This small function simply makes a call to the table_row() function in /book/functions/tables.php. It's basically a shortcut so you can print a simple two-column row.

```
function print_row ($label="",$what="")
{
    $label = empty($label) ? "" : "<b>$label:</b>";
    print table_row($label,$what);
}
```

You can think of the arguments as names and values.

FETCH_STAFF () If you've looked at some of the other applications in this book, this type of function should be clear.

```
function fetch_staff ($username = "")
{
    $result = fetch_record("staff", "username", "'$username'");
    return $result;
}
```

It calls to /book/functions/db.php, where the `fetch_record()` creates a query, runs it, and then sets the columns returned by the query to global variables.

FETCH_CUSTOMER () See the previous function for an explanation.

```
function fetch_customer ($customer_id = "")
{
    $result = fetch_record("customers", "customer_id",
$customer_id);
    return $result;
}
```

FETCH_PROBLEM () This function, which essentially does the same thing as the previous three, takes a slightly different form. This is because the `fetch_record()` function can only assemble simple queries: one table is all it can manage. However, since the `set_result_vars()` function is the one that actually assigns the results of the query to globals, you can pass the results of a query directly to it.

```
function fetch_problem ($problem_id = "", $problem_code = "")
{
        $query = "select p.*
                , s.status
                , u.source
                from problems p
                left join status s on p.status_id = s.status_id
                left join sources u on p.source_id = u.source_id
        ";
        if (!empty($problem_id))
        {
                $query .= " where p.problem_id = $problem_id ";
        }
        else
        {
                $query .= " where p.problem_code = '$problem_code'
```

```
";
        }
        $result = safe_query($query);
        if (!$result) { die("no such problem: <pre>$query</pre>"); }
        set_result_variables($result);
        return $result;
}
```

Here you are gathering all the information associated with a single problem_id. For that, you need to join problems on the sources status tables.

FIND_CUSTOMER()   Remember that you would like to enable users to report their problems over the Web. In this application, we've decided that while there is a numeric primary key for each user, the application should be able to identify the user by either a phone number or an e-mail. So when a user enters information, you will need to check if someone with an identical e-mail or phone number has come along.

```
function find_customer($email=""
    ,$day_area="",$day_prefix="",$day_suffix=""
    ,$eve_area="",$eve_prefix="",$eve_suffix=""
)
{

    $where = "";
    $sep = "";
    if ($day_prefix != "")
    {
        // there must be a prefix for this to be a valid phone
number
        $where .= "
            (day_area = '$day_area'
                and day_prefix = '$day_prefix'
                and day_suffix = '$day_suffix'
            )
        ";

        // separate each part of the qualification with OR -
        // any part constitutes a valid match.
        $sep = " or ";
    }
    if ($eve_prefix != "")
    {
        // there must be a prefix for this to be a valid phone
        //number
```

```
        $where .= "
            $sep
            (eve_area = '$eve_area'
                and eve_prefix = '$eve_prefix'
                and eve_suffix = '$eve_suffix'
            )
        ";
        $sep = " or ";
    }
    if ($email != "")
    {
        $where .= "
            $sep
            (email = '$email')
        ";
    }
    if ($where == "")
    {
        // nothing to look for
        return FALSE;
    }

    // run a query with the constructed qualification
    // and return the result
    $query = "select * from customers
        where $where
        order by customer_id
    ";
    $result = safe_query($query);
    return $result;
}
```

With this function you will know if the user has an existing record that can be used or that might need to be updated.

Notice the grouping of the portions of the where clause. It is looking for any one of three circumstances, each of which must meet a few criteria. If the e-mail, day-time phone and evening phone fields are filled in, this function will create a query that looks like this:

```
select * from customers
where (day_area = '415'
        and day_prefix = '555'
        and day_suffix = '0410' )
    or (eve_area = '212'
        and eve_prefix = '555'
```

```
                and eve_suffix = '9999' )
            or (email = 'jay@trans-city.com')
order by customer_id
```

 TIP If you were interested, you could set a cookie to make identifying the user a bit easier.

PRESENT_DUPS()   You need to plan for a couple of eventualities: if there are identical e-mail addresses or phone numbers, but some other personal information has changed, you need to let the user either update the database or discard the data. This function spots the redundancy and alerts the user.

```
function present_dups ($result)
{
    // we have to start the call entry form inside the function -
    // use a global variable to indicate that this was done.
    global $in_form;
    $in_form = 1;

    // start the form
    print start_form("create_call.php");

    print paragraph("<b>"
        ."We may have found you in our database."
        ." Please let us know what you would like to do:"
        ."</b>"
    );

    print start_table();

    // for each customer record in the result set
    while ($row = mysql_fetch_array($result,MYSQL_ASSOC))
    {
        // print out the ID value for the record in a radio field,
        // allowing the user to choose only one if more than
        // one is displayed.
        print table_row(
```

```
        radio_field(
            "customer_id"
            , $row["customer_id"]
            , "<b>Use this row</b>"
        )
        , "<b>Record #".$row["customer_id"]."</b>"
);

// print out the name & address information from this record
print table_row("",$row["firstname"]." ".$row["lastname"]);
if (!empty($row["address"]))
{
    print table_row("",$row["address"]);
}
if (!empty($row["address2"]))
{
    print table_row("",$row["address2"]);
}
if ( !empty($row["city"]) || !empty($row["state"])
    || !empty($row["zip"])
)
{
    print table_row(""
        , $row["city"].", ".$row["state"]." "
            .$row["zip"]
    );
}
if (!empty($row["day_prefix"]))
{
    $daycell = "Day: "
        .$row["day_area"]
        ." "
        .$row["day_prefix"]
        ."-"
        .$row["day_suffix"]
    ;
    if (!empty($row["day_ext"]))
    {
        $daycell .= " ".$row["day_ext"];
    }
    if (!empty($row["day_start"]))
    {
```

```
                        $daycell .= " from ".$row["day_start"];
                }
                if (!empty($row["day_end"]))
                {
                        $daycell .= " until ".$row["day_end"];
                }
                print table_row("",$daycell);
        }
        if (!empty($row["eve_prefix"]))
        {
                $evecell = "Eve: "
                        .$row["eve_area"]
                        ." "
                        .$row["eve_prefix"]
                        ."-"
                        .$row["eve_suffix"]
                ;
                if (!empty($row["eve_ext"]))
                {
                        $evecell .= " ".$row["eve_ext"];
                }
                if (!empty($row["eve_start"]))
                {
                        $evecell .= " from ".$row["eve_start"];
                }
                if (!empty($row["eve_end"]))
                {
                        $evecell .= " until ".$row["eve_end"];
                }
                print table_row("",$evecell);
        }
        if (!empty($row["email"]))
        {
                print table_row("",$row["email"]);
        }

        // print out a checkbox field allowing the user to
        // indicate that this record should be overwritten
        // with the information from the form.
        print table_row(""
                , checkbox_field(
                        "override"
```

```
                    , $row["customer_id"]
                    , "<b>Override this entry with the new"
                         ." information in the form below.</b>"
                )
            );

            // print out a checkbox field allowing the user to
            // indicate that this record should be merged
            // with the information from the form and the result
            // written back to the database.
            print table_row(""
                , checkbox_field(
                    "merge"
                    , $row["customer_id"]
                    , "<b>Merge this entry with the new"
                         ." information in the form below.</b>"
                )
            );
        }
        print end_table();

        // print out a final radio field indicating that, rather than
        // using any of the records found in the database, a new record
        // should be created.
        print paragraph(radio_field(
            "add_as_new"
            , "yes"
            , "Create a new record with the information in the form
below."
        ));

    }
```

All the duplicate rows are printed, and the user can choose what to do with the data. You can see this in action if you go to the index.php page of this application and attempt to enter two different tickets with, say, the same phone number. Figure 13-6 gives an example.

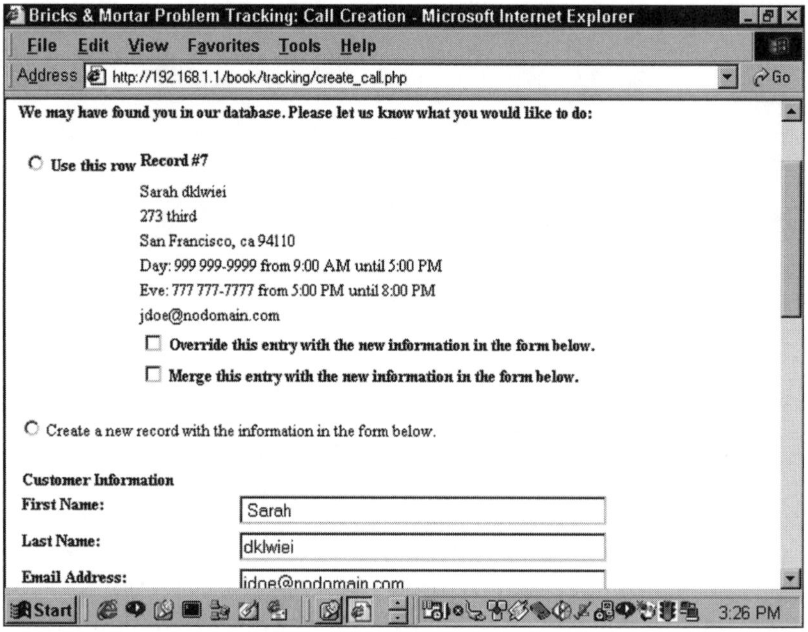

Figure 13-6: Form for updating customer information

HISTORY_ENTRY()   When a staff member enters an update on a problem, the step is stored in the history table. If the entry is "public" the user will be e-mailed with the update; if not, there will be no e-mail.

Notice the interesting query. Here the insert contains a select statement. The only thing this select is actually getting is the source_id related to the variable $source. All the rest of the insert information comes from variables.

```
function history_entry
($problem_id="",$entry_type_id="",$entered_by=""
    ,$source="",$notes=""
)
{
    if (empty($problem_id)) { return FALSE; }

    if (empty($entered_by)) { $entered_by = "customer"; }

    // create a record in the history table, getting the ID value
    // of the source from the sources table.
    $query = "insert into history

(problem_id,entry_type_id,entered_by,source_id,notes)
            select '$problem'_id,$entry_type_id,'$entered_by',
```

```
                     source_id, '$notes'
            from sources where source = '$source'
    ";
$result = safe_query($query);
if ($result)
{
    // get the ID value of the new history record
    // (automatically assigned by MySQL).
    $entry_id = mysql_insert_id();

    // get the email address of
    // the customer who opened this call
    // if this was a public history
    // entry, and if the email address
    // is not empty
    $cresult = safe_query("select c.email
        from problems p, customers c, history h, entry_types et
        where h.entry_id = $entry_id
        and et.entry_type_id = h.entry_type_id
        and et.entry_type = 'public'
        and h.problem_id = p.problem_id
        and p.customer_id = c.customer_id
        and c.email != '' and c.email is not null
    ");
    if ($cresult && mysql_num_rows($cresult))
    {
        // we have a valid email address - use it to
        // notify the customer that the call record
        // has been updated.
        list($email) = mysql_fetch_array($cresult);
        notify_customer('$problem_id',$email,$notes);
    }
}

// return the result of the creation of the new history record
return $result;
}
```

If the update is public, the notify_customer() function is run.

NOTIFY_CUSTOMER()   This function constructs an e-mail and sends it.

```
function notify_customer ($problem_id="", $email="", $notes="",
$problem_code="")
{
```

```
        // the Apache global variable $SERVER_NAME is the name
        // of the server we're running on, minus any port number.
        global $SERVER_NAME;

        // remove any HTML tags and backslashes from $notes.
        $notes = stripslashes(cleanup_text($notes));

        if (empty($problem_code))
        {
                $result = safe_query("select problem_code from
                        problems
                        where problem_id = $problem_id
                ");
                $problem_code = mysql_result($result,0);
                if (empty($problem_code))
                {
                        $problem_code = create_problem_code();
                        safe_query("update problems
                                set problem_code = '$problem_code'
                                where problem_id = $problem_id
                        ");
                }
        }
        // build an absolute URL calling the problem_status.php page
        // to check on this problem
        $problem_url =
regular_url("problem_status.php?problem_code=$problem_code");

        // set the body of the email
        $msgtext = <<<EOQ

Problem Update:

$notes

You can check the current status of this problem at

$problem_url
Thanks for your patience.

EOQ;

        // set the headers of the email
        $headers = "From: webmaster@".$SERVER_NAME."\n"
                ."Reply-To: webmaster@".$SERVER_NAME."\n"
                ."X-Mailer: PHP/".phpversion()
```

```
            ;

            // send the email
            return mail($email, "Problem Update", $msgtext, $headers);
}
```

 PHP will have to be able to find sendmail or another SMTP-compliant mail server in order for this to work. Check your php.ini file is you're having problems.

STATUS_CHANGE()   The status of a problem is going to be something like "open," "closed," or "pending." If it changes you are going to want to mark the exact change and record something like "status changed to closed by John." The change should be recorded in the history table.

```
function status_change($problem_id=""
    ,$new_status_id=""
    ,$old_status_id=""
    , $entered_by="customer"
)
{
    if (empty($problem_id) || empty($new_status_id)
        || $old_status_id == $new_status_id
    )
    {
        return;
    }

    if (empty($entered_by)) { $entered_by = "customer"; }

    // get the ID of the entry_type 'public', and construct
    // a string containing the new status value and either
    // the real name of the staff member who made the change,
    // or the value of $entered_by if no matching staff
    // member is found. for example, if the staff member Joe Blow
    // closes a call, the notes field will be set to
    // "Status set to Closed by Joe Blow". if a customer
    // re-opens a call, notes will be set to
    // "Status set to Re-opened by customer".

    // all of this depends on the value in $new_status_id
    // being a valid ID of a record in the status table.
    $query = "select et.entry_type_id
```

```
                     , concat('Status set to '
                        , ns.status
                        , ' by '
                        , ifnull(t.staff_name,'$entered_by')
                     ) as notes
                        from entry_types et, status ns
                left join staff t on t.username = '$entered_by'
                where et.entry_type = 'public'
                and ns.status_id = $new_status_id
                ";
        $result = safe_query($query);
        if ($result)
        {
            // $new_status_id is a valid status ID - use the
            // history_entry() to make an entry in the history table
            // recording the status change, and send email notifiying
            // the user.
            list($entry_type_id, $notes) = mysql_fetch_array($result);
            history_entry($problem_id, $entry_type_id, $entered_by
                , 'program', $notes
            );
        }
    }
}
```

DISPLAY_CALL_LIST()   This is another function of convenience. It prints the results of a query along with a header row.

```
function display_call_list($query="",$subtitle="Call List"
    , $script="edit_problem.php"
)
{
    if ($query == "") { return; }
    $result = safe_query($query);
    if (!$result) { return; }

    $calls = 0;
    while ($row = mysql_fetch_array($result))
    {
        if ($calls == 0)
        {
            // we want to print out the table header only once,
            // and only if there is at least one row -
            // do it when processing the first row
            // of the result set.
```

```
            print subtitle($subtitle);

            print start_table();

            print table_row(
                "<b>Problem #</b>"
                , "<b>Date</b>"
                , "<b>Customer</b>"
                , "<b>Problem</b>"
                , "<b>Source</b>"
                , "<b>Status</b>"
            );
        }
        $calls++;

        // print out information about the call, including
        // a link to the given script for updating its
        // status and history.
        print table_row($row["problem_id"]
            , $row["entry_dt"]
            , anchor_tag($script."?problem_id="
                    .$row["problem_id"]
                , $row["firstname"]." ".$row["lastname"]
            )
            , $row["summary"]
            , $row["source"]
            , $row["status"]
        );
    }
    if ($calls > 0)
    {
        // there was at least one call, so the table was opened -
        // close it.
        print end_table();
    }
}
```

CREATE_PROBLEM_CODE()   This function creates a unique and highly random 8-character alphanumeric code.

```
function create_problem_code()
{
        return substr(md5(uniqid(rand())),0,8);
}
```

Scripts

Here are the pages that are actually called by URLs and the includes.

CALL_ENTRY.PHP

This page does little but call the call_entry_form.php, which is discussed next.

Remember, it is possible that this form will be accessed by a staff member who is logged in. Note that staff members should start at the staff.php page to log in. Or again, you may want to work with cookies to determine staff members.

If either a staff member or a user is identified, all the information regarding the user is set to globals with the appropriate fetch function.

```
include "header.php";

if ($use_staff_name == "yes")
{
    db_authenticate("staff", "Bricks and Mortar Support");
    fetch_staff($PHP_AUTH_USER);
}

$page_title = $default_page_title.": Call Entry";
include "start_page.php";

if (!empty($customer_id))
{
    // a customer ID value was submitted - get the customer's
    // contact information from the database.
    fetch_customer($customer_id);
}

// call the script that actually displays the call entry form.
include "call_entry_form.php";

include "end_page.php";
```

CALL_ENTRY_FORM.PHP

Mostly this form makes calls to the functions in your /book/functions/ folder. It prints the form shown in Figure 13-1 and determines the default information in the form. The call_entry.php page will include this page.

The form will be submitted to the create_call.php page, which is discussed next.

```
if (!$in_form)
{
```

```
    // if the user has submitted the form once and existing
    // contact information was found for the customer,
    // the present_dups() function (defined in functions.php)
    // will have already started the form, in order to
    // display the contact records to the user. in this case,
    // the function will set the global variable $in_form to 1.
    // if $in_form is not set, begin the form here.
    print start_form("create_call.php");
}

print start_table();

// print out the customer's contact information.
print table_row(table_cell("<b>Customer
Information</b>",array("colspan"=>2)));

print_row("First Name", text_field("firstname","$firstname",40));
print_row("Last Name", text_field("lastname","$lastname",40));
print_row("Email Address", text_field("email","$email",40));
print_row("Street Address", text_field("address","$address",40));
print_row("", text_field("address2","$address2",40, 40));
print_row("City", text_field("city","$city",40, 40));
print_row("State/Zip", text_field("state","$state",2, 2)
    ." "
    .text_field("zip", "$zip", 5, 5)
    ."-"
    .text_field("zip4", "$zip4", 4, 4)
);

// by default, daytime phone numbers cover the hours of 9 AM to 5
PM.
if (empty($day_start)) { $day_start = "9:00 AM"; }
if (empty($day_end)) { $day_end = "5:00 PM"; }

print_row("Daytime Phone", "("
    .text_field("day_area","$day_area",3,3)
    .") "
    .text_field("day_prefix","$day_prefix",3,3)
    .text_field("day_suffix","$day_suffix",4,4)
    ." "
    ."<b>Ext:</b>\n"
    .text_field("day_ext","$day_ext",5,5)
    ." "
    ."<b>Hours:</b>\n"
    .text_field("day_start","$day_start",8,8)
```

```
        .text_field("day_end","$day_end",8,8)
);

// by default, evening phone numbers cover the hours of 5 PM to 8
PM.
if (empty($eve_start)) { $eve_start = "5:00 PM"; }
if (empty($eve_end)) { $eve_end = "8:00 PM"; }

print_row("Evening Phone", "("
    .text_field("eve_area","$eve_area",3,3)
    .") "
    .text_field("eve_prefix","$eve_prefix",3,3)
    .text_field("eve_suffix","$eve_suffix",4,4)
    ." "
    ."<b>Ext:</b>\n"
    .text_field("eve_ext","$eve_ext",5,5)
    ." "
    ."<b>Hours:</b>\n"
    .text_field("eve_start","5:00 PM",8,8)
    .text_field("eve_end","8:00 PM",8,8)
);

// spacer row to separate the two main areas of the form - we have
// to use a blank space ( ) to fill out the table cell, or it
// won't show up (much).
print table_row(table_cell(" ",array("colspan"=>2)));

// print out fields for describing the problem.
print table_row(table_cell("<b>Problem
Description</b>",array("colspan"=>2)));

if (!empty($use_staff_name))
{
    // if a staff member is entering a problem record, record
    // the fact in hidden fields.
    print_row("Entered by", $username
        .hidden_field("entered_by", $username)
        .hidden_field("use_staff_name", $use_staff_name)
    );

    // allow the staff member to indicate the original source of the
    // problem report.
    print_row("Source"
        , db_select_field("source_id", "sources", "source_id",
"source")
```

```
        );
}

print_row("Brief summary of problem"
    , textarea_field("summary",$summary, 40, 2)
);

print_row("Complete Problem Description"
    , textarea_field("problem",$problem, 40, 15)
);

print end_table();


print paragraph(
    submit_field("submit","Submit Problem Report")
    , reset_field()
);


print end_form();
```

CREATE_CALL.PHP

This page is long, if not terribly complicated. I will discuss interesting parts as they present themselves. When you're looking at it, it's easiest to know the variety of actions it can accomplish. Here's an overview of the logic in the page:

```
customer or staff comes to call_entry
    if customer_id is available
        fetch that record
        display it in the form
    else
        display blank form

    if email or phone number have no match in db
        create new customer address
    else
        if more than one records match
            present records to customer
            allow customer to:
                - create new record with new info
                - use an existing record
                - override an existing record with new info
                - merge new info with an existing record;
```

```
                        where existing has values and new
                        does not, existing will be used
                      - mark one of the records as a duplicate
                        to be purged; calls tied to it
                        will be linked to the record
                        used for this call
                 present new info in form to allow for updating
         else
             if no new info overrides existing record
                 use existing record
             else
                 present record to customer
                 allow customer to:
                     - create new record with new info
                     - use existing record
                     - override existing record with new info
                     - merge new info with existing record;
                       where existing has values and new
                       does not, existing will be used
                 present new info in form to allow for updating
```

Armed with this overview, you should be able to read through the source of this page, which of course is on the CD-ROM, without much difficulty.

STAFF.PHP

This is where you expect the staff members to log into the application. Note the use of the staff_authenticate() function, which calls the authenticate() function you've been using throughout the book. Before a staff member can log in, he or she must enter a valid password and username.

The page is going to show two lists of queries, a list of calls owned by the currently logged-in staff member, and a list of unowned calls, probably stuff that has been entered over the Web.

```
include "header.php";
staff_authenticate();

fetch_staff($PHP_AUTH_USER);

$page_title = $default_page_title.": $PHP_AUTH_USER";
include "start_page.php";

// first, get a list of all open unowned calls and display them,
// in the hopes that the user might grab one.
$query = "select c.customer_id, c.firstname, c.lastname
        , p.problem_id
```

```
        , date_format(p.entry_dt, '%Y-%c-%e %l:%i %p') as entry_dt
        , p.source_id, p.summary, p.entered_by
        , s.status
        , so.source
     , p.entry_dt as real_entry_dt
    from customers c, problems p, status s, sources so
    where p.status_id = s.status_id and s.status = 'Opened'
        and p.customer_id = c.customer_id
        and p.source_id = so.source_id
    order by real_entry_dt desc
";
display_call_list($query, "Unowned Calls");
```

The above query retrieves a list of calls that are marked "Opened." Note that "Opened" will be the status only for unowned calls. As soon someone performs an action, the status will change. The display_call_list() function prints the results of the query, if there are any.

If you remember back to the Defining the Database section, we had to use some trickery to get a listing of the most recent entries to calls that belong to a specific user. We need to create that make shift table we talked about, but before we do that, we need to clear out any old data that may be in there.

```
safe_query("delete from calls where username = '$PHP_AUTH_USER'");
```

Then we load up the temporary table with data that is needed for the join.

```
safe_query("insert into calls (username, problem_id, entry_dt)
    select p.owner
        , h.problem_id
        , max(h.entry_dt) as entry_dt
    from problems p, history h
    where p.problem_id = h.problem_id
        and p.owner = '$PHP_AUTH_USER'
    group by p.problem_id
");
```

Finally, we perform the following on the newly loaded table.

```
$query = "select c.customer_id, c.firstname, c.lastname
        , p.problem_id, p.source_id, p.entered_by
        , date_format(h.entry_dt, '%Y-%c-%e %l:%i %p') as entry_dt
        , h.notes as summary
        , s.status
        , so.source
```

```
        , h.entry_dt as real_entry_dt
    from customers c, problems p, status s, sources so
        , history h, calls m
    where p.status_id = s.status_id and s.status != 'Closed'
        and p.customer_id = c.customer_id
        and p.source_id = so.source_id
        and p.problem_id = h.problem_id
        and p.owner = m.username
        and h.entry_dt = m.entry_dt
        and h.problem_id = m.problem_id
        and m.username = '$PHP_AUTH_USER'
    order by real_entry_dt desc
";
display_call_list($query, "Open Calls");

// print out a link to allow the user to create a new call
print paragraph(anchor_tag("call_entry.php?use_staff_name=yes","Call
Entry"));

include "end_page.php";
```

EDIT_PROBLEM.PHP

This is the final file in this application. It is fairly brief and the source code on the
CD-ROM should be readable.

Summary

The application presented in this chapter is very useful, since just about every information services department at every company will have some sort of system to track
user complaints. As we stated at the beginning of this chapter, the problem tracking
system presented here is fairly generic. However, it can definitely be the basis for a
more detailed application that you'd custom design for use in the workplace.

Chapter 14

Shopping Cart

IN THIS CHAPTER

- Creating a secure site
- Working with PHP sessions
- Communicating with a credit-card authorization service

OK, FRIENDS. THIS IS IT, the final application in this book. I don't know about you, but I'm a little weepy. Sure, there were hard times. But all in all I feel great about what we've accomplished, and I hope you do too.

But before we start reminiscing, there's some more work to be done. You are going to learn what you need to create a shopping cart application using PHP and MySQL. But unlike with the other applications in this book, it's really impossible to talk about what you need for this application without delving into some other topics. In addition to understanding the schema and the PHP code, you'll need to have a basic understanding of know how to maintain state between pages. (If you don't know what that means, don't worry, I'll get to it momentarily.) Also, you will need to know how to securely process credit-card transactions.

 Don't read another sentence if you have not read through Chapter 10. You must understand how the catalog works before you can take this on. For reasons that shouldn't be too tough to understand, we built the shopping cart atop the catalog.

Determining the Scope and Goals of the Application

Anyone familiar with the Web knows what a shopping cart does. But it will be a bit easier to understand what the code for this application is doing if I explicitly state some of the goals of the shopping cart.

First, the application is going to have to display your wares; for this you will reuse the code from Chapter 10. Further, users will have to be able to choose items that they want to buy. Obvious, I know. Note what must happen after a user chooses an item: the exact item must be noted, and the user should have the opportunity to continue shopping. The server must remember what has been ordered. As the user continues to browse, the server must keep track of the user and allow him or her to check out with his or her requested items.

This requires you to use some method for maintaining state. That is, the Web server will need to remember who the user is as he/she moves from page to page. Now, if you remember back to the Introduction, the Web and the HTTP protocol that the Web makes use of is stateless. That is, after responding to an HTTP request, the server completely and totally forgets what it served to whom. The server takes care of requested information serially – one at a time as requests come in. There is no persistence, no connection that lasts after a page has been served.

In order to give your site memory, so that, in this case, the cart can remember who ordered what, some information that identifies the user must be sent with each page request. On the Web there are exactly three ways to store this information:

◆ You can set a cookie, and then each time a request is made, the information stored in the cookie will be sent to the server. Note that the browser stores the cookie information in a small text file and sends the information to the server with each request.

The setcookie() function is covered in Chapter 6.

◆ You can place hidden form elements on every page, and then design your pages so that the navigation is done through form submit buttons.

◆ Or you can tack on some sort of unique identifier to the querystring, so that with each page request the URL identifies the user.

But, as they have done with everything else in PHP, the developers have made maintaining state relatively painless. As with ColdFusion and ASP, they have included a facility for sessions. (Only sessions in PHP are much better.) If you are unfamiliar with the term, sessions automate the process of tracking users during a visit. They will be discussed in further detail later in the chapter.

The other major challenge in this application is to securely gather user information from the user – specifically data that will allow for the authorization of credit-card purchases. Information will need to be gathered over a connection that is relatively secure, and then that information will need to be verified by a qualified institution. This is going to require some new configurations and the use of some custom tools.

What do you need?

Since you are building this application atop the catalogue, much of the code and information should be very familiar. The one notable thing that is going to be added to every page is a button that lets people go directly to the checkout. Figure 14-1 shows an example.

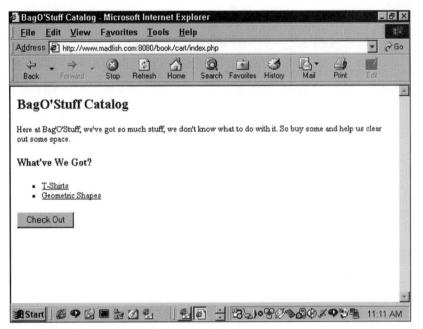

Figure 14-1: Category page with checkout button

On the pages that list the items, there must be a set of forms that will enable people to indicate the items they would like to purchase. Figure 14-2 shows a page that will allow people to add items to their shopping carts by pressing the Order! button.

Then there must be a page that lists all of the items currently in the cart. This page should enable people to add or subtract quantities of an item, or remove items entirely. The page in Figure 14-3 should do the trick.

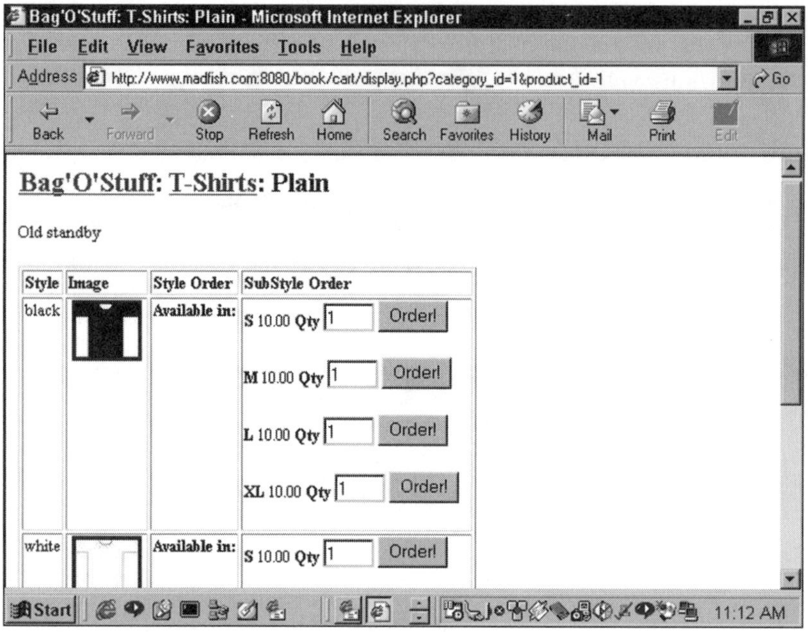

Figure 14-2: Item pages with order buttons

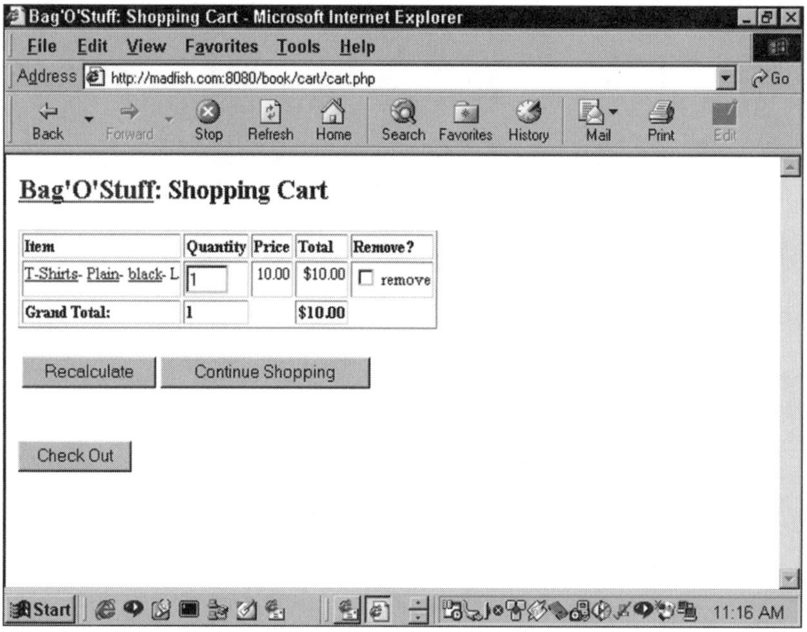

Figure 14-3: The cart page

Then, toward the end of the process, there will be a page that gathers user information and preferences. Depending on your specific needs, you may require something more complex than what is shown in this chapter. But at least the fields shown in Figure 14-4 are a good start. This page should indicate errors if the information is false or if the authorization of the credit card is rejected by the processing agency.

![Checkout page screenshot showing a Microsoft Internet Explorer window titled "Check Out". The address bar reads https://madfish.com:444/book/cart/checkout.php?sessid=7cc2358cf2a38f67b0e8644a996dc991. The page shows fields for Zip, Phone, Shipping Info with a Shipping Method table, Credit Card Info, and an ORDER NOW! button.]

Shipping Info

Shipping Method	Per Order	Per Item	Total for This Order
⊙ US Mail	$2.00	$0.50	$2.50
○ UPS 2nd Day	$5.00	$1.00	$6.00
○ UPS Next Day	$10.00	$1.00	$11.00

Credit Card Info

Credit Card: ⊙ American Express ○ Diners Club ○ Discover ○ MasterCard ○ Visa
Number:
Expires: 1 ▾ 2000 ▾

ORDER NOW!

Figure 14-4: Checkout page

Finally, there should be a receipt — a page that confirms the order and tells the user what the order number is.

Some information that might be important to you is not included with the code here. For instance, there are no administrative pages for adding or deleting shipping methods. At this point, you've probably seen enough admin pages to know how to create one for yourself.

What do you need to prevent?

There are essentially two things you need to be careful about here. The first is making sure you can track your users from page to page. The second is keeping credit-card numbers and other personal information away from prying eyes.

The Data

The database used here will be added to the catalog database. Information about goods will still come from the tables reviewed there, while information on orders will be stored in the tables shown here.

The data schema here, represented in Figure 14-5, offers few surprises.

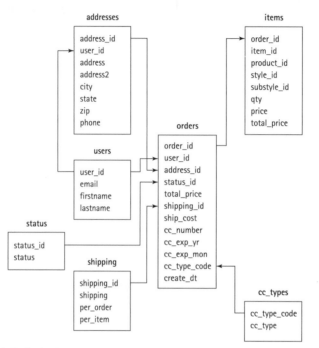

Figure 14-5: Cart schema

A couple of things here are worth noting. First notice how the order is really the center of the works. Every table, in one way or another, is related to the order. The order table stores a user_id, address_id, and all the needed payment information. Notice that the order table has a one-to-many relationship with the items table. That's because each order can have many items, which makes sense.

 Think about whether or not you want to store credit-card numbers in your database. We have included a column for the credit card number, but that doesn't mean you should use it. First consider if your box is secure enough. If you're not sure of the answer, the answer is no. If you are using a shared server, maybe a secure server offered by your ISP, you should consider it unsafe for storing credit card numbers. Other people will have access to that box and they will be able to see what you've written to the database. Keep in mind that there is no requirement that you store the credit-card numbers anywhere. You can simply validate the number and then drop it from memory. If it is never written to a disk, it will be very hard for anyone to steal.

Notice that user and address information is separated. This is so you can enable a single user (who will identify him- or herself by an e-mail address) to supply two addresses — maybe work and home.

The shipping table will store options you supply for moving your goods. It might have options for UPS, USPS, and Fed Ex, if you choose. I'll talk a little more about these options in the "Code Overview" section.

The status table will enable you to note if the order is backordered, shipped, or cancelled, or has any other status that might come up in your shop.

And the cc_types table stores credit cards that you're willing to accept.

```
# Table structure for table 'addresses'
#

CREATE TABLE addresses (
    address_id int(11) NOT NULL auto_increment,
    user_id int(11) NOT NULL,
    address varchar(40),
    address2 varchar(40),
    city varchar(40),
    state char(2),
    zip varchar(10),
    phone varchar(20),
    PRIMARY KEY (address_id),
    KEY address_user_key (user_id)
);
# --------------------------------------------------------
#
# Table structure for table 'cc_types'
#

CREATE TABLE cc_types (
    cc_type_code char(3) NOT NULL,
    cc_type varchar(30) NOT NULL
);

# --------------------------------------------------------
#
# Table structure for table 'orders'
#
```

```
CREATE TABLE orders (
    order_id int(11) NOT NULL auto_increment,
    user_id int(11) NOT NULL,
    address_id int(11) NOT NULL,
    status_id tinyint(4) NOT NULL,
    total_price decimal(10,2) DEFAULT '0.00' NOT NULL,
    shipping_id tinyint(4) NOT NULL,
    ship_cost decimal(10,2) DEFAULT '0.00' NOT NULL,
    cc_number varchar(30) NOT NULL,
    cc_exp_yr int(11) NOT NULL,
    cc_exp_mon tinyint(4) NOT NULL,
    cc_type_code char(3) NOT NULL,
    create_dt timestamp(14),
    PRIMARY KEY (order_id),
    KEY order_user_key (user_id)
);
# --------------------------------------------------------
#
# Table structure for table 'shipping'
#

CREATE TABLE shipping (
    shipping_id tinyint(4) NOT NULL auto_increment,
    shipping varchar(20) NOT NULL,
    per_order decimal(10,2) DEFAULT '0.00' NOT NULL,
    per_item decimal(10,2) DEFAULT '0.00' NOT NULL,
    PRIMARY KEY (shipping_id)
);


# --------------------------------------------------------
#
# Table structure for table 'status'
#

CREATE TABLE status (
    status_id tinyint(4) NOT NULL auto_increment,
    status varchar(20) NOT NULL,
    PRIMARY KEY (status_id)
);
# --------------------------------------------------------
#
# Table structure for table 'users'
#
```

```
CREATE TABLE users (
   user_id int(11) NOT NULL auto_increment,
   email varchar(255) NOT NULL,
   firstname varchar(40),
   lastname varchar(40),
   PRIMARY KEY (user_id),
   UNIQUE user_email_key (email)
);
```

Configuration Overview

This application is specialized enough to require its own configuration. All of the challenges discussed earlier (maintaining state, secure gathering of credit-card information, and processing of credit cards) not only require specialized code, they require some unique installation options.

Configuring for encryption and security

If you have a lot of experience with Apache and its related tools, this may not be too big a deal, or if you are using an ISP and don't have the authority to install programs on a box, then you won't need to worry about the specialized installation necessary to work with e-commerce.

But in any case, you should have an idea of the tools you'll need to get all of this working. First I will cover the basic theories behind encryption and Web security. I will then cover some of the mandatory tools for your Apache installation. Finally, I will cover some of the options for maintaining state and processing credit card transactions offered in PHP.

ENCRYPTION AND SECURITY THEORY

One of the best things about working around the Web is having first-hand knowledge of the work done by people far, far smarter than myself. Some of the most intense, complex and brain-intensive work being done is in the realm of security. This is algorithm-heavy stuff, and to really understand how the protocols work, you need to know quite a bit of math. Luckily, you don't need to have an advanced degree to understand the theories; and putting the stuff into practice really isn't too bad.

PUBLIC-KEY/PRIVATE-KEY ENCRYPTION   Machines on the Web make use of a Public-key/Private-key security scheme. Basically this means that computers that wish to communicate using encrypted data must have two keys to encrypt and decrypt data. First there is the Public key. As the name suggests the Public key is not hidden. It is available to all those you wish to communicate with. So everybody out there who wishes to communicate with you securely will have a copy of your Public key.

You might think that this is potentially dangerous. After all, everyone has access to your Public key, and thus they'll understand how you encrypted your data. But actually, it's just fine, because the messages can only be decrypted by the Private key. The Private key is kept . . . well . . . private. No one else has access to it.

So, for example, say you are going process a credit card with a bank. You will have access to the bank's Public key, with which you will encrypt the information. But because of the complex algorithms involved, only the Private key held by the bank can decrypt the data.

CERTIFICATES   Even with the Public key/Private key safeguards, the banks will have one major concern: that the messages they are getting are not from the sources they appear to be from. That is, if you are running `sofamegastore.com`, the bank needs to make sure that the request for credit-card authorization for that loveseat is actually from Sofa Megastore, not someone who is pretending to be Sofa Megastore. This requires a third party.

The encrypted messages that you send and receive will have a signature of sorts, but that signature must be verified. For this reason, organizations that wish to communicate over the Web make use of organizations that distribute certificates that verify the sender of a message. So it should make sense that you need to go to one of these organizations to get your Public and Private keys.

Probably the best-known organization involved in security certificates is VeriSign. You can find out about their offerings at this site: `http:// www.verisign.com/products/site/ss/index.html`.

SECURE PROTOCOL   HTTP by its very nature is open to eavesdropping. Packets that move across the Internet's routers are full of messages just waiting to be sniffed and read. Normally, the fact that you can easily read data sent via HTTP is a good thing. It makes the transfer and rendering of information quite easy. However, in cases where you need security, HTTP won't work well.

For example, if you are giving credit-card information to a site — say the commerce site you set up — you want to make sure that the information is unreadable. In order to do that, you need to make use of the Secure Socket Layer, or SSL. SSL is an additional protocol by which the keys and certificates from your site will be transferred to a browser or another server. Over SSL, your browser will be able to verify the certificate from your site so that it knows you are who you say you are. And sites will be able to verify each other.

All the encryption in the world will not stop someone who has hacked into your box or has legitimate access. Most credit-card theft is done by dishonest employees with too much access.

This has been a quick and dirty introduction to Web security. If you would like to learn more, I suggest starting with this page, and following any interesting links provided there: `http://www.modssl.org/docs/2.6/ssl_overview.html`

Encryption and security tools

Given what you have just read about encryption and security, it probably stands to reason that you are going to need some new tools. Here's a basic rundown.

First off, you are going to need to add SSL to Apache. As with everything else discussed in this book, adding SSL does not require you to pay for specialized software. All you need to do is install Apache with mod_ssl. You can read more about it at `http://www.mod_ssl.org`. To get SSL to work with Apache in the United States, you will need an additional piece of software called rsaref from RSA.

The installation of these tools with Apache is well documented in INSTALL.SSL file, so we won't cover it here. If you are having trouble getting mod_ssl, PHP, and MySQL to work for you, we recommend this site, which goes through the installation step by step: `http://www.devshed.com/Server_Side/PHP/SoothinglySeamless/page8.html`.

Make sure you read about the credit-card authorization options in the following section before you configure Apache with PHP.

But before any of this will work for you, you are going to need to get a certificate. As I already mentioned, VeriSign is the most frequently used certification organization. And if you use a VeriSign certificate along with the PayfloPro (which is a service of VeriSign) functions described below, you may be able to get a good deal. Thwate, which used to be the second-largest certification organization, is now owned by VeriSign. Other options in this area can be found at the following URL: `http://dmoz.org/Computers/Security/Public_Key_Infrastructure/PKIX/Tools_and_Services/Third_Party_Certificate_Authorities/`.

Configuring for credit-card authorization

When Apache is configured with SSL your site will be able to talk to browsers securely. If the URL starts with `https://`, the browser knows to look on Port 443 and to look for a certificate. However, there is still the question of how your site will talk with the entity that will process credit cards and either accept or reject the transaction. PHP has many great features for dealing with other sites. For instance, `fopen()` is URL-aware. But none of the filesystem or URL functions work with SSL, so you will need to make use of a specialized function set or a program outside of PHP.

I wholeheartedly recommend you look at some of the new options available in PHP4 before deciding on which payment processing services to use. I'll cover them briefly here.

PAYFLOPRO

If you decide to use Verisign to process credit cards, you will want to make use of these functions. You will need to install a code library that you will get from Verisign. You will then need to compile PHP so that it will recognize the new functions. Details can be found at `http://www.php.net/manual/ref.pfpro.php`.

PayfloPro is very easy to work with. A function or two will process your request and you will get back a response. Once that response is compared to a set of known codes, you will know whether or not the transaction succeeded. This is very nice and will help keep your code very clean.

CYBERCASH

Similarly, to make use of Cybercash, you will need to do a custom installation of PHP, using the libraries that come with the PHP distribution found at `http://www.php.net/manual/ref.cybercash.php`. The functions that come with PHP are not as clean as those that work with PayfloPro. However, there is a nice library in /ext/cybercash of your PHP installation that should make credit-card processing relatively easy.

CURL:

This acronym stands for Client URL Library functions. It is a code library that you can use for communicating over the Internet using just about any protocol out there. It supports Gopher, Telnet, and (the best for our purposes) HTTPS.

You can now access this library through PHP functions if you installed PHP using with the `--with-curl` flag. You will first have to download the library from `http://curl.haxx.se/`.

We don't think the cURL functions are as clean as the PayflowPro functions. However, the are open-source. We'll cover the functions in the Code Breakdown section.

Configuring for session handling

When I start breaking down the code, you will see the exact functions you need to work with sessions. But while you are reading about configuration options, it's best to cover the different ways sessions can be implemented in PHP. But first a little on what sessions in PHP actually do.

Say you want to track the activity of your users across a number of pages, as with this shopping cart. You need to remember who has put what in a cart. To accomplish this, you could pass some rather complex variables via a cookie that held the all of the elements and their prices. But this is kind of messy, and it may expose more of the workings of your application than you are comfortable exposing. Moreover, the cookie specification (`http://www.netscape.com/newsref/std/cookie_spec.html`) allows for only 20 cookies per domain and only 4 bytes per cookie.

A better idea is give each person who visits your site a unique identifier, some value that identifies who that person is. Then, as the user adds items to the cart, information associated with the unique identifier can be stored on the server. If you were to code a function that stored the information by hand, you might create a unique string that would be put in a cookie; then, in some directory on the server, you could have a file that has the same name as the unique user ID. Within that file you could store all the variables associated with the user. For example, you might have an array of items that a specific user put in his or her cart.

In fact, this is almost exactly what sessions do. When you indicate in your code (or by settings in your php.ini) that you'd like to start a session, PHP will create a unique identifier and an associated file, which is stored on the server (the location is set in the php.ini, and by default is in the /tmp directory). Then as a user moves from page to page, all the variable information that the user chooses can be stored in the file on the server, and all the script needs to keep track of is the unique identifier.

There are many configuration options when it comes to sessions, but probably the most important decision is where the session id will be propagated, in a URL or in a cookie. Most e-commerce sites make use of cookies. However, there is the chance that some of your users will not be able to use your site properly if they have their browsers set to reject cookies. For this reason, in PHP it is very easy to add the session id to the querystring. There are two ways to go about it.

The code `<?= SID ?>` will print the session id. To append the session id to a URL, you would have to manually add it, like this:

```
<a href=mydomain.com?sid=<?=SID?>
```

This can make for some tedious work if you want to put the session id on every link in your site. However, if you compile PHP with the flag `--enable-trans-sid`, the session id will be automatically appended to every relative link in your pages once a session has been started.

Code Overview

As you might have guessed by now, there are two function sets used here that are relatively unique: the functions that deal with sessions and the functions associated with the cURL library. I will cover both sets of functions in some detail in this section.

First, though, I need to make another note about the advantages of the object-oriented approach. When you read Chapter 10 (you did read Chapter 10, right?) you saw some of the principles of object-oriented programming in practice. Specifically, you should have noticed how inheritance is used. When a class inherits the properties and methods of a parent class, it has access to all of the methods and properties of the parent.

In this application, you are extending the code you used in the catalog, so it makes sense that this application would create classes that extend the classes used in the catalog. Please be sure you are familiar with the catalog classes in Chapter 10 before proceeding.

Session functions

If you head over to the session page in the PHP manual (http://www.php.net/manual/ref.session.php), you will find 16 different functions. Depending on your needs, you may have to use a majority of these, but in many circumstances you could get away with using a single function: session_register(). We'll explain.

There are many functions and settings regarding sessions that we don't cover here. As always, make sure to check the manual.

The first thing you will need to do is let PHP know that you wish to start a session. You can do that explicitly by using session_start(). Then you will need to let PHP know what variables you want to store. You can do this with session_register("variable_name"). Take the following page, for example:

The start session() and session_register() functions should be at the very top of your PHP pages. These functions send cookies, which are a type of HTTP header. If you attempt to send any type of header after text has been sent to the browser, you will get an error.

```
<?
session_start();
session_register("mystring");

$mystring = "testing for a string";
?>
```

When accessed the first time, this page will start a session, and depending on the configuration either the script will send a cookie or a session id will be appended to relative links. The `session_register` command tells PHP to search the session file for the variable `$mystring`. If it exists, it will become available as a global, or if you wish you can access it through the $HTTP_SESSION_VARS array. After the page is processed the most current value for the registered variables is written to the session file. So if you have another page that contains the following code:

```
<?
session_start();
session_register("mystring");

echo $mystring;
?>
```

It will print "testing for a string".

The fact is that the `session_start()` function isn't really necessary; if you have a `session_register()` in your code, PHP is smart enough to start the session for you.

Note that although in the preceding code the variable is a simple string, you are by no means limited to a string. Simple arrays, complex arrays, and objects are all viable session variables.

Here are some other session functions that you may find useful.

SESSION_DESTROY()
This function kills a session and all of the variables associated with it.

SESSION_UNREGISTER()
This function erases the value of a variable in the session file.

SESSION_SET_SAVE_HANDLER()
This interesting function allows you to set your own methods for storing, retrieving, and writing your own session handlers.

```
void session_set_save_handler (string open, string close, string
read, string write, string destroy, string gc)
```

For a good deal of the time, the file-based session management in PHP will be fine. However, there are a couple of circumstances in which it may not suit you. If you happen to be working in a clustered environment, where several machines are serving the same site, writing to the local filesystem really won't work. Similarly, your SSL-enabled Apache installation may sit on a different box than your main server.

In this case a better choice is to have all of the machines connect to the same database, and to have your database (MySQL, of course) store the session data. It was unnecessary for us to make use of this function when we created this application because we were only working with one physical server. However, if you need to store session data in a MySQL database, you can use the functions in Appendix G.

SESSION_ENCODE()

In order to write variables to a database, the variables needs to be put in a format that makes sense to the database. That is what the `session_encode` function does. You can see examples of this in Appendix G.

```
$str = session_encode( string)
```

SESSION_DECODE()   This function reverses the process of encoding, so that the variable is turned into a representation that PHP can work with. You can see examples of this in Appendix G.

cURL functions

You can use the cURL library for many things, but for the shopping cart application, you are only concerned with one piece of functionality: communicating with a credit-card validation service. Basically, the application will send a secure message over HTTPS, and the service that validates credit cards will send back a response, which can then be processed in PHP.

There are only four cURL functions to work with.

CURL_INIT()

This function returns an integer that is similar to the result identifier returned by `mysql_connect()` or the file pointer returned by `fopen()`. In this case, it's called the cURL handle, or ch. In the sole argument of this function you indicate the URL you wish to access.

```
int curl_init ([string url])
```

For example:

```
$cc_company_url =
"https://secure.process.site/transact.dll?exp=foo&cardtype=bar
$ch = curl_init($cc_company_url);
```

Note that this function only starts the cURL session. The call to the URL doesn't happen until the `curl_exec()` function is executed.

CURL_SETOPT( )

```
bool curl_setopt (int ch, string option, mixed value)
```

Before you execute the communication, there are over 40 options you can set for cURL. Many of these aren't really necessary, given the quality of PHP's function set. Others aren't really relevant to the application presented here. See the manual (`http://www.php.net/manual/ref.curl.php`) if you'd like to see the full list of cURL's functions. For the sake of this application, all you need is to have the results of the https request returned to a PHP variable. For that you can use the CURLOPT_RETURNTRANSFER option.

```
curl_setopt($ch, CURLOPT_RETURNTRANSFER, 1);
```

CURL_EXEC( )

This function executes the transfer. The one argument should be the results of the `curl_init()` function and you should set all the necessary options.

```
bool curl_exec (int ch)
```

CURL_CLOSE( )

This function finishes the cURL connection using the curl handle:

```
void curl_close (int ch)
```

In the end, this set of functions will conduct the transaction and return a result to the $data variable.

```
$ch = curl_init($authorize_net_url);
curl_setopt($ch, CURLOPT_RETURNTRANSFER, 1);
$data = curl_exec($ch);
curl_close($ch);
```

Dealing with the credit-card processor

You are going to need to get some information directly from the entity processing the transaction. Most processing companies that we've seen work similarly. You send them a request with all the expected credit card information: number, expiration date, address, and so forth, and they send you some codes in response.

Your PHP script will need to compare the codes it receives with the values you get from the processing agency.

For this application you will use Authorize.net as the credit card processor, which seems to work just fine.

 Remember to look into the `PayfloPro` and `Cybercash` functions before settling on a payment method.

Code Breakdown

As with the Catalog, here you'll start by looking at the classes that will come into play in this application. Again, the files accessed via the URLs are very high-level files; all the tough work is done in the Class files.

A peek at classes.php will show the classes of interest here:

```
include "cart_base_class.php";
include "../catalog/category_class.php";
include "../catalog/product_class.php";
include "../catalog/style_class.php";
include "../catalog/substyle_class.php";

include "cart_category_class.php";
include "cart_product_class.php";
include "cart_style_class.php";
include "cart_substyle_class.php";

include "user_class.php";
include "address_class.php";
include "order_class.php";
include "item_class.php";
```

As already mentioned, one of the goals of this application is to make use of the classes we created in the catalog. We want to write as little new code as possible. So the new classes here will inherit the methods and properties in the classes we already created.

One class from Chapter 10 doesn't quite do enough for inclusion in the cart. That is the Base class. We're going to create another Base class with some extended functionality. Then all we have to do is make sure that the categories that extend Base call our new version. This is easily done with includes. In our classes.php file we include the new Base class, and then, when a class that extends Base is included, it sees the new class. When you look at the classes.php file, remember that the entire content of each of the included files is sucked into this file when it is parsed by PHP.

It will be easier to get a feel for the inheritance chain with some visual representation. Figure 14-6 shows the inheritance chain.

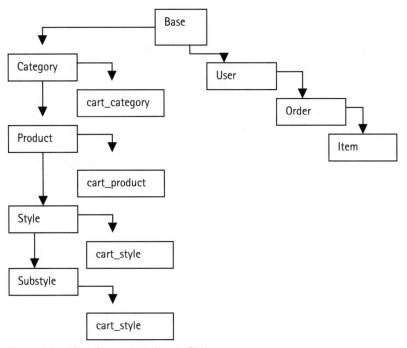

Figure 14-6: Cart Classes Inheritance Chain

As you can see from this figure, inheritance can be a bit more complicated than a straight hierarchy. Keep this figure handy as you read through this chapter and the source files on the CD-ROM.

Classes

The first classes we will discuss are on the right-hand side of Figure 14-6.

These classes have methods that look very much like the methods in the Category, Product, and other classes from Chapter 10. Those worked well because there is a natural hierarchy when dealing with products: categories contain products, products contain styles, and styles contain sub-styles. For a shopping cart there is a hierarchy of user information: a user can have many addresses, many orders can go to an address, and many items can belong in a single order.

Given this similarity it makes sense to create classes for user information that mimic the classes seen in Chapter 10. You will see what I mean when I get to the User class

Let's start at the top of the chain, looking at the changes to the Base class.

BASE CLASS

PHP classes do not support multiple inheritance. If they did, we could create a class named CartBase as an extension of Base, and then have the Catalog class extend both Base and CartBases. Since this isn't possible, we copied all of the methods from the Base class in the catalog (`sql_format()`, function `set_image_src ()`, `set_thumb_src()`, `construct()`, and `base()`). All of these methods are described in Chapter 10. We added a single method, which prints a form.

METHOD ORDER_FORM()   There's nothing terribly special in this form. It will print all the data necessary to gather information on an item to be put in the shopping cart.

```
function order_form ()
{
    $output = start_form("cart.php")
        ."<b>".$this->item."</b>"
        ." "
        .$this->price
        ." "
        ."<b>Qty</b> "
        .text_field("quantity",1,4,4)
        ." "
        .submit_field("order_item","Order!")
        .hidden_field("category_id",$this->category_id)
        .hidden_field("product_id",$this->product_id)
        .hidden_field("style_id",$this->style_id)
        .hidden_field("substyle_id",$this->substyle_id)
        .hidden_field("price",$this->price)
```

```
        .end_form()
    ;
    $output .= "\n";
    return $output;
}
```

USER CLASS

As mentioned, this class will look very much like the classes from the catalog. Here's the vital information on this class:

Class Name: User
Extends Base
Default Properties:

- ◆ $ addresses

Methods:

- ◆ User. The class constructor. Takes two arguments: $parent and $atts. Calls the Base() method, assigning each element of the $atts array to Object properties.

- ◆ FetchUser. Takes one argument, $user_id. Creates object properties for every row in the user table associated with the $user_id.

- ◆ LoadUser. Takes one argument, $user_id. First runs FetchUser and then creates an array, each element of which is an object containing address information.

- ◆ SaveUser. Takes no arguments, assumes a $this->user_id exists. Will both update existing styles and create new ones as needed.

- ◆ DeleteUser. Takes no arguments. Removes a user from the database. It will force confirmation if there are related addresses. It will delete the user after confirmation is provided.

This should look familiar. You should expect to see the same sorts of data structures that were created in Chapter 10 and shown in Figures 10-11 and 10-12. Using this class you can expect an object created from the User class to contain an array called address, each element of which is an object containing complete address information.

CLASS ADDRESS

This looks very similar to the previous class.

Class Name: Address
Extends User
Default Properties:

- ◆ $orders

Methods:

- ◆ Address. Calls the Base() method, assigning each element of the $atts array to Object properties.

- ◆ FetchAddress. Takes one argument, $address_id. Creates object properties for every row in the user table associated with the $address_id.

- ◆ LoadAddress. Takes one argument, $address_id. First runs FetchOrder and then creates an array, each element of which is an object containing address information.

- ◆ SaveAddress. Takes no arguments, assumes a $this->order_id exists. Will both update existing styles and create new ones as needed.

- ◆ DeleteAddress. Takes no arguments. Removes a user from the database. It will force confirmation if there are related addresses. It will delete the user after confirmation is provided.

CLASS ORDER

Finally, in this class we add something new and interesting.

Class Name: Order

Extends Address

Default Properties:

- ◆ $items

Methods:

- ◆ Order. Calls the Base() method, assigning each element of the $atts array to Object properties.

- ◆ FetchOrder. Takes one argument, $order_id. Creates object properties for every row in the user table associated with the $order_id.

- ◆ LoadOrder. Takes one argument, $order_id. First runs FetchOrder and then creates an array, each element of which is an object containing address information.

- ◆ SaveOrder. Takes no arguments, assumes a $this->order_id exists. Will both update existing styles and create new ones as needed.

- ◆ DeleteOrder. Takes no arguments. Removes a user from the database. It will force confirmation if there are related addresses. It will delete the user after confirmation is provided.

- ◆ CalculateTotals. Takes no arguments. This method calculates total prices for each item of the order and for the order as a whole. Items that are flagged for deletion are removed from the items array property.

◆ ValidateCard. Takes no arguments. This method does not conduct a trans-action with a credit-card processing agency. It runs through a function (seen in Appendix G) that makes sure the credit card number supplied is potentially valid. If the credit card is not in a proper format, the method will return false.

◆ ChargeCard. Takes no arguments. Communicates with the credit-card processor.

◆ PrintOrder. Takes no arguments. Prints out the results of an order.

The ChargeCard method deserves some added discussion.

METHOD CHARGECARD() This method will make use of the cURL functions described earlier in this chapter. First we start by calculating the totals.

```
function ChargeCard()
{
    $this->CalculateTotals();
    $total_charged = $this->total_price + $this->ship_cost;
    $exp = sprintf("%02d/%04d",
        $this->cc_exp_mon, $this->cc_exp_yr);
```

The following code prepares a URL that we will use to communicate with authorize.net. For legal reasons we did not include the actual variables you will need to send to authorize.net to get a meaningful response. However, that information is available at the authorize.net site. Following that, we prepare an error message, just in case.

```
$authorize_net_url =
"https://url.to.authorize.net?var1=FALSE&var2=foo";

    $this->error = "connection to authorize.net failed";
```

Now it is time to make the connection and see if the credit card is verified. The cURL functions are a little strange at this point. They are fairly new and aren't quite as polished as some of the other function sets. But by the time you read this, there may be a PEAR (PHP Extension and Application Repository) class that makes dealing with cURL easier. Make sure to check in at the php.net site for the latest updates to the cURL functions.

```
    global $ch;
    $ch = curl_init($authorize_net_url);
    curl_setopt($ch, CURLOPT_RETURNTRANSFER, 1);
    $data = curl_exec($ch);
    curl_close($ch);
```

authorize.net returns a string of comma-separated values. The script will compare the results from the returned string against their known meanings (supplied by authorize.net). In the code that follows, the first element in the returned string is tested. If it has a value of 1, this method will return TRUE, meaning the transaction was successful.

```
$this->rvars = explode(",",$buffer);
$this->auth_result = $this->rvars[0];
$this->error = $this->rvars[3];
if ($this->auth_result != 1) { return FALSE; }
return TRUE;
}
```

CLASS ITEM

This class is at the base of the hierarchy.

Default Properties:

- none

Methods:

- Item. The class constructor. Takes two arguments: $parent and $atts. Calls the Base() method, assigning each element of the $atts array to Object properties.

- SaveItem. Takes no arguments, assumes a $this->item_id exists. Will both update existing styles and create new ones as needed.

CLASS CARTCATEGORY

This is the first of the new classes that directly extend the classes created for the catalog application.

Class Name: CartCategory
Extends Category
Default Properties:

- none

Methods:

- CartCategory. The class constructor. Calls the Base() method, assigning each element of the $atts array to Object properties.

- AddProduct. This method overwrites the AddProduct() method that is in the parent (Category) class. It creates an array, called $products, each member of which is an object formed by calling the CartProducts() class.

In creating the data structure in Chapter 10, you saw how the LoadCategory() method instantiated objects within an array. Instead of having the LoadCategory() class instantiate the object directly, we had LoadCategory() call another method, named AddProduct(), which instantiated the objects. By breaking out AddProduct() into its own separate method, we gained some flexibility, which becomes convenient in this application.

When you instantiate the CartCategory class, the AddProduct() method of this child class overwrites the AddProduct() method of the parent (Category) class. So if you write the following code:

```
$c = new CartCategory;
$c->LoadProduct($product_id);
```

you can be sure that the AddProduct() method from the CartCategory call will execute.

Here are the contents of AddProduct() method of the CartCategory class.

```
function AddProduct($parent,$atts)
{
    $this->products[] = new CartProduct($parent,$atts);
}
```

CLASS CARTPRODUCT

This is similar to the CartCategory class and includes a method for printing Products that is better for the shopping cart.

Class Name: CartProduct
Extends Product
Default Properties:

◆ none

Methods:

◆ CartProduct. The class constructor. Takes two arguments: $parent and $atts. Calls the Base() method, assigning each element of the $atts array to Object properties.

◆ AddStyle. This method overwrites the AddStyle() method that is in the parent (Product) class. It creates an array, called $styles, each member of which is an object formed by calling the CartStyles() class.

◆ PrintProdct. Takes no attributes. Overwrites the PrintProduct() method of the parent (Product) class.

CLASS CARTSTYLE

This is similar to the CartStyle class and includes a method for printing Styles that is better for the shopping cart.

Class Name: CartStyle
Extends Style
Default Properties:

- none

Methods:

- CartStyle. The class constructor. Takes two arguments: $parent and $atts. Calls the Base() method, assigning each element of the $atts array to Object properties.

- AddSubStyle. This method overwrites the AddSubStyle() method that is in the parent (Style) class. It creates an array, called $substyles, each member of which is an object formed by calling the CartSubStyles() class.

- PrintStyleRow. Takes no attributes. Overwrites the PrintStyleRow() method of the parent (Style) class.

CLASS CARTSUBSTYLE

This is similar to the CartSubStyle class and includes a method for printing substyles that is better for the shopping cart.

Class Name: CartSubStyle
Extends SubStyle
Default Properties:

- none

Methods:

- CartSubStyle. The class constructor. Takes two arguments: $parent and $atts. Calls the Base() method, assigning each element of the $atts array to Object properties.

- AddSubStyle. This method overwrites the AddSubStyle() method that is in the parent (Style) class. It creates an array, called $substyles, each member of which is an object formed by calling the CartSubStyles() class.

- PrintSubStyle. Takes three attributes, $style_price, $style_dsc, $product_dsc. Overwrites the PrintSubStyle() method of the parent (Style) class.

Scripts

These are the pages called by URLs and the includes. Once again, you will probably notice that there isn't a whole lot involved. Almost all of the work is done in the Classes.

DISPLAY.PHP
This will print out either a list of categories or a specific product.

```
include 'header.php';

if (empty($category_id))
{
    header("Location: index.php");
    exit;
}

$page_title = anchor_tag("index.php", "Bag'O'Stuff");

$c = new CartCategory;

if (empty($product_id))
{
    $c->LoadCategory($category_id);

    $page_title .= ": $c->category";
    include "start_page.php";

    $c->PrintCategory();
}
else
{
    $p = new CartProduct;
    $p->LoadProduct($product_id);
    $p->LoadStyles();
    $c->FetchCategory($p->category_id);
    $page_title .= ": "
        .anchor_tag("display.php?category_id=$c->category_id"
            , $c->category
        )
        .": $p->product"
    ;
```

```
        include "start_page.php";

        $p->PrintProduct();
}

include "end_page.php";
```

It doesn't get a whole lot more basic: If this page is to display a Category (not a product), a Category is loaded and then printed. The same will happen for a Product if appropriate. If you remember the display.php page from Chapter 10, you might notice that the only real difference is that the objects instantiated here are created from the classes new to this application. That gives us access to the new print methods, which were designed to work with this application.

CART.PHP
Here's the page that creates our shopping cart.

```
include "header.php";

session_register("cart");
session_register("last_item");

$page_title = anchor_tag("index.php","Bag'O'Stuff")."
Shopping Cart";

include "start_page.php";
include "cart_form.php";
include "end_page.php";
```

What? Expecting a little more code from your shopping cart? Well, most of it is in the include (cart_form.php). Just note here that the session is started. And that there are two session variables you will be tracking. The cart object, as you will see in a moment, is created with the Order class. Remember that when the two variables are registered on the page, two things happen. First, if they exist already, they are pulled into memory from the session file. Second, if they are changed in the course of the page, they will be written out with those changes at the end of the page.

Note that the $last_item variable holds the description of the last item ordered by the user. We use it to prevent multiple orders of the same item, typically caused by the user hitting the Order! button more than once. If the user wants two of an item instead of one, they can change the quantity for the item.

Now let's look at the include.

CART_FORM.PHP
As you can see here, if the cart does not exist in the session a new one will be instantiated. There are extensive in-line comments, which should help you get through this script.

```
// if $cart is not an Order object, make it one
if (!is_object($cart)) { $cart = new Order; }



// initialize the URL for displaying
// items from the cart with the name
// of the display script, formatted as
// an absolute URL to the regular
// (non-secure) server by the regular_url() function (defined in
// /book/functions/basic.php).
$href = regular_url("display.php");

if ($order_item == "Order!")
{
    // create a new CartSubStyle object. as the lowest class in our
    // class hierarchy (low == furthest from Base),
    // it is an extension
    // of all the other classes, and so can access
    // all of their methods.
    // we will use this to hold any new item to be
    // added to the cart.
    $t = new CartSubStyle;

    // the $last_item variable holds the description of the last
    // item ordered by the user. we use it to prevent multiple
    // orders of the same item, typically caused by an itchy
    // finger on the 'Order!' button. if the user wants two of
    // an item instead of one, they can change the quantity for
    // the item.

    // if the cart is empty, of course, there is no previously
    // ordered item - set $last_item to an empty string.
    if (count($cart->items) == 0) { $last_item = ""; }

    // the $item variable will be set to a description of the
    // ordered item. initialize it to an empty string.
    $item = "";

    if (!empty($product_id))
    {
        // we at least have a product ID.  get information about
        // the product category and its category from the database,
        // and add links to the category and product to the item
        // description.
        $t->FetchCategory($category_id);
```

```
            $href .= "?category_id=$t->category_id";
            $item .= anchor_tag($href,$t->category);

            $t->FetchProduct($product_id);
            $href .= "&product_id=$t->product_id";
            $item .= "- ".anchor_tag($href,$t->product);
        }
        if (!empty($style_id))
        {
            // we have a style ID. get information about the style
            // from the database and add the style name to the item
            // description. (styles are not individually displayed.)
            $t->FetchStyle($style_id);
            $item .= "- $t->style";
        }
        if (!empty($substyle_id))
        {
            // we have a substyle ID. get information about the substyle
            // from the database and add the substyle name to the item
            // description. (substyles are not individually displayed.)
            $t->FetchSubStyle($substyle_id);
            $item .= "- $t->substyle";
        }

        if (!empty($item) && $last_item != $item)
        {
            // if we have an item description and it is not the
            // same as the last item ordered, add the new item
            // to the user's shopping cart.
            $cart->AddItem($cart, array(
                "item"=>$item
                , "product_id" => $product_id
                , "style_id" => $style_id
                , "substyle_id" => $substyle_id
                , "price" => $price
                , "quantity" => $quantity
            ));
        }

        // set $last_item to the item just ordered (if any)
        $last_item = $item;
    }
    elseif ($again == "please")
    {
        // which just means, we're coming from a submitted cart form,
```

```
      // where $again is set to "please" in a hidden field. we test
      // this, rather than the value of $submit as in other examples,
      // so the user can hit the ENTER key after typing in a new
      // quantity or checking remove boxes and get a recalculation,
      // without actually pressing the 'Recalculate' button.

      // for each item in the cart, set its quantity property
      // to the corresponding value from the $quantity[] array
      // built by PHP from the 'quantity[$row]' fields submitted
      // from the form.
      $quantity = (array)$quantity;

      reset($cart->items);
      while (list($row,) = each($cart->items))
      {
          // by adding 0 explicitly, PHP will set the value
          // of the quantity property to at least 0, even if,
          // for some reason, the user has set the field to
          // a blank value.
          $cart->items[$row]->quantity = $quantity[$row] + 0;
      }

      $remove = (array)$remove;
      while (list($row,$value) = each($remove))
      {
          // tag the item for removal by CalculateTotals()
          $cart->items[$row]->killme = $value;
      }
  }

// recalculate the total price for each item in the cart
$cart->CalculateTotals();

// display the contents of the shopping cart
print start_form();
print hidden_field("again","please");

print start_table(array("border"=>1));
print table_row("<b>Item</b>"
    , "<b>Quantity</b>"
    , "<b>Price</b>"
    , "<b>Total</b>"
    , "<b>Remove?</b>"
);
```

```php
    reset($cart->items);
    while (list($row,$item) = each($cart->items))
    {
        // display each item in the cart. the item description
        // will include links to the display page for the
        // various elements of the item (category, product,
        // style, as applicable). (see above where $item is
        // constructed.)

        // display the total price for each item as a US dollar
        // value (2 decimal places with a dollar sign in front).

        // display a checkbox allowing the user to remove an item
        // from the cart.
        print table_row($item->item
            , text_field("quantity[$row]",$item->quantity,3)
            , table_cell($item->price, array("align"=>"right"))
            , table_cell(money($item->total_price)
                , array("align"=>"right")
            )
            , checkbox_field("remove[$row]", "yes", "remove")
        );

        // keep a running total of the quantity and price of items
        // in the cart.
        $total_price += $item->quantity * $item->price;
        $total_quantity += $item->quantity;
    }

    // print out totals
    print table_row("<b>Grand Total:</b>"
        , "<b>$cart->total_quantity</b>"
        , ""
        , table_cell("<b>".money($cart->total_price)."</b>"
            , array("align"=>"right")
        )
    );

    print end_table();

    // the 'Continue Shopping' button displayed by the keep_shopping()
    // function (defined in functions.php) runs in its own form.
    // so we display it in an HTML table with the 'Recalculate'
    // button of the shopping cart form to keep them side-by-side.
    print start_table();
```

```
print table_row(
    submit_field("recalc","Recalculate")
        .end_form()

    ,
    //keep shopping is defined in the functions.php file
    keep_shopping($category_id,$product_id)
);
print end_table();
```

CHECKOUT.PHP

Now, finally, it's time to check out. Note that this is really the only file that needs to be on the secure server. There's no need for the catalog portions or even the cart page to be on a secure server, because there's really no information that needs to be protected. However, on this page we're going to be accepting credit card information.

Once again, there are extensive comments within the script to help you get through the page's logic.

```
include "header.php";

// if a session ID has been passed in, use it
if (isset($sessid)) { session_id($sessid); }

// get the session variables for the shopping cart and the user's
email address
session_register("cart");
session_register("email");

// if a value for 'email' was posted to the script from a form, use
that
// in preference to the session variable
if (!empty($HTTP_POST_VARS["email"])) { $email =
$HTTP_POST_VARS["email"]; }

// set up variables defining the values of the buttons of the form
// (defining the values once helps avoid errors caused by spleling
problems.)
$order_button = "ORDER NOW!";
$info_button = "Get My Info";

if (!is_object($cart))
{
    // if $cart isn't an Order class object (defined in
order_class.php),
    // we're not going to do much - the shopping cart will have no
```

```
    // items in it.  initialize it as one anyway, to keep the script
from
    // breaking.
    $cart = new Order;
}


// load any posted variables into the cart using the Construct()
// method of the Base class (defined in cart_base_class.php).
$cart->Construct($HTTP_POST_VARS);

if (!empty($zapthis) && is_array($zapthis))
{
    // if multiple addresses were found for the user from past
orders,
    // the user can ask to have one or more of the addresses removed
    // from the database. this is done by checking HTML checkbox
fields
    // named "zapthis[]", set to the ID values of the addresses.
    // if at least one of the checkboxes was set, PHP will return
    // the values in array variable $zapthis. (if no checkboxes
    // are checked, $zapthis is not necessarily empty, but it
    // will not be an array.)
    while (list(,$aid) = each($zapthis))
    {
        // delete the address records using the DeleteAddress()
        // method of the Address class (defined in
address_class.php)
        $cart->DeleteAddress($aid);
    }
}
if (!empty($usethis))
{
    // if multiple addresses were found for the user from past
orders,
    // the user can ask to use one of them for this order by
clicking
    // on a radio button field named "usethis", set to the ID value
    // of the address. if $usethis is set, get the address record
    // for the ID value, using the FetchAddress() method of the
    // Address class.
    if ($cart->FetchAddress($usethis))
    {
        // there is now one and only one address for this order
        $cart->address_count = 1;
    }
}
```

```php
if ($ordernow == $order_button)
{
    // the user hit the big ORDER button. validate their credit
    // card and charge it, using the ValidateCard() and ChargeCard()
    // methods of the Order class.
    if ($cart->ValidateCard() && $cart->ChargeCard())
    {
        // the charge went through - write the order to the
        // database using the SaveOrder() method of the Order class.
        $cart->SaveOrder();

        // redirect the user to the receipt page for a receipt
        // they can print or save to a file, and exit the script.
        //  pass on the ID value of the new order record and
        // the session ID that was passed in to this script.
        header("Location: receipt.php?order_id=$cart->order_id"
            ."&sessid=$sessid"
        );
        exit;
    }
}
elseif ($getdata == $info_button || (empty($cart->user_id) &&
!empty($email)))
{
    // either the user has asked to look up their information in the
    // database, or we don't yet have an ID value for the user but
    // do have an email address. use the LoadUser() method of the
    // User class (defined in user_class.php) to try looking up
    // address information stored for the user from past orders.
    $cart->LoadUser($email);
}

$page_title = "Check Out";
include "start_page.php";

// include the shopping cart form
include "cart_form.php";

// begin the order form. we pass on the session ID value that was
passed
// into this script as a GET-style argument because it makes it
easier
// to see if we're in the right session or not.
print start_form("checkout.php?sessid=$sessid");
```

```
// store the user ID of the user (if any)
print hidden_field("user_id",$cart->user_id);

print subtitle("User Info");

print start_table();

// display the user's email address, along with the button they
// can use to ask to check the database for address information.
print table_row("<b>Email:</b>",text_field("email",$cart->email,20)
    .submit_field("getdata",$info_button)
);

print table_row("<b>First Name:</b>",text_field("firstname",$cart-
>firstname,40,40));
print table_row("<b>Last Name:</b>",text_field("lastname",$cart-
>lastname,40,40));

print table_row("");

if ($cart->address_count == 1)
{
    // if we've only got one address, load its properties
    // as properties of the shopping cart. the easy case.
    $cart->Construct(get_object_vars(&$cart->addresses[0]));
}
elseif ($cart->address_count > 1)
{
    // we have more than one possible address from the database
    // for the user. the hard case.
    // begin building an HTML table to display them.
    $useme_cell = start_table(array("border"=>1));

    // begin building a list of address cells
    $useme_row = "";

    // walk through the array of addresses
    while (list($i,) = each($cart->addresses))
    {
        // use a reference to avoid copying the object
        $a = &$cart->addresses[$i];

        // build an HTML table cell containing the address
        // and fields for the user to indicate how they
```

```
        // would like to use it (if at all), and add the
        // cell to the row string.
        $useme_row .= table_cell(
            $a->PrintAddress()
            ."<br>"
            .radio_field("usethis"
                , $a->address_id
                , "Use this address"
            )
            ."<br>"
            .checkbox_field("zapthis[]"
                , $a->address_id
                , "Delete this address"
            )
        );
    }


    // add the address cells and close the table.
    // (note: this somewhat presumes there
    // won't be more than two or three addresses - the table
    // will get unwieldy otherwise.)
    $useme_cell .= table_row($useme_row);
    $useme_cell .= end_table();

    // display the addresses
    print table_row("",table_cell($useme_cell));
    print table_row("");
}


// these fields contain any address information that might have been
// directly entered by the user before the database was searched, or
// the information from an address from the database that has been
// selected by the user. in any case, *these* fields are what will
// be used in the order.
print table_row("<b>Address:</b>",text_field("address",$cart-
>address,40,40));
print table_row("",text_field("address2",$cart->address2,40,40));
print table_row("<b>City:</b>",text_field("city",$cart-
>city,40,40));
print table_row("<b>State:</b>",select_field("state",states(),$cart-
>state));
print table_row("<b>Zip:</b>",text_field("zip",$cart->zip,10,10));
print table_row("<b>Phone:</b>",text_field("phone",$cart-
>phone,20,20));
```

```
if (!empty($cart->address_id))
{
    // allow the user to create a new address
    print table_row(""
        , checkbox_field("save_as_new"
            , "yes"
            , "Save this as a new address"
        )
    );
}

print end_table();

// display the available shipping methods
print subtitle("Shipping Info");

print start_table();

print table_row(
    "<b>Shipping Method</b>"
    , table_cell("<b>Per Order</b>",array("align"=>"right"))
    , table_cell("<b>Per Item</b>",array("align"=>"right"))
    , table_cell("<b>Total for This
Order</b>",array("align"=>"right"))
);

// if no shipping method has been chosen, use the first one as a
default
if (empty($cart->shipping_id)) { $cart->shipping_id = 1; }

// get the list of shipping methods from the database
$result = safe_query("select shipping_id,shipping,per_item,per_order
    from shipping
");
while ($ship = mysql_fetch_object($result))
{
    // calculate the cost of using this method. we use a simplistic
    // system: a fixed cost per order, and a per item charge.
    $shiptotal = $ship->per_order + ($cart->total_quantity * $ship-
>per_item);

    // display the shipping method with a radio field allowing the
    // user to choose it
```

```
    print table_row(
        radio_field("shipping_id",$ship->shipping_id,$ship-
>shipping,$cart->shipping_id)
        , table_cell(money($ship-
>per_order),array("align"=>"right"))
        , table_cell(money($ship->per_item),array("align"=>"right"))
        , table_cell(money($shiptotal),array("align"=>"right"))
    );
}
print end_table();

// display payment information
print subtitle("Credit Card Info");

print start_table();

if ($cart->error)
{
    // if the user tried to place an order and there was an error
    // when validating or charging the card, display it here.
    print table_row(
        table_cell("<font color=red>$cart->error</font>"
            ,array("colspan"=>2)
        )
    );
    $cart->error = "";
}


// display a test card number in the form for this example by
default.
// it has a valid format, and since we're not really trying
// to charge any cards here, AuthorizeNet will accept it.
if (empty($cart->cc_number)) { $cart->cc_number = "4912-7398-07156";
}

// pick Visa as the default type, to match the default test card
number
if (empty($cart->cc_type_code)) { $cart->cc_type_code = "vis"; }

// use the db_radio_field() function (defined in
/book/functions/forms.php)
// to display the accepted credit card types as radio button fields
```

```php
print table_row("<b>Credit Card:</b>"
        ,
db_radio_field("cc_type_code","cc_types","cc_type_code","cc_type"
        , "cc_type_code",$cart->cc_type_code
    )
);

print table_row("<b>Number:</b>",text_field("cc_number",$cart-
>cc_number,20));

// set the variables used to enter the credit card expiration date

// set the $months array to a list of possible months
for ($i = 1; $i <= 12; $i++) { $months[$i] = $i; }

// set the $years array to a list of plausible years
for ($i = 2000; $i <= 2005; $i++) { $years[$i] = $i; }

// use January 2001 as a default expiration date
if (empty($cart->cc_exp_mon)) { $cart->cc_exp_mon = 1; }
if (empty($cart->cc_exp_yr)) { $cart->cc_exp_yr = 2001; }

print table_row("<b>Expires:</b>"
    , select_field("cc_exp_mon",$months,$cart->cc_exp_mon)
        .select_field("cc_exp_yr",$years,$cart->cc_exp_yr)
);
print end_table();

// save the ID of the address used in this order (if any)
print hidden_field("address_id",$cart->address_id);

// display the order button
print paragraph(submit_field("ordernow",$order_button));

print end_form();

include "end_page.php";

?>
```

Summary

In this, the final application of the book, you've seen a few interesting things. You've learned that an application like a shopping cart requires some method of maintaining state. Probably the best way to maintain state with PHP for something like a shopping cart is with sessions.

If you wish to process credit cards, you will need a secure server, an SSL certificate, and a set of functions for processing cards. In this application we used the cURL functions for credit card processing, but there are two other function sets (PayfloPro and Cybercash) that you should look into.

The final thing to note in this chapter is how classes were used. By extending existing classes, and writing methods to overwrite previous methods, we were able to flexibly use large blocks of code.

Part V

Appendixes

Appendix A

HTML Forms

IF YOU WANT YOUR APPLICATIONS to take user data, you are going to need a place for them to enter the information. That requires HTML forms. HTML forms are easy enough to work with. There are several commonly used input types, and in browsers that make use of HTML 4.0 and Cascading Style Sheet there are some techniques that you can use to make your forms a bit fancier. A full discussion of everything you can do with forms is beyond the scope of this book. If you need more information on forms and how they can work with CSS or JavaScript, or some of the newer browser-specific form types, check out the documentation at http://microsoft.com or http://mozilla.org.

Form Basics

Each form is delimited by opening and closing `<form>` tags. The `<form>` tag takes the following attributes:

- action – This attribute specifies the URL of the page that a form will be sent to for processing. It can contain a relative URL (e.g., "myscript.php" or "../myfolder/myscript") or a complete URL (e.g., http://www.mydomain/myscript.php").

- method – This attribute indicates the HTTP request type the browser will send to the server. It must be set to either GET or POST. If you set it to GET, the name=value pairs will appear in the browser location bar (e.g., http://mypage.com?name1=value1&name2=value2). The advantage of using GET is that results can be bookmarked in the browser. The disadvantage is that the variables you send will be more transparent. If you set this attribute to POST the name=value pairs will not be visible. The default value is GET.

- name – This attribute is most useful for addressing portions of a form through JavaScript. The form name is not sent to the server when the form is submitted.

- enctype – The default is "application-x-www-form-urlencoded", and this will normally be fine. But if you are uploading files (using `<input type="file">`, you should use "multipart/form-data".

A typical form shell will look something like this:

```
<form name="myform" action="processor.php" method="post">
...
</form>
```

Input Types

Most of the work in your forms will be done by the input types. An input tag and the type attribute will determine what kind of form element is rendered in your browser. Every input type must have a name attribute. That's how you're going to pass variables to your scripts, so make sure you don't forget them. (To be absolutely accurate, you don't need to supply name attributes to submit and reset buttons.)

As a quick example, the following would create a simple form with a single text box and a submit button. The text box has the default value of "hello there", as shown in Figure A-1.

```
<form>
   <input type="text" size="50" maxlength="15"
    value="hello there"><br>
   <input type="submit" name="submit" value="OK?">
</form>
```

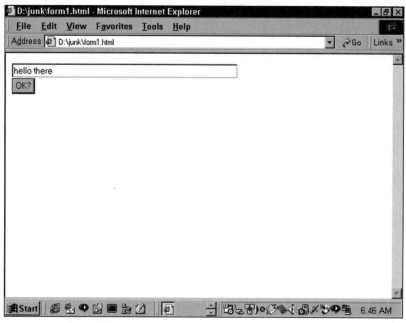

Figure A-1: Simple HTML form

The input types are as follows. Note that different input types have different attributes associated with them. Each of them takes a name attribute.

- Text – This type is shown in the above example. It can take these attributes:

    - Size, which indicates the length of the box rendered in the Web browser.

    - Maxlength, which limits the number of characters that can be input into the field. Keep in mind that older browsers will ignore maxlength, and even in newer browsers, you should not rely on this attribute to limit uploads. Check your upload_max_filesize item in your php.ini to set the limit on the server.

    - Value, which is the default value in the box. The user can override it by typing in different information.

- Password – This type is identical to the text field, except that the text that is typed into the box is shown as asterisks.

- Hidden – This type does not render on the screen. It is very useful for passing values between pages. The name and value attributes are all you need with hidden fields. Consider using hidden fields if you're uncomfortable with cookies or sessions. Note that by simply viewing the source of your Web page, a savvy user will be able to see your hidden form elements. Do not put any sensitive data in hidden form.

- Submit – This type places a submit button on the page. The text in the value attribute will appear on the submit button. When the form is submitted, the name and value of the submit button are passed along like all other form elements.

- Image – This type will serve the same purpose as the submit button, but it will allow you to specify an image to use instead of that ugly old submit button. Treat this form element as you would any <img> tag. Provide both scr and alt attributes.

- Reset – This type provides a button that, when pressed, alters your form to the state it was in when the page was initially loaded. The default text on the reset button is "Reset". By adding a value attribute, you can change the text on the reset button. A Reset button does not involve PHP or the server in any way.

- File – This type gives what looks like a textbox and a button with the text "browse" on it. When users hit browse, they are given a window that allows them to go through their operating system to find the file they would like to upload. If using this input type, be sure to change the form enctype attribute to "multipart/form-data". See Chapter 10 for a discussion of file uploads with PHP.

◆ Checkbox – The name and value of the checkbox will only be passed if the checkbox is checked when the form is submitted. If the word "checked" appears in the tag, the checkbox will be checked by default. Remember to use name=box_name[] to pass multiple checkboxes as an array. See Chapter 4 for a discussion of passing arrays with PHP.

◆ Radio – Radio buttons allow the user to select only one of several choices. Radio buttons with the same name attribute belong to the same group. The "checked" command signifies the default choice.

The following form makes use of most of the form elements we just covered, except for the image type. Figure A-2 shows how it is rendered in the browser.

```
<h2>Please Enter Personal Information</h2>
<form>
    <input type="text" size="25" maxlength="15" name="name"
value="Name Here"><br>
    <input type="password" size="25" maxlength="15" name="password"
value=""><br>
    <input type="hidden" value="you can't see me">
    <input type="checkbox" name="telemmarket" value="yes" checked>If
checked, I have permission to clear out your bank account.
    <p>
    <b>What is your eye color?</b><br>
    <input type="radio" name="eye_color" value="blue"
checked>blue<br>
    <input type="radio" name="eye_color" value="green">green<br>
    <input type="radio" name="eye_color" value="brown">brown<br>
    <input type="radio" name="eye_color" value="red">red<br>
    <input type="submit" name="submit" vaule="submit">    
 
    <input type="Reset">
</form>
```

Select, multiple select

The select form element creates drop-down boxes and (to use the Visual Basic term) list boxes. To create drop-down boxes, you must have an opening <select> tag with a name attribute. Within the select element, <option> tags will indicate possible choices. Each of these will have a value attribute.

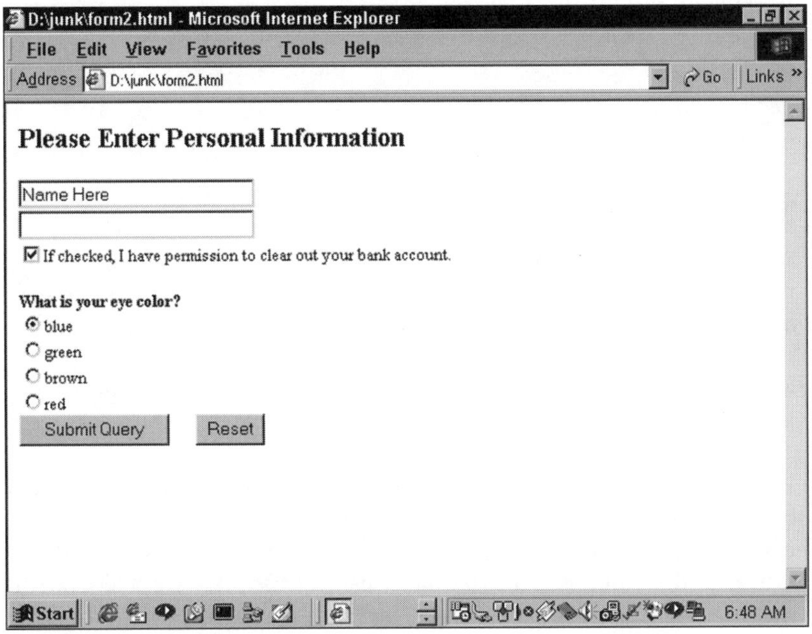

Figure A-2: More form elements

The following HTML creates a drop-down box with 3 elements.

```
<form name="tester" action="script.php" method="get">
   <select name="dinner">
      <option value="1">chicken
      <option value="2">fish
      <option value="3">vegetarian
   </select>
</form>
```

By adding the word "multiple" to the select element you enable the user to pick more than one of the choices. The size attribute determines how many of the options are visible at one time.

The following code creates a list box with 3 visible elements. Figure A-3 shows how this HTML looks in the browser.

```
<form name="tester" action="script.php" method="get">
   <select name="side_dishes" multiple size=3>
      <option value="1">potato
      <option value="2">pasta
```

```
            <option value="3">carrot
            <option value="4">celery
            <option value="5">mango
    </select>
</form>
```

Textarea

The textarea element creates a large block for text entry. Add a row and column attribute to specify the size of the box. Textarea is different from other form elements in that opening and closing tags surround the default text. For instance:

```
<textarea name="mytext" rows="5" colums="20">Here's the default
text</textarea>
```

Keep in mind that if you have spaces or hard returns between your <textarea> tags, those characters will be carried to the form element.

Add the wrap attribute to change how text wraps when it reaches the end of a line in the box. If the value is wrap=physical, carriage returns are added at the end of line; if the value is wrap=virtual, the lines will appear to wrap but will be submitted as a single line. This is almost always the best choice.

These attributes came about from the folks at Netscape, and you still may need to use them. The official W3C HTML 4.0 attribute values for wrap are none, hard, and soft.

Figure A-3 adds the select, multiple select and textarea elements to a form with this code.

```
<h2>Please Enter Personal Information</h2>
<form>
<fieldset id="fieldset1"
    style="postion:absolute;
    width:300;
    height:100;
    top:20;
    left:10;"
      >
<legend>Food Questions</legend>
<b>What did you eat for dinner?</b><br>
    <select name="dinner">
        <option value="1">chicken
        <option value="2">fish
        <option value="3">vegetarian
    </select><br>
```

```
<b>Any Side dishes?</b><br>
   <select name="side_dishes" multiple size=3>
      <option value="1">potato
      <option value="2">pasta
      <option value="3">carrot
      <option value="4">celery
      <option value="5">mango
   </select>
<br>
<b>How are you feeling about dinner?</b><br>
<textarea name="mytext" rows="5" colums="20">
Here's the default text</textarea>
</fieldset>
<p>
<button>
   <img src="disk.gif" width="32" height="32" border="0"
alt="disk"><br>
   Pretty Little Button
</button>
</form>
```

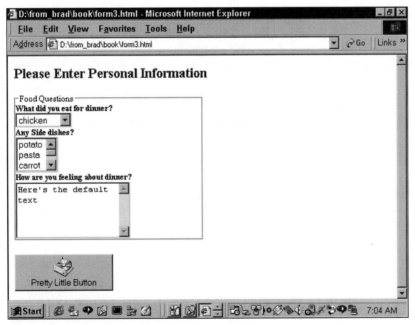

Figure A-3: Additional form elements

Other attributes

With HTML 4.0 and the newest browsers some additional attributes have been introduced. Make sure to test these as part of your QA process because they will not work on all browsers.

ACCESSKEY

An accesskey is the same as a hotkey. If this attribute appears in a form element, the user can hit (on a PC) Alt and the designated key to be brought directly to that form element. The hotkey is generally indicated by underlining of the hot letter.

```
<input type="text" name="mytext" acceskey="m"><u>M</u>y text box.
```

TABINDEX

Users can use the Tab key to move through form elements. The tabindex attribute specifies the order in which focus will move through form elements.

Other elements

Internet Explorer 5 and Mozilla support a couple of new and seldom-used form elements that you might want to consider using.

BUTTON

The button is a fancier version of the submit button. It allows for both text and an image to be put on the same button. There are opening and closing <button> tags, and everything inside of them appears on the button. Figure A-3 shows an example of the button.

FIELDSET AND LEGEND

These are nice for grouping elements in forms. All text and tags within the <fieldset> tags will be surrounded by a thin line. Text within the <legend> tags will serve as the caption for that grouping.

Figure A-3 shows all of the form types.

In the year 2001, it is still not a great idea to use most of the HTML 4.0 form elements and attributes. Generally speaking, they add very little, and they may look very strange on many browsers.

Appendix B

Brief Guide to PHP/MySQL Installation and Configuration

WHEN INSTALLING MySQL AND PHP, you are faced with all kinds of options. The variety of operating systems and installation options creates more permutations than could possibly be handled in this book. Luckily, installation procedures for both packages are documented well in each package's respective documentation.

In this appendix we will cover the basic installation and configuration of MySQL and PHP on Windows 98 and Unix systems. I'm assuming that you will be using the Apache Web server on all platforms. For the Unix installation, this book will document only the method of compiling the source code. If you wish to use RPMs for your installation, you should consult the online manuals.

Windows 98 Installation

Start by copying the MySQL binaries from the CD-ROM accompanying this book or the `mysql.com` site to your local drive. Do the same for Apache and PHP (the appropriate download sites here are `http://www.apache.org/dist` and `http://www.php.net/download`). The names of the files will be something like the following (they may be slightly different, depending on the version you are using):

- mysql-3.23.22-beta-win.zip
- apache_1_3_9_win32.exe
- php-4.0.1pl2-Win32.zip

Start by unzipping the mysql file and php files with your favorite unzip tool. (If you don't have one, we recommend Winzip, at `http://www.winzip.com/`.) Unzip them into a directory you find convenient. We prefer using a separate directory for each.

Start with MySQL. In the directory where you unzipped the file, you will have a file named setup.exe. Execute that file. Choose a directory (e.g. d:\mysqlinstall) where you want it installed, and then in the next screen select a Typical installation. (You may wish to examine the custom options, but with the Windows install there are very few real options.)

At this point your MySQL installation is complete. To test it, go to the DOS prompt and move to the directory you specified for your MySQL installation. Then move to the subcategory named \bin. If you then type **mysqld**, the mysql daemon should start. To test if your daemon is working, start up the mysql command-line client by typing **mysql**. If the monitor starts up and looks like Figure B-1, MySQL is working properly.

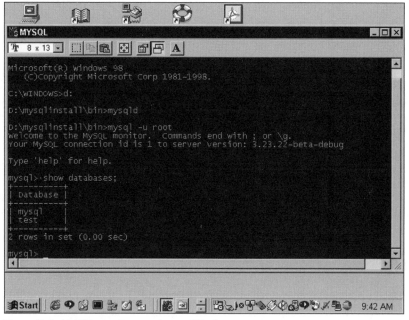

Figure B-1: MySQL monitor running on Windows

Next, you should install Apache.

This requires little more than double-clicking on the executable you copied from the CD or the apache.org site. The installation is pretty easy: all you really need to do is select a directory where you would like Apache to be installed. When it's completed, an Apache Group item will be added to the Start menu.

 Don't start up Apache just yet. A little more configuration information will follow.

Now on to PHP. You should have a folder into which you unzipped all the PHP files. In that folder copy MSVCRT.DLL and PHP4TS.DLL to c:\windows\system. Then rename php.ini-dist to php.ini and keep it in the same directory were you have the php.exe file.

All you need to do at this point is make sure that Apache is aware of PHP and that PHP is aware of MySQL.

First go to the directory where you installed Apache, find the httpd.conf file within the \conf directory, and open it in a text editor. Add these three lines to the file:

```
ScriptAlias /php4/ "d:/php4/"
AddType application/x-httpd-php4 .php
Action application/x-httpd-php4 "/php4/php.exe"
```

Note that we indicated the d: drive because that's how we set up our own system. The c: drive will work just as well.

The first line indicates the path where PHP resides. The second tells Apache what file extensions must be parsed as PHP, and the third gives the path to the php executable file. Note using this type of installation, PHP will run as an executable, not an Apache server module.

If you would like other file extensions to by parsed by PHP, simply add another AddType line to the conf file; for example:

```
AddType application/x-httpd-php4 .phtml
```

There are a couple of other alterations you may have to make to your httpd.conf file. If the server refuses to start, you may need to add something to the Server Name directive. If you are using TCP/IP in your local area network, you may need to add the IP address of your machine, for instance:

```
ServerName 192.168.1.2
```

Or if your machine is not networked, you may want to user the following ServerName

```
ServerName 127.0.0.1
```

If you also have Personal Web Server running on your machine, you may wish to change the port on which Apache runs. By default, Web servers listen on Port 80, but you can change that by altering the Port line in the httpd.conf to something else — perhaps 8080.

And that should do it. Start Apache through the Start Menu. Add a file to your \htdocs folder that contains the phpinfo() function. When you call that function you should see that everything is working properly, and that there is an entry for MySQL. Figure B-2 shows the results of phpinfo().

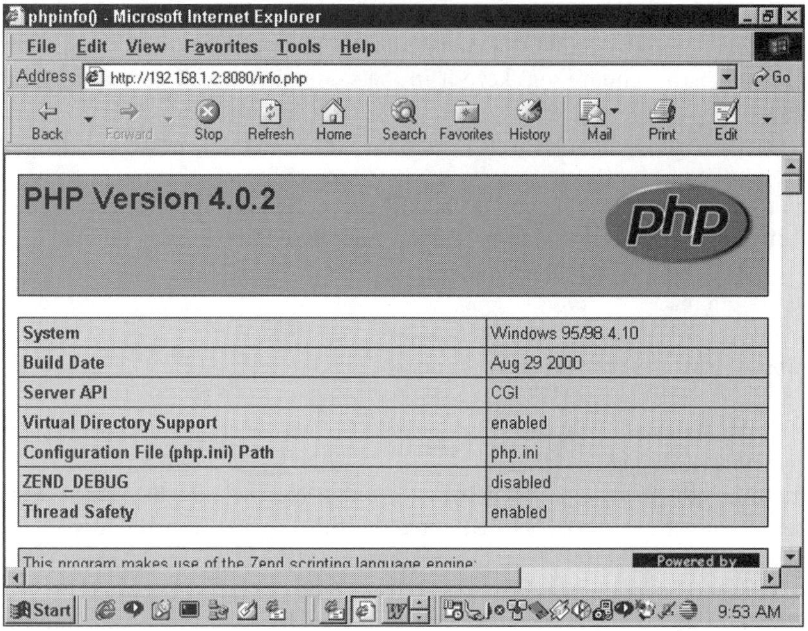

PHP Version 4.0.2

System	Windows 95/98 4.10
Build Date	Aug 29 2000
Server API	CGI
Virtual Directory Support	enabled
Configuration File (php.ini) Path	php.ini
ZEND_DEBUG	disabled
Thread Safety	enabled

This program makes use of the Zend scripting language engine:

Figure B-2: phpinfo() on Windows

Note that you don't need to make any alterations in the php.ini file to make PHP work with MySQL. MySQL support is, in fact, built into PHP for Windows.

If you uncomment the directive extension=php_mysql.dll, you will have all kinds of problems getting a PHP page to load.

These are the basics you need to get going with PHP and MySQL on Windows. Note that you can also install PHP as an ISAPI filter for Internet Information Server (IIS) and PWS. The instructions for doing so are included in the readme.txt file included in the PHP zip file. As of this writing, running PHP as an IIS filter is not recommended in a production environment.

Installation on Unix

On Unix, there are far more options you may wish to avail yourself of. You may wish to install by compiling the source code yourself or (on Linux) by using rpm files. This appendix will only cover compiling from source. We strongly recommend that you do not use rpm files. The convenience that rpms sometimes offer does not extend to this type of configuration.

There are a variety of libraries and optional functions that you can compile into PHP, and additional libraries and functions are being added all the time. In this quick guide, we will cover only some highlights.

If you have other priorities, need rpms, or wish to include options not covered here, seek out the documentation in the online manuals. This really isn't a very difficult install procedure, and you should be able to customize as you see fit with minimal effort. First stop, MySQL.

MySQL Installation

Complete information on MySQL installation can be found in Chapter 4 of the MySQL online manual: `http://www.mysql.com/documentation/mysql/bychapter/manual_Installing.html`. Check it out if you are having problems.

You will need to get the .tar.gz file either from the accompanying CD-ROM or from `http://www.mysql.com/downloads/`. Copy it to a directory you wish to work in and then unpack this file with the following command:

```
gunzip mysql-3.23.22.tar.gz
tar xf mysql-3.23.22.tar
```

This will create a directory with the name of the mysql distribution (for instance mysql-3.23.22). Use `cd` to move into the directory. Note that the exact version may be different, depending on the when you download the software.

The first step is to run configure. There are many options you can set with configure flags. To get a complete list run `./configure --help`.

In the installations I've run, I've found it convenient to specify the --prefix. If you do not specify a prefix, /usr/local will be used, and this is almost always perfectly fine. Additionally, mysql allows you to specify the location of any of the subdirectories (the data directory, the bin directory, etc). Usually that will not be necessary. Normally you can run

```
./configure --prefix=/path/to/installation
```

If you need to make use of database transactions in your applications, you will need to make use of the Berkeley Database (BDB) tables. At the time of this writing, this feature is still in beta release. You can get the BDB tables from `http://www.mysql.com/downloads`.

If you want to use BDB tables you would run the following configure line, not the one shown previously.

```
./configure --prefix=/path/to/installation --with-berkeley-db=/path/to/files
```

Next, run the following two commands:

```
make
make install
```

That's it. You should now have a directory that contains all of your files and subfolders.

The next thing you want to do is cd into the bin directory and run the following command:

```
./mysql_install_db
```

This creates your default databases and permissions tables. You should now be able to start the mysql daemon using the safe_mysql command from the /bin directory.

By default, mysql uses port 3306 and keeps the all important socket file at /tmp/ myslq.sock. This is generally OK. PHP will look for the socket file in this location. However, if you have multiple installations of MySQL you will need to change the port and socket location, which can be a pain. You will need to play with your my.cnf file. See Chapter 4 of the MySQL manual for more information.

PHP/Apache

On Unix, PHP will be loaded as an Apache module. Thus the installation of the two will need to be done in concert. Once again, there are many, many installation options. You can create PHP as an executable for use with CGI or command-line processing, as a shared Apache module (apxs), or for DSO. Here we will only cover installation as an Apache module.

Start by unpacking both Apache and PHP.

```
gunzip apache 1.3.x.tar.gz
tar xf apache1.3.x.tar
gunzip php-4.02.tar.gz
tar xf php-4.02
```

Here "x" is the version number of apache.

Use cd to move into the Apache directory and run configure, specifying the path where you would like Apache installed.

```
./configure --prefix=/path/to/apache
```

This 'preps' Apache to set up machine-specific information that PHP needs to compile. You'll come back later and finish up the Apache installation.

Then move to the directory holding PHP. Here there are a variety of flags you may or may not wish to specify. We would suggest using the following:

```
./configure --with-mysql=/path/to/mysql --enable-trans-id --enable-
track-vars
```

Here, the three flags do the following:

- `--with-mysql` — You may know that client libraries for MySQL will be automatically installed even if you don't specify `--with-mysql`. However, if you installed MySQL someplace other than /usr/local, you will need to use this flag and specify the directory. It's good practice to specify this anyway.

- `--enable-track-vars` — If this flag exists, variables from GET, POST, and COOKIES will be available in the appropriate arrays, HTTP_GET_VARS, HTTP_POST_VARS, HTTP_COOKIE_VARS.

- `--enable-trans-sid` — This option allows for Session ID to be included automatically in URLs after a session is started. The Shopping Cart in Chapter 10 makes use of this option.

Additionally, you may wish to include one or more of the following flags:

- `--with-gd=path/to/gd` — The GD functions allow you to create images on the fly, using nothing but code. GD requires a library from `http://www.boutell.com/gd/`.

- `--with-config-file-path=/path/to/file` — The php.ini file specifies many options for the PHP environment. PHP expects to find the file in /usr/local/lib/php.ini. If you wish to change the location, use this flag.

- `--with-curl/with-pfpro/with-cybyercash` — If you wish to use any of these libraries to process credit-card transactions, you will need to download the appropriate library and specify the location of that library with a path, for example, `--with-pfpro--path/to/pfpro`.

There are many other flags and libraries that you can incorporate into PHP. Please see the online manual (`http://www.php.net/manual/install-unix.php`) or run --configure --help for the latest and most complete list.

After running `configure`, run the following two commands:

```
make
make install
```

Now you will need to go back to the Apache directory and rerun the `configure` command:

```
./configure --prefix=/path/to/apache --activate-module=
src/modules/php4/libphp4.a
```

Note that the libphp4.a will not yet exist. It will be created after the compiling is completed.

Now it's time to run the great twosome.

```
make
make install
```

Apache should now be installed in the directory you specified.

Now move back to the PHP directory and copy the file named php-ini.dist to /usr/local/lib/php.ini (or to the directory you specified in the `--config-file-path` flag).

The final step is to go into the /conf directory of your Apache installation and open the httpd.conf file. There you should uncomment the following line:

```
AddType application/x-httpd-php .php
```

Then move into the /bin directory and start Apache.

```
./apachectl start
```

Your installation should now be complete.

 PHP will look for the socket to MySQL in /tmp/mysql.sock. If you have more than one MySQL installation and need PHP to connect to the socket in another location, you will need to specify that in the `mysql_connect()` function.

```
mysql_connect("localhost:/path/to/mysql.sock",
"username", "password");
```

PHP Configuration

The php.ini file is extremely large, and has more options than we can cover here. A full list of options and potential settings can be found at `http://www.php.net/manual/configuration.php`. Here are a few highlights.

MySQL configuration entries

The following are some of the MySQL configuration entries.

```
mysql.allow_persistent   =
mysql.max_persistent     =
mysql.max_links    =
mysql.default_port   =
mysql.default_host   =
mysql.default_user   =
mysql.default_password   =
```

If you want to forbid persistent connections, change that setting to Off, or if you want to limit the number of persistent links to MySQL, change the setting on max_persistent and max_links from –1 to an appropriate number. Persistent connections are explained in Chapter 6, in the discussion of the mysql_pconnect() function.

You can use the default_user, default_host, and default_password entries if you want to save yourself the trouble of entering these strings in your mysql_connect() command. Note that putting your MySQL password here is a probably a very bad idea.

ERROR REPORTING

This specifies the error reporting level.

```
error_reporting =
```

The default value here is 7, and generally that will be fine. The following is a list of the other potential values. If you indicate a number that is the sum of any of these values, all of the values that create the sum will be used. For instance 7 includes 1, 2, and 4.

1 = Normal errors

2 = Normal warnings

4 = Parser errors

8 = Notices

Note if you include 8, you will get a lot of messages, including things like uninitialized.

MAGIC QUOTES

```
magic_quotes_gpc
magic_quotes_runtime
```

If the first is set to On, all single quotes ('), double quotes ("), backslashes (\) and NULLs will be prepended with a backslash immediately upon being uploaded from a form element. This will make doing your inserts into MySQL a lot easier.

If set to On, data retrieved from the filesystem or a database will automatically be escaped with backslashes.

EXECUTION TIME

```
max_execution_time = 30
memory_limit = 8388608
```

These settings are intended to protect you in the event of an infinite loop or an endlessly recursive function. All scripts will automatically be terminated if they reach either of these limits. If you want to have a script you expect to take more than 30 seconds, you can set the maximum execution time within a script with the set_time_limit () function. This can contain the number of seconds; if you wish to specify no limit, use set_time_limit(0).

AUTO PREPEND AND APPEND

```
auto_prepend_file    =
auto_append_file     =
```

With these settings you can specify files that will automatically be included at the start and end of your php files. It may be useful for connection information or common headers.

INCLUDE PATH

```
include_path
```

This should contain a list of paths separated by colons (:). These paths will automatically be searched for every include() and require().

SESSION

There are many session settings you may with to change. Here are a few of them:

```
session.save_handler    = files
session.save_path       = /tmp
session.use_cookies     = 1
session.auto_start      = 0
```

Appendix H contains a set of functions for using MySQL for session handling. If you wish to use it, you must set the session.save.handler to user.

save_path indicates where in the filesystem PHP will save session information.

If use_cookies is set to 0, you must use another means of storing cookies, either by using <?=SID ?> or by configuring PHP--with-trans-sid

Finally, if auto_start is set to 1, sessions will be started automatically on every page.

Appendix C

MySQL Utilities

THIS APPENDIX PRESENTS A BRIEF OVERVIEW of some of the MySQL administrative utilities. These are the tools that you'll use to build and maintain your databases. Whether or not you'll have access to them depends on the exact version number you are running.

The best place to get the full details about the tools you have available to you is the Docs subdirectory of your local installation of MySQL. (Note: This is the install directory, not the data directory.) You can also check the online version of the MySQL documentation at `http://www.mysql.com/documentation/`

But be warned — the online manuals always document the most recent version of MySQL, which at the time of this writing is the beta release 3.23.

If you're running the production release, 3.22, many of the features you'll read about on the Web site won't be available to you. I've marked off version 3.23 enhancements in this document where I could. You can always find out just what your version of a tool supports by running it with the `--help` option (e.g., `mysql --help`).

mysql

This is the command-line interface to MySQL; it allows you to run any arbitrary SQL command, as well as the MySQL-specific commands like `describe table`. It's a tool you should get to know. You can use it to test out or debug queries for your code, create your database, create tables, add columns to existing tables — everything, really. It also has some batch-oriented options that make it handy to use in maintenance scripts, or as a quick no-frills reporting tool.

Syntax:

```
mysql [options] [database name] [<inputfile] [>outputfile]
```

If you just type `mysql`, you'll start the tool up, but you won't be anywhere. When you try to do anything that involves interaction with a database, you'll get this error:

```
ERROR 1046: No Database Selected
```

To select one, type

```
use databasename;
```

use' is one of the mysql tool's built-in commands. Type `help` to see a list of them:

```
help    (\h)    Display this text
?       (\h)    Synonym for 'help'
clear   (\c)    Clear command
connect (\r)    Reconnect to the server. Optional arguments are  and
host
edit    (\e)    Edit command with $EDITOR
exit    (\q)    Exit mysql. Same as quit
go      (\g)    Send command to mysql server
ego     (\G)    Send command to mysql server; Display result
vertically
print   (\p)    Print current command
quit    (\q)    Quit mysql
rehash  (\#)    Rebuild completion hash
status  (\s)    Get status information from the server
use     (\u)    Use another database. Takes database name as
argument

** new in 3.23:
source  (\.)    Execute a SQL script file. Takes a file name as an
argument
```

Of course, it's simpler if you just give a database name on the command line. But this command does let you switch between databases in a single session.

Once you're in a database, you can run an SQL statement by typing it in, followed by a semicolon, 'go' (this may not work by default in 3.23 installations) '\g', or '\G', and hitting return/enter.

Table C-1 list some of the more useful command-line options.

TABLE C-1 COMMON MYSQL COMMAND-LINE CLIENT OPTIONS, PART I

Flag	Alternate Flag	Description
-?	--help	Display this help and exit
-B	--batch	Print results with a tab as separator, each row on a new line. Doesn't use history file.
-D,	--database=..	Database to use; this is mainly useful in the my.cnf file, to specify a default database.

Flag	Alternate Flag	Description
e	--execute=...	Execute command and quit. (Output like with --batch)
-E	--vertical	Print the output of a query (rows) vertically. Without this option you can also force this output by ending your statements with \G.

Vertical means that each field of each row is on a line by itself. For instance, looking at the STATUS table from the problem-tracking example, here is a standard query and output:

```
mysql> select * from status
    -> go
+-----------+-------------+
| status_id | status      |
+-----------+-------------+
|         1 | Opened      |
|         2 | In Progress |
|         3 | Closed      |
|         4 | Re-opened   |
+-----------+-------------+
```

Here is the same query with vertical output:

```
mysql> select * from status
    -> go
*************************** 1. row ***************************
status_id: 1
status: Opened
*************************** 2. row ***************************
status_id: 2
status: In Progress
*************************** 3. row ***************************
status_id: 3
status: Closed
*************************** 4. row ***************************
status_id: 4
status: Re-opened
```

If you're feeding the output of your queries to another program for processing, like a Perl script, this form can be much easier to parse.

Tables C-2 and C-3 list additional mysql command-line client options.

TABLE C-2 COMMON MYSQL COMMAND-LINE CLIENT OPTIONS, PART II

Flag	Alternate Flag	Description
-f	--force	Continue even if we get a SQL error.
-h	--host=...	Connect to the given host.
-H	--html	Produce HTML output.
-L	--skip-line-numbers	Don't write line number for errors. Useful when one wants to compare result files that include error messages.
-n	--unbuffered	Flush buffer after each query.
-p[password]	--password[=...]	Password to use when connecting to server. If password is not given on the command line, you will be prompted for it. Note that if you use the short form (-p) you can't have a space between the option and the password.

Examples:

```
mysql -u root -pfoobar
```

or

```
mysql --username=root --password=foobar
```

TABLE C-3 COMMON MYSQL COMMAND-LINE CLIENT OPTIONS, PART III

Flag	Alternate Flag	Description
-P	--port=...	TCP/IP port number to use for connection.
-q	--quick	Don't cache result, print it row by row. This may slow down the server if the output is suspended. Doesn't use history file. If you have problems due to insufficient memory in the client, use this option. It forces mysql to use mysql_use_result() rather than mysql store result() to retrieve the result set.

Flag	Alternate Flag	Description
-r	--raw	Write column values without escape conversion. Used with `--batch`
--safe-mode (new to 3.23)		Sends the following command to the MySQL server when opening the connection: SET SQL_SAFE_UPDATES=1,SQL_SELECT_ LIMIT=#select_limit#, SQL_MAX_JOIN_SIZE=#max_join_size#" where `#select_limit#` and `#max_join_size#` are variables that you can set from the mysql command line.

The effect of the previous command is:

◆ You are not allowed to do an UPDATE or DELETE if you don't have a key constraint in the WHERE part. One can however force an UPDATE/DELETE by using LIMIT: UPDATE table_name SET not_key_column='some value' WHERE not_key_column='some value' LIMIT 1;

◆ All big results are automatically limited to #select_limit# rows.

◆ SELECTs that will probably need to examine more than #max_join_size row combinations will be aborted.

Table C-4 lists additional mysql command-line client options.

TABLE C-4 COMMON MYSQL COMMAND-LINE CLIENT OPTIONS, PART IV

Flag	Alternate Flag	Description
-t	--table	Output in table format. This is default in non-batch mode.
-u	--user=#	User for login if not current user.
-w	--wait	Wait and retry if connection is down instead of aborting.

mysqladmin

This is the command-line utility for performing administrative tasks.
   Syntax:

```
mysqladmin [OPTIONS] command command....
```

The mysqladmin commands are listed in Table C-5:

TABLE C-5 MYSQLADMIN COMMANDS

Command	Description
create databasename	Create a new database.
drop databasename	Delete a database and all its tables.
extended-status	Gives an extended status message from the server.
flush-hosts	Flush all cached hosts.
flush-logs	Flush all logs.
flush-tables	Flush all tables.
flush-privileges	Reload grant tables (same as reload).
kill id,id,...	Kill mysql threads.
password *newpassword*	Change old password to the string *newpassword*.
ping	Check if mysqld is alive.
processlist	Show list of active threads in server.
reload	Reload grant tables.
refresh	Flush all tables and close and open logfiles.
shutdown	Take server down.
status	Give a short status message from the server.
variables	Print variables available.
version	Get version info from server.
slave-start (new to 3.23)	Start slave replication thread.
slave-stop (new to 3.23)	Stop slave replication thread.

Each command can be shortened to its unique prefix. For example:

```
mysqladmin proc stat
+----+-------+-----------+----+-------------+------+-------+------+
| Id | User  | Host      | db | Command     | Time | State | Info |
+----+-------+-----------+----+-------------+------+-------+------+
| 6  | monty | localhost |    | Processlist | 0    |       |      |
+----+-------+-----------+----+-------------+------+-------+------+
Uptime: 10077  Threads: 1  Questions: 9  Slow queries: 0  Opens: 6
Flush tables: 1  Open tables: 2  Memory in use: 1092K  Max memory
used: 1116K
```

Table C-6 shows the columns created by the `mysqladmin status` command.

TABLE C-6 COLUMNS CREATED BY MYSQLSADMIN STATUS COMMAND

Column name	Description
Uptime	Number of seconds the MySQL server has been up.
Threads	Number of active threads (clients).
Questions	Number of questions from clients since mysqld was started
Slow queries	Queries that have taken more than 'long_query_time' seconds.
Opens	How many tables 'mysqld' has opened.
Flush tables	Number of 'flush ...', 'refresh' and 'reload' commands.
Open tables	Number of tables that are open now.
Memory in use	Memory allocated directly by the mysqld code (only available when *MySQL* is compiled with --with-debug).
Max memory used	Maximum memory allocated directly by the mysqld code (only available when MySQL is compiled with –with-debug).

In MySQL 3.23, if you do `myslqadmin shutdown` on a socket (in other words, on a computer where `mysqld` is running), `mysqladmin` will wait until the `MySQL pid-file` is removed to ensure that the mysqld server has stopped properly.

Table C-7 presents some of the more useful or common command-line options.

TABLE C-7 MYSQLSADMIN COMMAND-LINE OPTIONS

Flag	Alternate Flag	Description
-?	--help	Display help and exit.
-#	--debug=...	Output debug log. Often this is d:t:o,filename.
-f	--force	Don't ask for confirmation on drop database; with multiple commands, continue even if an error occurs.
-h	--host=#	Connect to host.
-p[...]	--password[=...]	Password to use when connecting to server. If password is not given on the command line, you will be prompted for it. Note that if you use the short form -p you can't have a space between the option and the password.
-P	--port=...	Port number to use for connection.
-I	--sleep=sec	Execute commands again and again with a sleep between.
-r	--relative	Show difference between current and previous values when used with -i. Currently works only with extended-status.
-s	--silent	Silently exit if one can't connect to server.
-t	--timeout=...	Timeout for connection to the mysqld server.
-w	--wait[=retries]	Wait and retry if connection is down.
-W (Windows only)	--pipe	Use named pipes to connect to server.
-E	--vertical	Print output vertically. Is similar to -relative, but prints output vertically.

mysqldump

This is the command-line utility for dumping out schema information and data from your databases. This is what you would use to back up your database, or move it from one machine to another.

The output from `mysqldump` will most commonly be a script of SQL commands, to create tables and then insert data into them. mysqldump can also create plain data files (i.e., a tab-delimited file) from your tables.

Syntax:

```
mysqldump [OPTIONS] database [tables]
```

or, as of 3.23:

```
mysqldump [OPTIONS] --databases [OPTIONS] DB1 [DB2 DB3...]
mysqldump [OPTIONS] --all-databases [OPTIONS]
```

A typical use of `mysqldump` would look like this:

```
mysqldump --opt mydatabase > backup-file.sql
```

You can read this back into MySQL with the `mysql` command-line tool:

```
mysql mydatabase < backup-file.sql
```

or, as of 3.23:

```
mysql -e "source /patch-to-backup/backup-file.sql" mydatabase
```

You could also use it to copy data from one MySQL server to another:

```
mysqldump --opt mydatabase | mysql --host=remote-host mydatabase
```

Table C-8 lists the command-line options:

TABLE C-8 MYSQLDUMP COMMAND-LINE OPTIONS

Flag	Alternate Flag	Description
-?	--help	Display this help message and exit.
-a	--all	Include all MySQL specific create options.
--add-locks		Add LOCK TABLES before and UNLOCK TABLE after each table dump (to get faster inserts into MySQL).

Continued

TABLE C-8 MYSQLDUMP COMMAND-LINE OPTIONS *(Continued)*

Flag	Alternate Flag	Description
--add-drop-table		Add a DROP TABLE IF EXISTS statement before each CREATE TABLE statement.
--allow-keywords		Allow creation of column names that are keywords. This option works by prefixing each column name with the table name.
-c	--complete-insert	Use complete insert statements (with column names).
--delayed		Insert rows with the INSERT DELAYED command.
-F	--flush-logs	Flush log file in the MySQL server before starting the dump.
-f	--force	Continue even if you get a SQL error during a table dump.
-h	--host=..	Dump data from the MySQL server on the named host. The default host is localhost.
-l	--lock-tables	Lock all tables before starting the dump.
-t	--no-create-info	Don't write table creation info.
-d	--no-data	Don't write any row information for the table.
--opt		Same as –quick --add-drop-table --add-locks –extended-insert --lock-tables. Should give you the fastest possible dump for reading into a MySQL server.
-p[...]	--password[=...]	Password to use when connecting to server. If password is not given on the command line, you will be prompted for it. Note that if you use the short form `-p' you can't have a space between the option and the password.
-P	--port=port_num	The TCP/IP port number to use for connecting to a host.

Flag	Alternate Flag	Description
`-q`	`--quick`	Don't buffer query, dump directly to stdout.
`-T path-to-some-directory,`	`--tab=path-to-some-directory`	For each table, creates a table_name.sql file containing the SQL CREATE commands, and a table_name.txt file containing the data from the table.

Here's an example of the `-T` flag on a Unix installation:

```
mysqldump -T . tracking problems
```

This will create two files in the current directory (that's what '.' means): 'problems.sql' and 'problems.txt'. 'problems.sql' will have the SQL statements to create the 'problems' table. 'problems.txt' is a tab-delimited (the default format) copy of the data now in the 'problems' table in the 'tracking' database.

This only works if mysqldump is run on the same machine as the mysqld daemon. The format of the .txt file is made according to the --fields-xxx and --lines--xxx options.

Table C-9 lists more mysqldump command-line options.

TABLE C-9 MORE MYSQLDUMP COMMAND-LINE OPTIONS

Flag	Alternate Flag	Description

`--fields-terminated-by=...`
`--fields-enclosed-by=...`
`--fields-optionally-enclosed-by=...`
`--fields-escaped-by=...`
`--lines-terminated-by=...`
		These options have the same meaning as the corresponding clauses for the LOAD DATA INFILE statement.

Continued

TABLE C-9 MORE MYSQLDUMP COMMAND-LINE OPTIONS *(Continued)*

Flag	Alternate Flag	Description
`-u user_name,`	`--user=` `user_name`	The MySQL user name to use when connecting to the server.

`-w`	`--where=`
	`'where-`
	`condition'`
		Dump only selected records; Note that QUOTES are mandatory!
		
		Example:
		
		`--where=`
		`user='jimf'"`
		`"-wuserid>1"`
		`"-wuserid<1"`

Table C-10 displays the mysqldump command line options that are new to version 3.23.

TABLE C-10 MYSQLDUMP COMMAND-LINE OPTIONS NEW IN VERSION 3.23

Flag	Alternate Flag	Description
`-A`		
	`--all-databases,`	Dump all the databases. This is the same as `--databases` with all databases selected.
`-B`		
	`--databases`	Dump several databases. Note the difference in usage; in this case no tables are given. All name arguments are regarded as database names. USE db_name; will be included in the output before each new database.
`-e`	`--extended-insert`	Use the new multiline INSERT syntax.

Flag	Alternate Flag	Description
`-n`	`--no-create-db`	'CREATE DATABASE IF NOT EXISTS db_name;' will not be put in the output. The above line will be added otherwise, if --databases or --all-databases option was given.
`--tables`		Overrides option –databases (-B).
`-O`		net_buffer_length=#, where # < 24M When creating multi-row-insert statements (as with option --extended-insert or --opt), mysqldump will create rows up to net_buffer_length length. If you increase this variable, you should also ensure that the max_allowed_packet variable in the MySQL server is bigger than the net_buffer_length.

mysqlimport

The `mysqlimport` tool provides a command line interface to the `'LOAD DATA INFILE'` SQL statement. Most options to `mysqlimport` correspond directly to the same options to `'LOAD DATA INFILE'`.

Syntax:

```
mysqlimport [options] database textfile1 [textfile2....]
```

For each text file named on the command line, `mysqlimport` strips any extension from the filename and uses the result to determine which table to import the file's contents into. For example, files named patient.txt, patient.text, and patient would all be imported onto a table named patient.

You typically use `mysqlimport` to bring data into a MySQL database from some other source – another DBMS, a spreadsheet, or the like. You can also use it together with the `mysqldump` tool. Take the example I gave earlier:

```
mysqldump -T . tracking problems
```

This created two files, problems.sql and problems.txt. To reload the problems table from these files, you could do as follows:

```
mysql tracking <problems.sql
mysqlimport tracking problems.txt
```

Some of the most common or useful command-line options are shown in Table C-11.

TABLE C-11 MYSQLIMPORT COMMAND-LINE OPTIONS

Flag	Alternate Flag	Description
-?	--help	Display a help message and exit.
-d	--delete	Empty the table before importing the text file.
--fields-terminated-by=... --fields-enclosed-by=... --fields-optionally-enclosed-by=... --fields-escaped-by=... --lines-terminated-by=...		These options have the same meaning as the corresponding clauses for 'LOAD DATA INFILE'.
-f	--force	Ignore errors. For example, if a table for a text file doesn't exist, continue processing any remaining files. Without '--force', mysqlimport exits if a table doesn't exist.
-h host_name	--host=host_name	Import data to the MySQL server on the named host. The default host is 'localhost'.
-l	--lock-tables	Lock all tables for writing before processing any text files. This ensures that all tables are synchronized on the server.
-L	--local	Read input files from the client. By default, text files are assumed to be on the server if you connect to 'localhost' (the default host).

Flag	Alternate Flag	Description
-p[...]	--password[=...]	Password to use when connecting to server. If password is not given on the command line, you will be prompted for it. Note that if you use the short form `-p` you can't have a space between the option and the password.
-P port_num	--port=port_num	The TCP/IP port number to use for connecting to a host. (This is used for connections to hosts other than 'localhost', for which Unix sockets are used.)
-I -r	--ignore --replace	The --replace and --ignore options control handling of input records that duplicate existing records on unique key values. If you specify --replace, new rows replace existing rows that have the same unique key value. If you specify --ignore, input rows that duplicate an existing row on a unique key value are skipped. If you don't specify either option, an error occurs when a duplicate key value is found, and the rest of the text file is ignored.
-s	--silent	Silent mode. Write output only when errors occur.
-u user_name	--user=user_name	The MySQL user name to use when connecting to the server. The default value is your Unix login name.
-c	--columns=...	This option takes a comma-separated list of field names as an argument. The field list is passed to the LOAD DATA INFILE MySQL sql command, which mysqlimport calls MySQL to execute. For more information, please see 'LOAD DATA INFILE'.

Other Utilities

Please check the /bin directory for other utilities that come with MySQL. If you are using 3.23 you will want to look at myisamchk and myisampack. The first repairs corrupted tables and the second will ensure that tables are set up as efficiently as possible. These utilities only work with the MyISAM tables. If you are using 3.22, you will need to use of the isamchk utility, which operates on the ISAM tables used in this version of MySQL.

Appendix D

MySQL User Administration

THIS APPENDIX WILL TEACH you to work with MySQL's grant tables, which control permissions in MySQL.

Administration of any relational database management system (RDBMS) requires some work. Each system presents its own unique methods for administration and difficulties when it comes to tasks like adding and deleting user accounts, backing up, and assuring security. Administering MySQL isn't especially difficult, but it can be a bit bewildering at first.

This book focuses on applications development, not server administration. Thus extensive details on administration are beyond the scope of this tome. If you are responsible for backup and security of your server, you should delve deep into the MySQL online manual, focusing on Chapters 21 (for backup) and Chapter 6 (for security).

For the purposes of this book, and we hope also for you, the application developer, it is enough to know a bit about user administration and the methods for assigning rights for users.

Grant Tables

MySQL user rights are stored in a series of tables that are automatically created with the MySQL installation. These tables are kept in a database called mysql. If you start up the MySQL daemon (with `mysqld`) and the MySQL monitor (with `mysql`), and run the query `show databases` just after installation, you will see two databases, test and mysql.

Running the `show tables` query on the mysql database lists the tables that store user permissions.

```
mysql> use mysql

Database changed
mysql> show tables;
+-----------------+
| Tables in mysql |
+-----------------+
| columns_priv    |
```

```
| db              |
| func            |
| host            |
| tables_priv     |
| user            |
+-----------------+
6 rows in set (0.00 sec)

mysql>
```

Each of these tables corresponds to a level of access control. You can create any number of users, and users can be allowed access from any variety of hosts. For each user/host combination, you can grant access to an entire database, to specific tables within a database, or to a number of columns within a table. Additionally, these tables grant administrative privileges. Users can be given permission to add and drop databases or permission to grant other users permissions.

In practice you will want to grant no more permissions than necessary. You want to protect your data from the overzealous and the incompetent. The best way to do that with MySQL is to use the proper grant table when assigning rights, keeping the following in mind: Rights are granted in a hierarchical way. Rights granted in the user table will be universal. If a user is granted drop privileges in the user table, that user will be able to drop any table in any database in that MySQL installation.

Then there is the db table, which grants privileges on a database-specific basis. Using this table, you can grant rights for an entire database. For any one table or set of tables, make use of the tables_priv table. Finally, the columns_priv table allows you to grant rights on specific columns within a table. If you don't need to grant rights to an entire table, see that rights are assigned in the columns_priv table.

Recent releases of MySQL make use of a couple of very convenient commands that make creating users and assigning rights fairly easy. I'll discuss these commands after a brief look at the user, db, tables_priv, and columns_priv tables.

user table

Every user who needs to get at MySQL must be listed in this table. Rights may be granted elsewhere, but without a listing here, the user will be refused a connection to the database server. Here is the listing of columns in the user table.

```
mysql> show columns from user;
+-----------------+-----------+------+-----+---------+-------+
| Field           | Type      | Null | Key | Default | Extra |
+-----------------+-----------+------+-----+---------+-------+
| Host            | char(60)  |      | PRI |         |       |
| User            | char(16)  |      | PRI |         |       |
| Password        | char(16)  |      |     |         |       |
```

```
| Select_priv     | enum('N','Y') |       |   | N |   |   |
| Insert_priv     | enum('N','Y') |       |   | N |   |   |
| Update_priv     | enum('N','Y') |       |   | N |   |   |
| Delete_priv     | enum('N','Y') |       |   | N |   |   |
| Create_priv     | enum('N','Y') |       |   | N |   |   |
| Drop_priv       | enum('N','Y') |       |   | N |   |   |
| Reload_priv     | enum('N','Y') |       |   | N |   |   |
| Shutdown_priv   | enum('N','Y') |       |   | N |   |   |
| Process_priv    | enum('N','Y') |       |   | N |   |   |
| File_priv       | enum('N','Y') |       |   | N |   |   |
| Grant_priv      | enum('N','Y') |       |   | N |   |   |
| References_priv | enum('N','Y') |       |   | N |   |   |
| Index_priv      | enum('N','Y') |       |   | N |   |   |
| Alter_priv      | enum('N','Y') |       |   | N |   |   |
+-----------------+---------------+-------+---+---------+-------+
17 rows in set (0.00 sec)

mysql>
```

As you must have seen by now, the PHP `mysql_connect()` function takes three arguments: username, host, and password. In the preceding code you will see the corresponding field names. MySQL identifies a user by the combination of the username and host. For instance, user jay can have a different set of rights for each host that he uses to connect to MySQL. If you or your PHP scripts are accessing MySQL from the local machine, you will usually assign a host of localhost.

The other columns are intuitively named. As you can see, all but the Host, User, and Password columns allow only Y or N as column values. As we mentioned earlier, any of these rights that are set to Y will be granted to every table of every database. Most of the columns' names correspond to SQL statements (e.g. delete, create, and so forth).

The user table also contains a set of columns that grant administrative rights. These columns are File_priv, Grand_pirv, Process_priv, Reload_priv, and Shutdown_priv. The following is a brief explanation of the meaning of these columns. If you are security-minded, grant these rights sparingly.

- ◆ File_priv – If granted, this privilege allows the database server to read and write files from the file system. You will most often use it when loading a file into a database table.

- ◆ Grant_priv – A user with this right will be able to assign his privileges to other users.

- ◆ Process_priv – This right gives a user the ability to view and kill all running processes and threads.

♦ Reload_priv – Most of the privileges granted by this column are not covered in the course of this book. This privilege is most often used with the `mysqladmin` utility to perform flush commands. See the MySQL online manual for more details.

♦ Shutdown_priv – Allows the user to shut down the daemon using `mysqladmin shutdown`.

db table

For database-specific permissions, the db table is where you will be doing most of your work. The following is a list of columns from the db table:

```
mysql> show columns from db;
+-----------------+---------------+------+-----+---------+-------+
| Field           | Type          | Null | Key | Default | Extra |
+-----------------+---------------+------+-----+---------+-------+
| Host            | char(60)      |      | PRI |         |       |
| Db              | char(32)      |      | PRI |         |       |
| User            | char(16)      |      | PRI |         |       |
| Select_priv     | enum('N','Y') |      |     | N       |       |
| Insert_priv     | enum('N','Y') |      |     | N       |       |
| Update_priv     | enum('N','Y') |      |     | N       |       |
| Delete_priv     | enum('N','Y') |      |     | N       |       |
| Create_priv     | enum('N','Y') |      |     | N       |       |
| Drop_priv       | enum('N','Y') |      |     | N       |       |
| Grant_priv      | enum('N','Y') |      |     | N       |       |
| References_priv | enum('N','Y') |      |     | N       |       |
| Index_priv      | enum('N','Y') |      |     | N       |       |
| Alter_priv      | enum('N','Y') |      |     | N       |       |
+-----------------+---------------+------+-----+---------+-------+
13 rows in set (0.01 sec)

mysql>
```

This works like the user table, except that permissions granted here will only work for the database specified in the db column.

tables_priv and columns_priv

These two tables look pretty similar, and to save a bit of space, I'll only show the tables_priv table.

```
mysql> show columns from tables_priv;
+-------------+---------------+------+-----+---------+-------+
| Field       | Type          | Null | Key | Default | Extra |
```

```
+-------------+---------------+------+-----+---------+-------+
| Host        | char(60)      |      | PRI |         |       |
| Db          | char(60)      |      | PRI |         |       |
| User        | char(16)      |      | PRI |         |       |
| Table_name  | char(60)      |      | PRI |         |       |
| Grantor     | char(77)      |      | MUL |         |       |
| Timestamp   | timestamp(14) | YES  |     | NULL    |       |
| Table_priv  |set('Select','Insert','Update',           |       |
|             | 'Delete','Create','Drop','Grant',         |       |
|             | 'References','Index','Alter')             |       |
|             |               |      |     |         |       |
| Column_priv | set('Select','Insert',       |         |       |
|             |    'Update','References')     |         |       |
+-------------+---------------+------+-----+---------+-------+
8 rows in set (0.00 sec)
```

For users who only get access to a table or set of tables within a database, the exact rights will be stored in this table. Note the use of the set column type for table_priv and column_priv tables. All of the rights available to a specific user will be crammed into these two cells.

 At a couple of points in the course of this book, we advised against using the set column type. In fact the db table is a good example of where set makes sense. There are few potential values for the column and the number of potential values is not likely to change.

Grant and Revoke Statements

Since the tables discussed above are regular MySQL tables, you can alter them with the SQL statements you are already familiar with. But consider the nightmare that would be. If you wanted to grant a new user table-level access, you would first need to insert a row into the user database with an SQL statement that looked like this:

```
INSERT INTO user (Host, User, Password, Select_priv, Insert_priv,
Update_priv, Delete_priv, Create_priv, Drop_priv, Reload_priv,
Shutdown_priv, Process_priv, File_priv, Grant_priv, References_priv,
Index_priv, Alter_priv) VALUES ('localhost', 'juan', 'password',
'N', 'N', 'N', 'N', 'N', 'N', 'N', 'N', 'N', 'N', 'N', 'N', 'N',
'N')
```

Then you'd need to grant specific rights with another insert statement to another table.

If you are thinking you could script these functions with a Web front end, that is definitely a possibility. But you'd want to be very careful, because the script would have the equivalent of root access to the database, which could be very unsafe.

Happily, the MySQL has some built-in statements that make user administration a whole lot easier. Knowing the grant and revoke statements will save you from having to send individual queries.

Grant

Before we get into specifics of this statement, take a look at the statement that would grant all rights on the database named guestbook to user jim; jim's password will be pword.

```
mysql> grant all on guestbook.* to jim@localhost
identified by "pword";
```

This command will make all the necessary changes to the user and db tables.

The first part of the grant statement can take the word all, or it can take any of the options listed in the user table. Most often, you will be granting rights to use SQL statements (select, create, alter, delete, drop, index, insert, and update).

The second portion (on guestbook in the example) identifies where privileges will be applied: universally, to a single database, to tables, or to columns. Table D-1 shows how to indicate where privileges should be applied.

TABLE D-1 PERMISSION LEVEL

Identifier	Meaning
grant all on *.*	Universal rights; inserted into the user table
grant all on database.*	Applies to all tables in a single database
grant all on database.table_name	Rights apply to a single table
grant all(col1, col2) on database.table_name	Rights apply only to specific columns in a specific database and table.

The third portion (to jim@localhost in the example) indicates the user to be given access. As we mentioned earlier, MySQL needs both a name and a host. In the grant statement, these are separated by the @ symbol.

Finally the `identified by` portion gives the user a password.

Here are a few more examples of grant statements.

```
grant select, update, insert  on guestbook2k.guestbook to
alvin@localhost identified by "pword";
```

The preceding statement allows alvin to view, update, and insert records into the table guestbook in database guestbook2k.

```
grant select, update (name, url)  on guestbook2k.guestbook to
chipmunk@localhost identified by "Mel12068";
```

With the preceding statement, the user can only view and update two columns (name and URL). No deletes or inserts allowed.

```
grant all on *.* to josh@localhost identified by "pword";
```

The preceding statement gives this user all privileges. This means that `josh@ localhost` is even allowed to grant privileges to other users.

Revoke

If you want to remove some of a user's privileges, you can use the `revoke` statement. To remove shutdown privileges from a user who had been granted all privileges, like josh above, you could run the following:

```
revoke Shutdown on *.* from josh@localhost;
```

Notice that the word `from` is used in the revoke statement in place of `to`. Otherwise revoke works just like grant.

Note that to remove a user entirely you must run a delete statement against the user table. Since the user is identified by a name and host, the following should do it:

```
delete from user where user='user' and host='host'
```

Viewing grants

Starting in version 3.23.4, MySQL incorporated the show grants statement, which allows you to see the exact grants available at a given time. All you need to know is the user name and host.

```
mysql> show grants for jayg@localhost;
+------------------------------------------------------------+
| Grants for jayg@localhost                                  |
+------------------------------------------------------------+
```

```
| GRANT ALL PRIVILEGES ON my_test.* TO 'jayg'@'localhost'     |
+-------------------------------------------------------------+
1 row in set (0.00 sec)
```

Reloading grants

The grant tables are loaded into memory when the MySQL daemon is started. Changes made to the grant tables that did not make use of the grant command will not take effect until you restart the program or tell MySQL to reload the table with the `flush` command.

Simply run:

```
flush privileges
```

Appendix E

PHP Function Reference

AT THIS POINT, PHP contains more functions than could possibly be listed in this book, and the function list is growing daily. Tables E-1 to E-43 are lists of just some of the functions available. Keep up with the online manual at www.php.net/manual to see the most current list.

TABLE E-1 PHP INFORMATION FUNCTIONS

Function	Returns	Action
phpinfo(void)	void	Outputs a page of useful information about PHP and the current request
phpversion(void)	string	Returns the current PHP version
phpcredits(void)	void	Prints the list of people who've contributed to the PHP project

TABLE E-2 VARIABLE TYPE FUNCTIONS

Function	Returns	Action
intval(mixed var [, int base])	int	Gets the integer value of a variable using the optional base for the conversion
doubleval(mixed var)	double	Gets the double-precision value of a variable
strval(mixed var)	string	Gets the string value of a variable
gettype(mixed var)	string	Returns the type of the variable

Continued

TABLE E-2 VARIABLE TYPE FUNCTIONS *(Continued)*

Function	Returns	Action
settype(string var, string type)	int	Sets the type of the variable. Returns 1 if the conversion is successful
is_bool(mixed var)	bool	Returns true if variable is a Boolean
is_long(mixed var)	bool	Returns true if variable is a long (integer)
is_double(mixed var)	bool	Returns true if variable is a double
is_string(mixed var)	bool	Returns true if variable is a string
is_array(mixed var)	bool	Returns true if variable is an array
is_object(mixed var)	bool	Returns true if variable is an object
is_numeric(mixed value)	bool	Returns true if value is a number or a numeric string

TABLE E-3 QUOTE SETTING FUNCTIONS

Function	Returns	Action
set_magic_quotes_ runtime(int new_setting)	int	Sets the current active configuration setting of magic_quotes_runtime and returns the previous setting
get_magic_quotes_ runtime(void)	int	Gets the current active configuration setting of magic_quotes_runtime
get_magic_quotes_ gpc(void)	int	Gets the current active configuration setting of magic_quotes_gpc

TABLE E-4 DATETIME FUNCTIONS

Function	Returns	Action
time(void)	int	Returns current UNIX timestamp
mktime(int hour, int min, int sec, int mon, int day, int year)	int	Composes UNIX timestamp for a date
gmmktime(int hour, int min, int sec, int mon, int day, int year)	int	Gets UNIX timestamp for a GMT date
date(string format [, int timestamp])	string	Formats a time/date
gmdate(string format [, int timestamp])	string	Formats a GMT/CUT date/time
localtime([int timestamp [, bool associative_ array]])	array	If the associative_array argument is set to 1, returns the results of the C system call localtime as an associative array; otherwise returns a regular array
getdate([int timestamp])	array	Gets date/time information
checkdate(int month, int day, int year)	bool	Returns 1 if it is a valid date
strftime(string format [, int timestamp])	string	Formats a local time/date according to locale settings
gmstrftime(string format [, int timestamp])	string	Formats a GMT/CUT time/date according to locale settings
strtotime(string time, int now)	int	Converts string representation of date and time to a timestamp. Will accept strings in most typical date formats. For example, YYYY-MM-DD and MM/DD/YYYY
microtime(void)	string	Returns a string containing the current time in seconds and microseconds
gettimeofday(void)	array	Returns the current time as array
getrusage([int who])	array	Returns an array of usage statistics taken from the getrusage Unix command. See your Unix man page for further details

TABLE E-5 DIRECTORY FUNCTIONS

Function	Returns	Action
opendir(string path)	int	Opens a directory and return a dir_handle
dir(string directory)	class	Returns an object with three methods (read, rewind, and close) and two properties (handle and path)
closedir([int dir_handle])	void	Closes directory connection identified by the dir_handle
chdir(string directory)	int	Changes the current directory
getcwd(void)	string	Gets the current directory
rewinddir([int dir_handle])	void	Rewinds dir_handle back to the start
readdir([int dir_handle])	string	Readsdirectory entry from dir_handle

TABLE E-6 FILESYSTEM FUNCTIONS

Function	Returns	Action
diskfreespace(string path)	double	Gets free diskspace for filesystem that path is on, in bytes
chown(string filename, mixed user)	bool	Changes file owner. Returns TRUE on success, otherwise FALSE
chgrp(string filename, mixed group)	bool	Changes file group. Returns TRUE on success, otherwise FALSE
chmod(string filename, int mode)	bool	Changes file mode. Retruns TRUE on success, otherwise FALSE
touch(string filename [, int time])	bool	Sets modification time of file
clearstatcache(void)	void	Clears file stat cache
fileperms(string filename)	int	Gets file permissions in octal
fileinode(string filename)	int	Gets file inode
filesize(string filename)	int	Gets file size

Function	Returns	Action
`fileowner(string filename)`	int	Gets file owner's userid
`filegroup(string filename)`	int	Gets file's groupid
`fileatime(string filename)`	int	Gets last access time of file
`filemtime(string filename)`	int	Gets last modification time of file
`filectime(string filename)`	int	Gets inode modification time of file
`filetype(string filename)`	string	Gets file type
`is_writable(string filename)`	int	Returns true if file can be written
`is_readable(string filename)`	int	Returns true if file can be read
`is_executable(string filename)`	int	Returns true if file is executable
`is_file(string filename)`	int	Returns true if file is a regular file
`is_dir(string filename)`	int	Returns true if file is directory
`is_link(string filename)`	int	Returns true if file is symbolic link
`file_exists(string filename)`	bool	Returns true if filename exists
`lstat(string filename)`	array	Gives information about a file or symbolic link. The returned array contains the following elements: device, inode; inode protection mode; number of links; user id of owner; group id owner; device type if inode device; size in bytes; time of last access; time of last modification; time of last change; blocksize for filesystem I/O; number of blocks allocated
`stat(string filename)`	array	Gives information about a file, the same as described in lstat

TABLE E-7 EXECUTION FUNCTION

Function	Returns	Action
exec(string command [, array output [, int return_value]])	int	Executes an external program
system(string command [, int return_value])	int	Executes an external program and displays output
passthru(string command [, int return_value])	void	Executes an external program and displays raw output. Will usually be used with something like PBMPlus
escapeshellcmd(string command)	string	Escapes shell metacharacters

TABLE E-8 FILE MANIPULATION FUNCTIONS

Function	Returns	Action
flock(int fp, int operation [, int wouldblock])	bool	Locks a file so that it is not accessible by other PHP scripts. The locking will not keep other processes from opening the file
get_meta_tags(string filename [, int use_include_path])	array	Extracts all <meta> tag content attributes from a file and returns an array
file(string filename [, int use_include_path])	array	Reads entire file into an array, with each line as an array element
tempnam(string dir,	string	Creates a unique filename in a string prefix)directory
tmpfile(void)	int	Creates a temporary file that will be deleted automatically after a call the fclose() function or at the end of the script
fopen(string filename, string mode [, int use_include_path])	int	Opens a file or a URL and returns a file pointer

Function	Returns	Action
fclose(int fp)	int	Closes an open file pointer
popen(string command, string mode)	int	Executes a command and opens either a read or a write pipe to it
pclose(int fp)	int	Closes a file pointer opened by popen()
feof(int fp)	int	Tests for end-of-file on a file pointer
set_socket_blocking(int socket_descriptor, int mode)	int	Sets blocking/non-blocking mode on a socket
socket_set_timeout(int socket_descriptor, int seconds, int microseconds)	bool	Sets timeout on socket read to seconds + microseconds
socket_get_status(resource socket_descriptor)	array	Returns an array describing socket status. The array contains four elements: timed_out (bool), blocked (bool), eof (bool), and unread bytes (int)
fgets(int fp, int length)	string	Gets a line from file pointer
fgetc(int fp)	string	Gets a character from file pointer
fgetss(int fp, int length [, string allowable_tags])	string	Gets a line from file pointer and strips HTML tags
fscanf(string str, string format [, string ...])	mixed	Formats a file using the specified format
fwrite(int fp, string str [, int length])	int	Implements a binary-safe file write
fflush(int fp)	int	Flushes output
set_file_buffer(int fp, int buffer)	int	Sets file write buffer; the default size is 8 kb
rewind(int fp)	int	Moves the position of a file pointer to the beginning of a file
ftell(int fp)	int	Gets file pointer's read/write position

Continued

TABLE E-8 FILE MANIPULATION FUNCTIONS *(Continued)*

Function	Returns	Action
fseek(int fp, int offset [, int whence])	int	Seeks the position of a file pointer
mkdir(string pathname, int mode)	int	Creates a directory
rmdir(string dirname)	int	Removes a directory
readfile(string filename [, int use_include_path])	int	Outputs a file or a URL
umask([int mask])	int	Returns or changes the umask. See the Unix man page on umask for further details
fpassthru(int fp)	int	Outputs all remaining data from a file pointer
rename(string old_name, string new_name)	int	Renames a file
unlink(string filename)	int	Deletes a file, similar to the C unlink function
ftruncate (int fp, int size)	int	Truncates file to the size indicated in the second argument
fstat(int fp)	int	Returns the same information as stat() (described eariler) on a file handle
copy(string source_file, string destination_file)	int	Copies a file
fread(int fp, int length)	int	Conducts a binary-safe file read
fgetcsv(int fp, int length)	array	Gets line from file pointer and parses for CSV fields
realpath(string path)	string	Returns the resolved path, from root. Works on symbolic links and references using .. or .

TABLE E-9 PRINT FUNCTIONS

Function	Returns	Action
sprintf(string format [, mixed arg1 [, mixed ...]])	string	Returns a formatted string
printf(string format [, mixed arg1 [, mixed ...]])	int	Outputs a formatted string
print_r(mixed var)	void	Prints out information about the specified variable
var_dump(mixed var)	void	Dumps a string representation of the variable to output

TABLE E-10 HTTP HEADER FUNCTIONS

Function	Returns	Action
header(string header)	void	Sends a raw HTTP header
setcookie(string name [, string value [, int expires [, string path [, string domain [, string secure]]]]])	void	Sends a cookie
headers_sent(void)	int	Returns true if headers have already been sent; returns false otherwise

TABLE E-11 HTML FUNCTIONS

Function	Returns	Action
htmlspecialchars(string string)	string	Converts special characters (ampersand, double quotes, single quotes, less than, and greater than) to HTML entities
htmlentities(string string)	string	Converts all applicable characters to HTML entities
get_html_translation_table([int whichone])	array	Returns the internal translation table used by htmlspecialchars and htmlentities

TABLE E-12 MAIL FUNCTION

Function	Returns	Action
mail(string to, string subject, string message [, string additional_ headers])	int	Sends an e-mail message

TABLE E-13 RANDOM NUMBER FUNCTIONS

Function	Returns	Action
srand(int seed)	void	Seeds random number generator
rand([int min, int max])	int	Returns a random number
getrandmax(void)	int	Returns the maximum value a random number can have
mt_srand(int seed)	void	Seeds Mersenne Twister random number generator

Function	Returns	Action
mt_rand([int min, int max])	int	Returns a random number from Mersenne Twister
mt_getrandmax(void)	int	Returns the maximum value a random number from Mersenne Twister can have

TABLE E-14 REGULAR EXPRESSION FUNCTIONS

Function	Returns	Action
ereg(string pattern, string string [, array registers])	int	Conducts a regular expression match
eregi(string pattern, string string [, array registers])	int	Case-insensitive regular expression match
ereg_replace(string pattern, string replacement, string string)	string	Replaces regular expression
eregi_replace(string pattern, string replacement, string string])	string	Conducts a case-insensitive replace regular expression
split(string pattern, string string [, int limit])	array	Splits string into array by regular expression
spliti(string pattern, string string [, int limit])	array	Splits string into array by a case-insensitive regular expression
sql_regcase(string string)	string	Makes regular expression for case-insensitive match

TABLE E-15 STRING MANIPULATION FUNCTIONS

Function	Returns	Action
bin2hex(string data)	string	Converts the binary representation of a number to hex
strspn(string str, string mask)	int	Finds length of initial segment consisting entirely of characters found in mask
strcspn(string str, string mask)	int	Finds length of initial segment consisting entirely of characters not found in mask
rtrim(string str)	string	Alias for chop()
chop(string str)	string	Strips trailing white space
trim(string str)	string	Strips white space from the beginning and end of a string
ltrim(string str)	string	Strips white space from the beginning of a string
wordwrap(string str [, int width [, string break]])	string	Wraps buffer to selected number of characters using the specified width. The line is broken with the character in the third argument or \n. If no width is given, the string will be broken at 75 characters
explode(string separator, string str [, int limit])	array	Splits a string on string separator and returns array of components
implode(array src, string glue)	string	Joins array elements by placing glue string between items and returns one string
join(array src, string glue)	string	Alias for implode()
strtok([string str,] string token)	string	Tokenizes a string
strtoupper(string str)	string	Makes a string uppercase
strtolower(string str)	string	Makes a string lowercase
basename(string path)	string	Returns the filename component of the path

Function	Returns	Action
dirname(string path)	string	Returns the directory name component of the path
strstr(string haystack, string needle)	string	Finds first occurrence of a string within another
strchr(string haystack, string needle)	string	Alias for strstr()
stristr(string haystack, string needle)	string	Finds first occurrence of a string within another (case-insensitive)
strpos(string haystack, string needle [, int offset])	int	Finds position of first occurrence of a string within another
strrpos(string haystack, string needle)	int	Finds position of last occurrence of a character in a string within another
strrchr(string haystack, string needle)	string	Finds the postion of the last occurrence of a character in a string within another
chunk_split(string str [, int chunklen [, string ending]])	string	Splits a line by inserting, by default, \r\n every 76 chracters. The length of the chunks and the separation string can be indicated
substr(string str, int start [, int length])	string	Returns part of a string, as specified by the start position and length. If the length is a negative number, position is determined from the end of the string
substr_replace(string str, string repl, int start [, int length])	string	Replaces part of a string with another string
quotemeta(string str)	string	Returns a string with the following characters prepended by a backslash: . \ + * ? [^] ($)
ord(string character)	int	Returns ASCII value of character
chr(int ascii)	string	Converts ASCII code to a character

Continued

TABLE E-15 STRING MANIPULATION FUNCTIONS *(Continued)*

Function	Returns	Action
ucfirst(string str)	string	Makes a string's first character uppercase
ucwords(string str)	string	Makes the first character of every word in a string uppercase
strtr(string str, string from, string to)	string	Translates characters in str using given translation tables
strrev(string str)	string	Reverses a string
similar_text(string str1, string str2 [, double percent])	int	Returns the number of charcters that are the same in the two strings. By using a referenced varaible in the third argument, the precentage of similar characters is passed to the third argument
addcslashes(string str, string charlist)	string	Escapes all chars mentioned in charlist with backslashes
addslashes(string str)	string	Escapes single quotes, double quotes, and backslash characters in a string with backslashes
stripcslashes(string str)	string	Strips backslashes from a string. Uses C-style conventions
stripslashes(string str)	string	Strips backslashes from a string
str_replace(string needle, string str, string haystack)	string	Replaces all occurrences of needle in haystack with str
hebrev(string str [, int max_chars_per_line])	string	Converts logical Hebrew text to visual text
hebrevc(string str [, int max_chars_per_line])	string	Converts logical Hebrew text to visual text with newline conversion
nl2br(string str)	string	Inserts HTML line breaks after each newline
strip_tags(string str [, string allowable_tags])	string	Strips HTML and PHP tags from a string
setlocale(string category, string locale)	string	Sets locale information

Function	Returns	Action
parse_str(string encoded_string)	void	Parses GET/POST/COOKIE data and sets global variables
str_repeat(string input, int mult)	string	Returns the input string repeated `mult` times
count_chars(string input [, int mode])	mixed	Returns info about what characters are used in input string. If mode is 0, an associative array is returned with the byte value as key and the number of ocurrences as value.
strnatcmp(string s1, string s2)	int	Returns the result of string comparison using "natural" algorithm
strnatcasecmp(string s1, string s2)	int	Returns the result of a case-insensitive string comparison using "natural" algorithm
substr_count(string haystack, string needle)	int	Returns the number of times a substring occurs in the string
str_pad(string input, int pad_length [, string pad_string [, int pad_type]])	string	Returns input string padded on the left or right to specified length with `pad_string`
sscanf(string str, string format [, string ...])	mixed	Implements an ANSI C-compatible sscanf

TABLE E-16 URL FUNCTIONS

Function	Returns	Action
parse_url(string url)	array	Parses a URL and returns its components in an associative array. The array elements are: scheme (e.g., http), host (e.g., www.mydomain.com), path (e.g., /index.php), query, which is the entire querystring.

Continued

TABLE E-16 URL FUNCTIONS *(Continued)*

Function	Returns	Action
urlencode(string str)	string	URL-encodes string
urldecode(string str)	string	Decodes URL-encoded string
rawurlencode(string str)	string	URL-encodes string. See Chapter 6 for the difference between this and urlencode().
rawurldecode(string str)	string	Decodes URL-encoded string

TABLE E-17 VARIABLE SERIALIZING FUNCTIONS

Function	Returns	Action
serialize(mixed variable)	string	Returns a string representation of variable (which can later be unserialized)
unserialize(string variable_representation)	mixed	Takes a string representation of variable and recreates it

TABLE E-18 MISCELLANEOUS FUNCTIONS

Function	Returns	Action
ip2long(string ip_address)	int	Converts a string containing an (IPv4) Internet Protocol dotted address into a proper address
long2ip(int proper_address)	string	Converts an (IPv4) Internet network address into a string in Internet standard dotted format
getenv(string varname)	string	Gets the value of an environment variable
putenv(string setting)	void	Sets the value of an environment variable by using a format of putenv("ENV_VAR=$foo");

Function	Returns	Action
`flush(void)`	void	Flushes the output buffer
`sleep(int seconds)`	void	Delays for a given number of seconds
`usleep(int micro_seconds)`	void	Delays for a given number of microseconds
`get_current_user(void)`	string	Gets the name of the owner of the current PHP script
`get_cfg_var(string option_name)`	string	Gets the value of a PHP configuration option
`is_resource(mixed var)`	bool	Returns true if variable is a resource
`error_log(string message, int message_type [, string destination] [, string extra_headers])`	int	Sends an error message to an error log, TCP port, or file
`call_user_func(string function_name [, mixed parmeter] [, mixed ...])`	mixed	Calls a user function that is the first parameter
`call_user_method(string method_name, object object [, mixed parameter] [, mixed ...])`	mixed	Calls a user method on a specific object where the first argument is the method name, the second argument is the object, and the subsequent arguments are the parameters
`register_shutdown_function(string function_name)`	void	Registers a user-level function to be called on request termination
`highlight_file(string file_name)`	void	Outputs a PHP source file with syntax highlights
`highlight_string(string string)`	void	Syntax highlights a string
`ini_get(string varname)`	string	Gets a configuration option
`ini_set(string varname, string newvalue)`	string	Sets a configuration option, returns false on error and the string of the old value of the configuration option on success

Continued

TABLE E-18 MISCELLANEOUS FUNCTIONS *(Continued)*

Function	Returns	Action
ini_restore(string varname)	string	Restores the value of a configuration option specified by varname to its original value set in the php.ini
connection_aborted(void)	int	Returns true if client disconnected
connection_timeout(void)	int	Returns true if script timed out
connection_status(void) bitfield	int	Returns the connection status
ignore_user_abort(boolean value)	int	Sets whether you want to ignore a user abort event or not
getservbyname(string service, string protocol)	int	Returns port associated with service (protocol must be tcp or udp)
getservbyport(int port, string protocol)	string	Returns service name associated with port (protocol must be "tcp" or "udp")
getprotobyname(string name)	int	Returns protocol number associated with name as per /etc/protocols
getprotobynumber(int proto)	string	Returns protocol name associated with protocol number proto
get_loaded_extensions(void)	array	Returns an array containing names of loaded extensions
extension_loaded(string extension_name)	bool	Returns true if the named extension is loaded
get_extension_funcs(string extension_name)	array	Returns an array with the names of functions belonging to the named extension

TABLE E-19 ARRAY FUNCTIONS

Function	Returns	Action
krsort(array array_arg [, int sort_flags])	int	Sorts an array reverse by key

Function	Returns	Action
`ksort(array array_arg` `[, int sort_flags])`	int	Sorts an array by key
`natsort(array array_arg)`	void	Sorts an array using natural sort. The difference between a natural sort and a normal sort is described here: `http://www.linuxcare.com.au/projects/natsort/`
`natcasesort(array` `array_arg)`	void	Sorts an array using case-insensitive natural sort
`asort(array array_arg` `[, int sort_flags])`	void	Sorts an array and maintains index association
`arsort(array array_arg` `[, int sort_flags])`	void	Sorts an array in reverse order and maintains index association
`sort(array array_arg` `[, int sort_flags])`	void	Sorts an array
`rsort(array array_arg` `[, int sort_flags])`	void	Sorts an array in reverse order
`usort(array array_arg,` `string cmp_function)`	void	Sorts an array by values using a user-defined comparison function
`uasort(array array_arg,` `string cmp_function)`	void	Sorts an array with a user-defined comparison function and maintains index association
`uksort(array array_arg,` `string cmp_function)`	void	Sorts an array by keys using a user-defined comparison function

`array_walk(array input,`
`string funcname`
`[, mixed userdata])`
	int	Applies a user function to every member of an array

`count(mixed var)`	int	Counts the number of elements in a variable (usually an array)
`end(array array_arg)`	mixed	Advances array argument's internal pointer to the last element and returns it

Continued

TABLE E-19 ARRAY FUNCTIONS *(Continued)*

Function	Returns	Action
prev(array array_arg)	mixed	Moves array argument's internal pointer to the previous element and returns it
next(array array_arg)	mixed	Moves array argument's internal pointer to the next element and returns it
reset(array array_arg)	mixed	Sets array argument's internal pointer to the first element and returns it
current(array array_arg)	mixed	Returns the element currently pointed to by the internal array pointer
key(array array_arg)	mixed	Returns the key of the element currently pointed to by the internal array pointer
min(mixed arg1 [, mixed arg2 [, mixed ...]])	mixed	Returns the lowest value in an array or a series of arguments
max(mixed arg1 [, mixed arg2 [, mixed ...]])	mixed	Returns the highest value in an array or a series of arguments
in_array(mixed needle, array haystack [, bool strict])	bool	Checks if the given value exists in the array
extract(array var_array, int extract_type [, string prefix])	void	Imports variables into symbol table from an array
compact(mixed var_names [, mixed ...])	array	Creates an array containing variables and their values
range(int low, int high)	array	Creates an array containing the range of integers from low to high (inclusive)
shuffle(array array_arg)	int	Randomly shuffles the contents of an array. The random number generator must first be seeded with srand()

Function	Returns	Action
`array_push(array stack, mixed var [, mixed ...])`	int	Pushes elements onto the end of the array
`array_pop(array stack)`	mixed	Pops an element off the end of the array
`array_shift(array stack)`	mixed	Pops an element off the beginning of the array
`array_unshift(array stack, mixed var [, mixed ...])`	int	Pushes elements onto the beginning of the array
`array_splice(array input, int offset [, int length [, array replacement]])`	array	Removes the elements designated by `offset` and `length` and replaces them with supplied array
`array_slice(array input, int offset [, int length])`	array	Returns elements specified by `offset` and `length`
`array_merge(array arr1, array arr2 [, array ...])`	array	Merges elements from passed arrays into one array
`array_merge_recursive (array arr1, array arr2 [, array ...])`	array	Recursively merges elements from passed arrays into one array.
`array_keys(array input [, mixed search_value])`	array	Returns just the keys from the input array, optionally only for the specified `search_value`
`array_values(array input)`	array	Returns just the values from the input array
`array_count_values(array input)`	array	Returns the value as key and the frequency of that value in input as value
`array_reverse(array input)`	array	Returns a new array with the order of the entries reversed
`array_pad(array input, int pad_size, mixed pad_value)`	array	Returns a new array padded with `pad_value` to size `pad_size`
`array_flip(array input)`	array	Returns array with key <-> value flipped

Continued

TABLE E-19 **ARRAY FUNCTIONS** *(Continued)*

Function	Returns	Action
`array_unique(array input)`	array	Removes duplicate values from array
`array_intersect(array arr1, array arr2 [, array ...])`	array	Returns the entries of `arr1` that have values that are present in all the other arguments
`array_diff(array arr1, array arr2 [, array ...])`	array	Returns the entries of `arr1` that have values that are not present in any of the other arguments
`array_multisort(array ar1 [, SORT_ASC|SORT_DESC [, SORT_REGULAR|SORT_ NUMERIC|SORT_STRING]] [, array ar2 [, SORT_ASC| SORT_DESC [, SORT_REGULAR| SORT_NUMERIC|SORT_ STRING]], ...])`	bool	Sorts multiple arrays at once (works like the ORDER BY clause in SQL). Retruns TRUE on success, FALSE on failure.
`array_rand(array input [, int num_req])`	mixed	If the second argument is blank or set to 0, this will return a single key form the input array. If the second argument is greater than 0, it will return an array, each element of which is a random key from the input array.

TABLE E-20 **MYSQL FUNCTIONS**

Function	Returns	Action
`mysql_connect([string hostname[:port][:/path/to/ socket]] [, string username] [, string password])`	int	Opens a connection to a MySQL Server. Returns FALSE on failure

Function	Returns	Action
mysql_pconnect([string hostname[:port][:/path/ to/socket]] [, string username] [, string password])	int	Opens a persistent connection to a MySQL Server
mysql_close([int link_ identifier])	int	Closes a MySQL connection. Does not effect persistent connections
mysql_select_db(string database_name [, int link_identifier])	int	Selects a MySQL database
mysql_create_db(string database_name [, int link_identifier])	int	Creates a MySQL database
mysql_drop_db(string database_name [, int link_identifier])	int	Drops (deletes) a MySQL database
mysql_query(string query [, int link_identifier])	int	Sends an SQL query to MySQL
mysql_db_query(string database_name, string query [, int link_ identifier])	int	Sends an SQL query to MySQL
mysql_list_dbs([int link_identifier])	int	Lists databases available on a MySQL server
mysql_list_tables(string database_name [, int link_identifier])	int	Lists tables in a MySQL database
mysql_list_fields(string database_name, string table_name [, int link_ identifier])	int	Lists MySQL result fields
mysql_error([int link_ identifier])	string	Returns the text of the error message from the previous MySQL operation

Continued

TABLE E-20 MYSQL FUNCTIONS *(Continued)*

Function	Returns	Action
mysql_errno([int link_identifier])	int	Returns the number of the error message from previous MySQL operation
mysql_affected_rows([int link_identifier])	int	Gets number of affected rows in previous MySQL operation
mysql_insert_id([int link_identifier])	int	Gets the number generated from the previous INSERT operation, where there is an auto_increment column
mysql_result(int result, int row [, mixed field])	int	Gets result data
mysql_num_rows(int result)	int	Gets number of rows in a result
mysql_num_fields(int result)	int	Gets number of fields in a result
mysql_fetch_row(int result)	array	Gets a result row as an enumerated array
mysql_fetch_object(int result [, int result_type])	object	Fetches a result row as an object
mysql_fetch_array(int result [, int result_type])	array	Fetches a result row as an associative array, a numeric array, or both.
mysql_data_seek(int result, int row_number)	int	Moves internal result pointer. Creates an error if given an invalid row
mysql_fetch_lengths(int result)	array	Gets max data size of each column in a result
mysql_fetch_field(int result [, int field_offset])	object	Gets column information from a result and returns as an object
mysql_field_seek(int result, int field_offset)	int	Sets result pointer to a specific field offset. The next call to mysql_fetch_field() will use this offset
mysql_field_name(int result, int field_index)	string	Gets the name of the specified field in a result
mysql_field_table(int result, int field_offset)	string	Gets name of the table the specified field is in

Function	Returns	Action
mysql_field_len(int result, int field_offet)	int	Returns the length of the specified field
mysql_field_type(int result, int field_offset)	string	Gets the type of the specified field in a result
mysql_field_flags(int result, int field_offset)	string	Gets the flags associated with the specified field in a result
mysql_free_result(int result)	int	Frees result memory

TABLE E-21 ASPELL FUNCTIONS

Function	Returns	Action
aspell_new(string master [, string personal])	int	Loads a dictionary
aspell_suggest(aspell int, string word)	array	Returns array of suggestions
aspell_check(aspell int, string word)	bool	Returns TRUE if a word is valid, FALSE if it is not
aspell_check_raw(aspell int, string word)	int	Returns TRUE if word is valid

To use the aspell functions, you need the aspell library from http://metalab.unc.edu/kevina/aspell/. That PHP is configured with --with-aspell

TABLE E-22 BCMATH FUNCTIONS

Function	Returns	Action
bcsub(string left_operand, string right_operand [, int scale])	string	Returns the difference between two arbitrary-precision numbers
bcmul(string left_operand, string right_operand [, int scale])	string	Returns the multiplication of two arbitrary-precision numbers
bcdiv(string left_operand, string right_operand [, int scale])	string	Returns the quotient of two arbitrary-precision numbers (division)
bcmod(string left_operand, string right_operand)	string	Returns the modulus of the two arbitrary-precision operands
bcpow(string x, string y [, int scale])	string	Returns the value of an arbitrary-precision number raised to the power of another
bcsqrt(string operand [, int scale])	string	Returns the square root of an arbitrary-precision number
bccomp(string left_operand, string right_operand [, int scale])	string	Compares two arbitrary-precision numbers
bcscale(int scale)	string	Sets default scale parameter for all bc math functions

Use of the bcmath functions requires PHP to be complied with --enable-bc-math.

TABLE E-23 CALENDAR FUNCTIONS

Function	Returns	Action
jdtounix(int jday)	int	Converts Julian Day to Unix timestamp

Function	Returns	Action
`jdtogregorian(int juliandaycount)`	string	Converts a Julian Day count to a Gregorian calendar date
`gregoriantojd(int month, int day, int year)`	int	Converts a Gregorian calendar date to Julian Day count
`jdtojulian(int juliandaycount)`	string	Converts a Julian Day count to a Julian calendar date
`juliantojd(int month, int day, int year)`	int	Converts a julian calendar date to julian day count
`jdtojewish(int juliandaycount)`	string	Converts a Julian Day count to a Jewish calendar date
`jewishtojd(int month, int day, int year)`	int	Converts a Jewish calendar date to a Julian Day count
`jdtofrench(int juliandaycount)`	string	Converts a Julian Day count to a French Republic calendar date
`frenchtojd(int month, calendar int day, int year)`	int	Converts a French Republic date to Julian Day count
`jddayofweek(int juliandaycount [, int mode])`	mixed	Returns name or number of day of week from Julian Day count
`jdmonthname (int juliandaycount, int mode)`	string	Returns name of month for Julian Day count

 Use of the calendar functions requires PHP to complied with --enable-calendar.

TABLE E-24 COM FUNCTIONS

Function	Returns	Action
com_load(string module_name)	int	Loads a COM module
com_invoke(int module, string handler_name [, mixed arg [, ...]])	mixed	Invokes a COM module
com_propget(int module, string property_name)	mixed	Gets properties from a COM module
com_propput(int module, string property_name, mixed value)	bool	Puts the properties for a module

 These will work when PHP is installed with IIS or PWS.

TABLE E-25 CYBERCASH FUNCTIONS

Function	Returns	Action
cybercash_encr (string wmk, string sk, string inbuff)	array	Returns an associative array with the elements errcode and, if errcode is false, outbuff (string), outLth (long) and macbuff (string)
cybercash_decr (string wmk, string sk, string inbuff)	array	Returns an associative array with the elements errcode and, if errcode is false, outbuff (string), outLth (long) and macbuff (string)
cybercash_base64_encode (string inbuff)	string	Encodes a string in a way that Cybercash will accept
cybercash_base64_decode (string inbuff)	string	Decodes a string received from Cybercash

Use of the cybercash functions requires the Cybercash libraries and that PHP be configured --with-cybercash. You can see an example of how to use these functions with the following class: http://www.zend.com/codex.php?id= 115&single=1.

Table E-26 DBASE FUNCTIONS

Function	Returns	Action
dblist(void)	string	Describes the dbm-compatible library being used
dbmopen(string filename, string mode)	int	Opens a dbm database
dbmclose(int dbm_identifier)	bool	Closes a dbm database
dbminsert(int dbm_identifier, string key, string value)	int	Inserts a value for a key in a dbm database
dbmreplace(int dbm_identifier, string key, string value)	int	Replaces the value for a key in a dbm database
dbmfetch(int dbm_identifier, string key)	string	Fetches a value for a key from a dbm database
dbmexists(int dbm_identifier, string key)	int	Tells if a value exists for a key in a dbm database
dbmdelete(int dbm_identifier, string key)	int	Deletes the value for a key from a dbm database
dbmfirstkey(int dbm_identifier)	string	Retrieves the first key from a dbm database
dbmnextkey(int dbm_identifier, string key)	string	Retrieves the next key from a dbm database

PHP must be compiled --with-dbase in order to use these functions.

TABLE E-27 DBA FUNCTIONS

Function	Returns	Action
dba_popen(string path, string mode, string handlername [, string ...])	int	Opens path using the specified handler in mode persistently
dba_open(string path, string mode, string handlername [, string ...])	int	Opens path using the specified handler in mode
dba_close(int handle)	void	Closes database
dba_exists(string key, int handle)	bool	Determines whether the specified key exists
dba_fetch(string key, int handle)	string	Fetches the data associated with key
dba_firstkey(int handle)	string	Resets the internal key pointer and returns the first key
dba_nextkey(int handle)	string	Returns the next key
dba_delete(string key, int handle)	bool	Deletes the entry associated with the key
dba_insert(string key, string value, int handle)	bool	Inserts value as key, returns false if key already exists
dba_replace(string key, string value, int handle)	bool	Inserts value as key, replaces key if key already exists already
dba_optimize(int handle)	bool	Optimizes (e.g. cleans up, vacuums) database
dba_sync(int handle)	bool	Synchronizes database

PHP must be compiled with --enable-dba in order to use these functions.

TABLE E-28 **FTP FUNCTIONS**

Function	Returns	Action
ftp_login(int stream, string username, string password)	int	Logs into the FTP server
ftp_pwd(int stream)	string	Returns the present working directory
ftp_cdup(int stream)	int	Changes to the parent directory
ftp_chdir(int stream, string directory)	int	Changes directories
ftp_mkdir(int stream, string directory)	string	Creates a directory
ftp_rmdir(int stream, string directory)	int	Removes a directory
ftp_nlist(int stream, string directory)	array	Returns an array of filenames in the given directory
ftp_rawlist(int stream, string directory)	array	Returns a detailed listing of a directory as an array of output lines
ftp_systype(int stream)	string	Returns the system type identifier
ftp_fget(int stream, int fp, string remote_ file, int mode)	int	Retrieves a file from the FTP server and writes it to an open file
ftp_pasv(int stream, int pasv)	int	Turns passive mode on or off

Continued

TABLE E-28 FTP FUNCTIONS *(Continued)*

Function	Returns	Action
`ftp_get(int stream, string local_file, string remote_file, int mode)`	int	Retrieves a file from the FTP server and writes it to a local file
`ftp_fput(int stream, string local_file, string remote_file, int mode)`	int	Stores a file from an open file to the FTP server
`ftp_put(int stream, string remote_file, string local_file, int mode)`	int	Stores a file on the FTP server
`ftp_size(int stream, string path)`	int	Returns the size of the file, in bytes or –1 on error
`ftp_mdtm(int stream, string path)`	int	Returns the last modification time of the file or –1 on error
`ftp_rename(int stream, string src, string dest)`	int	Renames the given file to a new path
`ftp_delete(int stream, string path)`	int	Deletes a file
`ftp_site(int stream, string cmd)`	int	Sends a SITE command to the server
`ftp_quit(int stream)`	int	Closes the FTP stream

 PHP must be compiled --with-ftp in order to have access to these functions.

The gd functions can make and manipulate images on the fly and can work with several types of image formats: jpeg, gif, png, and WBMP (used for protable devices). Note that Unisys holds the patent to the type of compression used in gif images. When they started enforcing the patent, libraries such as GD had to drop their support of gif images. There, if you want to use the GD functions with gif images, you will need a version of the GD libraries older than 1.6. However, these older libriaries do not support png files. Versions later than 1.6 do support png.

TABLE E-29 GD FUNCTIONS

Function	Returns	Action
imagecreate(int x_size, int y_size)	int	Creates a new image
imagetypes(void)	int	Returns the types of images supported in a bitfield — 1=gif, 2=jpeg, 4=png, 8=wbmp
imagecreatefromgif (string filename)	int	Creates a new image from GIF file or URL
imagecreatefromjpeg (string filename)	int	Creates a new image from JPEG file or URL
imagecreatefrompng (string filename)	int	Creates a new image from PNG file or URL
imagecreatefromwbmp (string filename)	int	Creates a new image from WBMP file or URL
imagegif(int im [, string filename])	int	Outputs GIF image to browser or file
imagepng(int im [, string filename])	int	Outputs PNG image to browser or file
imagejpeg(int im [, string filename [, int quality]])	int	Outputs JPEG image to browser or file
imagewbmp(int im [, string filename])	int	Outputs WBMP image to browser or file
imagedestroy(int im)	int	Destroys an image
imagecolorallocate(int im, int red, int green, int blue)	int	Allocates a color for an image, will usually be assigned to a variable for later use.

Continued

TABLE E-29 GD FUNCTIONS *(Continued)*

Function	Returns	Action
imagepalettecopy(int dst, int src) blue)	int	Copies the palette from the src image onto the dst imz the pallete to the specified color
imagecolorclosesthwb(int im, int red, int green, int blue)	int	Gets the index of the color with the hue, whiteness and blackness nearest to the given color
imagecolordeallocate(int im, int index)	int	De-allocates a color for an image
imagecolorresolve(int im, int red, int green, int blue)	int	Gets the index of the specified color or its closest possible alternative
imagecolorexact(int im, int red, int green, int blue)	int	Gets the index of the specified color. Returns –1 if the color does not exist
imagecolorset(int im, int col, int red, int green, int blue)	int	Sets the color for the specified palette index
imagecolorsforindex (int im, int col)	array	Gets the colors for an index, in red, green, and blue
imagegammacorrect (int im, double inputgamma, double outputgamma)	int	Applies a gamma correction to a GD image
imagesetpixel(int im, int x, int y, int col)	int	Sets a single pixel; the x and y coordinates start at the top left, and col is the color for the pixel
imageline(int im, int x1, int y1, int x2, int y2, int col)	int	Draws a line
imagedashedline(int im, int x1, int y1, int x2, int y2, int col)	int	Draws a dashed line
imagerectangle(int im, int x1, int y1, int x2, int y2, int col)	int	Draws a rectangle

Function	Returns	Action
imagefilledrectangle (int im, int x1, int y1, int x2, int y2, int col)	int	Draws a filled rectangle
imagearc(int im, int cx, int cy, int w, int h, int s, int e, int col)	int	Draws a partial ellipse
imagefilltoborder(int im, int x, int y, int border, int col)	int	Fills the image *im*, to the borders specified by x and y coordinates with the color in the fifth argument
imagefill(int im, int x, int y, int col)	int	Floods fill starting at the x and y coordinates using the color specified in the fourth argument
imagecolorstotal(int im)	int	Returns the number of colors in an image's palette
imagecolortransparent (int im [, int col])	int	Defines a color as transparent. Returns the identifier of the new color
imageinterlace(int im [, int interlace])	int	Enables or disables interlace
imagepolygon(int im, array point, int num_points, int col)	int	Draws a polygon. The array will take the following form: points[0] = x0, points[1] = y0, points[2] = x1, points[3] = y1
imagefilledpolygon(int im, array point, int num_points, int col)	int	Draws a filled polygon
imagefontwidth(int font)	int	Gets font width
imagefontheight(int font)	int	Gets font height
imagechar(int im, int font, int x, int y, string c, int col)	int	Draws a character

Continued

TABLE E-29 GD FUNCTIONS *(Continued)*

Function	Returns	Action
imagecharup(int im, int font, int x, int y, string c, int col)	int	Draws a character rotated 90 degrees counterclockwise
imagestring(int im, int font, int x, int y, string str, int col)	int	Draws a string horizontally
imagestringup(int im, int font, int x, int y, string str, int col)	int	Draws a string vertically — rotated 90 degrees counterclockwise
imagecopy(int dst_im, int src_im, int dst_x, int dst_y, int src_x, int src_y, int src_w, int src_h)	int	Copies part of an image
imagecopymerge(int src_im, int dst_im, int dst_x, int dst_y, int src_x, int src_y, int src_w, int src_h, int pct)	int	Merges one part of an image with another
imagecopyresized(int dst_im, int src_im, int dst_x, int dst_y, int src_x, int src_y, int dst_w, int dst_h, int src_w, int src_h)	int	Copies and resizes part of an image
imagesx(int im)	int	Gets image width
imagesy(int im)	int	Gets image height
imagettfbbox(int size, int angle, string font_file, string text)	array	Gives the bounding box of a text using TrueType fonts
imagettftext(int im, int size, int angle, int x, int y, int col, string font_file, string text)	array	Writes text to the image using a TrueType font
imagepsloadfont (string pathname)	int	Loads a new font from specified file

Function	Returns	Action
`imagepsfreefont (int font_index)`	bool	Frees memory used by a font
`imagepsextendfont (int font_index, double extend)`	bool	Extends or condenses (if extend < 1) a font
`imagepstext(int image, string text, int font, int size, int xcoord, int ycoord [, int space, int tightness, double angle, int antialias])`	array	Draws a text string over an image
`imagepsloadfont(string pathname)`	int	Loads a new font from specified file
`imagepsfreefont(int font_index)`	bool	Frees memory used by a font
`imagepsencodefont(int font_index, string filename)`	bool	Changes a font's character encoding vector
`imagepsextendfont(int font_index, double extend)`	bool	Extends or condenses (if extend < 1) a font
`imagepsslantfont(int font_index, double slant)`	bool	Slants a font
`imagepstext(int image, string text, int font, int size, int xcoord, int ycoord [, int space, int tightness, double angle, int antialias])`	array	Rasterizes a string over an image
`imagepsbbox(string text, int font, int size [, int space, int tightness, int angle])`	array	Returns the bounding box needed by a string if rasterized
`imagepsbbox(string text, int font, int size [, int space, int tightness, int angle])`	array	Returns the bounding box needed by a string if rasterized

Use of these functions requires the GD library from `http://www.boutell.com/gd/` and for PHP to be compiled --with-gd.

TABLE E-30 IMAP FUNCTIONS

Function	Returns	Action
`imap_open(string mailbox, string user, string password [, int options])`	int	Opens an IMAP stream to a mailbox
`imap_popen(string mailbox, string user, string password [, int options])`	int	Opens a persistant IMAP stream to a mailbox
`imap_reopen(int stream_id, string mailbox [, int options])`	int	Reopens an IMAP stream to a new mailbox
`imap_close(int stream_id [, int options])`	int	Closes an IMAP stream
`imap_append(int stream_id, string folder, string message [, string flags])`	int	Appends a new message to a specified mailbox
`imap_num_msg(int stream_id)`	int	Gives the number of messages in the current mailbox
`imap_ping(int stream_id)`	int	Checks if the IMAP stream is still active
`imap_num_recent(int stream_id)`	int	Gives the number of recent messages in current mailbox
`imap_expunge(int stream_id)`	int	Permanently deletes all messages marked for deletion
`imap_headers(int stream_id)`	array	Returns headers for all messages in a mailbox
`imap_body(int stream_id, int msg_no [, int options])`	string	Reads the message body

Function	Returns	Action
`imap_fetchtext_full(int stream_id, int msg_no [, int options])`	string	Reads the full text of a message
`imap_mail_copy(int stream_id, int msg_no, string mailbox [, int options])`	int	Copies specified message to a mailbox
`imap_mail_move(int stream_id, int msg_no, string mailbox [, int options])`	int	Moves specified message to a mailbox
`imap_createmailbox (int stream_id, string mailbox)`	int	Creates a new mailbox
`imap_renamemailbox (int stream_id, string old_name, string new_name)`	int	Renames a mailbox
`imap_deletemailbox (int stream_id, string mailbox)`	int	Deletes a mailbox
`imap_list(int stream_id, string ref, string pattern)`	array	Reads the list of mailboxes
`imap_getmailboxes(int stream_id, string ref, string pattern)`	array	Reads the list of mailboxes and returns a full array of objects containing name, attributes, and delimiter
`imap_check(int stream_id)`	object	Gets mailbox properties
`imap_delete(int stream_id, int msg_no [, int flags])`	int	Marks a message for deletion
`imap_undelete(int stream_id, int msg_no)`	int	Removes the delete flag from a message

Continued

TABLE E-30 IMAP FUNCTIONS *(Continued)*

Function	Returns	Action
`imap_headerinfo(int stream_id, int msg_no [, int from_length [, int subject_length [, string default_ host]]])`	object	Reads the headers of the message
`imap_rfc822_parse_headers (string headers [, string default_host]) imap_headerinfo()`	object	Parses a set of mail headers contained in a string and returns an object, much like
`imap_lsub(int stream_id, string ref, string pattern)`	array	Returns a list of subscribed mailboxes
`imap_getsubscribed(int stream_id, string ref, string pattern)`	array	Returns a list of subscribed mailboxes, in the same format as `imap_getmailboxes()`
`imap_subscribe(int stream_id, string mailbox)`	int	Subscribes to a mailbox
`imap_unsubscribe(int stream_id, string mailbox)`	int	Unsubscribes from a mailbox
`imap_fetchstructure(int stream_id, int msg_no [, int options])`	object	Reads the full structure of a message
`imap_fetchbody(int stream_id, int msg_no, int section [, int options])`	string	Gets a specific body section. The different portions of the IMAP body are defined in the IMAP RFC
`imap_base64(string text)`	string	Decodes BASE64-encoded text
`imap_qprint(string text)`	string	Converts a quoted-printable string to an eight-bit string
`imap_8bit(string text)`	string	Converts an eight-bit string to a quoted-printable string
`imap_binary(string text)`	string	Converts an eight-bit string to a base64 string

Function	Returns	Action
imap_mailboxmsginfo(int stream_id)	object	Returns info about the current mailbox
imap_rfc822_write_ address(string mailbox, string host, string personal)	string	Returns a properly formatted e-mail address given the mailbox, host, and personal info
imap_rfc822_parse_ adrlist(string address_ string, string default_ host)	array	Parses an address string
imap_utf8(string string)	string	Converts a string to UTF-8
imap_utf7_decode(string buf)	string	Decodes a modified UTF-7 string
imap_utf7_encode(string buf)	string	Encodes a string in modified UTF-7
imap_setflag_full(int stream_id, string sequence, string flag [, int options])	int	Sets flags on messages
imap_clearflag_full (int stream_id, string sequence, string flag [, int options])	int	Clears flags on messages
imap_sort(int stream_id, int criteria, int reverse [, int options])	array	Sorts an array of message headers
imap_fetchheader(int stream_id, int msg_no [, int options])	string	Gets the full, unfiltered header for a message
imap_uid(int stream_id, int msg_no)	int	Gets the unique message ID associated with a standard sequential message number
imap_msgno(int stream_id, int unique_msg_id)	int	Gets the sequence number associated with a UID

Continued

Table E-30 IMAP FUNCTIONS *(Continued)*

Function	Returns	Action
imap_status(int stream_id, string mailbox, int options)	object	Gets status info from a mailbox
imap_bodystruct(int stream_id, int msg_no, int section)	object	Reads the structure of a specified body section of a specific message
imap_fetch_overview(int stream_id, int msg_no)	array	Reads an overview of the information in the headers of the given message sequence
imap_mail_compose(array envelope, array body)	string	Creates a MIME message based on given envelope and body sections
imap_mail(string to, string subject, string message [, string additional_headers [, string cc [, string bcc [, string rpath]]]])	int	Sends an e-mail message
imap_search(int stream_id, string criteria [, long flags])	array	Returns a list of messages matching the given criteria. The criteria are listed on the manual page: http://www.php.net/manual/function.imap-search.php
imap_alerts(void)	array	Returns an array of all IMAP alerts generated since the last page load or since the last imap_alerts() call, whichever came last; the alert stack is cleared after imap_alerts() is called
imap_errors(void)	array	Returns an array of all IMAP errors generated since the last page load, or since the last imap_errors() call, whichever came last; the error stack is cleared after imap_errors() is called
imap_last_error(void)	string	Returns the last error generated by an IMAP function; the error stack is NOT cleared after this call

Function	Returns	Action
imap_mime_header_decode (string str)	array	Decodes MIMEheader element in accordance with RFC 2047 and returns array of objects containing charset encoding and decoded text

 Use of the IMAP functions requires the IMAP libraries and PHP to be installed --with-imap. The functions will work with a POP3 server as well.

TABLE E-31 INTERBASE FUNCTIONS

Function	Returns	Action
ibase_connect(string database [, string username] [, string password] [, string charset] [, int buffers] [, int dialect] [, string role])	int	Opens a connection to an InterBase database and returns a connection identifier
ibase_pconnect(string database [, string username] [, string password] [, string charset] [, int buffers] [, int dialect] [, string role])	int	Opens a persistent connection to an InterBase database
ibase_close([int link_identifier])	int	Closes an InterBase connection
ibase_commit([int link_identifier,] int trans_number)	int	Commits transaction

Continued

TABLE E-31 INTERBASE FUNCTIONS *(Continued)*

Function	Returns	Action
`ibase_rollback([int link_identifier,] int trans_number)`	int	Rolls back transaction
`ibase_query([int link_identifier,] string query [, int bind_args])`	int	Executes a query
`ibase_prepare([int link_identifier,] string query)`	int	Prepares a query for later execution
`ibase_fetch_row(int result [, int blob_flag])`	array	Fetches a row from the results of a query
`ibase_fetch_object(int result [, int blob_flag])`	object	Fetches an object from the results of a query
`ibase_free_result(int result)`	int	Frees the memory used by a result
`ibase_execute(int query [, int bind_args [, int ...])`	int	Executes a previously prepared query
ibase_free_query(int query)	int	Frees memory used by a query
`ibase_timefmt(string format)`	int	Sets the format of timestamp, date, and time columns returned from queries
`ibase_num_fields(int result)`	int	Gets the number of fields in result
`ibase_field_info(int result, int field_number)`	array	Gets information about a field
`ibase_blob_add(int blob_id, string data)`	int	Adds data into created blob

PHP must be installed --with-ibase in order for these functions to work. Please check the current documentation on PHP interbase functions, because as of the time of this writing, this API was under a lot of flux.

TABLE E-32 MHASH FUNCTIONS

Function	Returns	Action
mhash_count()	int	Gets the number of available hashes
mhash_get_block_size (int hash)	int	Gets the block size of hash
mhash_get_hash_name(int hash)	string	Gets the name of hash
mhash(int hash, string data)	string	Computes hash function on data, using the hash in the first argument.

Use of these functions requires the mhash library from http://mhash.
sourceforge.net/. PHP must be compiled --with-mhash.

The msql database is another open-source SQL database server. It is not actively maintained and has some limitiations that make it a poor choice when compared to MySQL, PostGRES, or Interbase. Note that msqp and MySQL have almost identical function sets.

TABLE E-33 MSQL FUNCTIONS

Function	Returns	Action
msql_connect([string hostname[:port]] [, string username] [, string password])	int	Opens a connection to an mSQL Server
msql_pconnect([string hostname[:port]] [, string username] [, string password])	int	Opens a persistent connection to an mSQL Server

Continued

TABLE E-33 MSQL FUNCTIONS *(Continued)*

Function	Returns	Action
msql_close([int link_identifier])	int	Closes an mSQL connection
msql_select_db(string database_name [, int link_identifier])	int	Selects an mSQL database
msql_create_db(string database_name [, int link_identifier])	int	Creates an mSQL database
msql_drop_db(string database_name [, int link_identifier])	int	Drops (deletes) an mSQL database
msql_query(string query [, int link_identifier])	int	Sends an SQL query to mSQL
msql_list_dbs([int link_identifier])	int	Lists databases available on an mSQL server
msql_list_tables(string database_name [, int link_identifier])	int	Lists tables in an mSQL database
msql_list_fields(string database_name, string table_name [, int link_identifier])	int	Lists mSQL result fields
msql_error([int link_identifier])	string	Returns the text of the error message from previous mSQL operation
msql_result(int query, int row [, mixed field])	int	Gets result data
msql_num_rows(int query)	int	Gets number of rows in a result
msql_num_fields(int query)	int	Gets number of fields in a result
msql_fetch_row(int query)	array	Gets a result row as an enumerated array
msql_fetch_object(int query [, int result_type])	object	Fetches a result row as an object
msql_fetch_array(int query [, int result_type])	array	Fetches a result row as an associative array

Function	Returns	Action
msql_data_seek(int query, int row_number)	int	Moves internal result pointer
msql_fetch_field(int query [, int field_offset])	object	Gets column information from a result and returns as an object
msql_field_seek(int query, int field_offset)	int	Sets result pointer to a specific field offset
msql_field_name(int query, int field_index)	string	Gets the name of the specified field in a result
msql_field_table(int query, int field_offset)	string	Gets name of the table the specified field is in
msql_field_len(int query, int field_offet)	int	Returns the length of the specified field
msql_field_type(int query, int field_offset)	string	Gets the type of the specified field in a result
msql_field_flags(int query, int field_offset)	string	Gets the flags associated with the specified field in a result
msql_free_result(int query)	int	Frees result memory
msql_affected_rows(int query)	int	Returns number of affected rows

TABLE E-34 MSSQL FUNCTIONS

Function	Returns	Action
mssql_connect([string servername [, string username [, string password]]])	int	Establishes a connection to a MS-SQL server, returns a connection identifier
mssql_pconnect([string servername [, string username [, string password]]])	int	Establishes a persistent connection to a MS-SQL server

Continued

TABLE E-34 MSSQL FUNCTIONS *(Continued)*

Function	Returns	Action
mssql_close([int connectionid])	int	Closes a connection to a MS-SQL server
mssql_select_db(string database_name [, int conn_id])	bool	Selects a MS-SQL database
mssql_query(string query [, int conn_id])	int	Performs an SQL query on a MS-SQL server database
mssql_free_result(string result_index)	int	Frees a MS-SQL result index
mssql_get_last_message (void)	string	Gets the last message from the MS-SQL server
mssql_num_rows(int mssql_result_index)	int	Returns the number of rows fetched in from the result ID specified
mssql_num_fields(int mssql_result_index)	int	Returns the number of fields fetched in from the result ID specified
mssql_fetch_row(int result_id)	array	Returns an array of the current row in the result set specified by result_id
mssql_fetch_object(int result_id)	object	Returns an object of the current row in the result set specified by result_id
mssql_fetch_array(int result_id)	array	Returns an associative array of the current row in the result set specified by result_id
mssql_data_seek(int result_id, int offset)	int	Moves the internal row pointer of the MS-SQL result associated with the specified result identifier to pointer to the specified row number
mssql_fetch_field(int result_id [, int offset])	object	Gets information about a certain field in a query result
mssql_field_length(int result_id [, int offset])	int	Gets the length of a MS-SQL field

Function	Returns	Action
mssql_field_name(int result_id [, int offset])	string	Returns the name of the field given by offset in the result set given by result_id
mssql_field_type(int result_id [, int offset])	string	Returns the type of a field
mssql_field_seek(int result_id, int offset)	bool	Moves pointer to the specified field offset
mssql_result(int result_id, int row, mixed field)	string	Returns the contents of one cell from a MS-SQL result set
mssql_min_error_severity(int severity)	void	Sets the lower error severity
mssql_min_message_severity(int severity)	void	Sets the lower message severity

TABLE E-35 PERL COMPATIBLE REGULAR EXPRESSION FUNCTIONS

Function	Returns	Action
preg_match(string pattern, string subject [, array subpatterns])	int	Performs a Perl-style regular expression match
preg_match_all(string pattern, string subject, array subpatterns [, int order])	int	Performs a Perl-style global regular expression match
preg_replace(string| array regex, string|array replace, string|array subject [, int limit])	string	Performs a Perl-style regular expression replacement
preg_split(string pattern, string subject [, int limit [, int flags]])	array	Splits string into an array using a perl-style regular expression as a delimiter

Continued

TABLE E-35 PERL COMPATIBLE REGULAR EXPRESSION FUNCTIONS *(Continued)*

Function	Returns	Action
preg_quote(string str, string delim_char)	string	Quotes regular expression characters plus an optional character
preg_grep(string regex, array input)	array	Searches array and returns entries that match regex

TABLE E-36 POSTGRES FUNCTIONS

Function	Returns	Action
pg_connect([string connection_string] | [string host, string port [, string options [, string tty,]] string database)	int	Opens a PostgreSQL connection
pg_pconnect([string connection_string] | [string host, string port [, string options [, string tty,]] string database)	int	Opens a persistent PostgreSQL connection
pg_close([int connection])	bool	Closes a PostgreSQL connection
pg_dbname([int connection])	string	Gets the database name
pg_errormessage([int connection])	string	Gets the error message string
pg_options([int connection])	string	Gets the options associated with the connection
pg_port([int connection])	int	Returns the port number associated with the connection
pg_tty([int connection])	string	Returns the tty name associated with the connection
pg_host([int connection])	string	Returns the host name associated with the connection

Function	Returns	Action
pg_exec([int connection,] string query)	int	Executes a query
pg_numrows(int result)	int	Returns the number of rows in the result
pg_numfields(int result)	int	Returns the number of fields in the result
pg_cmdtuples(int result)	int	Returns the number of affected tuples
pg_fieldname(int result, int field_number)	string	Returns the name of the field
pg_fieldsize(int result, int field_number)	int	Returns the internal size of the field
pg_fieldtype(int result, int field_number)	string	Returns the type name for the given field
pg_fieldnum(int result, string field_name)	int	Returns the field number of the named field
pg_result(int result, int row_number, mixed field_name)	mixed	Returns values from a result identifier
pg_fetch_row(int result, int row)	array	Gets a row as an enumerated array
pg_fetch_array(int result, int row [, int result_type])	array	Fetches a row as an array
pg_fetch_object(int result, int row [, int result_type])	object	Fetches a row as an object
pg_fieldprtlen(int result, int row, mixed field_name_or_number)	int	Returns the printed length
pg_fieldisnull(int result, int row, mixed field_name_or_number)	int	Tests if a field is NULL

Continued

TABLE E-36 POSTGRES FUNCTIONS *(Continued)*

Function	Returns	Action
pg_freeresult(int result)	int	Frees result memory
pg_getlastoid(int result)	int	Returns the last object identifier
pg_trace(string filename [, string mode [, resource connection]])	bool	Enables tracing of a PostgreSQL connection
pg_untrace([int connection])	bool	Disables tracing of a PostgreSQL connection
pg_locreate(int connection)	int	Creates a large object
pg_lounlink([int connection,] int large_obj_id)	void	Deletes a large object
pg_loopen([int connection,] int objoid, string mode)	int	Opens a large object and returns fd
pg_loclose(int fd)	void	Closes a large object
pg_loread(int fd, int len)	string	Reads a large object
pg_lowrite(int fd, string buf)	int	Writes a large object
pg_loreadall(int fd)	void	Reads a large object and sends straight to browser
pg_loimport(string filename [, resource connection])	int	Imports large object direct from filesystem
pg_loexport(int objoid, string filename [, resource connection])	bool	Exports large object directly to filesystem
pg_setclientencoding ([int connection,] string encoding)	int	Sets client encoding
pg_clientencoding ([int connection])	string	Gets the current client encoding

Use of these functions requires that PHP be compiled --with-postgres.

TABLE E-37 SESSION FUNCTIONS

Function	Returns	Action
session_set_cookie_ params(int lifetime [, string path [, string domain]])	void	Sets session cookie parameters
session_get_cookie_ params(void)	array	Returns the session cookie parameters
session_name([string newname])	string	Returns the current session name; if newname is given, the session name is replaced with newname
session_module_name ([string newname])	string	Returns the current module name used for accessing session data; if newname is given, the module name is replaced with newname
session_set_save_handler (string open, string close, string read, string write, string destroy, string gc)	void	Sets user-level functions
session_save_path([string newname])	string	Returns the current save path passed to module_name; if newname is given, the save path is replaced with newname
session_id([string newid])	string	Returns the current session id; if newid is given, the session id is replaced with newid
session_register(mixed var_names [, mixed ...])	bool	Adds variable names to the list of variables stored by the session

Continued

TABLE E-37 SESSION FUNCTIONS *(Continued)*

Function	Returns	Action
session_unregister (string varname)	bool	Removes varname from the list of variables stored by the session
session_is_registered (string varname)	bool	Checks if a variable is registered in session
session_encode(void)	string	Serializes the current setup and returns the serialized representation
session_decode(string data)	bool	Deserializes data and reinitializes the variables
session_start(void)	bool	Begins session — reinitializes freezed variables, registers browsers, and so forth
session_destroy(void)	bool	Destroys the current session and all data associated with it
session_unset(void)	void	Unsets all registered variables

 Session functions are described in more detail in Chapter 14.

TABLE E-38 DNS FUNCTIONS

Function	Returns	Action
gethostbyaddr(string ip_address)	string	Gets the Internet host name corresponding to a given IP address
gethostbyname(string hostname)	string	Gets the IP address corresponding to a given Internet host name
gethostbynamel(string hostname)	array	Returns a list of IP addresses that a given host name resolves to

Function	Returns	Action
checkdnsrr(string host [, string type])	int	Checks DNS records corresponding to a given Internet host name or IP address
getmxrr(string hostname, array mxhosts [, array weight])	int	Gets MX records corresponding to a given Internet host name

TABLE E-39 MATH FUNCTIONS

Function	Returns	Action
abs(int number)	int	Returns the absolute value of the number
ceil(double number)	int	Returns the next highest integer value of the number
floor(double number)	int	Returns the next lowest integer value of the number
round(double number [, int precision])	double	Returns the number rounded to specified precision
sin(double number)	double	Returns the sine of the number in radians
cos(double number)	double	Returns the cosine of the number in radians
tan(double number)	double	Returns the tangent of the number in radians
asin(double number)	double	Returns the arc sine of the number in radians
acos(double number)	double	Return the arc cosine of the number in radians
atan(double number)	double	Returns the arc tangent of the number in radians

Continued

Table **E-39 MATH FUNCTIONS** *(Continued)*

Function	Returns	Action
atan2(double y, double x)	double	Returns the arc tangent of y/x, with the resulting quadrant determined by the signs of y and x
pi(void)	double	Returns an approximation of pi
pow(double base, double exponent)	double	Returns base raised to the power of exponent
exp(double number)	double	Returns e raised to the power of the number
log(double number)	double	Returns the natural logarithm of the number
log10(double number)	double	Returns the base-10 logarithm of the number
sqrt(double number)	double	Returns the square root of the number
deg2rad(double number)	double	Converts the number in degrees to the radian equivalent
rad2deg(double number)	double	Converts the radian number to the equivalent number in degrees
bindec(string binary_number)	int	Returns the decimal equivalent of the binary number
hexdec(string hexadecimal_number)	int	Returns the decimal equivalent of the hexadecimal number
octdec(string octal_number)	int	Returns the decimal equivalent of an octal string
decbin(int decimal_number)	string	Returns a string containing a binary representation of the number
decoct(int decimal_number)	string	Returns a string containing an octal representation of the given number
dechex(int decimal_number)	string	Returns a string containing a hexadecimal representation of the given number

Function	Returns	Action
base_convert(string number, int frombase, int tobase)	string	Converts a number in a string from any base <= 36 to any base <= 36.
number_format(double number [, int num_decimal_ places [, string dec_ seperator, string thousands_seperator]])	string	Formats a number with grouped thousands

TABLE E-40 MD5

Function	Returns	Action
md5(string str)	string	Calculates the md5 hash of a string

TABLE E-41 OUTPUT BUFFERING

Function	Returns	Action
ob_start(void)	void	Turns on output buffering
ob_end_flush(void)	void	Flushes (sends) the output buffer and turns off output buffering
ob_end_clean(void)	void	Cleans (erases) the output buffer and turns off output buffering
ob_get_contents(void)	string	Returns the contents of the output buffer
ob_implicit_flush([int flag])	void	Turns implicit flush on/off and is equivalent to calling flush() after every output call

TABLE E-42 PAYFLOW PRO FUNCTIONS

Function	Returns	Action
pfpro_version()	string	Returns the version of the Payflow Pro library
pfpro_init()	void	Initializes the Payflow Pro library
pfpro_cleanup()	void	Shuts down the Payflow Pro library
pfpro_process_raw(string parmlist [, string hostaddress [, int port, [, int timeout [, string proxyAddress [, int proxyPort [, string proxyLogon [, string proxyPassword]]]]]]])	string	Performs a raw Payflow Pro transaction
pfpro_process(array parmlist [, string hostaddress [, int port, [, int timeout [, string proxyAddress [, int proxyPort [, string proxyLogon [, string proxyPassword]]]]]]])	array	Performs a Payflow Pro transaction using arrays

 Use of these functions requires payflo pro libraries from verisign and PHP to compile with --with-payflo.

TABLE E-43 CURL FUNCTIONS

Function	Returns	Action
curl_version (void)	string	Returns the CURL version string
curl_init ([string url])	int	Initializes a CURL session

Function	Returns	Action
`curl_setopt (int ch, string option, mixed value)`	bool	Sets an option for a CURL transfer
`curl_exec (int ch)`	bool	Performs a CURL session
`curl_close (int ch)`	void	Closes a CURL session

 Use of these functions requires the curl library and PHP to be compiled -- with-curl. The cURL functions are discussed in more detail in Chapter 14.

Appendix F

Regular Expressions Overview

REGULAR EXPRESSIONS provide a means for pattern matching in strings. Patterns may be as simple as a literal string or a literal string with a wildcard character, or they can grow to be very complex. How complex? Check out the following example, which is intended for e-mail validation. If you're new to regular expressions this may look bad, but to tell the truth, it's not nearly nasty enough. In fact to properly validate an e-mail, it takes about 200 lines of regular expressions. See Appendix G for an e-mail validation function that's quite a bit more complete.

```
^[_\.0-9a-z-]+@([0-9a-z][0-9a-z-]+\.)+[a-z]{2,3}$
```

When you're working with PHP and MySQL there are three variants of regular expressions you might need to use, the regular PHP functions, the Perl-compatible regular expression functions and MySQL regular expression functions. The PHP `ereg()`, `eregi()`, `ereg_replace()`, and `eregi_replace()` functions use the patterns described here.

The Perl Compatible Regular Expressions (PCRE) are quite different in places, and they offer some functionality that can't be replicated with the standard `ereg()` functions. After you have a good feel for regular expressions, you should probably head over to this page to view some of the differences for yourself: `http://www.perl.com/pub/doc/manual/html/pod/perlre.html`. The major PCRE functions are `preg_match()`, `preg_match_all()`, and `preg_replace()`.

Finally, there is another slight variant of the regular expressions used in MySQL, which is described in Appendix I of the MySQL manual.

Literal Patterns

The simplest possible pattern match is to a series of known characters. For instance, to match "jay" within a string, you could do this.

```
$str = "this is a string with my name: jay";
if ( ereg("jay", $str))
{
    echo "pattern found";
}
```

```
else
{
    echo "string not found";
}
```

This will test true and print "pattern found". However, with a simple string like this, you wouldn't need a regular expression. One of PHP's string functions would work and be a good deal faster. For example, in the preceding example, `strstr($str, "jay")` would work equally well.

Characters

In regular expressions you can make use of the following characters.

\n — Newline

\t — Tab

\r — Return

\f — Form feed

^ (Shift-6) — Start of string

$ — End of string

. (dot) — Matches any non-newline character.

So if you needed to match the word "jay" at the end beginning of a string, you could do this:

```
ereg("^jay", $str)
```

And if you wanted to make sure there was nothing before or after "jay" in the string, you could do the following:

```
ereg("^jay$", $str)
```

Notice the meaning of the dot (.). It stands for any non-newline character. If you wanted to print whatever four characters followed "jay" in a string, you could do the following:

```
ereg("jay(....)", $str, $arr);
echo $arr[1];
```

Note that the parentheses here represent a substring. When `ereg()` is processed and there is a match, the array in the third argument will contain the entire matched string (including substrings) in `$arr[0]`, and each additional substring indicated by parentheses will be assigned to an additional array element. So in the preceding example, the four characters following "jay" will be in `$arr[1]`.

 The array created in the optional third argument of `ereg()` will always contain 10 elements. The first element is the entire matched string. It can only place nine matched substrings in the other array elements. If there are fewer than 9 substrings indicated, those elements will be willed with empty strings.

Character Classes

Often you will need to see if a string contains a group of characters. For instance, you may need to make sure that a single character·or given set of characters is alphanumeric or consists of a digit or digits. For this, you will make use of character classes. You can make use of the built-in character classes or make your own. The built-in character classes are surrounded by two sets of brackets. Character classes of your own making will be surrounded by a single set of brackets.

Built-in character classes

`[[:alpha:]]` — Any letter, upper or lower case

`[[:digit:]]` — Digits (0-9)

`[[:space:]]` — Matches any whitespace character, including spaces, tabs, newlines, returns, and form feeds

`[[:upper:]]` — Matches only uppercase letters

`[[:lower:]]` — Matches only lowercase letters

`[[:punct:]]` — Matches any punctuation mark

`[[:xdigit:]]` — Matches possible hexadecimal characters

For example, say you wanted to make sure a letter contained punctuation after "Dear Sir or Madam" salutation.

```
ereg("Madam[[:punct:]]", $str);
```

Note that if you use the carat symbol (^) within a character class it has the effect of saying not. So, `ereg("Madam[^[:punct]]", $str)` would match only if Madam is not followed by a punctuation mark.

> The carat symbol can get confusing because it has two distinct meanings. At the beginning of a regular expression it indicates the start of a string. So the following regular expression will match only a string in which a digit is the first character:
>
> `^[[:digit]]`
>
> But if the carat is not in the first position in the regular expression, it means "not." The following regular expression would match a string that does not contain any digits.
>
> `[^[:digit:]]`
>
> And to put it all together, the following matches a string that starts with a digit but has a second character that is not a digit.
>
> `^[[:digit:]][^[:digit:]]`

Self-made character classes

Using brackets, you can construct your own character classes either by using ranges of characters or by mixing characters of your choosing. Here are some typical ranges:

- ◆ a-z – Any lowercase letter
- ◆ A-Z – Any uppercase letter
- ◆ 0-9 – Any digit

Note that these are the ones you will see most frequently, but a range could contain a-m or 0-4 if you wished.

These ranges must be put within brackets to become character classes. So

`[a-zA-Z]`

is identical to `[[:alpha:]]`.

Self-made classes don't have to contain a range; they can contain any characters you wish.

`[dog0-9]`

This class will match the letters d, o, or g, or any digit.

```
$str="drat";
if(ereg("^[dog0-9]", $str))
{
    echo "true";
}else{
    echo "false";
}
```

This code will print "true", because the first character in $str is in the class I've defined. If we replaced the d in drat with a b, this code would print "false".

 TIP If you need to include a hyphen within a class, the hyphen must be the final character before the closing bracket of the class. For example [a-zA-Z-]

Multiple Occurrences

The real fun in regular expressions comes when you deal with multiple occurrences. This is when the syntax starts getting a little thick. I'll start by looking at three commonly used special characters.

◆ * (asterisk) – Zero or more of the previous character

◆ + – One or more of the previous character

◆ ? – Zero or one of the previous character

Note that if you want to match any of these characters literally, you will need to escape it with a backslash. So, for example, if you want to match the querystring of a URL, say, `http://www.mysqlphpapps.com/index.php?foo=mystring`, you could do the following:

```
\?.*$
```

The first two characters (\?) match the question mark character (?). Note that it matches the literal question mark because it is escaped with a backslash. If it were not escaped, the question mark would have the meaning given in the previous listing. Then the dot matches any a non-newline character. The asterisk matches zero or more of the pervious character. So the combination .* will match any number of characters until a newline. You will see the .* combination frequently. The dollar sign is the end of string character. So .*$ matches every non newline character to the end of the string.

You would probably want to use a regular expression like the previous one if you need to make use of the querystring in some other context

```
$str="http://domain.com/index.php?foo=mystring&bar=otherstring";
//see the use of the parenthesized substring
//this will assign the matched portion to $array[1]
if (ereg("\?(.*)$", $str, $array) )
{
    echo "The querystring is ", $array[1];

}
```

Now that you have the querystring in the variable $array[1], you do further processing on it.

Before you incorporate this code into your script, note that you don't have to. You could use the Apache variable $QUERY_STRING or the PHP HTTP_GET_VARS array.

Moving on, since the plus sign means one or more of the previous character,

```
[0-9]+
```

will match a single digit or multiple digits. In the following statement:

```
if (ereg("jay[0-9]+", $str) )
```

jay1 will test true, but jayg will test false, jay2283092002909303 will test true because it's still "jay" followed by one or more numbers. Even, jay8393029jay will test true.

If you need to get more specific about the number of characters you need to match, you can make use of curly braces.

- ◆ {3} – If there is a single digit within brackets, it indicates that you wish to match exactly that number of the previous character. j{3} matches only jjj.

- ◆ {3, 5} – If there are two digits, it indicates an upper and lower limit to the matches of the previous character. j{3,5} will match jjj, jjjj, and jjjjj only.

- ◆ {3, } – If there is a comma and there is no second integer, it will match as many times or more of the previous character. So j{3, } will match jjj, jjjj, or jjjjjjj, and so on.

Specifying "Or"

If you want to specify one combination of characters or another, you need to make use of the pipe character (|). Most often, you will use the pipe with parentheses, which group portions of strings. If you wanted to match either jay or brad within a string, you could use the following:

```
(jay|brad)
```

Or you might want to check that URLs had a suffix you were familiar with:

```
(com|org|edu)
```

Example Regular Expressions

This has been a pretty quick review of regular expressions. If you're interested, there have been entire books written on the subject. To get you more comfortable with regular expressions, lets look at a practical example.

Say you want to write a regular expression that matches the contents of an href attribute of an anchor tag. An example anchor looks something like this:

```
<a href="../my_link.php">this is my link text</a>
```

At first, you might tempted to look at this link and think all you need to do is match everything after the href=" to the closing quotation mark. Something like this:

```
if (ereg('<a href="(.*)"', $anchor, $array))
{
    echo $array[1];
}
```

However, you really can't be sure that the href will immediately follow the <a; there could be another attribute or perhaps a javascript event prior to the href. So you'd need to account for that in your regular expression.

```
if (ereg('<a.*href="(.*)"', $anchor, $array))
{
    echo $array[1];
}
```

We've seen anchor tags where a space existed prior to and following the equal sign. So we need to account for occasions when the space exists and when it doesn't.

```
if (ereg('<a.*href[[:space:]]?=[[:space:]]?"(.*)"',
$anchor, $array))
{
    echo $array[1];
}
```

Since the question mark character means "zero or one of the previous character", the pairing [[:space:]]? means there can be one whitespace character or none. If you wanted to allow for more than one whitespace character, you could use [[:space:]]+.

Finally, we need to deal with the actual contents of the href attribute. So far, we've only accounted for cases where the link destination is delimited by double quotes. But at the very least, we should account for delimiters of either double quotes or single quotes. To do that, we'll need to put double quotes and single quotes within a character class. Because we've surrounded the entire regular expression with single quotes, we will need to escape single quotes within the regular expression with backslashes. The class will be ["\'].

```
if (ereg('<a.*href[[:space:]]?=[[:space:]]?["\'](.*)["\']',
        $anchor, $array))
{
    echo $array[1];
}
```

To be even more complete, the regular expression should account for cases when no quotation mark at all is used to delimit value of the href. For example, browsers are just fine with a tag like this: <a href=mylink.php>. In a case like this, it might be a good idea to use the greater than sign to mark the end of the string. All you would need to do is add the greater than sign to the last character class

```
if (ereg('<a.*href[[:space:]]?=[[:space:]]?["\']?(.*)["\'>]',
        $anchor, $array))
{
    echo $array[1];
}
```

However, this presents some problems that you may not have anticipated. Imagine that this previous code is attempting to match this string: <a href = ../ my_link.php>this is my link text</a>. When you add the greater than sign to the character class, the regular expression will not match the first greater than sign — it will match to the final greater than sign in the string. This is known as greedy matching, and using `ereg()` or `ereg_replace()` there is no way around greedy matching.

In a circumstance when you need to match the first occasion of a character in a string, you will need to make use of the PCRE functions. Using PCRE, the combination .*? will match all characters until the first occasion of the character you indicated. This series

```
.*?["\'>]
```

will match everything until the first double quote, single quote or greater than sign. With `preg_match()` the final function would look like this:

```
if
(preg_match('/<a.*href[[:space:]]?=[[:space:]]?["\']?(.*?)["\'>]/i',
        $anchor, $array))
{
    echo $array[1];
}
```

Appendix G

Helpful User-Defined Functions

THIS APPENDIX CONTAINS a series of PHP functions and classes that you might find useful in creating your scripts. It will start with a run-through of the base functions kept in the /book/functions folder.

Base Functions Set Used in this Book

We discuss these in detail in Chapter 9, but we include them here for quick reference.

from functions/basic.php

These functions deal with authentication and text manipulation.

AUTHENTICATE()
This function sends a "401 Unauthorized" header. The default string is "Secure Area".

```
void authenticate ([string realm], [string error_message])
```

DB_AUTHENTICATE()
This function attempts to run 401-type authentication and verify the results against a given database table. The default table is mysql.users. It makes calls to `authenticate()` to send the 401 header.

```
void db_authenticate([string table [, string realm [, string error
message [, string username field name [, string password field
name]]]]])
```

CLEANUP_TEXT()
This function removes HTML and PHP tags using the `strip_tags()` function and replaces <, >, &, and " characters with their HTML entities. If the second argument is not empty, strip_tags will not be run and only the HTML entity replacement will occur. The third argument can specify tags that should not be removed.

517

```
string cleanup_text ([string value [, string preserve [, string
allowed_tags]]])
```

GET_ATTLIST()

This function uses the PHP function `htmlspecialchars()` to convert special HTML characters in the first argument (&,",<, and >) to their equivalent HTML entities. If the optional second argument is empty, any HTML tags in the first argument will be removed. The optional third argument lets you specify specific tags to be spared from this cleansing. The format for the argument is "<tag1><tag2>".

```
string get_attlist (array attributes,[array default attributes])
```

MAKE_PAGE_TITLE()

This function will clean up a string to make it suitable for use as the value of an HTML <TITLE> tag, removing any HTML tags and replacing all HTML entities with their literal character equivalents by using get_html_translation_table (HTML_ENTITIES).

```
string make_page_title (string string)
```

MONEY()

This function will format the sole argument as a standard U.S. dollars value, rounding any decimal value two decimal places for cents and prepending a dollar sign to the returned string. Commas will server as thousands separators.

```
string money ([mixed value])
```

STATES()

This function returns an associative array, the key being the two-letter abbreviation of the states, the value being the state name.

```
array states(void)
```

from functions/db.php

These are common functions that will help work with MySQL databases.

DBCONNECT()

Creates a connection to a MySQL server and selects a database. Defaults are, from left to right, "test", "nobody", "", "localhost". If the connection fails, an error message prints and the script ends.

```
void dbconnect ([string database name [, string user name [, string
password [, string server name]]]])
```

SAFE_QUERY()

This function will return a result identifier if a `mysql query()` runs successfully; otherwise it will print the `mysql_error()` message, the error number, and the query text of the query sent to the function.

```
int safe_query (string query)
```

SET_RESULT_VARIABLES ()   The sole argument of this function should be the identifier returned as the result of a `mysql_query()` (or if you are using these functions, `safe_query()`). The query should have returned only a single row. Each column returned for the row is turned into a global variable, with the column name being the variable name and the result being the variable value.

```
void set_result_variables (int result identifier)
fetch_record()
int fetch_record (string table name, mixed key, mixed value)
```

This function will select values from the MySQL table specified by the first argument. If the optional second and third arguments are not empty, the select will get the row from that table where the column named in the second argument has the value given by the third argument. The second and third arguments may also be arrays, in which case the query builds its where clause using the values of the second argument array as the table column names and the corresponding values of the third argument array as the required values for those table columns. If the second and third arguments are not empty, the data from the first row returned (if any) are set to global variables by the `set_result_variables()` function (described previously).

DB_VALUES_ARRAY()   This function builds an associative array out of the values in the MySQL table specified in the first argument. The data from the column named in the second argument will be set to the keys of the array. If the third argument is not empty, the data from the column it names will be the values of the array; otherwise, the values will be equal to the keys. If the third argument is not empty, the data will be ordered by the column it names; otherwise, they will be ordered by the key column. The optional fourth argument specifies any additional qualification for the query against the database table; if it is empty, all rows in the table will be retrieved.

If either the first or second argument is empty, no query is run and an empty array is returned. The function presumes that whoever calls it knows what they're about, e.g., that the table exists, that all the column names are correct, etc.

```
array db_values_array ([string table name [, string value field [,
string label field [, string sort field [, string where clause]]]]])
```

from functions/html.php

These functions create common HTML elements, including anchors and unordered lists.

FONT_TAG()
This function creates an HTML font tag. Default size is 2, default font face is sansserif. Any additional attributes in the third argument will be added to the tag. It is expecting an associative array, the key of which will be the name of the attribute; the value of the array element will be the attribute value.

```
string font_tag ([int size [, string typeface [, array
attributes]]])
```

ANCHOR_TAG()
This function creates an HTML anchor tag. The first argument is the href value, the second is the string to be surrounded by the anchor. It is expecting an associative array, the key of which will be the name of the attribute; the value of the array element will be the attribute value.

```
string anchor_tag ([string href [, string text [, array
attributes]]])
```

IMAGE_TAG()
This function returns an HTML image tag (<img>). The first argument gives the URL of the image to be displayed. Additional attributes may be supplied as an array in the third argument.

```
string image_tag ([string src [,array attributes]])
```

SUBTITLE()
This function returns an HTML <h3> tag. It is used for the titles of secondary areas within pages in our examples. The reason to display these via a function, rather than just literal <h3> tags, is to enable you to change the format of these subtitles in one place, instead of in each script.

```
string subtitle(string string)
```

PARAGRAPH()
This function will return a string inside HTML paragraph (<p>) tags. Attributes for the <p> tag may be supplied in the first argument. Any additional arguments will be included inside the opening and closing <p> tags, separated by newlines.

```
string paragraph ([array attributes [, mixed ...]])
```

UL_LIST()

This function returns an HTML unordered (bulleted) list (`<ul>` tags). If the argument is an array, then each value from the array will be included as a list item (`<li>`) in the list. Otherwise, the argument will simply be included inside the `<ul>` tags as is.

```
string ul_list(mixed values)
```

From functions/forms.php

These functions create all common form elements, as well as the opening and closing `<form>` tags.

START_FORM()

This function returns an HTML `<form>` tag. If the first argument is empty, the value of the global Apache variable SCRIPT_NAME is used for the 'action' attribute of the `<form>` tag. Other attributes for the form can be specified in the optional second argument; the default method of the form is "post". The behavior of this function on servers other than Apache is not known. It's likely that it will work, as SCRIPT_NAME is part of the CGI 1.1 specification.

```
string start_form ([string action, [array attributes]])
```

END_FORM()

This function returns a closing form tag.

```
string end_form(void)
```

TEXT_FIELD()

Returns an HTML `<input type=text>` form element. Default size is 10.

```
string text_field ([string name [, string value [, int size [, int
maximum length]]]])
```

TEXTAREA_FIELD()

This function returns an HTML textarea field. The default size is 50 columns and 10 rows, and the default wrap mode is 'soft', which means no hard newline characters will be inserted after line breaks in what the user types into the field. The alternative wrap mode is 'hard', which means that hard newlines will be inserted.

```
string textarea_field([string name [, string value [, int cols [,
int rows [, string wrap mode]]]]])
```

PASSWORD_FIELD()

This function returns an HTML password field. This is like a text field, but the value of the field is obscured (only stars or bullets are visible for each character). The default size of the field is 10. A starting value and maximum data length may be supplied.

```
string password_field ([string name [, string value [, int size [,
int maximum length]]]])
```

HIDDEN_FIELD()

This function returns an HTML hidden form element. A name and value may be supplied.

```
string hidden_field ([string name [, string value]])
```

FILE_FIELD()

This function returns an HTML file field form element.

```
string file_field([string name])
```

This function returns an HTML file field. These are used to specify files on the user's local hard drive, typically for uploading as part of the form. (See http://www.zend.com/manual/features.file-upload.php for more information about this subject.)

SUBMIT_FIELD()

This function returns an HTML submit field. The value of the field will be the string displayed by the button displayed by the user's browser. The default value is "Submit".

```
string submit_field ([string name [, string value]])
```

IMAGE_FIELD()

This function returns an HTML image field. An image field works likes a submit field, except that the image specified by the URL given in the second argument is displayed instead of a button.

```
string image_field ([string name [, string src [, string value]]])
```

RESET_FIELD()

This function returns an HTML reset form element.

```
string reset_field ([string name, [string value]])
```

CHECKBOX_FIELD()

This function returns an HTML checkbox field. The optional third argument will be included immediately after the checkbox field, and the pair is included inside an HTML <nobr> tag – meaning that they will be displayed together on the same line. If the value of the second or third argument matches that of the fourth argument, the checkbox will be 'checked' (i.e., flipped on).

```
string checkbox_field ([string name [, string value [, string label
[, string match]]]])
```

RADIO_FIELD()

This function returns an HTML radio button field. The optional third argument will be included immediately after the radio button, and the pair is included inside an HTML <nobr> tag – meaning that they will be displayed together on the same line. If the value of the second or third argument matches that of the fourth argument, the radio button will be 'checked' (i.e., flipped on).

```
string radio_field ([string name [, string value [, string label [,
string match]]]])
```

SELECT_FIELD()

This function returns an HTML select field (a popup field). If the optional second argument is an array, each key in the array will be set to the value of an option of the select field, and the corresponding value from the array will be the displayed string for that option. If the key or the value from the array matches the optional third argument, that option will be designated as the default value of the select field.

```
string select_field ([string name [, array items [, string default
value]]])
```

DB_SELECT_FIELD()

This function returns an HTML select field (popup field), based on the values in the MySQL database table specified by the second argument, as returned by the db_values_array() function (defined previously).

```
string db_select_field ([string name [, string table name [, string
value field [, string label field [, string sort field [, string
match text [, string where clause]]]]]]])
```

DB_RADIO_FIELD()

This function returns a list of HTML radio button fields, separated by a non-breaking space HTML entity ( ) and a newline, based on the values in the MySQL database table named by the second argument, as returned by the db_values_array() function (defined previously).

```
string db_radio_field (string name, string table name, string value
field, string label field, string sort field, [string match text],
[string where clause])
```

From functions/tables.php

These functions create opening and closing ⟨table⟩ tags, as well as ⟨tr⟩ and ⟨td⟩ tags.

START_TABLE()

This function returns an opening HTML ⟨table⟩ tag, inside an opening paragraph (⟨p⟩) tag. Attributes for the table may be supplied as an array.

```
string start_table([array attributes])
```

END_TABLE()

This function returns a closing table tag.

```
string end_table(void)
```

TABLE_ROW()

This function returns an HTML table row (⟨tr⟩) tag, enclosing a variable number of table cell (⟨td⟩) tags. If any of the arguments to the function is an array, it will be used as attributes for the ⟨tr⟩ tag. All other arguments will be used as values for the cells of the row. If an argument begins with a ⟨td⟩ tag, the argument is added to the row as is. Otherwise it is passed to the table_cell() function and the resulting string is added to the row.

```
string table_row ([array attributes], [indefinite number of string
arguments])
```

TABLE_CELL()

This function returns an HTML table cell (⟨td⟩) tag. The first argument will be used as the value of the tag. Attributes for the ⟨td⟩ tag may be supplied as an array in the second argument. By default, the table cell will be aligned left horizontally, and to the top vertically.

```
string table_cell ([string value [, array attributes]])
```

Additional Functions Not Used in this Book

Here are a couple of functions that may make dealing with common queries a bit easier.

insert_row()

This is a generic function to run SQL insert statements.

```
function insert_row($table="", $atts="")
{
    if(empty($table) || !is_array($atts))
    {
        return False;
    }
    else
    {
        while (list ($col, $val) = each ($atts))
        {
            //if null go to the next array item
            if ($val=="")
            {
                continue;
            }
            $col_str .= $col . ",";
            if (is_int($val) || is_double ($val))
            {
                $val_str .= $val . ",";
            }
            else
            {
            $val_str .= "'$val',";
            }
        }
        $query = "insert into $table
            ($col_str)
                values($val_str)";
        //trim trailing comma from both strings
        $query = str_replace(",)", ")", $query);
    }
    safe_query($query);

    return mysql_affected_rows();
}
```

This function takes two attributes: the first is the table name and the second should be an associative array, with the key being the column name and the value being the value to be inserted. Single quotes that should surround a string are will be included if the variable is not an integer or a double. The function returns FALSE if the query fails to perform an action. It will not work in all circumstances, because it doesn't check for the column type from the database. But it could be nice for creating pages quickly.

Empty values in the array are not added to the query. For columns left out of the query, MySQL will insert either null values or empty strings, depending on whether or not the column allows nulls.

Note that you can create the associative array from a set of variables using the compact() function. For example, the following will create an associative array named $array, and then insert a row into a table named mytable. It's assumed that you will have already connected to the database

```
$category="";
$category_id=6;
$category_name="my category";
$array=compact("category", "category_id", "category_name");
if (!insert_row("mytable", $array))
{
    echo "insert failed";
}
```

update_row()

The function will SQL update statements

```
function update_row($table="", $atts="", $where="")
{
    if(empty($table) || !is_array($atts))
    {
        return FALSE;
    }
    else
    {
        while(list ($col, $val) = each ($atts))
        {
            if ($val=="")
            {
                continue;
            }
            if(is_int($val) || is_double($val))
            {
```

```
            $str .= "$col=$val,";
        }
        elseif($val=="NULL" || $val=="null")
        {
            $str .= "$col=NULL,";
        }
        else
        {
            $str .= "$col='$val',";
        }
    }
}
$str = substr($str, 0, -1);
$query = "update $table set $str";
if (!empty($where))
{
    $query .= " where $where";
}
mysql_query($query) or
    die (mysql_error());
return mysql_affected_rows();
}
```

This function takes three arguments: `$table`, a string; `$atts`, an associative array containing keys of column names and values of values to be inserted; and `$where`, which is the condition, for example (`column_id = 1`).

Again, this is not robust enough to work in all circumstances.

delete_row()

This function takes two arguments: `$table`, the table name, and `$where`, the value in the `where` clause. It returns false on failure or 0 if nothing was deleted.

```
function delete_row($table="", $where="")
{
    if (empty($table) || empty($where))
    {
        return FALSE;
    }
    $query = "delete from $table where $where";
    mysql_query($query) or die (mysql_error());
    return mysql_affected_rows();
}
```

Function select_to_table()

This function takes a query and lays it out in a simple HTML table. It assumes that a database connection has already been made.

```
function select_to_table($query)
{
    $result=mysql_query($query);
    $number_cols = mysql_num_fields($result);
    echo "<b>query: $query</b>";
    //layout table header
    echo "<table border = 1>\n";
    echo "<tr align=center>\n";
    for ($i=0; $i<$number_cols; $i++)
    {
        echo "<th>" . mysql_field_name($result, $i). "</th>\n";
    }
    echo "</tr>\n";//end table header
    //layout table body
    while ($row = mysql_fetch_row($result))
    {
        echo "<tr align=left>\n";
        for ($i=0; $i<$number_cols; $i++)
        {
        echo "<td>";
            if (!isset($row[$i])) //test for null value
            {
              echo "NULL";
            }
            else
            {
              echo $row[$i];
            }
            echo "</td>\n";
        } echo "</tr>\n";
} echo "</table>";
}
```

enum_to_array()

This functions returns the values defined in an enum field into an array.

```
function enum_to_array($table="", $col = "")
{

    if (empty($table) || empty($col))
```

```
        { return False; }
        else
        {
            $query = "describe $table $col";
            $result = mysql_query($query);
            list( , $col) = mysql_fetch_array($result);
            echo $col;
            if (substr($col, 0, 4) != "enum")
            {
                return FALSE;
            }
            $col = str_replace ("'","" ,
                        substr($col, 5, -1)
            );
            $col = explode(",", $col);
        }
        return $col;
}
```

You can use the enum field type in MySQL to limit possible values in a column. This might be helpful for restricting column values to Y or N, for example. But to get at these values in PHP, you need to run one of the MySQL queries that retrieve column information. In the preceding example I use the describe query, and I assume that the column of interest will be included in the query.

The query returns 6 columns. In order, they are: Field, Type, Null, Key, Default, and Extra. The second, Type, contains the column type – something like enum('yes','no'). In the preceding function, this value is assigned to $col. That string can then be stripped of the extraneous parentheses and the letters enum. The remainder is exploded into an array.

You can then use the array however you wish, perhaps in a drop-down box.

Session handling with MySQL

If you wish to use these, set your session.save_handler to user in your php.ini. This set of functions is intended to work with a table that looks something like this:

```
create table sessions(
    session_id char(32) not null primary key,
    sess_data text,
    last_update timestamp
function mysql_session_open()
{
        mysql_pconnect("localhost", "root", "")
            or die (mysql_error());
        $db_sess = mysql_select_db("test")
```

```
                    or die (mysql_error());
}


//this function receives the session_id as the only argument
function mysql_session_read($id)
{
        $data = "";
         $query = "select sess_data from sessions
                where session_id = '$id'";
        $result= mysql_query($query) or die (mysql_error());
        if ($row = mysql_fetch_row($result) )
        {
                $data=session_decode($row[0]);
        }
        return $data;
}


//this takes the sessionid and the sesssion data
//as arguments
function mysql_session_write($id, $data)
{
    $data = session_encode($data);
    $query = "replace into sessions (session_id, sess_data)
        values ('$id', '$data')";
    mysql_query($query) or
        die(mysql_error());
    return true;
}


function mysql_session_close()
{
        return true;
}


//takes only the session id for an argument
function mysql_session_destroy($id)
{
        $query = "delete from sessions where session_id = '$id'";
        mysql_query($query) or
            die (mysql_error());
            return true;
}
```

```
//this function receives the maximum lifetime setting
//from php.ini. It is by default set to 1440 seconds.
//the session.gc_probability setting in the php.ini determines
//what percentage of the time this function will run.
function mysql_session_gc($time)
{
        $query = "delete from sessions where
                    last_update < ( subdate(now(),
                    INTERVAL $time SECOND) )";
        mysql_query($query) or
            die (mysql_error() )_;
}
session_set_save_handler(
        "mysql_session_open",
        "mysql_session_close",
        "mysql_session_read",
        "mysql_session_write",
        "mysql_session_destroy",
        "mysql_session_gc"
);
```

MySQL Backup

Dan Nedoborski wrote this script, which I planned on including. However, it is a bit lengthy for printed form. I recommend you go to his site and take a look for yourself.

```
http://www.ov-m.com/mysqlphpbak/
```

Validation

Here are a couple of the trickier items to validate properties.

E-mail validation

There are a lot of simple regular expressions to make sure a string more or less resembles the format of a proper e-mail address, but if you want something that is a bit more thorough, try this. It may not be entirely RFC-compliant, but it is pretty close. It is included in the /book/functions folder.

```
#CheckEmail
#
#mailbox     =  addr-spec                    ; simple address
#               /  phrase route-addr         ; name & addr-spec
```

```
#
#route-addr  =  "<" [route] addr-spec ">"
#
#route       =  1#("@" domain) ":"           ; path-relative
#
#addr-spec   =  local-part "@" domain         ; global address
#
#local-part  =  word *("." word)              ; uninterpreted
#                                             ; case-preserved
#
#domain      =  sub-domain *("." sub-domain)
#
#sub-domain  =  domain-ref / domain-literal
#
#domain-ref  =  atom                          ; symbolic reference
#
#atom        =  1*<any CHAR except specials, SPACE and CTLs>
#
#specials    =  "(" / ")" / "<" / ">" / "@"  ; Must be in quoted-
#               / "," / ";" / ":" / "\" / <">  ; string, to use
#               / "." / "[" / "]"              ; within a word.
#
#                                             ; ( Octal, Decimal.)
#CHAR        =  <any ASCII character>          ; ( 0-177,  0.-127.)
#ALPHA       =  <any ASCII alphabetic character>
#                                             ; (101-132, 65.- 90.)
#                                             ; (141-172, 97.-122.)
#DIGIT       =  <any ASCII decimal digit>      ; ( 60- 71, 48.- 57.)
#CTL         =  <any ASCII control             ; ( 0- 37,  0.- 31.)
#               character and DEL>             ; (    177,     127.)
#CR          =  <ASCII CR, carriage return>    ; (     15,      13.)
#LF          =  <ASCII LF, linefeed>           ; (     12,      10.)
#SPACE       =  <ASCII SP, space>              ; (     40,      32.)
#HTAB        =  <ASCII HT, horizontal-tab>     ; (     11,       9.)
#<">         =  <ASCII quote mark>             ; (     42,      34.)
#CRLF        =  CR LF
#
#LWSP-char   =  SPACE / HTAB                   ; semantics = SPACE
#
#linear-white-space =  1*([CRLF] LWSP-char)   ; semantics = SPACE
#                                             ; CRLF => folding
#
#delimiters  =  specials / linear-white-space / comment
#
#text        =  <any CHAR, including bare     ; => atoms, specials,
```

```
#                   CR & bare LF, but NOT        ; comments and
#                   including CRLF>              ; quoted-strings are
#                                                ; NOT recognized.
#
#quoted-string = <"> *(qtext/quoted-pair) <">; Regular qtext or
#                                                ;   quoted chars.
#
#qtext        = <any CHAR excepting <">,        ; => may be folded
#                "\" & CR, and including
#                linear-white-space>
#
#domain-literal = "[" *(dtext / quoted-pair) "]"
#
#
#
#
#dtext        = <any CHAR excluding "[",        ; => may be folded
#                "]", "\" & CR, & including
#                linear-white-space>
#
#comment      = "(" *(ctext / quoted-pair / comment) ")"
#
#ctext        = <any CHAR excluding "(",        ; => may be folded
#                ")", "\" & CR, & including
#                linear-white-space>
#
#quoted-pair  = "\" CHAR                         ; may quote any char
#
#phrase       = 1*word                           ; Sequence of words
#
#word         = atom / quoted-string
#

#mailbox      = addr-spec                        ; simple address
#              / phrase route-addr              ; name & addr-spec
#route-addr   = "<" [route] addr-spec ">"
#route        = 1#("@" domain) ":"              ; path-relative
#addr-spec    = local-part "@" domain           ; global address

#validate_email("insight\@bedrijfsnet.nl");

function print_validate_email ($eaddr="")
{
    $result = validate_email($eaddr) ? "is valid" : "is not valid";
    print "<h4>email address (".htmlspecialchars($eaddr).")"
```

```
$result</h4>\n";
}

function validate_email ($eaddr="")
{

    if (empty($eaddr))
    {
#print "[$eaddr] is not valid\n";
        return false;
    }
    $laddr = "";
    $laddr = $eaddr;

# if the addr-spec is in a route-addr, strip away the phrase and <>s

    $laddr = preg_replace('/^.*<\//','', $laddr);
    $laddr = preg_replace('/>.*$/','',$laddr);
    if (preg_match('/^\@.*:/',$laddr))      #path-relative domain
    {
        list($domain,$addr_spec) = preg_split('/:/',$laddr);
        $domain = preg_replace('/^\@/','',$domain);
        if (!is_domain($domain)) { return false; }
        $laddr = $addr_spec;
    }
    return(is_addr_spec($laddr));
}

function is_addr_spec ( $eaddr = "" )
{
    list($local_part,$domain) = preg_split('/\@/',$eaddr);
    if (!is_local_part($local_part) || !is_domain($domain))
    {
#print "[$eaddr] is not valid\n";
        return false;
    }
    else
    {
#print "[$eaddr] is valid\n";
        return true;
    }
}

#local-part  =  word *("." word)              ; uninterpreted
function is_local_part ( $local_part = "" )
```

```
{
    if (empty($local_part)) { return false; }

    $bit_array = preg_split('/\./',$local_part);
    while (list(,$bit) = each($bit_array))
    {
        if (!is_word($bit)) { return false; }
    }
    return true;
}


#word          =  atom / quoted-string
#quoted-string = <"> *(qtext/quoted-pair) <">; Regular qtext or
#                                            ;   quoted chars.
#qtext         =  <any CHAR excepting <">,    ; => may be folded
#                   "\" & CR, and including
#                   linear-white-space>
#quoted-pair =   "\" CHAR                      ; may quote any char
function is_word ( $word = "")
{

    if (preg_match('/^".*"$/i',$word))
    {
        return(is_quoted_string($word));
    }
    return(is_atom($word));
}

function is_quoted_string ( $word = "")
{
    $word = preg_replace('/^"/','',$word);    # remove leading quote
    $word = preg_replace('/"$/','',$word);    # remove trailing
quote
    $word = preg_replace('/\\+/','',$word);    # remove any quoted-
pairs
    if (preg_match('/\"\\\r/',$word))    # if ", \ or CR, it's bad
qtext
    {
        return false;
    }
    return true;
}


#atom         =  1*<any CHAR except specials, SPACE and CTLs>
```

```
#specials     =   "(" / ")" / "<" / ">" / "@"   ; Must be in quoted-
#                 / "," / ";" / ":" / "\" / <">  ;   string, to use
#                 / "." / "[" / "]"               ;   within a word.
#SPACE        =   <ASCII SP, space>               ; (    40,       32.)
#CTL          =   <any ASCII control              ; (  0- 37,  0.- 31.)
#                   character and DEL>            ; (   177,      127.)
function is_atom ( $atom = "" )
{

    if (
    (preg_match('/[\(\)\<\>\@\,\;\:\\\"\.\[\]]/',$atom))     #
specials
        || (preg_match('/\040/',$atom))                 # SPACE
        || (preg_match('/[\x00-\x1F]/',$atom))          # CTLs
    )
    {
        return false;
    }
    return true;
}


#domain       =   sub-domain *("." sub-domain)
#sub-domain   =   domain-ref / domain-literal
#domain-ref   =   atom                           ; symbolic reference
function is_domain ( $domain = "" )
{

    if (empty($domain)) { return false; }

# this is not strictly required, but is 99% likely sign of a bad
domain
    if (!preg_match('/\./',$domain)) { return false; }

    $dbit_array = preg_split('/./',$domain);
    while (list(,$dbit) = each($dbit_array))
    {
        if (!is_sub_domain($dbit)) { return false; }
    }
    return true;
}
function is_sub_domain ( $subd = "" )
{
    if (preg_match('/^\[.*\]$/',$subd))     #domain-literal
    {
```

```
            return(is_domain_literal($subd));
    }
    return(is_atom($subd));
}
#domain-literal =   "[" *(dtext / quoted-pair) "]"
#dtext          =   <any CHAR excluding "[",     ; => may be folded
#                       "]", "\" & CR, & including
#                       linear-white-space>
#quoted-pair =   "\" CHAR                        ; may quote any char
function is_domain_literal ( $dom = "")
{
    $dom = preg_replace('/\\+/','',$dom);        # remove quoted
pairs
    if (preg_match('/[\[\]\\\r]/',$dom))     # bad dtext characters
    {
        return false;
    }
    return true;
}


?>
```

You would probably want to put all of these functions in one file and then include it when needed. It returns 1 (for true) or nothing (for false). You'd probably want to use it like so:

```
if ( !validate_email("myaddress@mydomain.com") )
{
    echo "this is not a valid email";
}
```

Credit-card validation

Here's the credit-card validator we used in Chapter 14. You can find it in /book/ cart/ccval.php.

```
/*
**************************************************************
*
* CCVal - Credit Card Validation function.
*
* Copyright (c) 1999 Holotech Enterprises. All rights reserved.
* You may freely modify and use this function for
*  your own purposes.You may freely distribute it, without
*  modification and with this notice and entire header intact.
```

```
    * This function accepts a credit card number and, optionally,
    *  a code for a credit card name. If a Name code is specified,
    * the number is checked against card-specific criteria, then
    *  validated with the Luhn Mod 10 formula. Otherwise it is only
    *  checked against the  formula. Valid name codes are:
    *
    *    mcd - Master Card
    *    vis - Visa
    *    amx - American Express
    *    dsc - Discover
    *    dnc - Diners Club
    *    jcb - JCB
    *
    * A description of the criteria used in this function
    * can be found at
    * http://www.beachnet.com/~hstiles/cardtype.html.
    * If you have any
    * questions or comments, please direct them to
    * ccval@holotech.net
    *                                    Alan Little
    *                                    Holotech Enterprises
    *                                    http://www.holotech.net/
    *                                    September 1999
    *
    **********************************************************************
    /


function CCVal($Num, $Name = 'n/a')
{

// You can't get money from an empty card
    if (empty($Num)) { return FALSE; }

//  Innocent until proven guilty
    $GoodCard = TRUE;
//print "<h4>pre-code: GoodCard is ".($GoodCard ? "TRUE" :
"FALSE")."</h4>\n";

//  Get rid of any non-digits
    $Num = ereg_replace("[^[:digit:]]", "", $Num);

//  Perform card-specific checks, if applicable
    switch ($Name)
    {
```

```
        case "mcd" :
            $GoodCard = ereg("^5[1-5].{14}$", $Num);
            break;

        case "vis" :
            $GoodCard = ereg("^4.{15}$|^4.{12}$", $Num);
            break;

        case "amx" :
            $GoodCard = ereg("^3[47].{13}$", $Num);
            break;

        case "dsc" :
            $GoodCard = ereg("^6011.{12}$", $Num);
            break;

        case "dnc" :
            $GoodCard = ereg("^30[0-5].{11}$|^3[68].{12}$", $Num);
            break;

        case "jcb" :
            $GoodCard = ereg("^3.{15}$|^2131|1800.{11}$", $Num);
            break;
    }
//print "<h4>pre-luhn: GoodCard is ".($GoodCard ? "TRUE" :
"FALSE")."</h4>\n";

//  The Luhn formula works right to left, so reverse the number.
    $Num = strrev($Num);

    $Total = 0;

    for ($x=0; $x<strlen($Num); $x++)
    {
    $digit = substr($Num,$x,1);

//    If it's an odd digit, double it
        if ($x/2 != floor($x/2))
        {
            $digit *= 2;

//    If the result is two digits, add them
            if (strlen($digit) == 2)
            {
                $digit = substr($digit,0,1)
```

```
                                    + substr($digit,1,1)
                    ;
            }
        }


//    Add the current digit, doubled and added if applicable, to the
Total

        $Total += $digit;
    }


//  If it passed (or bypassed) the card-specific check and the Total
is
//  evenly divisible by 10, it's cool!
//print "<h4>post-luhn: Total = $Total</h4>\n";

    if ($GoodCard && $Total % 10 == 0) return TRUE; else return
FALSE;


}
```

?> recurse_directory

I wrote the following to help me take a look at all the documents installed on my Web server. It will print every document and provide a link to these documents.

```
function recurse_directory($path="")
{
    global $DOCUMENT_ROOT, $HTTP_HOST
    if (empty($path)) {$path = $DOCUMENT_ROOT;}
    if(!is_dir($path))
    {
        return FALSE;
    }

    $dir = opendir($path);
    echo "<ul>";
    while ($file = readdir($dir))
    {
        if ($file != "." && $file != "..")
        {
            if (is_dir($path . "/" .$file))
            {
```

```
                    echo "<li><b>$file</b></li>";
                    recurse_directory($path . "/" . $file, $base_url,
$path);
            }
            else
            {
                $url = "http://$HTTP_HOST/$path/$file";
                $url = str_replace("$DOCUMENT_ROOT", "", $url);
                echo "<li> <a href = \"$url\">$file</a></li>";

            }
        }
    }
    echo "</ul>";
}
recurse_directory();
?>
```

Appendix H

PHP and MySQL Resources

THIS APPENDIX PRESENTS SOME resources that should be extremely useful in increasing your knowledge of both PHP and MySQL.

PHP Resources

Here are some sights that are great for all things PHP.

PHP site

This site, located at `http://php.net`, along with its many international mirrors, should be your home away from home. From the home page, you can search the manual or one of the many mailing lists. Among the many helpful resources are:

◆ PHP Annotated Manual – (`http://www.php.net/manual/`) The online manual is really terrific; it includes user comments, some of which clarify the use of some of the trickier functions in PHP.

◆ Downloads – (`http://www.php.net/downloads`) Here you can find not only the various distributions, but an HTML manual that you can download and put on your local machine.

◆ Daily snapshots – (`http://snaps.php.net`) PHP is an active open-source project, and features and bug fixes are constantly added to the code base. Prior to official releases, you can get the most up-to-date code here. Source code is updated daily. Note this is best for the true hacker with a box devoted to development. If you have room for only one installation, get the most recent source code. A link to the most recent source is always on the home page of `http://www.php.net/`.

◆ Bug database – (`http://bugs.php.net`) Wondering if there is a problem with a function? Head over to this site to search through the bug reports. This is also a place where you can add bug reports. But be very sure that you've found a bug before submitting a report.

◆ FAQ: (`http://www.php.net/FAQ.php`) Before you post to any mailing list or start writing an application, read the FAQ.

PHP mailing lists

One of the great things about the Web, and about open source projects in particular, is the quality of the advice available on the mailing lists. There are many lists, covering many specific topics. The ones discussed in this section are all part of php.net and use the lists.php.net mail domain. You can subscribe to any of these lists on http://www.php.net/support.php, and they are all archived at http://marc.theaimsgroup.com/. The core developers do monitor the list, and respond to questions and complaints.

If you want to keep up with the goings-on of any of the lists but would rather not stuff up your mail box, you can also get to these mailing lists via a newsgroup reader. Just connect to news.php.net.

◆ PHP General – This is the generic support area. Over the course of a typical day over 100 e-mails are posted to this list. It is amazingly helpful, even if you don't have an interest in posting questions or supplying answers. Your comrades have some interesting techniques and knowledge, which they share daily.

Please practice good etiquette in posting to the mailing lists. First check one of the searchable archives to make sure your question is something resembling unique. And please, read the FAQ

◆ Database List – This one is a natural for most everyone reading this book.

◆ Installation List – If you are having problems getting PHP installed on your box, this is the place to go.

Zend.com

At the core of the PHP is the Zend engine. This engine was built by Zeev Suraski and Andi Gutmans. Their work is now the basis for a company that is offering products that make PHP even more powerful. By the time you are reading this book, it is likely that Zend products will include a cache, which could really increase speed, an optimizer, which could help make badly written code run faster, a compiler, which would make PHP unreadable (this is great if you're planning on distributing code that you would rather not be open source), and an Integrated Development Environment. And who wouldn't want that?

The Zend.com site includes some valuable resources:

◆ Change list (http://zend.com/zend/list_change_4.php) – Keep up on the evolution of PHP 4 here.

◆ Code gallery (http://zend.com/codex.php) – This is one of the better code galleries out there. Browse and see if there are functions that will make your life easier.

◆ Applications (http://zend.com/apps.php) – What? What you have here isn't enough?

◆ Tutorials (http://zend.com/zend/tut/) – Zend has a growing number of very informative tutorials that cover a variety of topics.

PHPBuilder.com

PHPbuilder is without question one of the best resources for PHP developers. Tim Perdue, who runs PHPbuilder, has a built a great base of articles that cover topics that include databases, cascading stylesheets, and other topics of interest to developers who work in the Web environment.

PHPbuilder also has discussion boards, job boards, and a code library. It is really worth checking with frequently.

PHPwizard.com

Earlier in the book, we recommended the phpmyadmin, a PHP tool for Web-based administration of MySQL. There are several other useful tools from Tobias Ratschiller and Till Gerken. Additionally, from their site you can find other great applications, including a Web-based administrative interface to PostGres, a Web-based e-mail client, and an add rotation application. There's a bunch of other good stuff available on their site as well.

 phpmyadmin is included on the CD-ROM that accompanies this book.

PEAR

PEAR stands for the PHP Extension and Application Repository. It is a set of code being written by some very skilled programmers who are trying to come up with a common set of well-written extensions the rest of us can incorporate into our own PHP applications. Stig Bakken, one of the core developers, is heading up the project.

At this point the only place to find PEAR code is the /pear directory of your PHP installation. As of the writing of this book, there were several components in PEAR, most of which were still undergoing quite a bit of work. There is a database abstraction layer, an XML processing class, and some code for directory searching. I suggest you browse the documentation in your own installation, and every now and then look in on the latest goings-on at `snaps.php.net`.

PHPclasses

A Portuguese programmer named Manual Lemos is among the most prolific PHP coders on the planet, and – God bless him – he shares his code at `http://phpclasses.upperdesign.com`. In fact, PHPclasses is now a code repository for anyone who has classes to share with the PHP world. The following are of particular note:

◆ Manual's Form Processing Class. This class provides a uniform method for creating and validating forms. It accounts for about every type of validation imaginable.

◆ Metabase – This is a very complete database abstraction layer.

◆ Mail Class. This class came to our attention too late to include on the CD. Word is, this makes the sending of e-mail with attachments quite a bit easier.

 Both Manual's Form Processing Class and Metabase are included on this book's CD-ROM.

PHP base library

The PHP base library has a fairly large user base – and it's no wonder. It's a very nice set of tools that you can easily add to your PHP system. Many people originally used this library because it was the easiest way to use Sessions in PHP3. Now, I would recommend using PHP's built-in session functions. But even so, there are authorization routines, user administration functions, and a template class that could save you some coding time.

`http://phplib.netuse.de/`

Binarycloud

The folks at Binarycloud are working on creating a common code base to help with rapid development of PHP applications. So far (as of September 2000) there isn't a lot of code to review. But their documentation looks really promising. I'd recommend checking in on `http://www.binarycloud.com` to see what they're up to.

Midgard

The Midgard project is building a content management system with PHP and MySQL. If you need content management, this is definitely worth a look: `http://www.midgard-project.com`. Or you can just work on the application we created in Chapter 12.

Phorum

Phorum.org has an excellent discussion server written in PHP and MySQL. You may want to compare it to the Application in Chapter 11.

Weberdev

Of the many Web development sites that have PHP articles, tutorials and code, Weberdev.com is among the most extensive: `http://www.weberdev.com/`.

Webmonkey

Both Brad and Jay have worked at Webmonkey. Jay is a former producer of the site, and Brad has written several articles. Check out its PHP-related material at `http://hotwired.lycos.com/webmonkey/programming/php/`.

Heyes Computing

Richard Heyes has created some pretty cool scripts. Take a look: `http://www.heyes-computing.net/scripts/index.html`.

MySQL Resources

There's no shortage of resources here either. I've mentioned mainly Web-based resources in this appendix; however, there is one hard-copy MySQL resource that I must mention. If this book hasn't covered enough of MySQL for your needs, get Paul Dubois' *MySQL* (New Riders, ISBN: 0-7357-0921-1). It is an excellent book.

MySQL.com

Predictably, this is probably the best place to find answers to any questions you might have about MySQL. Some specific portions of the site are worth particular note:

◆ Downloads (`http://www.mysql.com/downloads/`) – This is the place to find the latest version of MySQL in all the popular formats, including rpms, source code, and Windows binaries.

◆ Contributions (http://www.mysql.com/downloads/contrib.html) —
A lot of developers have put together tools that you might be able to
use when working with MySQL. Of these, the GUI clients are particularly
interesting.

◆ Documentation (http://www.mysql.com/documentation/) — The online
manual for MySQL is pretty good, and covers many things that this book
did not. Chapter 7, the language reference, should be bookmarked on
your browser.

 Both PHP and MySQL have downloadable HTML manuals. I keep them on
my local machine so I don't have to connect to the Web every time I have
a question.

Mailing lists

The MySQL mailing list is monitored by many of the core developers. If you have a
concern about the product and post it on the mailing list, someone who is working
on the product itself will surely see it. In addition, they're really a very nice bunch
of guys. Information about subscribing to any of the mailing lists can be found
here: http://www.mysql.com/documentation/lists.html. A searchable archive
of the mailing lists can be found here: http://lists.mysql.com.

General Client-Side Resources

Here are a few of the sites we the authors find ourselves returning to frequently.

Character entity reference

About the most comprehensive list we know of is found here: http://www.
hclrss.demon.co.uk/demos/ent4_frame.html.

Netscape's tag reference

If you are still dealing with the mess that is Netscape 4, this tag reference should be
of some assistance: http://developer.netscape.com/docs/manuals/htmlguid/
contents.htm.

CSS reference

CSS is very cool, but still kind of a pain to work with. This chart, compiled by Eric Meyer, is the most complete one of its kind: `http://webreview.com/wr/pub/guides/style/mastergrid.html`.

Apache References

Apache will likely be your Web server, and when you are new to it, it can be tricky.

Apache.org

This is the home site for the Apache Software Foundation, which now includes many interesting projects. In particular, there are some very cool things happening in the XML space. Apache can be opaque when you first come to it, but when you grow accustomed to using their documentation, you will see that it really isn't very difficult to work with.

Apachetoday.org

Quite a few of the Apache developers contribute text to this site. Definitely worth a look.

Appendix 1

MySQL Function Reference

MySQL HAS MANY FUNCTIONS, and only a portion of these was used in the course of the applications in this book. You should have a good idea of what MySQL functions are available, as you may find they come in handy at times.

String Comparison Functions

This set of functions should not be confused with PHP's string handling functions. Normally, if any expression in a string comparison is case-sensitive, the comparison is performed in a case-sensitive way.

LIKE

This function conducts a pattern match using basic SQL wildcard characters.

```
expr LIKE pat [ESCAPE 'escape-char']
RETURNS: int
```

With LIKE you can use the following two wildcard characters in the pattern: %, which matches any number of characters, even zero characters; and _, which matches exactly one character. To test for literal instances of a wildcard character, precede the character with the escape character. If you don't specify the ESCAPE character, \ is assumed. This function returns 1 (true) if the pattern is found or 0 (false) if not.

```
mysql> select 'jay greenspan' like 'jay%';
+-----------------------------+
| 'jay greenspan' like 'jay%' |
+-----------------------------+
|                           1 |
+-----------------------------+
1 row in set (0.00 sec)
```

REGEXP

This function performs a pattern match of a string expression (expr) against a regular expression (pat). See Appendix C for a discussion of regular expressions. But be aware that MySQL does not support regular expressions to the extent you will find in PHP.

```
expr REGEXP pat
```

or

```
expr RLIKE pat
RETURNS: int
```

REGEXP returns 1 (true) if the pattern is found or 0 (false) if not.

```
mysql> select name from guestbook where name regexp '^j.*g';
+---------------+
| name          |
+---------------+
| Jay Greenspan |
| Jay Green     |
+---------------+
2 rows in set (0.00 sec)

mysql>
```

STRCMP

```
STRCMP(expr1,expr2) (used in examples)
RETURNS: int
```

Returns 0 if the strings are the same, -1 if the first argument is smaller than the second, and 1 if the second argument is smaller than the first.

```
mysql> select strcmp('foo', 'bar');
+----------------------+
| strcmp('foo', 'bar') |
+----------------------+
|                    1 |
+----------------------+
1 row in set (0.11 sec)

mysql> select strcmp('bar', 'bar');
+----------------------+
```

```
| strcmp('bar', 'bar') |
+----------------------+
|                    0 |
+----------------------+
1 row in set (0.00 sec)

mysql> select strcmp('bar', 'foo');
+----------------------+
| strcmp('bar', 'foo') |
+----------------------+
|                   -1 |
+----------------------+
1 row in set (0.00 sec)

mysql>
```

Cast Operators

There is only one cast operator you will encounter in MySQL.

Binary

```
BINARY
RETURNS: 1
```

The BINARY operator casts the string following it to a binary string. This is an easy way to force a column comparison to be case-sensitive even if the column isn't defined as BINARY or BLOB. BINARY was introduced in MySQL 3.23.0.

```
mysql> select binary('Foo') = 'foo', binary('Foo') = 'Foo';
+----------------------+----------------------+
| binary('Foo') = 'foo' | binary('Foo') = 'Foo' |
+----------------------+----------------------+
|                    0 |                    1 |
+----------------------+----------------------+
1 row in set (0.06 sec)
```

Control Flow Functions

There are two functions that allow for varying results depending on conditions.

IFNULL

```
IFNULL(expr1,expr2) (used in examples)
RETURNS: type of expr1
```

If expr1 is not NULL, IFNULL() returns expr1; otherwise, it returns expr2. IFNULL() returns a numeric or string value depending on the context in which it is used.

```
mysql> select ifnull(1/0, 'exp 1 is null');
+----------------------------+
| ifnull(1/0, 'exp 1 is null') |
+----------------------------+
|                exp 1 is null |
+----------------------------+
1 row in set (0.00 sec)

mysql> select ifnull(1/1, 'exp 1 is not null');
+--------------------------------+
| ifnull(1/1, 'exp 1 is not null') |
+--------------------------------+
|                           1.00 |
+--------------------------------+
1 row in set (0.00 sec)
```

IF

```
IF(expr1,expr2,expr3) (used in examples)
```

If expr1 is TRUE (expr1 <> 0 and expr1 <> NULL) then IF() returns expr2; otherwise, it returns expr3. IF() returns a numeric or string value depending on the context in which it is used. expr1 is evaluated as an integer value, which means that if you are testing floating-point or string values, you should do so using a comparison operation.

```
mysql> select if(name like 'jay%', 'Yes', 'No') as 'Jay Names'
    -> from guestbook;
+-----------+
| Jay Names |
+-----------+
| Yes       |
| Yes       |
| No        |
| Yes       |
| No        |
| No        |
```

```
| No        |
+-----------+
10 rows in set (0.00 sec)
```

Mathematical Functions

All mathematical functions return NULL in case of an error.

ABS

This function returns the absolute value of X.

```
ABS(X)
RETURNS: type of X
```

SIGN

This function returns the sign of the argument as -1, 0, or 1, depending on whether X is negative, 0, or positive.

```
SIGN(X)
RETURNS: int
mysql> select sign(10), sign(-10), sign(0);
+----------+-----------+---------+
| sign(10) | sign(-10) | sign(0) |
+----------+-----------+---------+
|        1 |        -1 |       0 |
+----------+-----------+---------+
1 row in set (0.00 sec)
```

MOD

Modulo is like the % operator in C). It returns the remainder of N divided by M.

```
MOD(N,M) or N % M
RETURNS: int
mysql> select mod(10,3), mod(10,4);
+-----------+-----------+
| mod(10,3) | mod(10,4) |
+-----------+-----------+
|         1 |         2 |
+-----------+-----------+
1 row in set (0.05 sec)
```

FLOOR

This function returns the largest integer value not greater than X.

```
FLOOR(X) RETURNS: int
mysql> select floor(8.5);
+------------+
| floor(8.5) |
+------------+
|          8 |
+------------+
1 row in set (0.00 sec)
```

CEILING

This function returns the smallest integer value not less than X.

```
FUNCTION: CEILING(X)
RETURNS: int
mysql> select ceiling(8.5);
+--------------+
| ceiling(8.5) |
+--------------+
|            9 |
+--------------+
1 row in set (0.00 sec)
```

Round

This function returns the argument X, rounded to an integer.

```
Round ROUND(X [,D])

RETURNS: mixed
```

Returns the argument X, rounded to a number with D decimals. If D is 0, or does not exist, the result will have no decimal point or fractional part.

```
mysql> select round(8.53), round(8.47), round(8.534,2);
+-------------+-------------+----------------+
| round(8.53) | round(8.47) | round(8.534,2) |
+-------------+-------------+----------------+
|           9 |           8 |           8.53 |
+-------------+-------------+----------------+
1 row in set (0.33 sec)
```

TRUNCATE

TRUNCATE returns the number X, truncated to D decimals. If D is 0, the result will have no decimal point or fractional part.

```
TRUNCATE(X,D)
RETURNS: decimal
```

Example:

```
mysql> select truncate(8.53,0), truncate(8.43,0), truncate(8.534,2);
+------------------+------------------+------------------+
| truncate(8.53,0) | truncate(8.43,0) | truncate(8.534,2) |
+------------------+------------------+------------------+
|                8 |                8 |             8.53 |
+------------------+------------------+------------------+
1 row in set (0.05 sec)
```

EXP

This function returns the value of e (the base of natural logarithms) raised to the power of X.

```
EXP(X)
RETURNS: float
```

LOG

This function returns the natural logarithm of X. If you want the log of a number X to some arbitrary base B, use the formula LOG(X)/LOG(B).

```
LOG(X)
RETURNS: float
```

LOG10

LOG10 returns the base-10 logarithm of X.

```
LOG10(X)
RETURNS: float
```

POW(X,Y) or POWER(X,Y)

This function returns the value of X raised to the power of Y.

```
RETURNS: float
```

SQRT

This returns the non-negative square root of X.

```
SQRT(X)
RETURNS: float
```

PI

This returns an approximation of Pi.

```
Pi()
RETURNS: float
```

COS

COS returns the cosine of X, where X is given in radians.

```
COS(X)
RETURNS: float
```

SIN

SIN returns the sine of X, where X is given in radians.

```
SIN(X)
RETURNS: float
```

TAN

This returns the tangent of X, where X is given in radians.

```
TAN(X)
RETURNS: float
```

ACOS

This function returns the arc cosine of X — that is, the value whose cosine is X. It returns NULL if X is not in the range -1 to 1.

```
ACOS(X)
float
```

ASIN

This returns the arc sine of X – that is, the value whose sine is X. Returns NULL if X is not in the range -1 to 1.

```
ASIN(X)
RETURNS: float
```

ATAN

ATAN returns the arc tangent of X – that is, the value whose tangent is X.

```
ATAN(X)
RETURNS: float
```

ATAN2

ATAN2 returns the arc tangent of the two variables X and Y. The process is similar to calculating the arc tangent of Y/X, except that the signs of both arguments are used to determine the quadrant of the result.

```
ATAN2(X,Y)
RETURNS: float
```

COT

This function returns the cotangent of X.

```
COT(X)
RETURNS: float
```

RAND

This function returns a random floating-point value in the range 0 to 1.0.

```
RAND()
```

or

```
RAND(N)
RETURNS: float
```

If an integer argument N is specified, it is used as the seed value. You cant use a column with RAND() values in an 'order by clause because order by would evaluate the column multiple times. In MySQL 3.23, you can, however, do: select * from table_name order by rand(). This is useful to get a random sample. Note that a RAND() in a WHERE clause will be re-evaluated every time the WHERE is executed.

LEAST

With two or more arguments, this function returns the smallest (minimum-valued) argument.

```
LEAST(X,Y,...)
RETURNS: type of X
mysql> select least(2,7,9,1);
+----------------+
| least(2,7,9,1) |
+----------------+
|              1 |
+----------------+
1 row in set (0.00 sec)
```

GREATEST

GREATEST returns the largest (maximum-valued) argument. In MySQL versions prior to 3.22.5, you can use MAX() instead of GREATEST.

```
GREATEST(X,Y,...)
RETURNS: type of X
mysql> select greatest(2,7,9,1);
+-------------------+
| greatest(2,7,9,1) |
+-------------------+
|                 9 |
+-------------------+
1 row in set (0.00 sec)
```

DEGREES

This returns the argument X, converted from radians to degrees.

```
DEGREES(X)
RETURNS: float
```

RADIANS

This returns the argument X, converted from degrees to radians.

```
RADIANS(X)
RETURNS: float
```

String Functions

MySQL's string functions return NULL if the length of the result would be greater than the max_allowed_packet server parameter. This parameter can be set by starting MySQL with a command like this:

```
safe_mysqld -O max_allowed_packet=16M
```

For functions that operate on string positions, the first position is numbered 1.

ASCII

Returns the ASCII code value of the leftmost character of the string str. Returns 0 if str is the empty string. Returns NULL if str is NULL.

```
ASCII(str)
RETURNS: int
mysql> select ascii('\n');
+-------------+
| ascii('\n') |
+-------------+
|          10 |
+-------------+
1 row in set (0.00 sec)
```

ORD

If the leftmost character of the string str is a multi-byte character, this function returns the code of multi-byte character by returning the ASCII code value of the character in the format of: ((first byte ASCII code)*256+(second byte ASCII code))[*256+third byte ASCII code...]. If the leftmost character is not a multi-byte character, ORD returns the same value as the similar ASCII() function.

```
ORD(str)
RETURNS: int
```

CONV

This function converts numbers between different number bases.

```
CONV(N,from_base,to_base)
RETURNS: string
```

It returns a string representation of the number N, converted from base from_base to base to_base. It returns NULL if any argument is NULL. The argument N is interpreted as an integer, but may be specified as an integer or a string. The minimum base is 2 and the maximum base is 36. If to_base is a negative number, N is regarded as a signed number. Otherwise, N is treated as unsigned. CONV works with 64-bit precision.

```
mysql> select conv(3,10,2);
+--------------+
| conv(3,10,2) |
+--------------+
| 11           |
+--------------+
```

BIN

This function returns a string representation of the binary value of N, where N is a long (BIGINT) number. It is equivalent to CONV(N,10,2). Returns NULL if N is NULL.

```
BIN(N)
RETURNS: string
```

OCT

This function returns a string representation of the octal value of N, where N is a long (BIGINT) number. It is equivalent to CONV(N,10,8). It returns NULL if N is NULL.

```
OCT(N)
RETURNS: string
```

HEX

This function returns a string representation of the hexadecimal value of N, where N is a long (BIGINT) number. This is equivalent to CONV(N,10,16). Returns NULL if N is NULL.

```
HEX(N)
RETURNS: string
```

CHAR

This function interprets the arguments as integers and returns a string consisting of the ASCII code values of those integers. NULL values are skipped.

```
CHAR(N,...)
RETURNS: string
```

CONCAT

This function returns the string that results from the concatenation of the arguments. It returns NULL if any argument is NULL. CONCAT may have more than two arguments. A numeric argument is converted to the equivalent string form.

```
CONCAT(str1,str2,...) (used in examples)
RETURNS: string
```

This function is used in the following example to prepend a wildcard character onto the column in the where clause of a query.

```
select 1 from blocked_domains
    where '$REMOTE_HOST' like concat('%',domain)
    and release_dt is null
```

LENGTH

This function returns the length of the string str. Note that for CHAR_LENGTH(), multi-byte characters are only counted once.

```
LENGTH(str)
```

or

```
CHAR_LENGTH(str)
RETURNS: int
mysql> select length('mysql functions');
+-------------------------+
| length('mysql functions') |
+-------------------------+
|                      15 |
+-------------------------+
1 row in set (0.00 sec)
```

LOCATE

This function returns the position of the first occurrence of substring substr in string str. Returns 0 if substr is not in str. The optional third argument allows you to specify a starting position for the search.

```
LOCATE(substr,str [,pos])
```

or

```
POSITION(substr IN str)
RETURNS: int
```

The optional third argument specifies an offset to start the search.

```
mysql> select locate('s', 'mysql funcitons') as example1,
    -> locate('s', 'mysql funcitons',4) as example2;
+----------+----------+
| example1 | example2 |
+----------+----------+
|        3 |       15 |
+----------+----------+
1 row in set (0.00 sec)
```

INSTR

This function returns the position of the first occurrence of substring `substr` in string `str`. It is the same as `LOCATE()`, except that the arguments are swapped and no argument that indicates position is allowed.

```
INSTR(str,substr)
RETURNS: int
```

LPAD

This function returns the string `str`, left-padded with the string `padstr` until `str` is `len` characters long.

```
LPAD(str,len,padstr)
RETURNS: string
mysql> select lpad('foo', 15, 'k');
+----------------------+
| lpad('foo', 15, 'k') |
+----------------------+
| kkkkkkkkkkkkfoo      |
+----------------------+
1 row in set (0.00 sec)
```

RPAD

This function returns the string `str`, right-padded with the string `padstr` until `str` is `len` characters long.

```
RPAD(str,len,padstr)
RETURNS: string
```

LEFT

This function returns the leftmost `len` characters from the string `str`.

```
LEFT(str,len)
RETURNS: string
```

RIGHT

This function returns the rightmost `len` characters from the string `str`.

```
RIGHT(str,len)
RETURNS: string
```

SUBSTRING

This function returns a substring `len` characters long from string `str`, starting at position `pos`, and continuining for len number of characters. The variant form that uses `FROM` is ANSI SQL92 syntax.

```
SUBSTRING(str,pos[,len])
```

or

```
SUBSTRING(str FROM pos FOR len)
```

or

```
MID(str,pos,len) (used in examples)
RETURNS: string
mysql> select mid('mysqlfunctions',6,8);
+--------------------------+
| mid('mysqlfunctions',6,8) |
+--------------------------+
| function                 |
+--------------------------+
1 row in set (0.00 sec)
```

SUBSTRING_INDEX

This function returns the substring from string `str` after `count` occurrences of the delimiter `delim`. If `count` is positive, everything to the left of the final delimiter (counting from the left) is returned. If count is negative, everything to the right of the final delimiter (counting from the right) is returned.

```
SUBSTRING_INDEX(str,delim,count) (used in examples)
RETURNS: string
mysql> select substring_index('mysqlfunctionsmysql', 'fu', 1);
+----------------------------------------------+
| substring_index('mysqlfunctions', 'fu', 1) |
+----------------------------------------------+
| mysql                                        |
+----------------------------------------------+
1 row in set (0.00 sec)

mysql> select substring_index('mysqlfunctionsmysql', 'fu', -1);
+-----------------------------------------------------+
| substring_index('mysqlfunctionsmysql', 'fu', -1) |
+-----------------------------------------------------+
| nctionsmysql                                        |
+-----------------------------------------------------+
1 row in set (0.00 sec)
```

LTRIM

```
LTRIM(str)
RETURNS: string
```

RTRIM

This function returns the string str with trailing space characters removed.

```
RTRIM(str)
RETURNS: string
```

TRIM

This function returns the string str with all remstr prefixes and/or suffixes removed. If none of the specifiers BOTH, LEADING, or TRAILING are given, BOTH is assumed. If remstr is not specified, spaces are removed.

```
TRIM([[BOTH | LEADING | TRAILING] [remstr] FROM] str) (used in
examples)
RETURNS: string

mysql> select trim(both '\n' from '\n mystring');
+----------------------------------+
```

```
| trim(both '\n' from '\n mystring') |
+-----------------------------------+
|  mystring                         |
+-----------------------------------+
1 row in set (0.00 sec)
```

Note that remstr will exact match only the exact sequence of characters. So putting '\t\n\ in the remstr will remove only occurrences where tabs and newlines appear consecutively.

REPLACE

This function returns the string str with all occurrences of the string from_str replaced by the string to_str.

```
REPLACE(str,from_str,to_str)
RETURNS: string
```

SOUNDEX

This function returns a soundex string from str.

```
SOUNDEX(str)
RETURNS: string
```

Two strings that sound "about the same" should have identical soundex strings. A "standard" soundex string is four characters long, but the SOUNDEX() function returns an arbitrarily long string. You can use SUBSTRING() on the result to get a "standard" soundex string. All non-alphanumeric characters are ignored in the given string. All international alpha characters outside the A-Z range are treated as vowels.

SPACE

This function returns a string consisting of N space characters.

```
SPACE(N)
RETURNS: string
```

REPEAT

This function returns a string consisting of the string str repeated count times. If count <= 0, it returns an empty string. It returns NULL if str or count are NULL.

```
REPEAT(str,count)
RETURNS: string
```

REVERSE

This function returns the string `str` with the order of the characters reversed.

```
REVERSE(str)
RETURNS: string
```

INSERT

This function returns the string `str`, with the substring beginning at position `pos` and `len` characters long replaced by the string `newstr`.

```
INSERT(str,pos,len,newstr)
RETURNS: string
mysql> select insert('mysqlfunctions', 6,2,'FU');
+----------------------------------+
| insert('mysqlfunctions', 6,2,'FU') |
+----------------------------------+
| mysqlFUnctions                   |
+----------------------------------+
1 row in set (0.44 sec)
```

ELT

This function returns `str1` if `N` = 1, `str2` if `N` = 2, and so on. It returns `NULL` if `N` is less than 1 or greater than the number of arguments. `ELT()` is the complement of `FIELD()`.

```
ELT(N,str1,str2,str3,...)
RETURNS: string
mysql> select elt(2, 'foo', 'bar', 'foobar');
+------------------------------+
| elt(2, 'foo', 'bar', 'foobar') |
+------------------------------+
| bar                          |
+------------------------------+
1 row in set (0.00 sec)
```

FIELD

This function returns the index of `str` in the `str1`, `str2`, `str3`, ... list. It returns 0 if `str` is not found. `FIELD()` is the complement of `ELT()`.

```
FIELD(str,str1,str2,str3,...)
RETURNS: int
mysql> select field('foobar', 'foo', 'bar', 'foobar');
```

```
+-------------------------------------+
| field('foobar', 'foo', 'bar', 'foobar') |
+-------------------------------------+
|                                   3 |
+-------------------------------------+
1 row in set (0.01 sec)
```

LCASE

This function returns the string str with all characters changed to lowercase according to the current character set mapping (the default is ISO-8859-1 Latin1).

```
LCASE(str) or LOWER(str) (used in examples)
RETURNS: string
```

UCASE

This function returns the string str with all characters changed to uppercase according to the current character set mapping (the default is ISO-8859-1 Latin1).

```
UCASE(str) or UPPER(str)
RETURNS: string
```

LOAD_FILE

This function reads the file and returns the file contents as a string. The file must be on the server, and you must specify the full pathname to the file. The file must be readable by all and smaller than max_allowed_packet. If the file doesn't exist or can't be read, the function returns NULL.

```
LOAD_FILE(file_name)
RETURNS: string
```

Date and Time Functions

MySQL offers many functions for calculating dates. Of all of the MySQL functions available, these are the ones you will probably use most frequently.

The DATE_FORMAT function will allow you to format dates to take the form of MySQL timestamps. In addition, there are several functions that will easily allow you to get specific date information from a column. For example, to find the day of the week of all of the entires in a timestamp column, you could use the following.

```
mysql> select dayname(created) from guestbook;
+------------------+
```

```
| dayname(created) |
+------------------+
| Sunday           |
| Sunday           |
| Wednesday        |
| Sunday           |
| Sunday           |
| Wednesday        |
| Wednesday        |
| Wednesday        |
```

DAYOFWEEK

This function returns the weekday index for date (1 = Sunday, 2 = Monday, ... 7 = Saturday). These index values correspond to the ODBC standard.

```
DAYOFWEEK(date) (used in examples)
RETURNS: int
mysql> select dayofweek('2001-01-01');
+-------------------------+
| dayofweek('2001-01-01') |
+-------------------------+
|                       2 |
+-------------------------+
1 row in set (0.33 sec)
```

WEEKDAY

This function returns the weekday index for date (0 = Monday, 1 = Tuesday, ... 6 = Sunday).

```
WEEKDAY(date) (used in examples)
RETURNS: int
```

DAYOFMONTH

This function returns the day of the month for date, in the range 1 to 31.

```
DAYOFMONTH(date)
RETURNS: int
```

DAYOFYEAR

This function returns the day of the year for date, in the range 1 to 366.

```
DAYOFYEAR(date)
RETURNS: int
mysql> select dayofmonth('02-01-2000');
+-------------------------+
| dayofmonth('02-01-2000') |
+-------------------------+
|                      20 |
+-------------------------+
1 row in set (0.00 sec)
```

MONTH

This function returns the month for date, in the range 1 to 12.

```
MONTH(date)
RETURNS: int
```

DAYNAME

This function returns the full name of the weekday for date.

```
DAYNAME(date)
RETURNS: string
mysql> select dayname('10/01/2000');
+----------------------+
| dayname('10/01/2000') |
+----------------------+
| Wednesday            |
+----------------------+
1 row in set (0.00 sec)
```

MONTHNAME

This function returns the full name of the month for date.

```
MONTHNAME(date)
RETURNS: string
```

QUARTER

This function returns the quarter of the year for date, in the range 1 to 4.

```
QUARTER(date)
RETURNS: int
```

To find all of the people who signed your guestbook in the second quarter of the year, you could use this:

```
select name from guestbook where quarter(created) = 2;
```

WEEK

With a single argument, this function returns the week for date, in the range 0 to 53.

```
WEEK(date [, first])
RETURNS: int
```

The optional second argument allows you to specify whether the week starts on Sunday or Monday. The week starts on Sunday if the second argument is 0 and on Monday if the second argument is 1.

YEAR

This function returns the year for date, in the range 1000 to 9999.

```
YEAR(date) (used in examples)
RETURNS: int
```

YEARWEEK

This function returns year and week for a date, in the format YYYYWW. The second argument works exactly like the second argument in WEEK().

```
YEARWEEK(date [,first])
RETURNS: int
```

HOUR

This function returns the hour for time, in the range 0 to 23.

```
HOUR(time)
RETURNS: int
```

MINUTE

This function returns the minute for time, in the range 0 to 59.

```
MINUTE(time)
RETURNS: int
```

SECOND

This function returns the second for `time`, in the range 0 to 59.

```
SECOND(time)
RETURNS: int
```

PERIOD_ADD

This function adds `N` months to period `P` (in the format YYMM or YYYYMM) and returns a value in the format YYYYMM.

```
PERIOD_ADD(P,N)
RETURNS: int
```

Note that the period argument `P` is *not* a date value.

```
mysql> select period_add('200006',7);
+------------------------+
| period_add('200006',7) |
+------------------------+
|                 200101 |
+------------------------+
1 row in set (0.00 sec)
```

PERIOD_DIFF

This function returns the number of months between periods `P1` and `P2`. `P1` and `P2` should be in the format YYMM or YYYYMM.

```
PERIOD_DIFF(P1,P2)
RETURNS: int
```

Note that the period arguments `P1` and `P2` are *not* date values.

```
mysql> select period_diff('200106','200001');
+--------------------------------+
| period_diff('200106','200001') |
+--------------------------------+
|                             17 |
+--------------------------------+
1 row in set (0.00 sec)
```

DATE_ADD

These functions perform date arithmetic. They are new for MySQL 3.22.

```
DATE_ADD(date,INTERVAL expr type)
```

or

```
DATE_SUB(date,INTERVAL expr type)
```

or

```
ADDDATE(date,INTERVAL expr type)
```

or

```
SUBDATE(date,INTERVAL) (used in examples)
RETURNS: date
```

ADDDATE() and SUBDATE() are identical to DATE_ADD() and DATE_SUB(). In MySQL 3.23, you can use + and - instead of DATE_ADD() and DATE_SUB(). (See example.) date is a DATETIME or DATE value specifying the starting date. expr is an expression specifying the interval value to be added or substracted from the starting date. expr is a string; it may start with a - for negative intervals. type is a keyword indicating how the expression should be interpreted.

Table I-1 shows how the type and expr arguments are related.

TABLE I-1 DATE_ADD () OPERATORS

type	Meaning	Expected expr format value
SECOND	Seconds	SECONDS
MINUTE	Minutes	MINUTES
MINUTE_SECOND	Minutes and seconds	"MINUTES:SECONDS"
HOUR	Hours	HOURS
HOUR_SECOND	Hours, minutes, seconds	"HOURS:MINUTES:SECONDS"
HOUR_MINUTE	Hours and minutes	"HOURS:MINUTES"
DAY	Days	DAYS
DAY_SECOND	Days, hours, minutes, seconds	"DAYSHOURS:MINUTES:SECONDS"

type	Meaning	Expected expr format value
DAY_MINUTE	Days, hours, minutes	"DAYS HOURS:MINUTES"
DAY_HOUR	Days and hours	"DAYS HOURS"
MONTH	Months	MONTHS
YEAR	Years	YEARS
YEAR_MONTH	Years and months	"YEARS-MONTHS"

MySQL allows any punctuation delimiter in the expr format. The ones shown in the table are the suggested delimiters. If the date argument is a DATE value and your calculations involve only YEAR, MONTH, and DAY parts (that is, no time parts), the result is a DATE value. Otherwise, the result is a DATETIME value.

```
mysql> select '2001-01-01 13:00:00' + interval 10 m
+-------------------------------------------+
| '2001-01-01 13:00:00' + interval 10 minute |
+-------------------------------------------+
| 2001-01-01 13:10:00                       |
+-------------------------------------------+
1 row in set (0.39 sec)
mysql> select '2000-01-01 00:00:00' - interval 1 second;
+-----------------------------------------+
| '2000-01-01 00:00:00' - interval 1 second |
+-----------------------------------------+
| 1999-12-31 23:59:59                     |
+-----------------------------------------+
1 row in set (0.00 sec)
mysql> select date_add('2000-01-01 00:00:00', interval '1:1:1' hour_second);
+-------------------------------------------------------------+
| date_add('2000-01-01 00:00:00', interval '1:1:1' hour_second) |
+-------------------------------------------------------------+
| 2000-01-01 01:01:01                                         |
+-------------------------------------------------------------+
1 row in set (0.00 sec)
mysql> select date_sub('2000-01-01 00:00:00', interval '1' month);
+-----------------------------------------------+
| date_sub('2000-01-01 00:00:00', interval '1' month) |
+-----------------------------------------------+
```

```
| 1999-12-01 00:00:00                                    |
+--------------------------------------------------------+
1 row in set (0.00 sec)
```

If you specify an interval value that is too short (does not include all the interval parts that would be expected from the `type` keyword), MySQL assumes you have left out the leftmost parts of the interval value. For example, if you specify a `type` of `DAY_SECOND`, the value of `expr` is expected to have days, hours, minutes, and seconds parts. If you specify a value like `1:10`, MySQL assumes that the days and hours parts are missing and that the value represents minutes and seconds.

TO_DAYS

Given a date `date`, this function returns a daynumber (the number of days since year 0).

```
TO_DAYS(date) (used in examples)
RETURNS: int
```

`TO_DAYS()` is not intended for use with values that precede the advent of the Gregorian calendar (1582). Note that this is not the same as the PHP `mktime()` function, which gets the date as of January 1, 1970. See the MySQL UNIX_TIMESTAMP function if you need that information.

FROM_DAYS

Given a daynumber `N`, this function returns a `DATE` value.

```
FROM_DAYS(N) (used in examples)
RETURNS: date
```

`FROM_DAYS()` is not intended for use with values that precede the advent of the Gregorian calendar (1582).

DATE_FORMAT

This function formats the `date` value according to the `format` string.

```
DATE_FORMAT(date,format) (used in examples)
RETURNS: string
```

The specifiers in Table I-2 may be used in the `format` string.

Table 1-2 DATE_FORMAT SPECIFIERS

Specifier	Meaning
%M	Month name (January through December)
%W	Weekday name (Sunday through Saturday)
%D	Day of the month with English suffix (1st, 2nd, 3rd, etc.)
%Y	Year, numeric, four digits
%y	Year, numeric, two digits
%a	Abbreviated weekday name (Sun..Sat)
%d	Day of the month, numeric (00..31)
%e	Day of the month, numeric (0..31)
%m	Month, numeric (01..12)
%c	Month, numeric (1..12)
%b	Abbreviated month name (Jan..Dec)
%j	Day of year (001..366)
%H	Hour (00..23)
%k	Hour (0..23)
%h	Hour (01..12)
%I	Hour (01..12)
%l	Hour (1..12)
%i	Minutes, numeric (00..59)
%r	Time, 12-hour (hh:mm:ss [AP]M)
%T	Time, 24-hour (hh:mm:ss)
%S	Seconds (00..59)
%s	Seconds (00..59)
%p	AM or PM
%w	Day of the week (0=Sunday..6=Saturday)
%U	Week (0..53), where Sunday is the first day of the week
%u	Week (0..53), where Monday is the first day of the week

Continued

TABLE I-2 DATE_FORMAT SPECIFIERS *(Continued)*

Specifier	Meaning
%V	Week (1..53), where Sunday is the first day of the week; used with %X
%v	Week (1..53), where Monday is the first day of the week; used with %x
%X	Year for the week, where Sunday is the first day of the week, numeric, four digits, used with %V
%x	Year for the week, where Monday is the first day of the week, numeric, four digits, used with %v
%%	A literal %

All other characters are just copied to the result without interpretation.

```
mysql> select date_format('2001-01-01', '%W %M %d, %Y');
+-----------------------------------------+
| date_format('2001-01-01', '%W %M %d, %Y') |
+-----------------------------------------+
| Monday January 01, 2001                 |
+-----------------------------------------+
1 row in set (0.00 sec)

mysql> select date_format('2001-01-01 15:30:20',
    ->'%W %M %d, %Y %I:%i:%S %p');
+-----------------------------------------------------------+
| date_format('2001-01-01 15:30:20', '%W %M %d, %Y %I:%i:%S %p') |
+-----------------------------------------------------------+
| Monday January 01, 2001 03:30:20 PM                       |
+-----------------------------------------------------------+
1 row in set (0.00 sec)
```

As of MySQL 3.23, the % character is required before format specifier characters. In earlier versions of MySQL, % was optional.

TIME_FORMAT

This function is used like the DATE_FORMAT() function above, but the format string may contain only those format specifiers that handle hours, minutes, and seconds. If specifiers other than hours, minutes, and seconds are included, the function will return a NULL value.

```
TIME_FORMAT(time,format) (used in examples)
RETURNS: string
```

CURDATE

This function returns today's date as a value in YYYY-MM-DD or YYYYMMDD format, depending on whether the function is used in a string or numeric context.

```
CURDATE() or CURRENT_DATE (used in examples)
RETURNS: mixed
```

CURTIME

This function returns the current time as a value in HH:MM:SS or HHMMSS format, depending on whether the function is used in a string or numeric context.

```
CURTIME() or CURRENT_TIME
RETURNS: mixed
```

NOW

This function returns the current date and time as a value in YYYY-MM-DD HH:MM:SS or YYYYMMDDHHMMSS format, depending on whether the function is used in a string or numeric context.

```
NOW()
```

or

```
SYSDATE()
```

or

```
CURRENT_TIMESTAMP (used in examples)
RETURNS: string
```

UNIX_TIMESTAMP

If this function is called with no argument, it returns a Unix timestamp (seconds since 1970-01-01 00:00:00 GMT). If UNIX_TIMESTAMP() is called with a date argument, it returns the value of the argument as seconds since 1970-01-01 00:00:00 GMT. date may be a DATE string, a DATETIME string, a TIMESTAMP, or a number in the format YYMMDD or YYYYMMDD in local time.

```
UNIX_TIMESTAMP([date])
RETURNS: int
```

FROM_UNIXTIME

This function returns a representation of the unix_timestamp argument as a value in YYYY-MM-DD HH:MM:SS or YYYYMMDDHHMMSS format, depending on whether the function is used in a string or numeric context.

```
FROM_UNIXTIME(unix_timestamp) (used in examples)
RETURNS: string
```

From_Unixtime

This function returns a string representation of the Unix timestamp, formatted according to the format string. format may contain the same specifiers as those listed in the entry for the DATE_FORMAT() function.

```
FROM_UNIXTIME(unix_timestamp,format) (used in examples)
RETURNS: string
```

SEC_TO_TIME

```
SEC_TO_TIME(seconds)
RETURNS: string
```

Returns the seconds argument, converted to hours, minutes and seconds, as a value in HH:MM:SS or HHMMSS format, depending on whether the function is used in a string or numeric context.

TIME_TO_SEC

```
TIME_TO_SEC(time) (used in examples)
RETURNS: int
```

This function returns the time argument, converted to seconds.

Miscellaneous Functions

Here are a few other functions that don't fit under any of the previous categories.

Database

This function returns the current database name. If there is no current database, DATABASE() returns the empty string.

```
DATABASE()
RETURNS: string
```

User

This function returns the current MySQL username. In MySQL 3.22.11 or later, this includes the client hostname as well as the username.

```
USER()
or
SYSTEM_USER()
or
SESSION_USER() (used in examples)
RETURNS: string
```

VERSION

This function returns a string indicating the MySQL server version.

```
VERSION()
RETURNS: string
```

PASSWORD

This function calculates a password string from the plaintext password str.

```
PASSWORD(str) (used in examples)
RETURNS: string
```

   This is the function that encrypts MySQL passwords for storage in the Password column of the user grant table. PASSWORD() encryption is one-way. PASSWORD() does not perform password encryption in the same way that Unix passwords are encrypted. You should not assume that if your Unix password and your MySQL password are the same, PASSWORD() will result in the same encrypted value as is stored in the Unix password file. See ENCRYPT().

ENCRYPT

This function encrypts str using the Unix crypt() system call.

```
ENCRYPT(str[,salt])
RETURNS: string
```

   The salt argument should be a string with two characters. (As of MySQL 3.22.16, salt may be longer than two characters.) If crypt() is not available on your system, ENCRYPT() always returns NULL. ENCRYPT() ignores all but the first eight characters of str on most systems.

ENCODE

This function encrypts str using pass_str as the password.

```
ENCODE(str,pass_str)
RETURNS: binary string
```

To decrypt the result, use DECODE( ). The result is a binary string. If you want to save it in a column, use a BLOB column type.

DECODE

This function decrypts the encrypted string crypt_str using pass_str as the password. crypt_str should be a string returned from ENCODE( ).

```
DECODE(crypt_str,pass_str)
RETURNS: string
```

MD5

This function calculates an MD5 checksum for the string. The value is returned as a 32-character alpha-numeric string. This is the same as the md5() functions used by PHP.

```
MD5(string)
RETURNS: string
```

LAST_INSERT_ID

This function returns the last automatically generated value that was inserted into an AUTO_INCREMENT column.

```
LAST_INSERT_ID()
RETURNS: int
```

GET_LOCK

This function tries to obtain a lock with a name given by the string str, with a timeout of timeout seconds. Returns 1 if the lock was obtained successfully, 0 if the attempt timed out, or NULL if an error occurred (such as running out of memory or the thread being killed with mysqladmin kill). A lock is released RELEASE_LOCK( ) is executed, a new GET_LOCK( )a new GET_LOCK() is executed, or the thread terminates.

```
GET_LOCK(str,timeout)
RETURNS: int
```

RELEASE_LOCK

This function releases the lock named by the string `str` that was obtained with `GET_LOCK()`. It returns 1 if the lock was released, 0 if the lock wasn't locked by this thread (in which case the lock is not released) and `NULL` if the named lock didn't exist.

```
RELEASE_LOCK(str)
RETURNS: int
```

Functions for Use with GROUP BY Clauses

Most of the functions that are used with the GROUP BY clase were covered in Chapter 3. There are two additional functions which we did not cover there.

STD/STDDEV

This function returns the standard deviation of `expr`. It is an extension of ANSI SQL. The `STDDEV()` form of this function is provided for Oracle compatibility.

```
STD(expr)
```

or

```
STDDEV(expr)
RETURNS: float
```

BIT_OR

This function returns the bitwise `OR` of all bits in `expr`. The calculation is performed with 64-bit (`BIGINT`) precision.

```
BIT_OR(expr)
RETURNS: int
```

BIT_AND

This function returns the bitwise `AND` of all bits in `expr`. The calculation is performed with 64-bit (`BIGINT`) precision.

```
BIT_AND(expr)
RETURNS: int
```

Appendix J

What's on the CD-ROM

TO GET THE APPLICATIONS Sections III and IV working you first need to install Apache, PHP, and MySQL. You can find these applications on this book's CD-ROM in the /apache, /php, and /mysql directories. Each has subdirectories for Windows and Unix. Use whichever is appropriate. Then follow the instructions in Appendix B to install these applications.

Once Apache, PHP, and MySQL are installed, you will need to copy the PHP scripts that load the databases and run the applications. Copy the entire /book directory from the CD, with all of its subfolders, to the htdocs/ directory of your Apache installation.

The files that install the databases are kept in the book/install/ directory. If Apache is running on your system, all you will need to do to install the databases is open the correct URL in your browser: `http://yourdomain/book/install/index.php`. (If Apache is on your local machine, the acutal URL will likely be `http://localhost/book/install/index.php`).

Follow the instructions to install the databases you wish to use. Note that for the install script, you will need to enter a valid hostname, username, and password in the mysql_connect() function on the fourth line of the install/index.php file. You can then access all of the applications by moving to `http://yourdomain/book/index.html/`

You should then open the book/functions/db.php file. In the first function, change the `$user`, `$password`, and `$server` arguments to reflect strings that are valid for your MySQL installation.

Also on the CD, you will find the following:

◆ A PDF version of this book.

◆ Adobe Acrobat Reader 4.0.

◆ PHPmyadmin – This excellent utility gives MySQL a graphical user interface via a Web browser using PHP scripts.

◆ Manual Lemos' Form Creation and Validation Class – This is a very complete set of scripts for creating forms and validating form input.

◆ Manual Lemos' Database Abstraction Layer – This can be helpful if you need to access more than one database from your PHP scripts.

◆ PHP Base Library – A set of scripts useful for user authentication and other common processes.

◆ Scripts from Appendix G.

◆ PBMPlus – This utility for manipulating images is used in Chapter 10. It will only work on Unix systems.

All files with .php extensions can simply be copied to the Web server directory and will execute when the page is accessed.

Files with .tar.gz extensions are intended for Unix systems and must be uncompressed before you will be able to use them. Use the following commands:

```
gunzip filename.tar.gz
tar xf filename.tar
```

All files with .zip extensions must be uncompressed using a Windows zip utility such as WinZip (available at http://www.winzip.com).

Once you've uncompressed the packages, see the README or INSTALL files for installation instructions.

Index

Symbols & Numbers

!= (not equal), 98
$ (dollar sign), 71, 73
$1 variable, 180
$allowed_tags, 203
$bgcolor, 225
$category_id variable, 184
$date_array, 136
$DOCROOT, 180
$DOCUMENT_ROOT, 204
$errmsg, 201, 209
$GLOBALS, 178
$HTTP_GET_VARS array, 78
$HTTP_POST_VARS array, 78
$HTTP_SESSION_VARS, 375
$image_src property, catalog
    application, 269
$imagefile variable, 264
$imagefile_name variable, 264
$imagefile_size variable, 264
$imagefile_type variable, 264
$nbsp. *See* non-breaking spaces
$newuser, 303
$offset variable, 210
$olduser, 303
$PHP_AUTH_PSSWD, 201
$PHP_AUTH_PW, 302
$PHP_AUTH_USER, 201, 302
$preserve variable, 206
$query variable, 180
$rand_keys, 147
$REMOTE_ADDR, 329
$REQUEST_URI, 180
$result variable, 180
$row variable, 180, 206
$thumb_src property, catalog
    application, 269
$thumb_width property, catalog
    application, 269
$user_id, 304
$what, 303
$whatami property, catalog
    application, 269
&& logical operator, 98
&amp, 203
&quot, 203
* (asterisk), 46
.gif file extension, 216
.pbm file, 265
= (assignment operator), 72
== (comparison operator), 72, 98
=== (identical to), 98
!= (not equal to), 49, 99
" (double quote), 38

(hash), 188
% (percent sign), 38, 53
' (single quote), 38
< (less than), 49, 98
<<< (Here document delimiter), 73
<= (less than or equal to), 49, 98
<> (not equal to), 49
<?php marker, 171
<img> tag, 216
= (equal to), 49
> (greater than), 49, 98
>= (greater than or equal to), 49, 98
\ (backslash), 38, 73
\b (back space), 38
\n (newline), 38
\r (carriage return), 38
\t (tab), 38
_ (underscore), 38, 53
|| logical operator, 99
401 HTTP response code, 201, 302

A

Access, 21
add_numbers() function, 178
address class, 381–382
address_class.php, 378
addresses table, 367
addslashes() function, 39, 126
admin_get_winner.php, 242–243
admin_question.php, 238–242
admin_winners.php, 243–244
after reserved word, 36
age_ranges table, survey application,
    221
aggregate functions
    avg(), 59
    count(), 55–57
    group by predicate and, 54–55,
        59–61
    indexes and, 24
    max(), 59
    min(), 59
    sum(), 57–59
alter table statement
    attributes, 37
    change command, 37
    columns, adding and dropping, 36
    combining all changes into single
        command, 37
    indexes and, 34
    modify command, 37
    overview, 35
    table names, changing, 36
anchor_tag() function, 230
and logical operator, 98

and, adding to where clause, 50
anomalies
    delete, 8–9
    insert, 10
    remove, 10
    update, 5–8
answers table, survey application, 221
Apache
    DOCUMENT_ROOT variable, 87
    htdocs folder, 200
    HTTP_REFERER variable, 87
    HTTP_USER_AGENT variable, 88
    httpdconf file, 170
    REMOTE_ADDR variable, 88
    REMOTE_HOST variable, 88
    REQUEST_URI variable, 89
    SCRIPT_FILENAME variable, 89
    variables, 180
API. *See* application program interface
    functions
APPL_PHYSICAL_PATH variable, 89
application program interface (API)
    functions
    mysql_affected_rows(), 119
    mysql_close(), 122
    mysql_connect(), 115
    mysql_create_db(), 122
    mysql_data_seek(), 122
    mysql_drop_db(), 123
    mysql_errno(), 120
    mysql_fetch_array(), 117
    mysql_fetch_object(), 121
    mysql_fetch_row(), 118
    mysql_free_result(), 122
    mysql_insert_id(), 118
    mysql_list_dbs (), 123
    mysql_list_fields(), 124
    mysql_list_tables(), 123
    mysql_num_rows(), 119
    mysql_pconnect(), 116
    mysql_query(), 117
    mysql_result(), 120
    mysql_select_db(), 116
    overview, 111
applications design
    controlling access, 195, 220
    deleting entries, 195
    error handling, 198
    navigational elements, 195
    pages, required, 194, 216–219
    reset button, 194
    scope, determining, 193, 215–216
    security, 195–196, 220
    submit button, 194
    validation, 198, 220

Continued

my2cents.idgbooks.com

IDG Books Worldwide, Inc.
End-User License Agreement

READ THIS. You should carefully read these terms and conditions before opening the software packet(s) included with this book ("Book"). This is a license agreement ("Agreement") between you and IDG Books Worldwide, Inc. ("IDGB"). By opening the accompanying software packet(s), you acknowledge that you have read and accept the following terms and conditions. If you do not agree and do not want to be bound by such terms and conditions, promptly return the Book and the unopened software packet(s) to the place you obtained them for a full refund.

1. **License Grant.** IDGB grants to you (either an individual or entity) a nonexclusive license to use one copy of the enclosed software program(s) (collectively, the "Software") solely for your own personal or business purposes on a single computer (whether a standard computer or a workstation component of a multiuser network). The Software is in use on a computer when it is loaded into temporary memory (RAM) or installed into permanent memory (hard disk, CD-ROM, or other storage device). IDGB reserves all rights not expressly granted herein.

2. **Ownership.** IDGB is the owner of all right, title, and interest, including copyright, in and to the compilation of the Software recorded on the disk(s) or CD-ROM ("Software Media"). Copyright to the individual programs recorded on the Software Media is owned by the author or other authorized copyright owner of each program. Ownership of the Software and all proprietary rights relating thereto remain with IDGB and its licensers.

3. **Restrictions On Use and Transfer.**

   (a) You may only (i) make one copy of the Software for backup or archival purposes, or (ii) transfer the Software to a single hard disk, provided that you keep the original for backup or archival purposes. You may not (i) rent or lease the Software, (ii) copy or reproduce the Software through a LAN or other network system or through any computer subscriber system or bulletin-board system, or (iii) modify, adapt, or create derivative works based on the Software.

   (b) You may not reverse engineer, decompile, or disassemble the Software. You may transfer the Software and user documentation on a permanent basis, provided that the transferee agrees to accept the terms and conditions of this Agreement and you retain no copies. If the Software is an update or has been updated, any transfer must include the most recent update and all prior versions.

4. **Restrictions on Use of Individual Programs.** You must follow the individual requirements and restrictions detailed for each individual program in Appendix J of this Book. These limitations are also contained in the individual license agreements recorded on the Software Media. These limitations may include a requirement that after using the program for a specified period of time, the user must pay a registration fee or discontinue use. By opening the Software packet(s), you will be agreeing to abide by the licenses and restrictions for these individual programs that are detailed in Appendix J and on the Software Media. None of the material on this Software Media or listed in this Book may ever be redistributed, in original or modified form, for commercial purposes.

5. **Limited Warranty.**

   (a) IDGB warrants that the Software and Software Media are free from defects in materials and workmanship under normal use for a period of sixty (60) days from the date of purchase of this Book. If IDGB receives notification within the warranty period of defects in materials or workmanship, IDGB will replace the defective Software Media.

   (b) IDGB AND THE AUTHORS OF THE BOOK DISCLAIM ALL OTHER WARRANTIES, EXPRESS OR IMPLIED, INCLUDING WITHOUT LIMITATION IMPLIED WARRANTIES OF MERCHANTABILITY AND FITNESS FOR A PARTICULAR PURPOSE, WITH RESPECT TO THE SOFTWARE, THE PROGRAMS, THE SOURCE CODE CONTAINED THEREIN, AND/OR THE TECHNIQUES DESCRIBED IN THIS BOOK. IDGB DOES NOT WARRANT THAT THE FUNCTIONS CONTAINED IN THE SOFTWARE WILL MEET YOUR REQUIREMENTS OR THAT THE OPERATION OF THE SOFTWARE WILL BE ERROR FREE.

   (c) This limited warranty gives you specific legal rights, and you may have other rights that vary from jurisdiction to jurisdiction.

6. **Remedies.**

   (a) IDGB's entire liability and your exclusive remedy for defects in materials and workmanship shall be limited to replacement of the Software Media, which may be returned to IDGB with a copy of your receipt at the following address: Software Media Fulfillment Department, Attn.: *MySQL/PHP Database Applications*, IDG Books Worldwide, Inc., 10475 Crosspoint Blvd., Indianapolis, IN 46256, or call 1-800-762-2974. Please allow three to four weeks for delivery. This Limited Warranty is void if failure of the Software Media has resulted from accident, abuse, or misapplication. Any replacement Software Media will be warranted for the remainder of the original warranty period or thirty (30) days, whichever is longer.

(b) In no event shall IDGB or the authors be liable for any damages whatsoever (including without limitation damages for loss of business profits, business interruption, loss of business information, or any other pecuniary loss) arising from the use of or inability to use the Book or the Software, even if IDGB has been advised of the possibility of such damages.

(c) Because some jurisdictions do not allow the exclusion or limitation of liability for consequential or incidental damages, the above limitation or exclusion may not apply to you.

7. **U.S. Government Restricted Rights.** Use, duplication, or disclosure of the Software by the U.S. Government is subject to restrictions stated in paragraph (c)(1)(ii) of the Rights in Technical Data and Computer Software clause of DFARS 252.227-7013, and in subparagraphs (a) through (d) of the Commercial Computer – Restricted Rights clause at FAR 52.227-19, and in similar clauses in the NASA FAR supplement, when applicable.

8. **General.** This Agreement constitutes the entire understanding of the parties and revokes and supersedes all prior agreements, oral or written, between them and may not be modified or amended except in a writing signed by both parties hereto that specifically refers to this Agreement. This Agreement shall take precedence over any other documents that may be in conflict herewith. If any one or more provisions contained in this Agreement are held by any court or tribunal to be invalid, illegal, or otherwise unenforceable, each and every other provision shall remain in full force and effect.

GNU GENERAL PUBLIC LICENSE

Preamble

The licenses for most software are designed to take away your freedom to share and change it. By contrast, the GNU General Public License is intended to guarantee your freedom to share and change free software – to make sure the software is free for all its users. This General Public License applies to most of the Free Software Foundation's software and to any other program whose authors commit to using it. (Some other Free Software Foundation software is covered by the GNU Library General Public License instead.) You can apply it to your programs, too.

When we speak of free software, we are referring to freedom, not price. Our General Public Licenses are designed to make sure that you have the freedom to distribute copies of free software (and charge for this service if you wish), that you receive source code or can get it if you want it, that you can change the software or use pieces of it in new free programs; and that you know you can do these things.

To protect your rights, we need to make restrictions that forbid anyone to deny you these rights or to ask you to surrender the rights. These restrictions translate to certain responsibilities for you if you distribute copies of the software, or if you modify it.

For example, if you distribute copies of such a program, whether gratis or for a fee, you must give the recipients all the rights that you have. You must make sure that they, too, receive or can get the source code. And you must show them these terms so they know their rights.

We protect your rights with two steps: (1) copyright the software, and (2) offer you this license which gives you legal permission to copy, distribute and/or modify the software.

Also, for each author's protection and ours, we want to make certain that everyone understands that there is no warranty for this free software. If the software is modified by someone else and passed on, we want its recipients to know that what they have is not the original, so that any problems introduced by others will not reflect on the original authors' reputations.

Finally, any free program is threatened constantly by software patents. We wish to avoid the danger that redistributors of a free program will individually obtain patent licenses, in effect making the program proprietary. To prevent this, we have made it clear that any patent must be licensed for everyone's free use or not licensed at all.

The precise terms and conditions for copying, distribution and modification follow.

TERMS AND CONDITIONS FOR COPYING, DISTRIBUTION, AND MODIFICATION

0. This License applies to any program or other work which contains a notice placed by the copyright holder saying it may be distributed under the terms of this General Public License. The "Program", below, refers to any such program or work, and a "work based on the Program" means either the Program or any derivative work under copyright law: that is to say, a work containing the Program or a portion of it, either verbatim or with modifications and/or translated into another language. (Hereinafter, translation is included without limitation in the term "modification".) Each licensee is addressed as "you".

   Activities other than copying, distribution and modification are not covered by this License; they are outside its scope. The act of running the Program is not restricted, and the output from the Program is covered only if its contents constitute a work based on the Program (independent of having been made by running the Program). Whether that is true depends on what the Program does.

1. You may copy and distribute verbatim copies of the Program's source code as you receive it, in any medium, provided that you conspicuously and appropriately publish on each copy an appropriate copyright notice and disclaimer of warranty; keep intact all the notices that refer to this License and to the absence of any warranty; and give any other recipients of the Program a copy of this License along with the Program.

   You may charge a fee for the physical act of transferring a copy, and you may at your option offer warranty protection in exchange for a fee.

2. You may modify your copy or copies of the Program or any portion of it, thus forming a work based on the Program, and copy and distribute such modifications or work under the terms of Section 1 above, provided that you also meet all of these conditions:

   a) You must cause the modified files to carry prominent notices stating that you changed the files and the date of any change.

   b) You must cause any work that you distribute or publish, that in whole or in part contains or is derived from the Program or any part thereof, to be licensed as a whole at no charge to all third parties under the terms of this License.

c) If the modified program normally reads commands interactively when run, you must cause it, when started running for such interactive use in the most ordinary way, to print or display an announcement including an appropriate copyright notice and a notice that there is no warranty (or else, saying that you provide a warranty) and that users may redistribute the program under these conditions, and telling the user how to view a copy of this License. (Exception: if the Program itself is interactive but does not normally print such an announcement, your work based on the Program is not required to print an announcement.)

These requirements apply to the modified work as a whole. If identifiable sections of that work are not derived from the Program, and can be reasonably considered independent and separate works in themselves, then this License, and its terms, do not apply to those sections when you distribute them as separate works. But when you distribute the same sections as part of a whole which is a work based on the Program, the distribution of the whole must be on the terms of this License, whose permissions for other licensees extend to the entire whole, and thus to each and every part regardless of who wrote it.

Thus, it is not the intent of this section to claim rights or contest your rights to work written entirely by you; rather, the intent is to exercise the right to control the distribution of derivative or collective works based on the Program.

In addition, mere aggregation of another work not based on the Program with the Program (or with a work based on the Program) on a volume of a storage or distribution medium does not bring the other work under the scope of this License.

3. You may copy and distribute the Program (or a work based on it, under Section 2) in object code or executable form under the terms of Sections 1 and 2 above provided that you also do one of the following:

   a) Accompany it with the complete corresponding machine-readable source code, which must be distributed under the terms of Sections 1 and 2 above on a medium customarily used for software interchange; or,

   b) Accompany it with a written offer, valid for at least three years, to give any third party, for a charge no more than your cost of physically performing source distribution, a complete machine-readable copy of the corresponding source code, to be distributed under the terms of Sections 1 and 2 above on a medium customarily used for software interchange; or,

c) Accompany it with the information you received as to the offer to distribute corresponding source code. (This alternative is allowed only for noncommercial distribution and only if you received the program in object code or executable form with such an offer, in accord with Subsection b above.)

The source code for a work means the preferred form of the work for making modifications to it. For an executable work, complete source code means all the source code for all modules it contains, plus any associated interface definition files, plus the scripts used to control compilation and installation of the executable. However, as a special exception, the source code distributed need not include anything that is normally distributed (in either source or binary form) with the major components (compiler, kernel, and so on) of the operating system on which the executable runs, unless that component itself accompanies the executable.

If distribution of executable or object code is made by offering access to copy from a designated place, then offering equivalent access to copy the source code from the same place counts as distribution of the source code, even though third parties are not compelled to copy the source along with the object code.

4. You may not copy, modify, sublicense, or distribute the Program except as expressly provided under this License. Any attempt otherwise to copy, modify, sublicense or distribute the Program is void, and will automatically terminate your rights under this License. However, parties who have received copies, or rights, from you under this License will not have their licenses terminated so long as such parties remain in full compliance.

5. You are not required to accept this License, since you have not signed it. However, nothing else grants you permission to modify or distribute the Program or its derivative works. These actions are prohibited by law if you do not accept this License. Therefore, by modifying or distributing the Program (or any work based on the Program), you indicate your acceptance of this License to do so, and all its terms and conditions for copying, distributing or modifying the Program or works based on it.

6. Each time you redistribute the Program (or any work based on the Program), the recipient automatically receives a license from the original licensor to copy, distribute or modify the Program subject to these terms and conditions. You may not impose any further restrictions on the recipients' exercise of the rights granted herein. You are not responsible for enforcing compliance by third parties to this License.

7. If, as a consequence of a court judgment or allegation of patent infringement or for any other reason (not limited to patent issues), conditions are imposed on you (whether by court order, agreement or otherwise) that contradict the conditions of this License, they do not excuse you from the

conditions of this License. If you cannot distribute so as to satisfy simultaneously your obligations under this License and any other pertinent obligations, then as a consequence you may not distribute the Program at all. For example, if a patent license would not permit royalty-free redistribution of the Program by all those who receive copies directly or indirectly through you, then the only way you could satisfy both it and this License would be to refrain entirely from distribution of the Program.

If any portion of this section is held invalid or unenforceable under any particular circumstance, the balance of the section is intended to apply and the section as a whole is intended to apply in other circumstances.

It is not the purpose of this section to induce you to infringe any patents or other property right claims or to contest validity of any such claims; this section has the sole purpose of protecting the integrity of the free software distribution system, which is implemented by public license practices. Many people have made generous contributions to the wide range of software distributed through that system in reliance on consistent application of that system; it is up to the author/donor to decide if he or she is willing to distribute software through any other system and a licensee cannot impose that choice.

This section is intended to make thoroughly clear what is believed to be a consequence of the rest of this License.

8. If the distribution and/or use of the Program is restricted in certain countries either by patents or by copyrighted interfaces, the original copyright holder who places the Program under this License may add an explicit geographical distribution limitation excluding those countries, so that distribution is permitted only in or among countries not thus excluded. In such case, this License incorporates the limitation as if written in the body of this License.

9. The Free Software Foundation may publish revised and/or new versions of the General Public License from time to time. Such new versions will be similar in spirit to the present version, but may differ in detail to address new problems or concerns.

Each version is given a distinguishing version number. If the Program specifies a version number of this License which applies to it and "any later version", you have the option of following the terms and conditions either of that version or of any later version published by the Free Software Foundation. If the Program does not specify a version number of this License, you may choose any version ever published by the Free Software Foundation.

10. If you wish to incorporate parts of the Program into other free programs whose distribution conditions are different, write to the author to ask for

permission. For software which is copyrighted by the Free Software Foundation, write to the Free Software Foundation; we sometimes make exceptions for this. Our decision will be guided by the two goals of preserving the free status of all derivatives of our free software and of promoting the sharing and reuse of software generally.

NO WARRANTY

11. BECAUSE THE PROGRAM IS LICENSED FREE OF CHARGE, THERE IS NO WARRANTY FOR THE PROGRAM, TO THE EXTENT PERMITTED BY APPLICABLE LAW. EXCEPT WHEN OTHERWISE STATED IN WRITING THE COPYRIGHT HOLDERS AND/OR OTHER PARTIES PROVIDE THE PROGRAM "AS IS" WITHOUT WARRANTY OF ANY KIND, EITHER EXPRESSED OR IMPLIED, INCLUDING, BUT NOT LIMITED TO, THE IMPLIED WARRANTIES OF MERCHANTABILITY AND FITNESS FOR A PARTICULAR PURPOSE. THE ENTIRE RISK AS TO THE QUALITY AND PERFORMANCE OF THE PROGRAM IS WITH YOU. SHOULD THE PROGRAM PROVE DEFECTIVE, YOU ASSUME THE COST OF ALL NECESSARY SERVICING, REPAIR OR CORRECTION.

12. IN NO EVENT UNLESS REQUIRED BY APPLICABLE LAW OR AGREED TO IN WRITING WILL ANY COPYRIGHT HOLDER, OR ANY OTHER PARTY WHO MAY MODIFY AND/OR REDISTRIBUTE THE PROGRAM AS PERMITTED ABOVE, BE LIABLE TO YOU FOR DAMAGES, INCLUDING ANY GENERAL, SPECIAL, INCIDENTAL OR CONSEQUENTIAL DAMAGES ARISING OUT OF THE USE OR INABILITY TO USE THE PROGRAM (INCLUDING BUT NOT LIMITED TO LOSS OF DATA OR DATA BEING RENDERED INACCURATE OR LOSSES SUSTAINED BY YOU OR THIRD PARTIES OR A FAILURE OF THE PROGRAM TO OPERATE WITH ANY OTHER PROGRAMS), EVEN IF SUCH HOLDER OR OTHER PARTY HAS BEEN ADVISED OF THE POSSIBILITY OF SUCH DAMAGES.

END OF TERMS AND CONDITIONS